Indian Baskets of the Southwest

Clara Lee Tanner

Indian Baskets of the Southwest

THE UNIVERSITY OF ARIZONA PRESS
TUCSON

About the Author . . .

CLARA LEE TANNER, who joined the Anthropology Department of the University of Arizona in 1928, has become America's foremost expert on Indian crafts of the Southwest. Her previously published books include *Apache Indian Baskets, Prehistoric Southwestern Craft Arts,* and *Southwest Indian Craft Arts.* As Professor Emerita, she has continued to study, write, travel, and serve on the juries for Indian craft shows.

Frontispiece Photograph
A medley of colors and forms representative of southwestern baskets. Front: A wicker tray which reflects some of the bright colors used in this type of Hopi weaving *(Ray Manley collection).* Middle row, left to right: A tall, covered Papago piece which uses natural green and black *(ASM 19462);* Pimas employed black consistently with natural as in this tray *(ASME-540);* dyed black and red are always used in the Navajo wedding basket *(ASME-1433);* typical life forms combine with geometrics in this Apache-made black and natural jar *(ASM E-7358).* Far in the background is an elegant Havasupai jar made colorful with the addition of yellow and orange in great zigzags *(AHC 75.3.43).* *(Photo by Helga Teiwes.)*

Institutional sources of photographs, with abbreviations used in this work: AF, Amerind Foundation, Dragoon, Arizona; AHS, Arizona Historical Society, Tucson; ASM, Arizona State Museum, University of Arizona (Helga Teiwes, photographer), Tucson; LA, Laboratory of Anthropology, Museum of New Mexico Collections, Santa Fe; MNA, Museum of Northern Arizona, Flagstaff; SAR, School of American Research, Santa Fe; UCM, University of Colorado Museum, Boulder.

Second printing 1989

THE UNIVERSITY OF ARIZONA PRESS

This book was set in 12/13 Linotron 202 Trump.
Manufactured in the U.S.A.

Library of Congress Cataloging in Publication Data

Tanner, Clara Lee.
Indian baskets of the Southwest.

Bibliography: p.
Includes index.
1. Indians of North America—Southwest, New—Basket making. I. Title.
E78.S7T287 1983 746.41'2'08997078 83-5000

ISBN 0-8165-0811-9

To Donald B. Sayner
whose expertise and superb teaching
have inspired and qualified students in
the fields of scientific illustration

Contents

A Word From the Author

FOR MORE THAN TWENTY YEARS, I have been researching Indian basketry of the southwestern United States. In this book I attempt to bring together my own investigations, as well as scattered published material by other authors. There has previously been no single volume that covers the basketry of all the Indians of the American Southwest, although several very commendable books have been written on this craft as practiced by certain specific tribes. These include works by Roberts on the Apaches, Kissell on the Pima-Papagos, McKee on the Havasupais, and Breazeale and Cain on the Pimas. Other written source materials, ranging in length from a paragraph or two to many pages, are dispersed throughout many books, journals, and other publications.

The time span covered in this volume is largely the past century —from a little before 1880 to the 1980s. The area covered is Arizona and New Mexico, plus some parts of Utah, Colorado, and southeastern California. Tribes include all native southwestern historic groups.

Since 1970, during my most concentrated investigation of Indian basketry, I have analyzed baskets for every southwestern tribe, including hundreds of examples from each major group. Private collections, museums, art galleries, exhibits at Indian arts and craft shows, Indian craft shops, and Indian homes have provided the rich sources of the thousands of baskets involved in this study. Documentation is given where references were used, but the greater part of this study is based on the detailed analysis of vast numbers of baskets.

Throughout the text samples are mentioned. These are constituted of either a single comprehensive collection, say from a museum, or a number of baskets from several collections when no single collection offers a representative range. Often a collection, private or museum, reflects the collector more than the variety of products of a given tribe. Covering the full range of basketry for a tribal group is thus best accomplished by a selection of baskets.

This book is concerned primarily with basketry as a part of the material culture of southwestern Indians, as a form of craft art. Pertinent ethnological data are presented, but the prime objective is to record a commendable craft which contributes heavily to the roots of American art.

ACKNOWLEDGMENTS

A book with a single author's name attached appears to be a one-man production—but rarely is. Such books as *Indian Baskets of the Southwest* involve more individuals than most, from the editor of the press concerned to the contributor of the smallest bit of information.

Deep appreciation is expressed to many museums for the opportunity to work on their collections. The Arizona State Museum, Tucson (ASM) (and its multitribal collections), has been most cooperative through the years; to this institution and to its ever gracious and helpful personnel my warmest thanks, especially to Ellen Horn, Dianne Dittemore, and "behind the scene," its Director, Raymond Thompson. Over the years, too, the Museum of Northern Arizona, Flagstaff (MNA), has always made its collections available for research; most helpful has been Laura Allen. Other institutions have been equally cooperative in sharing their outstanding collections, including the Heard Museum, Phoenix; Southwest Museum, Los Angeles; Arizona State Archives, Phoenix, and their two fine collections (Elliott and Kingdon); the School of American Research (SAR) and particularly their excellent Indian Arts Fund Collections, Santa Fe; the Arizona Historical Society (AHS), especially their most unusual Sweeney collection of Havasupai baskets; the Laboratory of Anthropology (LA), with its broad coverage and its most helpful personnel. Other museums have been equally cooperative, particularly the Amerind Foundation (AF), Dragoon, Arizona; the Western Archeological and Conservation Center, Tucson; Taylor Museum, Colorado Springs, and Denver Art Museum, Denver, Colorado; and Wheelright Museum, Santa Fe, New Mexico. Appreciation is also expressed for the study use of many slides taken by Joe Ben Wheat, University of Colorado Museum (UCM).

Many traders or shop owners allowed me the privilege of working on their collections through the years—to each and all, named or not, my grateful thanks: Desert House Crafts, Tucson; Hubbell's Trading Post, Ganado, Arizona; Clay Locketts, then in Tucson; Dewey-Kofron, The Kiva Shop, and Woodards, all in Santa Fe; Rick Rosenthal, Mark Bahti, and Terry DeWald, Tucson; Don Hoels and Garlands, Sedona, Arizona; Russ Lindgren, Gallup, New Mexico; Dennis and Neva Kirkland, Casa Grande, Arizona; D. R. Truax, then at Forestdale, Arizona; several shops in Sells, Arizona; Fouts, Farmington, New Mexico; and the Fains, San Carlos, Arizona.

Through the years many collections of baskets at special exhibits have been made available for study. In particular I would like to recognize the following: the Gallup Intertribal Indian Ceremonials, Gallup, New Mexico; the Arizona State Fair Indian Art exhibits, Phoenix; O'Odham Tash, Casa Grande, Arizona; and the Indian Market, Santa Fe.

More private collections than can be mentioned were studied—to one and all involved my grateful thanks. Individuals frequently asked to remain anonymous but their baskets, be they few in number or numerous, are hereby acknowledged. Among many other important collections were those of the following: Don Hoel, Sedona; Ray Manley, Andrew M. Rupkey, Tom Beaham, Winston Reynolds, Bert Hatcher, and Dean Tillotson, all of Tucson, and Jolene Pierson, then living in Tucson. Other significant collections include those of Ray Dewey and Rex Arrowsmith of Santa Fe; Clay P. Bedford of Orinda, California; Jerry Collings of Paradise Valley, Arizona; the late Gertrude Hill Muir of Tempe, Arizona; H. S. Galbraith, Phoenix; and the late Mrs. E. E. Guenther, Whiteriver, Arizona.

Illustrations are of vital importance to any book concerned with any aspect of art. First, I wish to express my deep appreciation to Dr. Laurinda Queen for her fine drawings in Chapter 3, which give meaning to word descriptions in the text. The finished basket tends to hide much of the technical knowledge which goes into its making—these professional and explanatory illustrations should enlighten the reader on many such points. My thanks also to Nora Voutas who works quietly at her desk at the University of Arizona Press—she produced the numerous marginal sketches which also enhance text comments particularly in Chapters 4–8. And to Fritz Kaeser for the photographs of an old basket collection, my appreciation. Some of the Arizona State Museum pictures were produced by that superb photographer, Helga Teiwes; she is also responsible for the photograph used as the frontispiece. Ray Manley, of well-deserved renown, is responsible for the photograph on the back of the jacket, as well as photos in several chapters. Rene Verdugo is responsible for Arizona Historical Society (AHS) photographs, particularly of the very important Sweeney Collection. Fred Stimson, then at the School of American Research, took photographs of many of the Arizona State Museum and Museum of Northern Arizona baskets. The School of American Research has graciously permitted the use of these photos.

Always there are individuals who wittingly or unwittingly contribute to a publication. Thanks to Evelyn Schuff, Frances Kelly, and Joseph A. Fraps, who read the manuscript for me, and to Denwood Butler for scientific names of plants. To my husband, John, who so willingly and graciously helped in any way, from photographing baskets to driving me to exhibits—my greatest appreciation. Many on the University of Arizona Press staff—Marshall Townsend, Director before his retirement; Stephen Cox, present Director; Calvin Cook, book designer; Harrison Shaffer, Production and Design Manager; and most important of all my editor, Marie Webner, who has so pleasantly dealt with all problems—to each my thanks.

CLARA LEE TANNER

Chapter 1

Art in Basketry

THE COMBINATION of characteristics that expresses beauty differs from group to group and place to place. Beauty is a value, an emotional element that is not measurable. Art, the expression of man's sense of beauty, is a sensitive mirror of his inner self, of his thinking and his doing. In his art, man reveals his history. Among the Indians of the Southwest, whose culture is tribal, art is a formalized expression that combines emotion and intellectuality, technical skills and creative thought; it is guided by the patterns of the tribal culture in which the artist lives. The culture of the tribe is fundamental to the art and style of the artist, and style provides cultural identity as well as time classification.

The art of southwestern Indian basketry is a neolithic expression, for there is a continuity of basically simple materials and technologies out of the past to the present moment. It is a conventional art, for its design forms are controlled by the crossing of elements at right angles, and by other vagaries of the weaving process. It is a strictly decorative statement, for it came to life as embellishment for already established utility forms and has remained thus. Because it was decorative, it became an art of design. In basketry the social, political, economic, and religious aspects of each tribe's culture are molded into an artistic unity. Basket weaving was and is one of the great aesthetic expressions of many native Americans of the Southwest.

Appreciation of the art of a culture outside our own is very difficult; non-Indians can probably never fully appreciate the Indian's aesthetic values. The native himself does not verbalize about the aesthetic side of his art. He describes it in terms of technique, materials, and its utilitarian ends, but not in terms of aesthetic principles. By the 1970s an occasional individual had learned something about the theory of aesthetics, but the subject still lies outside the interests of tribal culture as a whole.

As a member of a tribe, each Indian artist is part of a relatively small community. His audience is knowledgeable, however, because most of his fellow tribesmen are also engaged in crafts. Tribal art is usually decorative; it is the result of expressing preferences in building upon acceptable elements, units, and motifs, or total art forms of the group. This manner of artistic expression creates the style of a group and labels the art form as belonging specifically to that tribe. Thus, Apache basketry art is concerned with a generous use of a great variety of units and motifs characteristically built up in an all-over style. Chemehuevi baskets, on the other hand, feature the discrete spacing of limited motifs.

All tribes in the Southwest have demonstrated changes in style within the hundred years of known basket making. Good craftsmanship has been fundamental to the development of style. The fine styles of basketry peculiar to the various tribes are the result of superior craftsmanship, the ability to completely visualize the finished article, and the patience to see the object through its final stages.

THE ROLE OF THE INDIVIDUAL WEAVER

Through the years the individual basket weaver has seldom been recognized. As each woman was the producer of essentials for her own household, it is understandable that the individual received little or no recognition in Indian crafts as a whole. Beginning in the 1880s, however, many southwestern tribes started to sell their products to the white man. In other crafts, particularly pottery, this eventuated in the first recognition of individual Indian artists: for instance, the Hopi potter Nampeo in the 1890s and María and Julián Martinez of San Ildefonso toward the end of World War I. Strangely, no equally outstanding names of basket weavers became known, a circumstance that persisted, with a few limited exceptions, into the 1970s.

Culture is the great director of the aesthetic, but progress in any craft art depends on the ability of creative individuals to develop the artistic potentials that exist within the framework of materials and technology. Style is the product of environment, cultural heritage, outside contacts, and individual creativity—all combined and channeled into an artistic expression that is the essence of tribal feeling.

Whether her name is known or not, the individual weaver plays a significant part in this development of style. She is responsible for the complete and automatic control of the technique; the aesthetic creativity of design is a reflection of her pleasure in her work. It is this marriage of skill and the aesthetic that makes a basket a work of art.

FACTORS INFLUENCING CHANGE AND DEVELOPMENT

The aesthetics of basketry vary from tribe to tribe and even from time to time within the cultural history of a single tribe. Sometimes the whim of a moment may become a fashion, as in the development of the wheat stitch by a Papago basket weaver. Perhaps she was weary of the plain split stitch and made something more out of it, something more appealing to her aesthetic sense. Others liked it, and some very interesting pieces have been decorated with the new stitch; it has inspired new creativity. At the same time, the more pedestrian split stitch, formerly used on storage baskets, has come into its own in the creation of beautiful pieces. The split stitch, as well as the plain open stitch, went out of favor when the storage basket did, only to reappear on occasional and much more artistic baskets. It has again come into high favor as a decorative device.

Spatial and temporal considerations also influence the aesthetics of basketry. Cultural well-being or depression finds expression in baskets, as in other art forms. A tribe living in an area where materials for basket weaving are sparse is not apt to produce baskets as aesthetically appealing as those produced by tribes living within easy reach of abundant and varied materials. The Chemehuevis, however, are an exception to this generalization. The culture which produced their basketry was at poverty level. However, baskets were their only developed craft and one which was essential to their gathering way of life. Although they had to trade at times for some of their materials, they have managed to produce some of the finest work in the Southwest.

The basic pattern of life of a group affects the direction taken by the aesthetic. The hard and difficult life of the Papagos is reflected in everything from heaviness of designs and shapes to extreme horizontal and vertical patterns, sometimes almost harsh. Pimas, on the other hand, found life comparatively easier, with the result that they use lighter designs, more diagonals, more delicate shapes. Apaches were often freer spirits; to them it was a delight to throw in an unnecessary bit of patterning, or to break the monotony of exact repetition. To the Hopis, the kachina cult was the most serious and significant aspect of their lives, and it is not surprising to find this subject in both coiled and wicker basketry. When commercial prospects became important to the Papagos, the weaver forsook the age-old forms, materials, and many of the designs, and conceded to the whims of the white man. Their new and easier way of life definitely affected the aesthetic.

Aesthetics are also dependent on the immediate environment. If there is no clay, there is not likely to be any pottery, and inferior clay cannot produce superior ceramics. The same is true of basketry materials; if there are no appropriate woody substances, the weaver must trade for them elsewhere or make the most of local, less desirable varieties. In earlier years, for example, the Papagos made long and difficult treks to the Pima groups along the Gila River to obtain the plentiful willow that grew there. When they no longer needed that sturdy material for baskets for their own hard uses, however, and when they realized at about the same time that the white man accepted the less substantial yucca, they switched without hesitation to making baskets of yucca, for this material grew abundantly about their villages. For the Hopis, yucca was the only material for coiled basketry readily available and they used it for many years, cutting finer stitching elements and tightening them to counter the inferiority of the material. Growing commercialization brought no need for the Hopis to change from yucca, for they had developed highly aesthetic expressions in this material.

There have been very few changes in methods of preparing materials for weaving. The Indian evolved a remarkable eye for equality of size and shape of sewing elements, and later historic years brought only minor refinements. One interesting development was a simple one: the use of a can lid with holes in it to equalize the sizes of wefts or to make them smaller, thus adding to the perfection of sewing.

RELIGION AND SYMBOLISM

Religion has been a driving force in all of man's art. It is known to have affected much southwestern art, but the extent to which religion may have influenced basketry may never be known. It can be said, however, that the Hopi kachina is woven into the basket with much more detail than is typical of almost all other life forms in tribal basketry.

Religious belief may curtail creativity, however, by setting standards from which little or no deviation is allowed. The Navajo wedding or ceremonial basket is a good example of such a standardized piece, although it is amazing how much variation could be incorporated into the specifications by a creative weaver. Religion was a strong factor which caused many Navajo women to stop weaving baskets as indicated in the limiting taboos discussed in Chapter 8; it was a religious concept which also became a rigid control of artistic feelings. Within the 1970s more Navajo women returned to basket production, seemingly without taboo controls; during these years creativity asserted itself in double bands of the traditional design or in totally new patterns. This development may foreshadow a real revival of the craft within this tribe.

Basketry design is responsive to symbolic attachments, which are usually but not always related to religion. A design is not symbolic merely because it has been given a name. Because patterns in basketry are dictated to a large extent by the technologies of the craft, symbolism is usually attached after the design is developed. A good example is the stepped pattern in black in the Navajo wedding basket. The step is one of the most natural results of crossing warps and wefts at right angles. There is a possibility that the Navajos borrowed this concept from the puebloans, perhaps then combining it with a well-established motif, the red band. It is also quite likely that the symbolic motif pertained to clouds, rain, and fertility among the puebloans, but meaning was transferred to curing by the Navajos. The same motif which was so limited in basketry could assume greater variety in another craft, such as textile weaving. That is what happened in Navajo blankets, where the stepped motif has been elaborated and has developed aesthetic qualities that were curtailed by the larger weaving elements of basket making.

Behind every symbol is community of thought; a specific meaning must be accepted not just by an individual but by the group to which he belongs. The Navajo and puebloan use of the same motif with different meanings illustrates the two ways in which design may become symbolic. The puebloans took the recognized symbol of stacked clouds and made it into an angular motif. The Navajos took an established basket theme, which resembled or was borrowed from the puebloans, and made it symbolic with their own meaning.

The same stepped motif is not uncommonly found in other basketry—for example, Papago and Apache. In both cases there may have been symbolic attachment in earlier years, but, with the increasing commercialization from 1900 on, this motif has become simply a design, with no symbolic meaning. The wide variety of uses to which the stepped motif has been put, particularly among the Apaches, testifies to aesthetic rather than symbolic development. The motif may be shallow or deep; it may be constituted of two, three, or many steps; it may be outlined, solid, or plain. Its use is far less varied by the Papagos than by the Apaches. Hopi variation consists almost entirely of the addition of dripping rain or of lightning, perhaps reflecting a connection with religious thought. But in the highly commercialized Hopi basket of the 1900s, these are named designs, not symbols.

COLOR AND CONTRAST

The use of color in basketry has varied through the years. Natural sources yielded few colors, usually only a basic light shade, black, and sometimes red. Another color or two might have been used in particular locales, but the use of additional colors has been largely in historic time. In the late nineteenth century, the native dyes were supplemented by anilines introduced by the white man. These were responsible for the bright reds and greens so popular at the turn of the century. Little can be said for their aesthetic value, but there were some significant tribal differences in their handling. Hopi expression was often poor, perhaps exaggerated by the very white yucca, large sizes of coils, and large designs in their baskets. Jicarilla Apache work was somewhat tempered by the addition of a blue-purple to the reds and greens of some pieces; also, the sumac which they used may not have contrasted so brilliantly with these colors. In Hualapai-Havasupai baskets the two colors glared against the white willow of which their baskets were woven; however, they, too, added other colors to relieve the sharp contrast of the red and green alone.

Before the mid-twentieth century, weavers began to experiment with colors and materials to achieve greater aesthetic effects. Some of the most interesting developments were in Hopi wicker basketry. A wide variety of vegetal dyes had long been used by the Hopis, but then they added anilines as well. Interestingly, they were so capable, so aesthetically sharp, that they could camouflage the two sources in a single basket. Beautiful native dyes could be as bright, as subtle, as dark, as the aniline colors. Such a variety of plants was explored that there were few colors in the spectrum unknown to these weavers. Hopi women made a conscious effort to explore every potential for color variation, such as leaving the material for a longer or shorter time in the dye bath, adding a second basic color source, "cooking" the wood for a longer or shorter period. This range of color was not accidental; it was carefully sought and put to excellent use.

There was also experimentation with combinations of materials for visual effects. Black, often from a different source, was common both prehistorically and historically. The basic aim was color and contrast, but sometimes texture differences resulted. Perhaps much of the choice in the aesthetic is subconscious. Why did the Pimas sometimes use a wheat straw foundation sewed with mesquite bark? They were probably not unaware that the soft red-brown of the sewing material brought out the pleasing sheen of the wheat straw. The Papagos used designs in white yucca against green bear grass in an open stitch; in time, perhaps as they became increasingly aware of the beauty of this contrast, they produced flowers, spiraling, or other more complex themes in these materials.

VARIATIONS IN WEAVE

Each of the three major weaves—coiled, wicker, and plaited—offers different potentials for aesthetic development. In the coiled technique, the fact that color, and therefore design, may be inserted at any point, made further exploration almost unnecessary. Yet experimentation flourished, and variations, including open coil, split stitch, and open stitch, were added. Each of these in turn was elaborated to add to decorative potentials. Wicker was also expanded; the Hopis developed plain wicker with color design to the highest degree of any comparable culture in the world. Experimentation with twined wicker resulted in vari-textured surfaces; by adding color and design to this background, the Apaches and others attained beautiful and sophisticated effects in their burden baskets. Although plaited weave offers few potentials for aesthetic development, great variety was attained by the Hopis in designing as simple a piece as the ring basket. In a few cases two weaves, such as wicker and plaited, were combined for decorative effect; the attractive piki tray testifies to this artistic accomplishment.

Some variations in the basic quality of the basket may be noted. Storage pieces were heavy walled, crudely woven. They had a purpose, a pedestrian one, and weaving these great jars was a pedestrian chore. Amazingly, some are regularly and evenly sewed, or even appealingly formed. In smaller baskets for everyday use, there is both inter- and intratribal variety in quality of wall and sewing. Pima coiled baskets are thin walled; Papago pieces are often coarse and heavy walled. The coiled baskets of the San Carlos Apaches often have heavier and thicker walls than do similar pieces by the White Mountain Apaches. Coils and stitches in Chemehuevi baskets tend to be regular and even; in some recent Navajo baskets, they are both irregular and uneven. Papago stitching at the turn of the century was close and tight, and coils were small in their utility baskets; in the 1960s and 1970s, coils were frequently wide, and stitching large and loose, in baskets produced for commerce. The aesthetic—or lack of it—responds to many influences.

VARIATIONS IN FORMS

Form is an expression which can be dull or highly artistic; it is a quality responsive to specific needs in the native situation. A water jar, for example, must have a relatively full body and a small neck. There will be some variation according to whether the jar is to sit on the floor or ground for storage of liquids or is to be carried on the back. In the former case a wider mouth may be required, particularly if people are to dip water out of the jar. The piece carried on the back, however, must have a small mouth, even a very small one, or water will splash out as the carrier jogs along. Burden baskets of the Havasupais were extremely wide brimmed to accommodate to a special grass which grew in their land; with a great swoop of the seedbeater, all the seeds from the tops of the generous plants could be gathered into these baskets. Apaches had no comparable seed-gathering problems, and their bucket-shaped carrying baskets sufficed for the fruits and nuts which they gathered and for other items carried in these pieces. Thus, necessity directed many shapes, but, once need was satisfied, forms were varied or refined in many and diverse directions. Beautiful biconical, small-necked Paiute water bottles are a delight to look at, and the refined lines of the great conical burden basket of the Havasupais exceed necessity, both of these baskets being expressions of the aesthetic sense of their respective tribes.

Trays have many shapes among the Indian tribes of the Southwest; they differ from tribe to tribe and, in some instances, differ greatly within a single tribe. Navajo wedding basket trays show little variation in form, though some may be rounded, some cone-shaped, a few more shallow or more deep. Apache tray baskets, however, run the gamut from very shallow to very deep, from a small to a wide flat base, from almost straight to curving to very rounded side walls. The Navajo form, like the design, probably responded to ceremonial requisites, while there were no restraints on the Apache tray beyond practical utility.

VARIATIONS IN DECORATION AND DESIGN

Decoration and design have, of course, the greatest aesthetic potential. Decoration was totally unnecessary to any basket, and, since it in no way interfered with the basic purpose of the piece, it was left to the whim and the ability of the weaver. There were, of course, certain pools of design which had evolved through the centuries in each tribal group. Often borrowed ideas were so completely incorporated into new expressions that they became an unidentifiable part of their adopted culture. The heavy cross in red, outlined in narrow black, with tiny squares at some or all of the corners, is used by Jicarillas, Navajos, and Rio Grande puebloans. Its tribal origin is unknown, however, obliterated by early and close contacts among these groups.

One of the amazing facts about basket design is that there is so little similarity from tribe to tribe. After all, technology dictated pattern to a degree, for that inevitable crossing of elements at right angles was certainly the controlling factor. Tribe after tribe controlled this circumstance in such a way as to use the same elements and units but to create designs essentially their own. Where there are close similarities, it is safe to say that there were contacts between the tribes involved, as in the case of the heavy cross mentioned above. Some of the Yavapais lived with the Apaches for twenty-five years, and the not surprising result is almost identical patterning in much of their basketry. Proximity alone would not have been sufficient, however. Yavapais and Apaches shared a comparable verve for life, a similarity in spirit, which was reflected in similarity in design. Although Hopis and Navajos were frequently in close contact, there was little exchange in basketry patterning because there was very little similarity in their respective approaches to the aesthetic, or to life. Navajos would have been more apt to do the borrowing, but their basket weaving was too heavily under the influence of taboo during many of their years of contact with the Hopis. And the Hopis were little inclined to borrow outside their own tribe. Kachinas were Hopi and could be used by any Hopi basket maker—even by makers of both wicker baskets and coiled work, which were done on different mesas. It is true that the Navajo wedding design was produced in Hopi baskets, but generally in baskets woven for sale or for use in an adopted ceremony, the Supai dance. Commercial and borrowed cultural concepts have indeed made strange bedfellows of many aesthetic ideas.

Although designs differ so greatly from tribe to tribe, the same cannot be said for the elements and units that make up the designs. The difference is in the ways in which the latter were used. The relatively large and simple geometrics possible in plaiting were very limited among the Jémez folk, but they were more extensively explored by the Hopis. The Hopis had a richer inheritance in these specific patterns, and possibly they were more inventive in design than the Jémez puebloans. Craft arts as a whole are richer among the Hopis. Artistic expression seems to have been curtailed in all the Rio Grande villages through contact with white men, but the Hopi pueblos experienced much less of this pressure. With so few standards to encourage her, the Jémez woman apparently ignored the aesthetic potential and produced the ring basket solely for utilitarian purposes.

In coiled basketry weave, wherein are the greatest aesthetic potentials, again the same fundamental elements and units are used by most tribes: squares, rectangles, lines and bands, triangles, diamonds, zigzags, circles. These are usually developed into tribal patterns based on the pool of design and the aesthetic bent of a group. Even life figures are related to these fundamental elements and units; among the Apaches and Yavapais, they are used to create simple but expressive humans and animals. The same elements appear totally different when coordinated to create Hopi kachinas, humans, and birds. A few of the Hopi animals, particularly the deer, are more like the Apache's than are other life forms, but they are not the same. The difference is partly due to differing aesthetic perspectives, but there is also the profoundly important religious aspect related to the more elaborate and detailed Hopi kachinas, birds, and certain clowns. Thus, it may be said that aesthetic attitude, modified by the religious, dominated some of the Hopi motifs. It is also true that there is a more extensive and more elaborate purely aesthetic base in Hopi crafts in general, and so it is not surprising to find this difference expressing itself in the life forms in their baskets.

A stylistic analysis can be based on design elements and their interrelationship in motifs and whole patterns. Tribal origin cannot always be determined on the basis of this analysis alone, however. Certain borderline cases need clarification by reference to form, rim finish, wall thickness, or even type of foundation. All observable factors put together sometimes cannot identify a given piece, especially some Apache-Yavapai or Pima–old Papago baskets. These are tribes that came together through intermarriage or trade and that eventually were using the same or very similar motifs, designs, and technologies.

UNITY

Unity has been posited as an important aspect of style. The Indian achieves a basic unity through perfection of technique combined with his feelings for the aesthetic. He has an innate sense of the artistic, a feeling for line, for mass, for space, for balance—all of which contribute to unity. In some tribal baskets artistry is controlled, perhaps even to sparseness, but other attributes may give this limited but unified expression a feeling of sophistication in its final form. Even the heavily designed Apache baskets, some almost to the point of *horror vacui*, are appealing, for these Indians also had that feeling of unity which demanded some balance in mass and line. The basic usefulness of the piece made for unity, as did decoration controlled by shape and technology. Whether decoration is symmetrical or asymmetrical is less significant than that the symmetry or asymmetry becomes a part of the whole. Asymmetrical volutes are cleverly adapted to plaques by the Hopis in such a way as to create a unified whole. The out-of-line character (an added figure or one different from all the others) in Apache basketry does not dispel unity, for even this alteration becomes a part of the whole in the inimitable Apache style of decoration.

Southwest Indian basket weavers expressed the aesthetic at many points, through the simple and complex; through refinements in materials, technologies, forms and designs; and in varied styles. Historically, this attainment represents a long, slow, and tedious process of development, but one marked by sure and steady steps along the way. High levels of artistry were realized, for in their devised methods of decorative expression, these weavers reached for and touched the topmost rungs of the aesthetic ladder in the basketry craft.

Chapter 2

The Southwest: Its Environment and Its People

DRAMAS OF GREAT significance to both geological and human history have been enacted in the Southwest, one of the most interesting parts of the United States. Here is found tremendous diversity in altitudes, from below sea level to 13,000 feet above; in scenery, from flat barren desert lands to high aspen-bearing mountains; and in animal life, from Glacial Age mammoths and mastodons to contemporary bears and mountain lions. Some of the most spectacular scenery in the world was formed here aeons ago: the Grand Canyon of the Colorado River, the red cliff walls of Canyons de Chelly and del Muerto, the unbelievable pinnacles and buttes of Monument Valley, and the incomparable vistas from the tops of Navajo Mountain or the San Francisco Peaks. In terms of the basketry covered in this book, the Southwest includes the states of Arizona and New Mexico (almost in their entirety), the better part of Utah, southerly and westerly portions of Colorado, western Texas, and southern Nevada—and on occasion, adjoining northern parts of the Mexican states of Sonora and Chihuahua, and eastern California.

PHYSICAL ENVIRONMENT

This total southwestern area has great diversity, despite a basic overall, semi-arid condition, despite a wide, overall distribution of plants peculiar to semi-arid climates. Rainfall is relatively low throughout the Southwest but varies from one section to another (sometimes such areas may not be too far apart). Plant life responds to this circumstance; accordingly, the basket weaver may find an abundance of material close at hand or she may have to travel far for certain plant sources.

The Southwest has been divided into three large geographic and environmental areas: a northerly Plateau, a central Mountain section, and a southern Desert. Each of these three areas is characterized by certain distinctive features relative to altitude, rainfall, and temperature, and, in turn, varied plant and animal life. All affected man. The Plateau includes southern Colorado and Utah, northern

Arizona, and northwestern New Mexico. Desert lands are in southern Arizona and New Mexico, while the Mountain area is between the Plateau and Desert.

CULTURAL ENVIRONMENT

Since craft arts respond to varied aspects of a culture, it is essential to have an understanding of the multiple peoples of the Southwest and their respective ways of life as a basis for this basket study. A few details of all the native cultures follow, from the first men living here, the Paleo-Indian, to the Indians of the 1980s. In sequence these include the earlier hunters and food gatherers, men who wandered more or less and who built no permanent residences, but men who were capable of maintaining life by living off the land. They were followed by sedentary populations whose lives were built on agriculture; therefore, they had permanent residences, they supported village life, and they developed most of the craft arts known to such stone-age farmers. It was their rich heritage which made possible the continued high cultural expressions of the historic native peoples of the Southwest. Among the latter were lineal descendants such as the Puebloans, but there were also some latecomers in the area such as the Navajos.

Paleo-Indians

The term Paleo-Indian or "Early Man" is applied to scattered wandering people in the Southwest who resided here from shortly before 10,000 B.C. to roughly 2,000 B.C. The way of life of these people would correspond roughly to that of the late Paleolithic men of the Old World. Both terms, Early Man and Paleo-Indian, include two quite different groups of men, the Paleowesterners and the Paleoeasterners.[1]

Paleoeasterners were wandering Big Game hunters who covered a great territory from the eastern part of the Southwest to the Eastern Seaboard. A wedge of their distribution extends into southeast Arizona. These men may or may not have produced baskets; their lives in the open air and their constant moving about would not support the preservation of this craft among them. Certainly no evidence of basketry has been recovered from any of the sites occupied by the Big Game hunters. In general, these hunters were of greater antiquity than other Paleo-Indians, for they are dated before as well as after 10,000 B.C.

On the other hand, quite a few examples of baskets, or fragments of them, have been excavated at sites occupied by Paleowestern men who appeared a little later in time than did the Paleoeasterners, for archaeologists date them from 8,000 to about 2,000 B.C. Significant habits of Paleowesterners include the hunting of small game, gathering of nuts, berries, and other foodstuffs, and living seasonally for long periods of time in caves. Gathering and seasonal cave habitation contribute importantly to the story of basketry.

The broad distribution of southwestern Paleowesterners would include parts of Nevada, Utah, and Arizona, and south into Mexico. In northern Utah, south of Salt Lake City, are important sites occupied by the Paleowesterners, including two caves, Hogup[2] and

Danger.[3] In these caves many feet of occupational debris have been excavated, with evidences of baskets found at several levels. It is very probable that the occupants of these and other caves moved about, stopping at desirable spots for the duration of a nut or berry "season." They left more evidences of their crafts than did the Big Game hunters, for the latter did not frequent caves. Basket making may well have been inspired by the necessity of gathering these foodstuffs, for some device was necessary for the collection and storage of such small commodities. Few or no such problems faced the Big Game hunters, for they ate the meat at the kill site or dragged some home to base camp.

These earliest men in the Southwest are significant to cultures of later times. Big Game hunters left a rich inheritance in stone tool making, but seemingly they disappeared along with the great mammoths, bison, and other large animals which had sustained them through the centuries. On the contrary, the men who lived off small game, and particularly foodstuffs which they gathered, were equipped for a different life. Although briefly, they had nonetheless settled down for certain periods of time. Undoubtedly they were aware of growth cycles and of crop maturation, for they wandered into certain areas at the proper time to reap the harvest of a given berry, fruit, or grass seeds. These were the men who were able to adapt early and simple cultivation to their food needs; they were able to settle down for ever longer periods of time, a necessity if they were to become agriculturists in the Southwest.

A prominent representative of this important transitional stage of development in the Southwest is the Cochise Culture[4], found basically in southern Arizona. For some years in its earlier phases it, too, nurtured the gathering of foods. Around postglacial lakes in southern Arizona some of these men reaped rich harvests of grass seeds. In time they came in contact with the idea of corn cultivation; this encouraged a more permanent settling down. The later introduction of beans made permanency of residence even more mandatory. Man was on his way to community life, certainly at midpoint in the last millennium B.C.

Cochise Culture merged into regional expressions, apparently feeding the three major groups of the Southwest, the Hohokam, centered in the Desert, Mogollon in the Mountain area, and Anasazi in the Plateau. In earliest levels of occupation of the first two groups, and not later than 300 B.C., there are evidences of the triple trait complex so significant to higher cultural development: cultivation, pottery, and permanent residences. These did not appear in the Anasazi area until several centuries later.

Prehistoric Sedentary Cultures

Hohokam[5] peoples occupied basically the southern and southeastern parts of Arizona; Mogollon[6] folk were located primarily in southwestern New Mexico and southeastern Arizona. Anasazis[7] started out in the "four corners" where Arizona, New Mexico, Colorado, and Utah meet, but they spread in all directions, most particularly to the south, southeast, and southwest. In some instances and as a result of their wanderings, all three cultures met and mixed, for example, in the Point of Pines area of east central Arizona.

Anasazi, Mogollon, and Hohokam peoples developed high-level neolithic cultures, each with features distinctive of their respective locales. Metallurgy was not known to them; however, a tiny copper bell which was made in Mexico was traded throughout the Southwest. Agriculture, with the cultivation of corn, beans, squash, and possibly tobacco, was basic to their lifeway. In each area dry farming was known, in the riverless lands of the southwesternmost Desert Hohokams and at divergent spots in both the Anasazi and Mogollan areas. This means basically that the people involved depended on rains for the growth and maturation of their crops. To be sure, the waters of arroyos or washes or lesser streams might be diverted to the fields when this was possible. Otherwise, dependence on rivers was developed with small or large canal systems carrying their waters to the planted grounds. Most elaborate canals, primary and secondary, were built by the River Hohokams. Developed canals were also utilized in the Anasazi, for example, in the Chaco Canyon area of northwestern New Mexico.

Although few evidences of basketry remain in River Hohokam sites, the consensus is that they were most vital to the building of canals. It is likely that lines of workmen carried away the dirt from the excavated ditches in large baskets. It should be mentioned also that simple agriculturalists the world over have developed basketry, and certainly the Southwest is no exception in this matter, for baskets were desirable for gathering, winnowing, parching, and storage of cultivated foodstuffs.

Typical neolithic craft arts were highly developed by all prehistoric southwestern peoples: pottery, basketry, textiles, jewelry, and many lesser ones. Baskets have been found in abundance in the Anasazi area, partly because some of these people were in the habit of occupying caves where perishables were often well preserved. An amazing basketry development occurred, with high design attainment in early years and great technological advancements during later times. Little basketry was found among the Mogollones and that usually in caves occupied by these people, and as indicated above, with even less among the Hohokams, for they lived almost entirely in the open and thus preservation of perishables would have been next to impossible.

Among the preserved basketry remains of the Anasazi[8] are found all the utility forms of later historic years: trays, bowls, water jars, burden baskets, and occasional others. All major techniques were also developed, including plaited, wicker, and coiled. Materials were also comparable in prehistoric times.

A rich heritage was passed down from prehistoric Anasazis to their lineal descendants, the historic puebloans. Some Mogollon people are thought to have migrated from their homes in the south to the Rio Grande, to add their blood and cultural inheritance to that of puebloans who had established themselves in this new homeland. Despite the fact that their culture had declined in some ways, the Hohokams left an inheritance of shallow-pit homes and numerous craft arts to their presumed descendants, the Pima and Papago Indians.

Latecomers to the Southwest, but still within the prehistoric past, were the Navajos and Apaches. It is questionable whether they came together or separately; at any rate, when the Spaniards arrived in 1540, these two tribes were recognized as separate groups.

Navajos, at least partially, were concentrated in the Gobernador country of northern and western New Mexico, and the Apaches were scattered more widely in both states. Ute and Paiute tribes may be descendants of the earliest folk of Anasazi culture, who were pushed to the fringes by more highly developed groups. Yuman-speaking tribes may be descendants of prehistoric populations of Western Arizona.

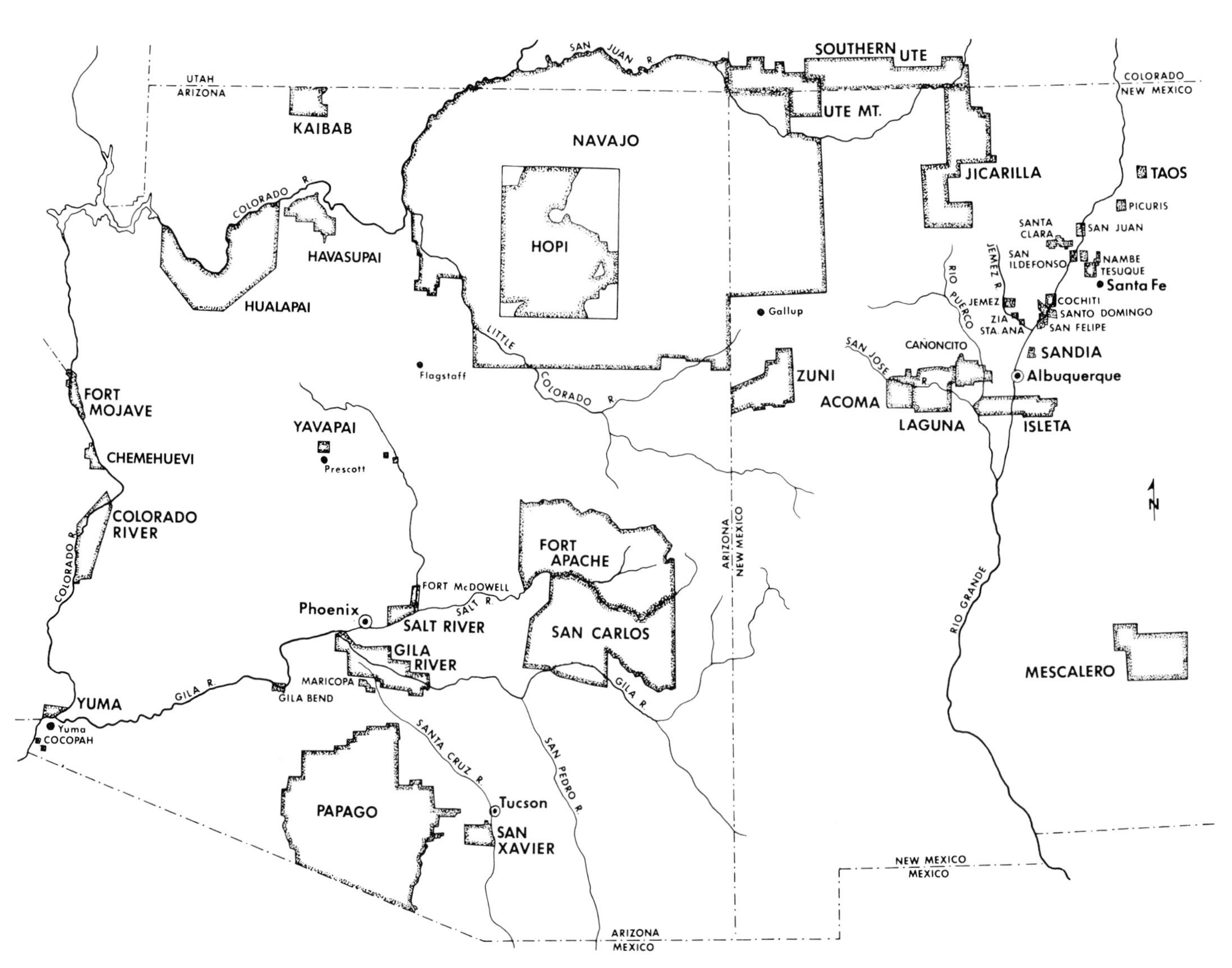

Fig. 2.1. Indian Reservations of the Southwest.

Historic Indians

Most of the contemporary Indians are, then, lineal descendants of these prehistoric peoples (Fig. 2.1). When the Spaniards arrived in 1540, the pueblo Indians were scattered up and down the Rio Grande from Taos to below Albuquerque; they were located in northwestern New Mexico, some 40 miles south of modern Gallup; they were concentrated in northeastern Arizona where the Hopi Indians still live to this day. Much shifting about has occurred through the years, with quite a diminution of village numbers in the Rio Grande, but an increase in settlements of both Zuñis and Hopis. The early Spaniards reported about seventy Rio Grande pueblos in all; there are not half that many today.

In southern Arizona are the two tribes thought to be related to the Hohokams, the Pimas and Papagos; their early historic simple, shallow pit houses testify to this relationship. Members of the Yuman-speaking group are widely scattered: Cocopas and Yumas along the lower Colorado River, Mohaves about midpoint of the north-south section of this same river, and farther along the Colorado, near the Grand Canyon, are the Hualapais and Havasupais. About 1700 a sixth tribal group of Yuman speakers, the Maricopas, moved into the area occupied by the Pimas; at some unknown date the last of this group, the Yavapais, wandered around southern Arizona, then settled in the vicinity of Prescott, Arizona. Utes and Paiutes roamed about and eventually settled parts of Utah, Colorado, and northwestern Arizona. Apaches were scattered in Arizona and New Mexico, and Navajos in the northern parts of the same two states. Formerly wanderers in eastern California, the Chemehuevis came to live near the Mohaves. All of these Yuman tribes seemingly inherited and carried on very simple cultures; several of them have been outstanding basket weavers. Today all are settled on reservations, most of them close to their original areas of occupation.

Why did some Indian tribes of the Southwest continue to make baskets through the years while others did not? What occurred in their lives to encourage or wipe out this craft? Their homes, other crafts, social, political, and religious organization, contact with the white man—all are significant in relation to the topic of basketry.

All Southwest Indian cultures have retained certain of the native ways, some of them in nature worship and in social organization, yet all have changed to a greater or lesser degree. In practically every case, economy has been affected, basically with the addition of cattle or sheep raising, with developed agriculture and new produce, and most significant to all tribes, by wage earning. It is likely that the last has been the greatest influence in connection with crafts, for women as well as men have been employed in a variety of wage-earning jobs; in many instances, this has definitely cut down on craft production. Increases in prices through aspects of commercialization, especially since the 1930s, have lured many craftspeople back into the fold. In fact, higher prices in the 1960s and particularly in the 1970s have turned numerous individuals into full-time craftsmen, a state not typical of many Indians before this later time.

Education became an influence after contact with Anglo-Americans. When reservations had been established, beginning in 1857, an effort was made to set up schools. In some instances this was most difficult, for example, with the Navajos, for this tribe was widely scattered over a vast area; however, eventually schooling was provided for all Indian children. This facet of life affected the crafts, particularly as young people went on to high school, and, in more recent years, to college. Resulting careers seldom allowed for participation in any aspect of the arts; for that matter, schooling in general discouraged native expressions.

Another development which struck heavily, and in part directly at basketry, was the coming of the railroads in the 1880s. Not only did they bring yardage goods, which curtailed weaving, and farming tools, which affected economy, but also pots and pans, which took the place of baskets in many tribes. The railroads also brought the first tourists, who encouraged a spurt of basket making among several tribes toward the end of the nineteenth century.

When Anglo-Americans became interested in native craft arts, it was natural that they would have an effect on them. The Museum of Northern Arizona influenced better basketry made by the Hopi Indians; white people, through an Arts and Crafts Guild, upped quality and quantity production of the Papago basket weaver. These two examples are supported by many others.

One aspect influential on all of these crafts is the so-called commercial. Trade was nothing new to these people, for they exchanged both raw and finished products long before the arrival of Europeans in the Southwest, and they were influenced by those with whom they traded. The same thing occurred with the arrival of Spaniards; why not with the Americans? Commercialization is often a two-way expression, for usually both give and take are involved. It can cause the degeneration of a craft or it can inspire superior workmanship. By the same token, the native can profit or lose by the transaction. Or, simultaneously and as a result of contact, certain individuals may be inspired to strike out in new directions while others follow the traditional ways in craft expressions.

Certainly the commercial has been influential on all southwestern crafts, including basketry. Some tribes had dropped basket weaving entirely before any opportunities for production for sales had developed. This was true in most of the Rio Grande villages except Jémez and among some of the Yuman-speaking tribes, particularly the Cocopas, Yumas, Mohaves, and Maricopas, and also with the Mescalero Apaches. However, other tribes were favorably affected at different times by commercialization, such as the Havasupais and Hualapais at the turn of the century and the former again during the 1930–40 years. Quite popular for sales about 1900 was Chemehuevi and Pima basketry, while Papago and Hopi baskets have been commercially successful not only at the turn of the century, but also from the 1940s throughout the 1970s. The general popularity of American Indian art in the late 1960s and 1970s was an influence on the revival of basket making among Pimas, Jicarilla Apaches, and, to a lesser degree, the Arizona Apaches. To be sure, this same influence furthered the already revived Hopi and Papago baskets.

Other influences of significance should be mentioned here also. Beginning in the later 1940s and accelerating into the late 1960s and the 1970s were museum and art gallery exhibits; some featured old baskets, some the latest work. Indian women were given prominence as they demonstrated their craft for public viewing. Some of these trends carried over into Indian craft shops, as well as such stores as J. C. Penney and Sears. And of course, a flood of publications appeared, especially in the 1970s; basketry was featured in such situations less often than some of the other crafts. Magazine articles, books, newspaper features, and others, either concerned with crafts in general or occasionally basketry alone, have focused the public's attention on this subject.

One important individual in much of this exposure of the Indian arts to the public was the Indian trader, both on and off reservations. These men were often influential in bettering the craft, paying higher prices for finer craftsmanship and for better forms and designs. Often the basket style which sold well became popular; a good example of this would be the miniature Pima basket of the early 1900s and the same made by Papagos in the 1960s and 1970s. Encouragement by traders and dealers to weave life forms in basketry has resulted in some interesting expressions by Papagos.

Collectors have also played a role in this story, although until recent years they have not been as significant in basketry as they have been in all the other major crafts. Whether the taste of the individual collector is good or bad, he may well encourage certain trends in basket weaving. The basket collector is usually more quiet and unobtrusive; therefore, one hears less about him. But frequently he has definite ideas and brings his influence to bear on the basket weavers; this is often reflected in what they produce. Even the "souvenir" or "gadget" buyer plays a part in this same way, often contributing his desire for a wide variety of baskets—and not always the best.

Generally speaking, tribal use has decreased greatly, but in a few instances it is very much in evidence. The Navajo wedding basket is a good example; here the influence has been in the direction of preserving a tray form and a dictated traditional design. Slightly comparable is the Hopi wedding plaque which traditionally a bride gives her groom; today more baskets are given in family exchange. In the first instance design potential, although not as standardized as the Navajo, is controlled more by tradition than are patterns in most other Hopi baskets. The Hopi "piki" tray remains flat and of two weaves; in this piece there is but a slight possibility for design variation. Forms for native uses which became too specialized to accommodate to change have generally disappeared; examples of this would include such pieces as Pima and Papago large granary baskets and Hopi and Zuñi peach baskets.

Change has marked the history of Southwest Indian basketry through the centuries, in response to culture variation and to contacts with other peoples. These changes are but hinted at in this chapter; many more have occurred. There have been periods of high attainment, periods of decline, all of this beginning in prehistoric times and continuing through the historic period. The miracle of it all is that basketry has survived, for in a vast majority of cases the Southwest Indians no longer use the products of their tribal basket weavers.

Chapter 3

Technological Background and Methods of Design Analysis

IN THIS CHAPTER on technology and design analysis, certain aspects of basketry will be dealt with on a broad base as background to the understanding of the craft when discussed under each tribe. Of first importance are the materials used, their general distribution, particularly as seen through tribal usage, and with examples of when they are gathered, what parts are used, how they are prepared, and the sources of colors. It is very important to understand the techniques themselves—plaited, wicker, and coiled—how they are executed and the variations in each weave, for the nature of baskets and their designs depend in large measure on these mechanics. The matter of form is significant; emphasis will be placed on native styles and what has happened to them historically, particularly in the light of native use value versus the commercialization of the craft. Design analysis is presented, for the understanding of decoration and its appreciation will be in proportion to the awareness on the part of the reader of specifics of style. In basketry there are well-established stylistic features, both on the prehistoric level and throughout historic times.

Before turning to these matters, the question may be asked: what is a basket? One dictionary definition states that a basket is "a receptacle made of twigs, rushes, thin strips of wood, or other flexible material woven together."[1] This definition is acceptable as far as it goes; to it will be added that herein the weaving of the receptacle is accomplished in one of three techniques, plaited, wicker, or coiled. In this book about baskets, emphasis will be placed on these methods and also on the category of container which includes anything from the very common tray, through bowls, burden baskets, water bottles, storage and other jars, to flat trays and plaques. The last, the plaque, is included, for this shape has become very popular, superseding certain other basket forms in some tribes which have commercialized the craft; too, it is often used to hold foods.

Not included in this book are certain pieces which are beyond the realm of definition of baskets as herein given, particularly as involving "woven in specific ways" and "a receptacle." Among these are cradle boards (the Papago coiled cradle is included), mats, shelves, bird cages, platforms, pot rests, and occasional other pieces. Small matlike pieces are woven for food trays, and for this reason are included. Another item is also included despite the fact that it is technically not woven in true coiled, but rather in coiled without foundation; it serves in the capacity of a burden basket. This is a Pima-Papago piece which is stiffened into basket form by the addition of heavy elements incorporated into the woven fabric.

MATERIALS

Materials are quite significant relative to the end product, the finished basket. Like peoples the world over, the Southwesterners were familiar with a wide variety of local plants so that, when it came to choosing what was necessary for basket weaving, they were able to select the more desirable ones for specific purposes. Undoubtedly there was some trial and error in earliest years, but by the time the first preserved specimens were made, their producers, the Paleo-Indians, had the situation quite well in hand.

The major plants used in basket making will be surveyed briefly in this chapter; exceptions include a few of such limited use and distribution that it would be more worthwhile to mention them under tribal discussions. The matter of when and how plant materials were gathered and prepared will be discussed here also, again with restricted problems left for the individual tribe involved. Sources of colors will be summarized, divided largely into natural and artificial types. Some specific colors used by individual tribes will also be left for later discussion.

Although the entire Southwest belongs to a semi-arid region, there are obvious differences which need to be taken into consideration in relation to plant distribution. For example, yucca is widely distributed, for it tends to grow in the higher elevations of the desert as well as in the mountain and plateau areas. Further, there are several varieties of yucca, some growing in limited regions. The same is true of other plants, with some significant limitations relative to location. This may explain why certain tribes used certain materials not known to other natives.

In this broad discussion of the plants used by southwestern basket makers, scientific names will usually not be included here.[2] Varieties of plants used will later be given in relation to specific types known to specific tribes, for there the scientific names will have greater significance.

Plants Used

Yucca was one of the most widely distributed of used native plants; it was employed by Utes in the north and Papagos in the south, and particularly by the Hopis in the northern area. The long leaves of this plant are gathered in the summer and bleached in the sun, usually until they are white; Papagos lay them out in long rows for the bleaching process. If yellow is desired for designing, the leaves are not left in the sun quite as long as for the white, or they may not be placed in the sun at all. Green, also used for designing, is the natural color of certain unbleached yucca leaves.

Devil's-claw, also called martynia, is another popular material; it provides the black for designs in Pima, Papago, Apache, Yavapai, Havasupai, and other tribal baskets. This widespread use reflects an equally widespread distribution. Among the Havasupai it is gathered in August, while among the Papagos gathering was done during the fall. Papagos have also been known to cultivate devil's-claw, for under such artificial conditions the pods grow to a greater length, which is an advantage to the weaver.

Among the Havasupai willow and cottonwood are gathered as young shoots, the former in March and April or in late August, and the latter in early spring or in July or August. Apaches also use these two materials; Pimas have always used willow, whereas Papagos used it until shortly after the turn of the century but rarely thereafter. Papagos had to travel to the Pima country for their willow supply, for this material did not grown on their dry desert lands. Far north, in New Mexico, are the Jicarillas; they used willow for foundation material and sometimes for sewing in coiled baskets. It is also indicated that willow was the material formerly used by a number of Rio Grande pueblo Indians in the making of their wicker basketry. Thus, there was a very wide distribution and use of this material, willow, and a little more restricted use of cottonwood.

Sumac is a fairly widely distributed plant. It is used by the Hopis and by Navajos, Western Apaches, Utes, Paiutes, Jicarillas, at Jémez, by Hualapais and Havasupais, and formerly at Zuñi, as construction material. Zuñis used the stems in sewing particularly, with the colored bark for designing. Williamson says that the Jémez Indians used sumac rods for the rims of their plaited baskets.[3]

Rabbitbrush of several varieties was used by the Hopis in the weaving of much of their wicker style basketry, especially for sewing but also often for the foundation. Zuñis also used the long stems of this plant as foundation in their wicker work.[4] Mountain mahogany or manzanita, which is gathered in the spring, is used rarely for design sewing material by the Pimas according to Jeancon and Douglas.[5] Used a little more extensively was squawberry: Apaches employed whole stems for foundations and split ones for sewing in some of their coiled work. It was also used by Havasupais for both coiled and twined work; of its use among these Indians it has been said that it stays "a lustrous white."[6] Jicarillas utilize squawberry for sewing in some of their coiled work; mulberry supplied material for both Western and Mescalero Apaches for some of their burden baskets and water bottles; and Yavapais and Hualapais use mulberry in coiled foundations and in twining.

Other Materials

In addition to the plants which are so basic and which comprise the greater part of the basket, there are a number of other materials used which need to be identified. Feathers, which are so important in some areas, were neglected in the Southwest; a few appeared on Chemehuevi baskets. Historically, beads were added to a limited number of Pima baskets. Historically, too, many other additions were made to some baskets, such as buckskin in the form of patches on vessel bottoms, or as decorative fringes, or to reinforce rims. When worn out, some basketry trays were patched, and any handy piece of cloth, buckskin, or other material would serve in such a situation, particularly among Apaches. Heavy wire rings for rims were sometimes substituted for heavy wooden ones in some baskets, for example, for Apache burden baskets or water bottles.

Tools for gathering and preparing materials and for making baskets have always been limited in number and simple in nature (Fig. 3.1). For years the Indian has used what was at hand, while later he acquired a few items from the white man; undoubtedly, well into historic times some out-of-the-way tribes employed what they had known for centuries. Perhaps most common was the stone knife; this was age-old and was used at one time by all the natives in cutting leaves and in preparing some of them for use. When metal knives, usually steel, became available, they were substituted, but any kind of knife convenient to a tribe or individual would find favor. The same principal applied to the only device used in the weaving process, the awl. Natively, the bone awl was widely distributed, both prehistorically and into historic times down to very recent years, but, depending on availability, other materials were sometimes substituted. Gifford[7] reports that among southeastern Yavapais "coiled baskets were sewed with an awl of yucca or mescal leaf point, or of hardwood; no bone awls were used." Metal awls eventually took over; makeshift awls, such as a nail set in a piece of wood, were not uncommon. Jeancon and Douglas[8] note that the Pimas "employed awls of bone, cactus thorn, or mesquite wood" in earlier years, later of steel.

Only one other tool, if it may be so called, has been added and used by the basket weaver. This is a twentieth-century addition employed for sizing the sewing splints—nothing more than a baking powder or other can lid. Into this is pierced a number of holes of different sizes, from very small to quite large. A weaver decides upon the proper size hole for preparing the material for a basket she is about to make and pulls the elements through that hole, thus gaining evenness and size not otherwise possible.

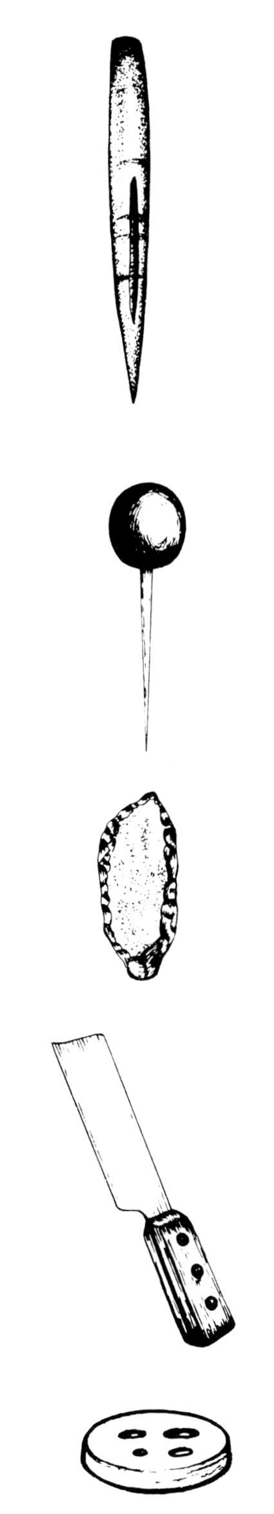

Fig. 3.1. Tools used by Apaches in basket making: stone and metal knives, bone and metal awls, tin can lid for sizing elements.

Preparation of Materials

As there was a proper time to gather materials, so was there a proper way to get them ready for use; generally, they were prepared for storage in the finished manner in which they were to be used. In a sense the entire element might be used, such as a narrow yucca leaf or whole rod, or this same leaf or round element might be split, or the bark split off the rod.

Willow and cottonwood shoots or other comparable round elements are generally worked in this manner. First, the stems are freed of their leaves and any other protuberances. If they have no heavy bark, then they may be ready to split for sewing material. The Havasupais split the rods three ways and remove the inner pith; the elements are now ready to store; most tribes do this splitting with teeth and fingernails. One observed Yavapai woman did her final sizing of the strips in a hole in a can lid as she moved along in the weaving process. Another commonly used material, martynia, is prepared in this way: the outer black is stripped off the 6″ to 8″ pods by the Yavapais and stored. Papagos gather the pods in the fall, after they have dried, and soften them by burying in damp earth or in water, and then strip off the outer black material. This may be used as it is, or split into narrower widths. The splints are tied together and stored.

Hopis clean the long shoots of the rabbitbrush which they use so abundantly, leaving them round for wicker warps and wefts; Zuñis also formerly cleaned smooth these remarkably slender and straight stems and used them in their round form. For foundation purposes, as used by several tribes, or for the ring in the Jémez plaited basket, large stems of the sumac are cleaned of all leaves, smoothed, and used in the natural round form. For sewing purposes, the Zuñis used to split the sumac rods three ways, leaving the colorful bark so that it could be manipulated for designing; this involved twisting so that the dark or light side came out as desired for the design. Mountain mahogany was worked in the same way.

Yucca and sotol are used in a variety of ways. The jagged edges of the sotol are first removed, then the material is further prepared like yucca. Both may be used for sewing in wider or narrower form; both were used in wide strips in plaiting. Yucca is also cut into very fine elements by the Hopis, a bundle of this to be used as the foundation of coiled baskets; bear grass is treated in like manner by the Papagos for the same purpose. The Pimas used cattails in a comparable way, gathering them in August, splitting them in long slender pieces, drying them, and tying them in bundles for storage. Hopis preserved a wider width in yucca strips to be used in the making of plaited baskets, while Papagos did the same for sewing coiled baskets.

Thus it appears that the majority of materials were prepared in specific ways, rolled or tied in lengths, and stored against future use. In a few instances, some last-minute work might be done as the weaving process moves along. Materials are always subjected to some kind of moisture when the weaver is ready to start her work. This differs according to conveniences in a given household: if no pans are available, the withes can be buried in damp sand; or a pail of water may be used and the elements may be kept in this during the weaving process; or it may be more convenient to wrap the elements in a wet towel or other old cloth.

Colors

Color in basketry is very often intimately related to natural material; in fact, some historic tribes never deviated from the use of native materials of natural colors. It was some time after the white man came before the Indian used aniline dyes in basketry, largely after 1880. Even then some tribes changed their minds about the lack of beauty of synthetic colors and went back to the softer native tones. Not a great deal of color was ever used in a single piece except for fairly recent Hopi and Jicarilla Apache examples, and some Havasupai work at the turn of the century. Many perfectly plain or simply decorated baskets were made in earlier years, but as commercialization took place, more and more designing occurred.

Obviously martynia or devil's-claw for the black was most popular among many tribes, as noted above. Too, the natural and black color combination was the dominant one. Red was second in popularity as a favorite with natural colors; the source of this was usually the outer bark of the root of a particular variety of yucca or of mountain mahogany, or, sometimes, of sumac. Other colors were not common but did appear here and there. Navajos combined rabbitbrush and cedar ashes to obtain a yellow dye; they also boiled the leaves of sumac to set other dye colors. Hopis, like the Papagos, used yucca bleached part way for a yellow color, or the inner leaves which supplied them with a natural green color; with dyed black and red or red-brown, they had a fair variety of colors to use in their coiled baskets.

When aniline dyes reached Southwest basket makers, Hopis took on a rather unhappy combination of these in red and green but quickly gave it up. The Jicarilla Apaches used the same colors but for a longer period of time. Also around the turn of the century the Havasupais and Hualapais were using commercial dyes in their basketry, the former featuring yellow, black, orange, red, pink, purple, green, and a coral color. Quite recently the Jicarilla Apaches again started using aniline colors on a large scale, this time including red, black, green, blue, brown, yellow, purple, and turquoise. Douglas cites as sources of the black and red or red-brown in the Navajo wedding basket made by this tribe, or woven by the Utes or Paiutes, as coal, resin, and sumac leaves for the black, and mountain mahogany, juniper roots, and alder bark for the red.[9]

A great variety of colors has been developed by the Hopis to dye splints for wicker baskets. The color range is limitless: reds, greens, yellows, purples, blues, pinks, and others, with many shades of each. These may be of native or commercial dyes; in fact, the two sources have been noted in single baskets. Variations in colors or shades might result from differences in length of time of boiling, periods of soaking, smoking time, and other such matters, as well as the source of the dye.

Mrs. Colton describes a typical dyeing process. She says that for a gold color the women gather whole plants, called by them Tu'i'tsma (*Pectis angustifolia*), and subject them to this processing: "The plants are packed into a kettle and well covered with water. This is brought slowly to a boil and kept boiling gently for several hours, refilling when necessary. It is then removed from the fire and strained through a cloth and squeezed out thoroughly. The resulting liquid is a clear yellow-brown."[10] The color is changed to old gold by the addition to the liquid of ground or melted native alum. A little additional boiling then takes place. Material to be dyed is placed in the dye bath which has been brought to a boil but the liquid is not allowed to continue boiling. When the proper shade has been attained, the material is removed and placed in the smoker.

Smoking sets colors, intensifies a shade, or completely changes a color. This is accomplished by the following procedure: Dirty wool is placed over charcoal or sometimes an open fire, or in a boiler arrangement to better control the smoke, and the wet element to be smoked is suspended above.[11] The elements are turned constantly until they are dry or have attained the proper color and are removed.[12] Both mineral and vegetal substances are used for these tribal dye colors; others will be noted under Hopi basketry.

It can be noted, then, that in the choice of materials, in their preparation, and in their application to a variety of baskets, the native woman is knowledgeable and ingenious. She knows the plants of her area, she knows what colors come from what sources, and she anticipates future activities related to basket making by collecting and storing material at the proper times. She is, indeed, a foresighted artist.

TECHNIQUES OF WEAVING

According to Douglas,[13] the Southwest is one of eleven distinctive areas of basketry distribution north of the Mexico–United States border. This area is unique in variety of technologies, plaiting, wicker, and coiling. He points out also that angular designs are dominant in all crafts, with right angles the most common, this in part because of a basic textile influence, including basketry. Although in the minority, curves are fairly abundant even in certain types of basketry.[14]

Many descriptions have been written relative to technology of basket weaving. Some are oversimplified and leave the reader with little idea of basic weaves, to say nothing of any variations of the same; others are over-elaborated, leading to confusion rather than enlightenment. Some are inaccurate. An effort will be made to combine the simplified and elaborate approaches in order to give the reader a more thorough but uncomplicated view of the major basket technologies, with some of their significant variations. Not all variations will be attempted here. There are, for example, some flurries which may be limited temporally, regionally, or tribally; these will be treated in appropriate spots in the ensuing pages. The surprising element in technology is that there are not more deviations from normal practices.

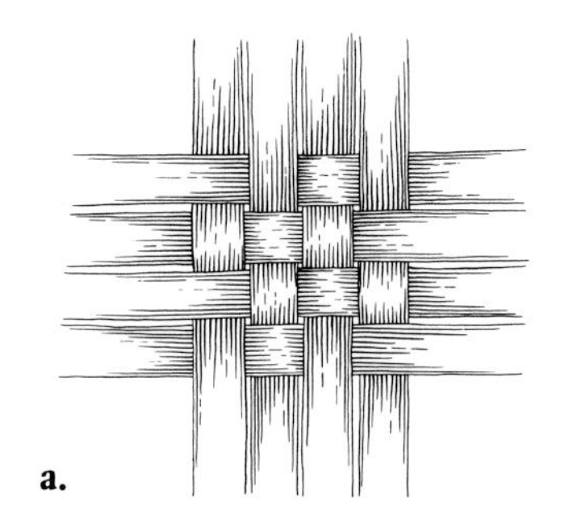

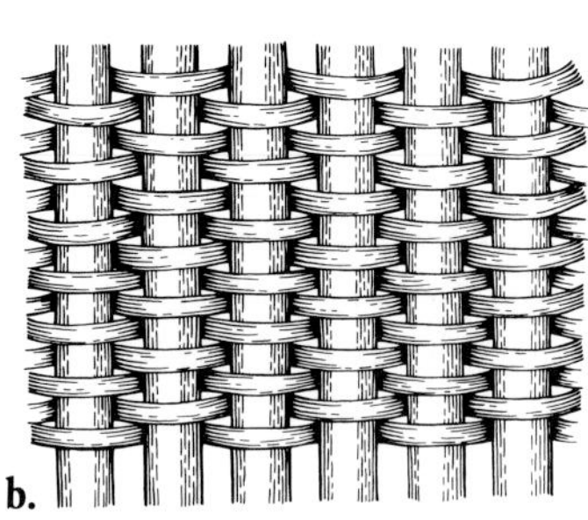

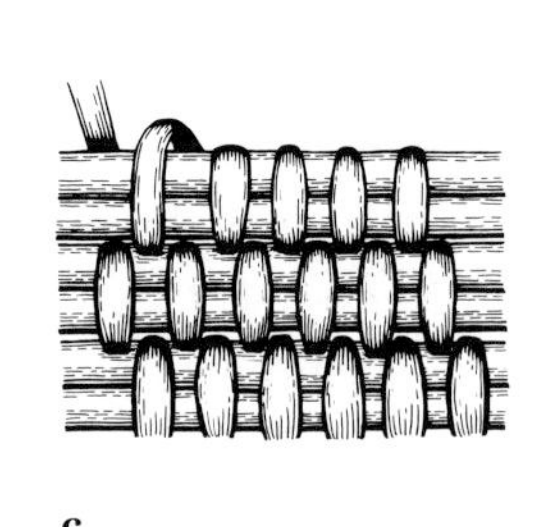

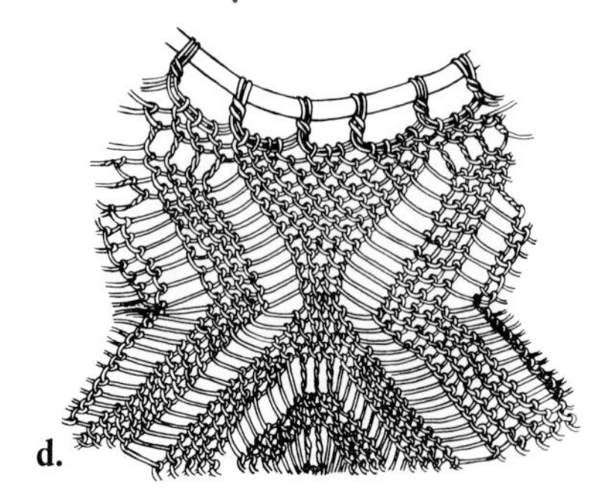

Fig. 3.2. Types of warps and wefts: (a) in plaited; (b) in wicker; (c) in coiled; (d) an example of a single-element style, coil-without-foundation.

Two elements are found in a majority of basket weaves, a warp and a weft (Fig. 3.2). One major exception to this would be coiled-without-foundation or lace weave, a technique in which a single element is used in the making of the container proper; as noted, the Papago burden basket was created in this manner. Warps generally serve as a foundation upon which the weft or filler is woven or sewed, or the weft holds warps together. Warps may be single or multiple, simple or complex, whereas wefts may be single, double, or triple. Warps are the stationary elements while wefts are the moving elements. Direction of each element (or lack of it) in relation to the weaver is significant in determining most techniques. Thus the components, action or lack of it, and direction of the two elements, warps and wefts, are significant factors in defining different techniques of weaving.

Basically, the three major weaves can be distinguished as follows: Plaiting, the simplest weave, is a process of crossing elements at right angles to form the basket structure. In this weave, as both elements are active, neither element is a true warp or weft in that neither retains a single directional position during the weaving process, nor can one element be distinguished from the other, for they are the same in size and shape. Wicker weave is one in which one or several stiff vertical element(s), warps, is (are) crossed in one of several ways by one or more equally or less stiff horizontal elements, wefts. Coiled weave is the process in which the two elements are related in this way: the warp can be varied in composition, is stationary and horizontal; and the weft, which is single and vertical, is wrapped about the warp and is caught or sewed into the preceding coil to form the continuous and joined fabric of the basket.

Plaiting

In a given piece of southwestern plaited basketry (see Fig. 3.2a) warps and wefts are almost invariably of the same material and size; usually they are flat, thus wider than they are thick. Cane, yucca leaves, and sotol are among the most common materials employed for plaiting. Natural colors are dominant, although occasional dyeing has been and still is practiced for plaited weave; black has been the more common color combined with natural; red and recently purple, green, and a bilious orange (commercial dyes) also have been used.

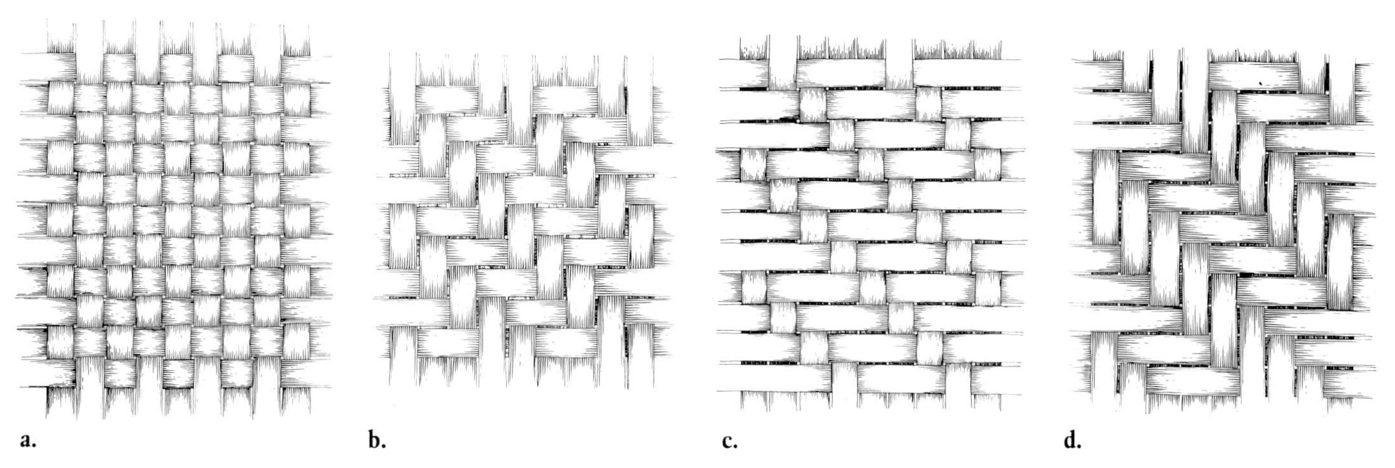

Fig. 3.3. Plaited weave, showing various alternations: (a) over-one-under-one; (b) over-two-under-two; (c) over-three-under-one; (d) over-three-under-three.

Variations in plaited weaving in the Southwest include plain and twilled (Fig. 3.3). Plain plaiting is a simple over-one-under-one alternation of elements; it is not conducive to designing except for the natural checkering which results from the regular and right-angle crossing of elements of equal sizes. Twill plaiting, on the other hand, is the result of crossing elements in various alternations, such as over-two-under-two, over-three-under-one, over-three-under-three, and others. Regular skipping in successive rows results in diagonal lines in the weave. With controlled manipulation of elements in continuous skipping, the weaver can produce diagonal lines over the entire basket; or with a back and forth alternation zigzags result; or, with various ordering by the weaver, squares, diamonds, chevrons, rectangles, or a variety of line patterns can be produced. Life forms are conspicuous by their absence in southwestern plaited basketry.

Patterns in this plaited weave are relatively large, yet there is some variation in size; obviously, design is limited to a few geometrics. Thus, it is evident that plaited technology, as a result of both element size and methodology, limits design development as a whole. Too, it should be stressed that patterning is produced in the weave proper; it may be emphasized in color. If color is used, a single dyed element goes all the way across a piece and becomes a part of design according to the chosen alternations in the weave.

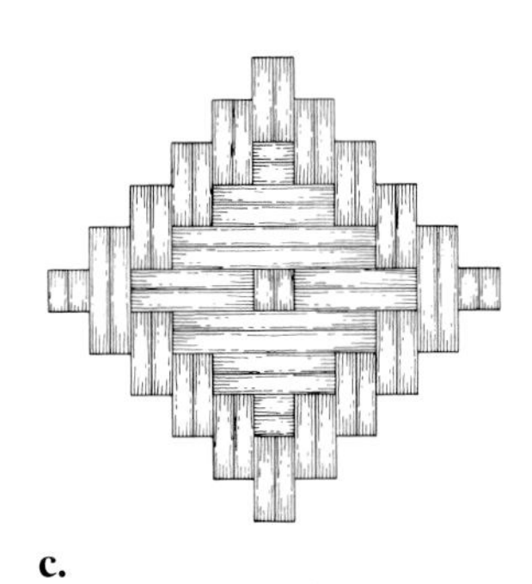

Fig. 3.4. Beginnings of plaited baskets: (a) two sets of three elements at right angles; (b) starting with two sets of two elements at right angles, the first woven so as to produce concentric squares; the second a cross in the bottom of the basket (adapted from Kissell, Fig. 15); (c) starting with over-two-under-two but immediately changing the rhythm creates a stepped diamond.

Despite a few local variations, the usual beginning of a plaited basket is accomplished by placing two sets of three or four parallel elements at right angles to each other, interlacing them in the alternation established in the mind of the weaver (Fig. 3.4). Weaving progresses by the addition of new elements above and below and to right and left of each set of the "starters," continuing to follow an established alternation. Each element is sufficiently long to accommodate to the full width and length or height of a given piece, for the introduction of short new elements during the weaving process is undesirable in these baskets, as this would weaken the structure. Throughout the piece all elements are active; this feature, plus equal size and pliability and lack of established direction for each, add to the impossibility of determining a distinct warp or weft in plaited weave.

Rims of plaited baskets vary according to several circumstances (Fig. 3.5). For example, in the so-called ring basket, a shallow piece, the weaver produces a square or oblong mat which is forced into a circular or oval ring made of a heavy withe, usually a whole, large wooden rod. Projecting edges of the mat are extended over the outside of this wooden rod and sewed or twined to the main part of the mat just below the rod. Irregularities are evened off by cutting. If a deep basket form is plaited, the rim may be finished off in an entirely different way; single- or double-rim endings may be woven in the latter style, which is the same as on mats, as is adequately described by Kissell. "The double edge is...made by bending one series of parallel elements to the front and downward and interplaiting them into the body plaiting on the front of the mat, and turning the second series to the back and downward and interplaiting them into the body plaiting on the back of the mat."[15] Each element is bent and woven obliquely at a ninety-degree angle into the main fabric. The single edge is accomplished by pursuing the first step described above and then the second series of elements is clipped off flush with the edge of the mat or basket.[16]

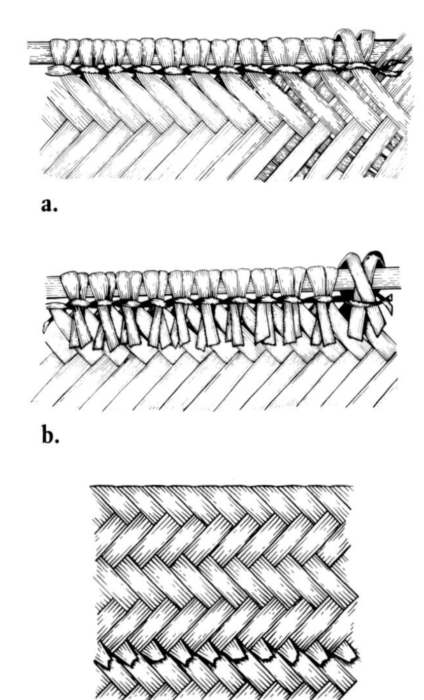

Fig. 3.5. Rims on plaited baskets may vary: (a and b) the common type, with a heavy withe or ring in top and twining immediately beneath (a) inside, and with ends cut off (b) outside. (c) No ring is added but elements are bent at a sharp angle and interwoven into basket rim.

Wicker Technique

In wicker weave, direction of warp is vertical while wefts are horizontal to the weaver; these positions are maintained by the basket maker as she constantly turns the developing basket.[17] Materials may be identical, such as whole rabbitbrush elements for both warps and wefts in some Hopi weaving, or they may differ, as in the heavier rod warps and lighter split-element wefts in Apache burden baskets: "Mulberry shoots are split in the same way as those of other wood, after the bark has been removed and the sap wood carefully scraped away."[18] Additional elements, usually quite large in size, may be used to strengthen the walls of a deep basket, as in Hopi and Zuñi peach baskets or in some Apache burden baskets. These are heavy withes, which are bent to conform to the basket shape; they consist of independent pieces, one each in the two ends of the rectangular or almost rectangular form of the peach basket, or they are made up of two pieces crossing in the center bottom of the Apache round burden type basket. These pieces are usually added during the weaving process.

In those instances where the whole rod is used in wicker weaving, it is the entire plant stem freed of its leaves and other projections and smoothed, with the bark left or removed as the weaver desires. When the bark is not removed, the weaving element may be twisted at desired points to create designs, for almost always the bark is darker than the split surface.

Because of the production of wicker baskets using vertical warps and horizontal wefts, in the flatter portions of the finished piece such as in a plaque or bottom of any form, the warps appear as spoke-like projections emanating from the center. Frequently the beginning of the Hopi basket is formed of three, four, or more elements or bundles of multiple elements, each bundle wrapped separately and all placed close together (Fig. 3.6). These are crossed at right angles by the same number, size, and quality of bundles, the wrapped portions forming a more or less square center from which the worker begins a circling process of weaving. At first, several splayed-out warps (all in a bundle) are crossed at a time by the moving wefts, with the number gradually decreased to the rim in a continuous over-one-under-one process. If a bowl form is to be made, the weaver bends the wall warps at a right angle, or nearly so, to the flat base, the tightened wefts holding them in position, and thus she continues to weave up the sides. Incidentally, in Hopi wicker the exterior base center (or bottom) is concave, the interior (or top) is convex due to the above described crossing of bundles of elements. Other types of beginnings appear, one in the Apache burden basket which is a "helter-skelter" crossing of several warps. Some Western Apache baskets are started in a more orderly arrangement, with three groups of two rods each wrapped a short distance, three groups of two each placed at right angles, and the two sets caught with stitching or tying, this forming a square. The wicker weave starts immediately, catching each of the elements of the sets and adding new warps as needed.

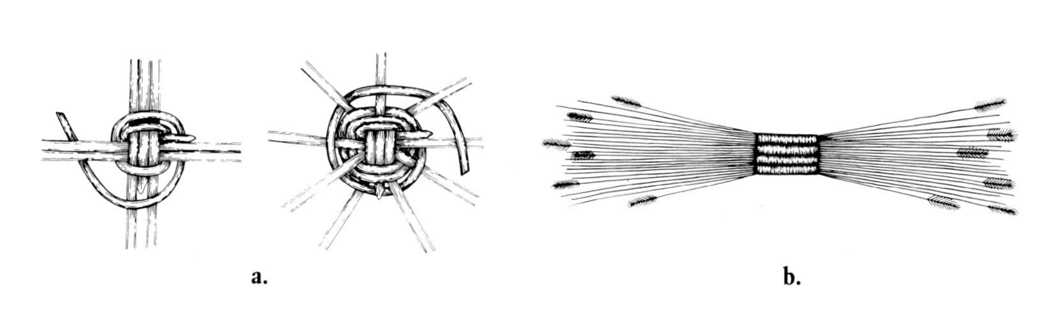

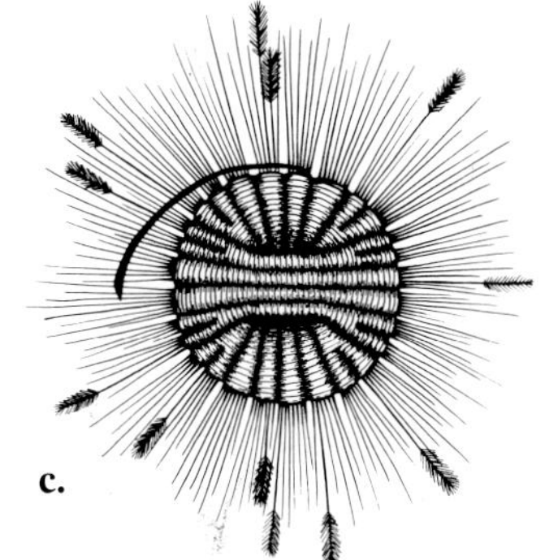

Fig. 3.6. Beginning of a wicker basket: (a) three rods one way, three the other, crossed, and weaving starts at once; (b) four bundles of fine elements are wrapped and sewed together; (c) a second such group of an equal number of elements is laid at right angles to the first and the weaving process continues (b and c after Underhill.)

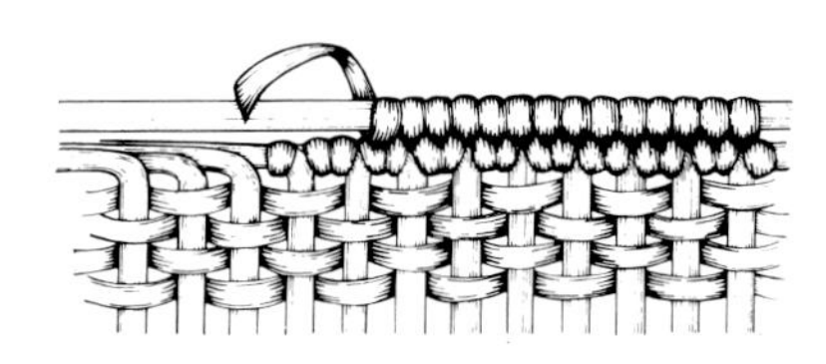

Fig. 3.7. Rims of wicker are finished in one of several ways: Warps may be bent to the left and sewed into position as here. An additional rod may be placed on the top and secured to the sewing below. Often some vertical warps are cut away and remaining ones bent and sewed.

When the weaver comes to the edge of her basket, she has all the warps projecting upright from the rim. These she will treat in one of several ways. She may cut off some even with the rim and bend the remaining warps, or bend all the warps (Fig. 3.7), to a horizontal position, wrapping them in a coil-like fashion as she finishes off the basket edge. Wrapping is often done in a totally different material; for example, a Hopi woman uses yucca, and the quality of her basket can be judged by the quality of this rim. A wooden withe may be formed into a ring, with the warps bent and bound along with the ring to form the edge. In some Apache burden baskets two such coiled rings may be added, and frequently in later historic years, one of the rings is or both are of heavy metal wire. The size of rod would dictate a more delicate or a heavier rim.

Many variations occur in wicker, some of these often given separate and major weave categories. Inasmuch as in all such weaves the basic relationship to the weaver is vertical warp and horizontal weft, and as materials are distinctly within simple wicker weave range in kind and quality, they are included here as variations of this style (Fig. 3.8). These include plain, plain and twill twined, and wrapped as the more common ones used in the Southwest.[19] Plain wicker is a simple over-under alternation of a single weft over one or more warps used as single elements. Twined wicker includes the use of both double and triple weft elements. In plain twined, two wefts are carried along together, one weft crossing over and one under alternate single warps, then twisting or "twining" about each other between warps. Triple twined uses three elements in like manner, producing a heavier "ridge." In twill twined, two warps are involved, with continuous skipping of one warp in each successive row; two or more wefts may be used. In wrapped weave, the weft element is literally wound or wrapped around each warp, alternating warps from one row to the next (see Fig. 3.8).

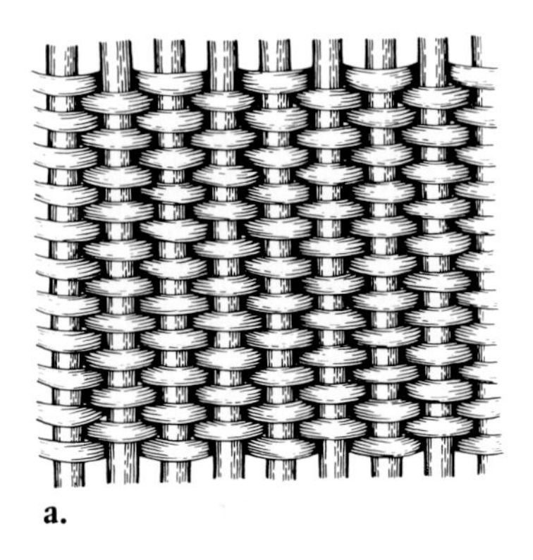

a.

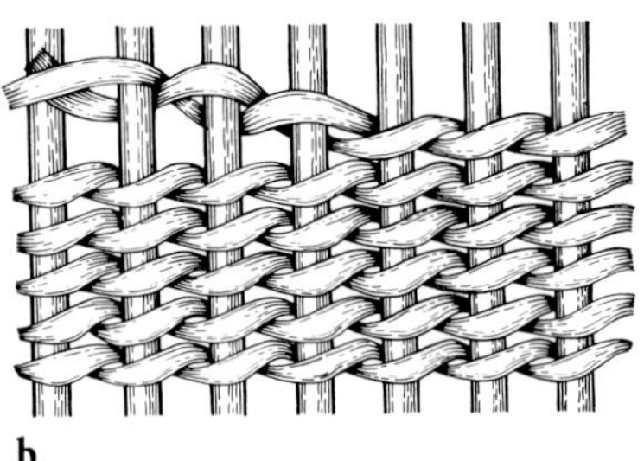

b.

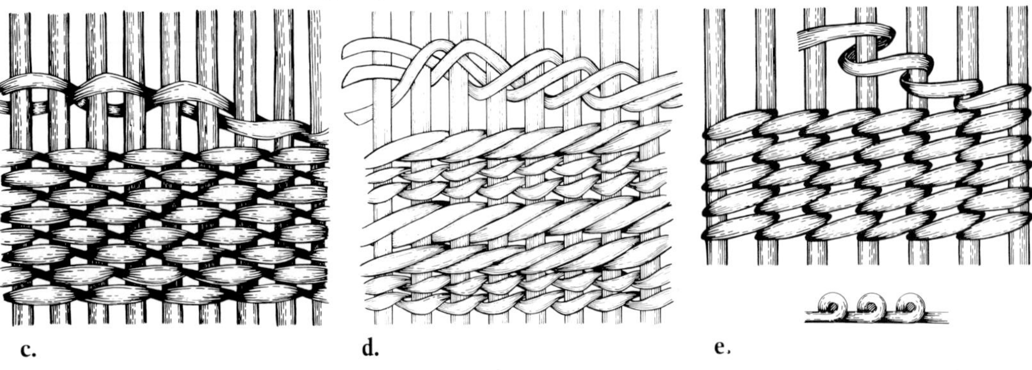

c. d. e.

Fig. 3.8. Types of wicker weave: (a) plain wicker, one weft over-one-under-one warp; (b) plain twined wicker, two wefts over-one-under-one and "twining" in between; (c) twill twined wicker, over-two-under-two, skipping one each time; (d) alternating two-weft and three-weft twined wicker; (e) wrapped twine, a literal wrapping of the weft about each warp, with detail showing top view of same.

Colored elements, either dyed or natural, may be introduced into any type of wicker weave. In plain wicker, Hopis have carried designing to a higher degree than any other Southwest tribe, including those using a great variety of both color and design. Geometrics possible in this weave include not only the typical horizontal lines, bands, small cogwheels, checkers, short diagonals, and other simple patterns, but also larger themes such as swirls, belt patterns, and elongated geometrics. Life forms were also developed by the Hopis, including birds, kachina heads or masks or complete kachina figures, and occasional other motifs.

The majority of Southwest Indian tribes have developed simple banded geometric patterns in wicker weave, using color or technology or both to produce them. Quite common is technology wherein one, two, or three rows of a weave different from that of the rest of the piece will create one or several subtle lines or bands. Often it is a three-element twine combined with a two-element twine (see Fig. 3.8d). Frequently this variation is not only productive of decorative effect but also the heavier bands may be placed at points of stress such as the edge at the bottom where it turns into the sidewall or a like situation where a jar shoulder is bent inward. Paiute water bottles and the Apache tus or water jar would illustrate the usage of these combined techniques.

Coiled Technique

Undoubtedly the most important of southwestern basketry techniques is coiling, for it is productive of the greatest variety of both forms and designs. The majority of the baskets of this area have been and still are made in this technique. Interestingly, coiling is more a process of sewing than true basket weaving, for a worker pierces a hole at some point into the previous coil with an awl and secures the current wrapped coil to it by passing the moving weft through the hole. In coiling, the stationary warp is held in a position horizontal to the weaver while the moving weft is vertical (or nearly so) to her. Again, as in other techniques, the weaver keeps turning her work in order to maintain these directions. In the vast majority of coiled basketry, sewing direction is counterclockwise; that is, the weaver sews from her right toward her left. The major exception to this is Chemehuevi basketry which is heavily clockwise in sewing direction. Some maintain that clockwise work found in a tribal style normally counterclockwise is the effort of a left-handed person.

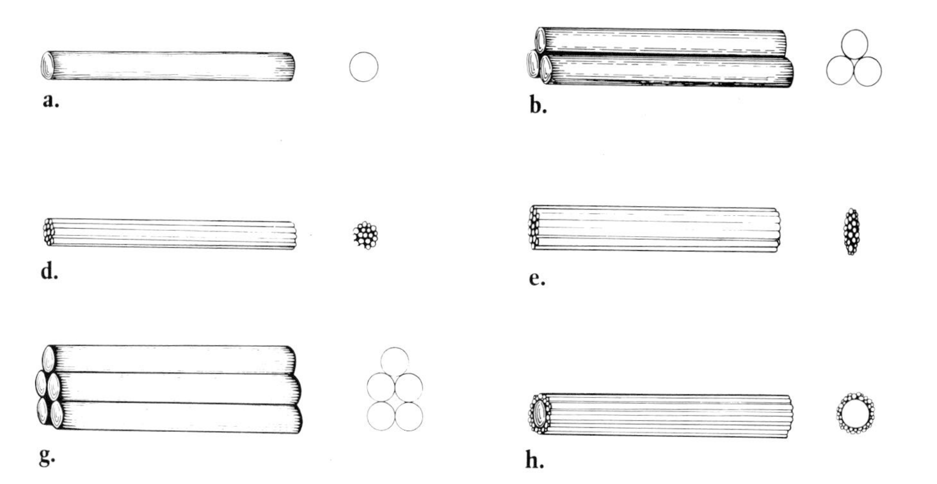

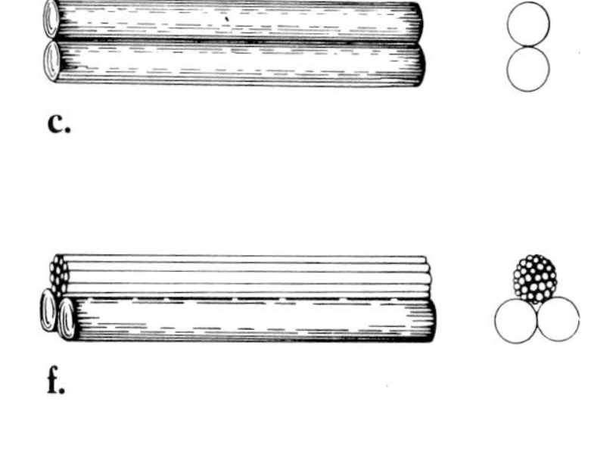

Fig. 3.9. Varieties of foundations in coiled weave: (a) single rod; (b) three rods, stacked; (c) two rods; (d) bundle of split elements, round; (e) bundle of split elements, flattened; (f) two rods and bundle; (g) five rods, stacked; (h) rod surrounded with bundle.

There is great variety in both the materials used and the nature of the warp (or coil) in this type of basketry: cottonwood, willow, or mulberry shoots, squawberry, yucca, grasses, bear grass, and devil's-claw are among the most commonly used. Rodlike shoots may be left whole or they may be split. One rod alone, or two rods stacked one on top of each other, or three or five stacked in pyramidal form may serve as the foundation (Fig. 3.9). Slatlike pieces may be incorporated with other elements to serve as further types of foundation. Quite common also are warps made of a bundle of shredded grass or yucca; less frequently used is a warp of a similar but small bundle combined in various ways with one or more rods.

Weft materials used in coiling also differ considerably. Varying widths of yucca leaves are employed, or of split willow, cottonwood, squawberry, or other such materials. It is known that formerly the native weaver depended solely on her eye for accuracy in preparing regular and even sewing splints. Many weavers still depend on the ability of the eye to gauge size and evenness of weft elements.

The nature of the size and shape of foundation and weft elements is significant in connection with the identification of tribal basketry styles. Hopis and Papagos use foundation bundles of shredded yucca or grasses, or bear grass, respectively. However, the Hopi woman forms her material into a large or smaller round bundle, while the Papago weaver flattens hers by hand manipulation or by pounding the coil. When willow was used in earlier years by the Papagos and when yucca was first introduced shortly after the turn of the century, coil size was quite small, with high counts up to six or seven to the inch; gradually, and in yucca, the size increased to result in three or four to the inch. Into the 1960s and 1970s, coil size increased greatly, some counting as low as one and one-half coils to the inch. This might seem to represent a technological degeneracy, and often it did; however, in some instances fine sewing countered large coils. This is particularly true of the Hopi fat coil which often counted not more than two to the inch; here very fine stitching resulted in technically excellent pieces and often excellent designing.

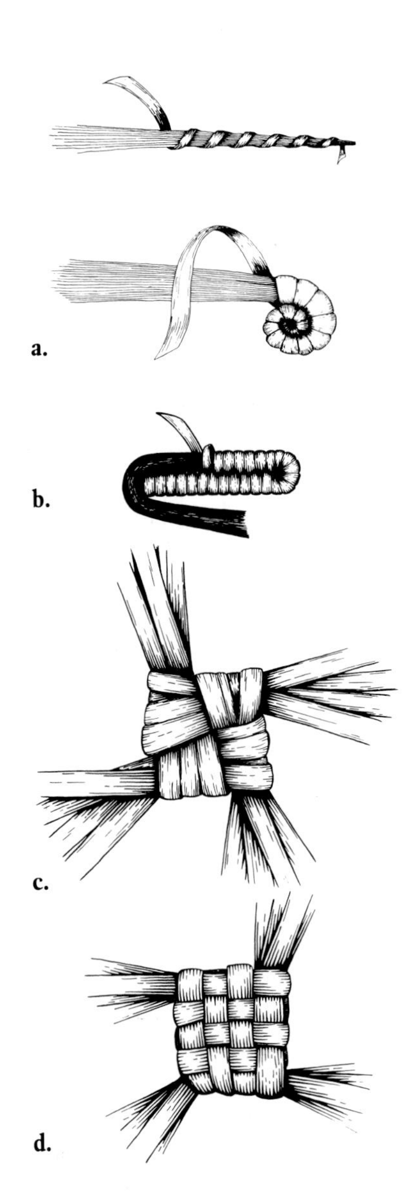

Fig. 3.10. Methods of beginning coiled baskets: (a) by wrapping a rod or bundle, forming it into a circle, and sewing; (b) following the same procedure but keeping a long beginning, this for an oval basket; (c) by tying a knot of three or four elements and sewing first coil into the knot; (d) by plaiting a small section, usually under 1″ on each side (or a knot on one side, plaiting on the opposite side).

Perhaps one of the most common foundations was that employing three round rods built up in pyramid form, this resulting in a round coil. This was the featured warp of all the coiled work of Western Apaches, Havasupais, Yavapais, Hualapais, and Chemehuevis. Inasmuch as small to medium rods were used, the coil was relatively small to medium in size. Jicarilla Apaches often used a five-rod foundation.

Preparation of weft materials is very significant in relation to design. This is well demonstrated in the detailed kachina figure on a Hopi piece, where stitches commonly count fourteen to the inch, as opposed to the simple and generalized life figures on Papago baskets, where stitches often count no more than three or four to the inch.

To start a coiled basket, varied methods have been devised by southwestern Indians (Fig. 3.10). Like other aspects of this craft, sometimes these can be significant relative to tribal identifications. Generally a given tribe leans toward a single method of starting a basket, but a few may work with several different techniques.

Perhaps the simplest, and certainly the most common beginning for a coiled basket, is a circle. However, there are variations within this method. The crudest weave, bird's nest, has a crude beginning. Several twigs are bent into a circle and stems are added first outside, then inside, with their leafy ends passed around previous twigs. Not so crude but still a coarse coil is accomplished by wrapping a bundle of wheat straw for about 4″, forming this into a circle, and beginning the coiling by space stitching the current coil to this first one. Almost all crude and coarse coils are used in the making of granaries or other large storage baskets, such as those woven by Cocopas, Pimas, and Papagos.

Of the more sophisticated coiled beginnings there are also several varieties. Jémez puebloans wrapped a piece of sumac around itself, tied this with a bit of string, and then attached a rod foundation by sewing into this circle, thus beginning the regular sewing. Or a coil can be started with two twigs which are wrapped with sewing material and made into a circle; then a third rod is added as the sewing continues. This shows a tiny, slender coil to start with, but it quickly becomes the thickness of the normal three-rod foundation; Yavapais follow this method. Where a bundle of material is used, essentially the same thing can be done. A smaller amount or the regular amount of material for the foundation is wrapped to start with; it is bent back or coiled around and the weaver progresses, sewing into this coiled circle. If the start is small, more material may be added as sewing continues. Hopis, Pimas, and Papagos may use one of the variations of this technique.

There are two additional methods used by Pimas and Papagos for beginning a coiled-style basket that are quite different from those just described. These include, first, the simple tying of the basic split elements of the foundation into a knot, bending the elements around the knot, and sewing into it. The second start involves plaiting a small section, usually under an inch square, and sewing the first coil into this. Sometimes a knot appears on one side and the ends of this are plaited for the beginning on the opposite side.[20]

Although not true coiled weaving, mention should be made of the coil-without-foundation burden basket of the Pimas and Papagos. The start for this is a ring of cordage to which is attached a first row of loops; then the weaver continues with further loops into this and into successive rows (see Fig. 3.2d). The end result is a conical basket which served as the chief burden carrier of these tribes.

Several methods of sewing in the coiled weave were developed prehistorically, most of them continuing down to the present. The technique of enclosing a current warp by passing the weft over it and securing it through an awl-punched hole to the coil below, as mentioned, is basic coiling. If the sewing is close together, the stitching is vertical; this is close coil (Fig. 3.11). If a weaver becomes careless, stitches may become more slanted. Or, if a weaver wishes, she may intentionally space out her stitches; the result can be labeled open stitching. Normal sewing is between stitches, and the current stitch is not involved with the one below: this is called non-interlocked or uninterlocked stitching (Fig. 3.12). However, if the weaver so chooses she can sew under the stitch in the coil below; this is called interlocked. Most Southwest coiled basketry is done in non-interlocked stitching.

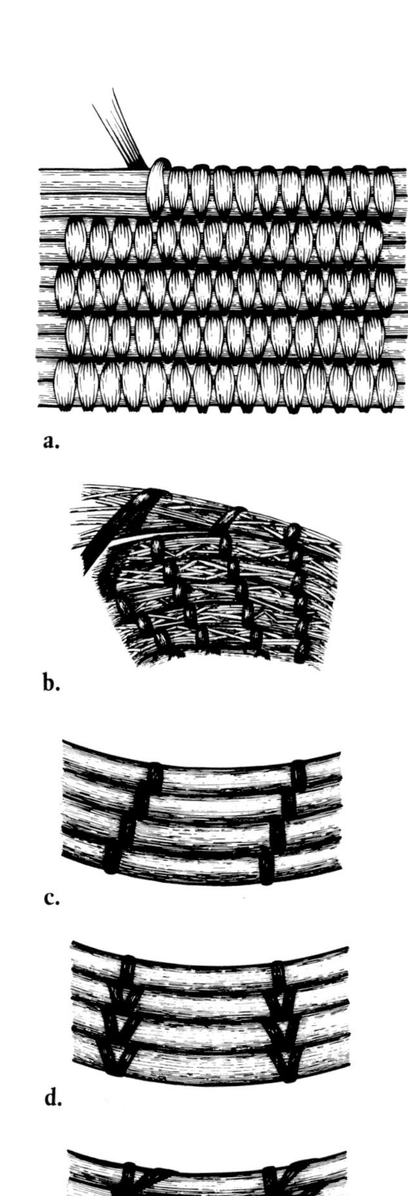

Fig. 3.11. Coiled weave, showing (a) close coiled where stitches touch or nearly touch; (b, c) open stitch coil, with stitches spaced out; (d) split stitch; (e) wheat stitch.

Rims on coiled pieces present an interesting facet of basketry, again often serving as a tribal diagnostic. Some rims definitely serve as a finishing touch to a basket; others leave a piece with an unfinished feeling, particularly in this coiled basketry. Some serve as a frame for design, whereas in other cases the lack of a definitive rim might suggest that design could escape momentarily.

The vast majority of Southwest coiled baskets are completed at the rim in the same stitch used in the creation of the object (Fig. 3.13); color then plays the significant role in definition or lack of it. Many tribes use a solid black rim, as in some of the Apache and

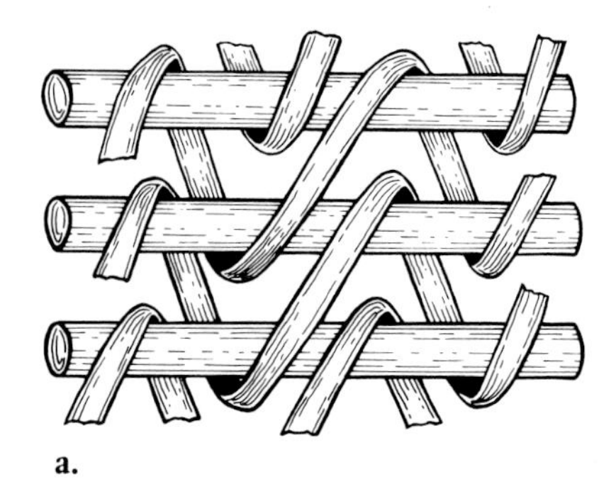

a.

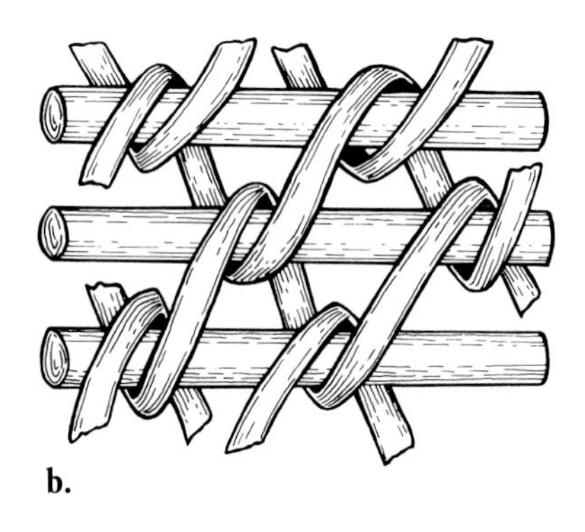

b.

Fig. 3.12. Types of stitch interrelationship in coiling: (a) non-interlocked stitching, where sewing goes between stitches below; (b) interlocked, where a stitch goes under a stitch below, whether in single rod, bundle, or other foundation.

Pima baskets, or all white or off-white, as exemplifed in Havasupai and some Hopi baskets. Apaches frequently alternate a black and white stitch in the rim coil; or a series of black stitches may alternate with a series of white stitches, as in occasional Apache or rare Havasupai baskets. Another device is to weave a plain white coil after the completion of the design, then top this with a black one, as in some Yavapai pieces. Quite a few weavers carry design into the rim, among others, the Hopis and Havasupais. Frequently, although not always, this lends a feeling that the basket is unfinished. The chief design motif or motifs may be so carried into the rim, again as is typical of many Havasupai and Hopi pieces; or a main theme and a lesser element may be treated in the same way. Or, less frequently, a small, secondary element alone may be worked at regular intervals into the rim, sometimes to give the feeling of a border or finishing touch, for frequently these are close together.

Less common than a single rim coil beyond the design is a white coil topped by another white or, as mentioned above, a black one. Rare is the use of a black coil, a white one, then alternating stitches of black and white as seen in a few Havasupai baskets. In a number of Chemehuevi ollas the weaver confined her design to a band on or near the widest diameter of the basket, then put many white coils above to the black or white rim coil.

A false braid or herringbone rim is to be noted on Navajo baskets whether made by the weavers of this tribe or by the Utes or Paiutes. Usually this braid went the full rim length, although in some tribal baskets it is to be found for the last inch or so only. In many Pima baskets and those produced by the Papago tribe up to and shortly after the turn of the century, a tight false braid was dominant on their willow baskets.

Papagos used a plain white or black rim or alternate black and white stitches on their yucca pieces for some years, along with their highly favored overstitching, usually in black, or later in green, on the white rim coil. This oversewing might be in one of several stitches, for example, cross stitching, or a combined long diagonal and a short vertical stitch, or just plain diagonal stitches close together or far apart (Fig. 3.13f, g, h).

Forms

In the vast majority of baskets around the world, form has responded to use values; once this utility is satisfied then the weaver is free to express herself as she wishes. To be sure, certain controls affect all workers, such as tribal values and styles, and always the weaver must respond to technique controls. It is amazing how many different variations can be and are developed within a single basket form.[21] The Southwest is no exception in this matter, for ingenuity is not limited to any part of the world.

Basket forms in the Southwest can be divided into two basic categories, native and introduced styles. The first group consists of forms which had been perfected and localized during prehistoric days. In prehistoric times there were some shapes that were so very specialized that they died when their use values ceased; then there were the good, reliable forms with use values which have survived to this day. The second category involves historically introduced shapes; most of these have come to the Indian by way of the Anglo-

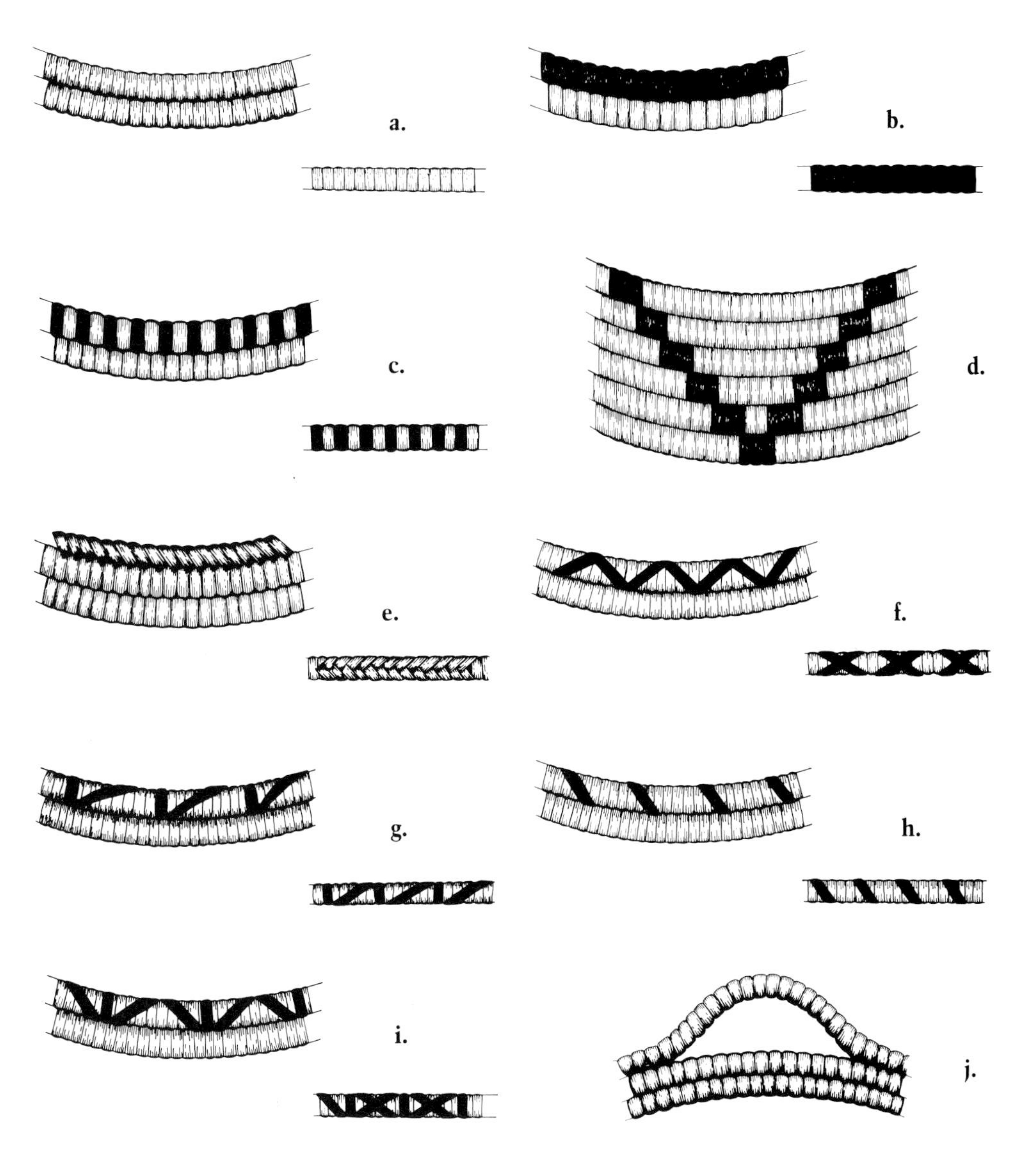

Fig. 3.13. Types of rim finish in coiled baskets: (a) of self material, natural or white; (b) all black stitching; (c) alternate black and white stitches; (d) design carried into rim; (e) braided rim, shallow or deeper; (f) cross stitch, from side to top; (g) long slanting and short vertical stitch; (h) diagonal stitch; (i) variations; (j) extended rim coil to make a handle.

Americans. In turn, some of these have been adapted into the Indian way of life but many more have been developed solely for white man's consumption.

Two basic native forms are the jar and the tray (Fig. 3.14). A distinction should be made immediately between a tray and a bowl, for all too frequently the latter name is applied to both forms. A tray is generally more shallow, it is characterized by a more sloping line from rim to base, and it is woven from the inside. Bowls, on the other hand, are deeper, often they have a straight or nearly straight line from rim to base, and frequently the weaver works from the outside. To be sure, there are borderline examples. For instance, there are bowls which are slightly more open or perhaps not so deep but are woven from the outside. When the shape is even more borderline and sewing is from the inside, identification becomes more difficult, as is true in almost all handicrafts.

Jars are quite varied in their uses; therefore, great variety is expressed in form. The basic form is a full body and a more or less restricted mouth. If use value is aimed at conveying or storing water, the mouth width proportion in relation to body is much smaller. If the jar is to be used for grain storage, a wider mouth is desirable. Other variations will reflect other use values. Then enters

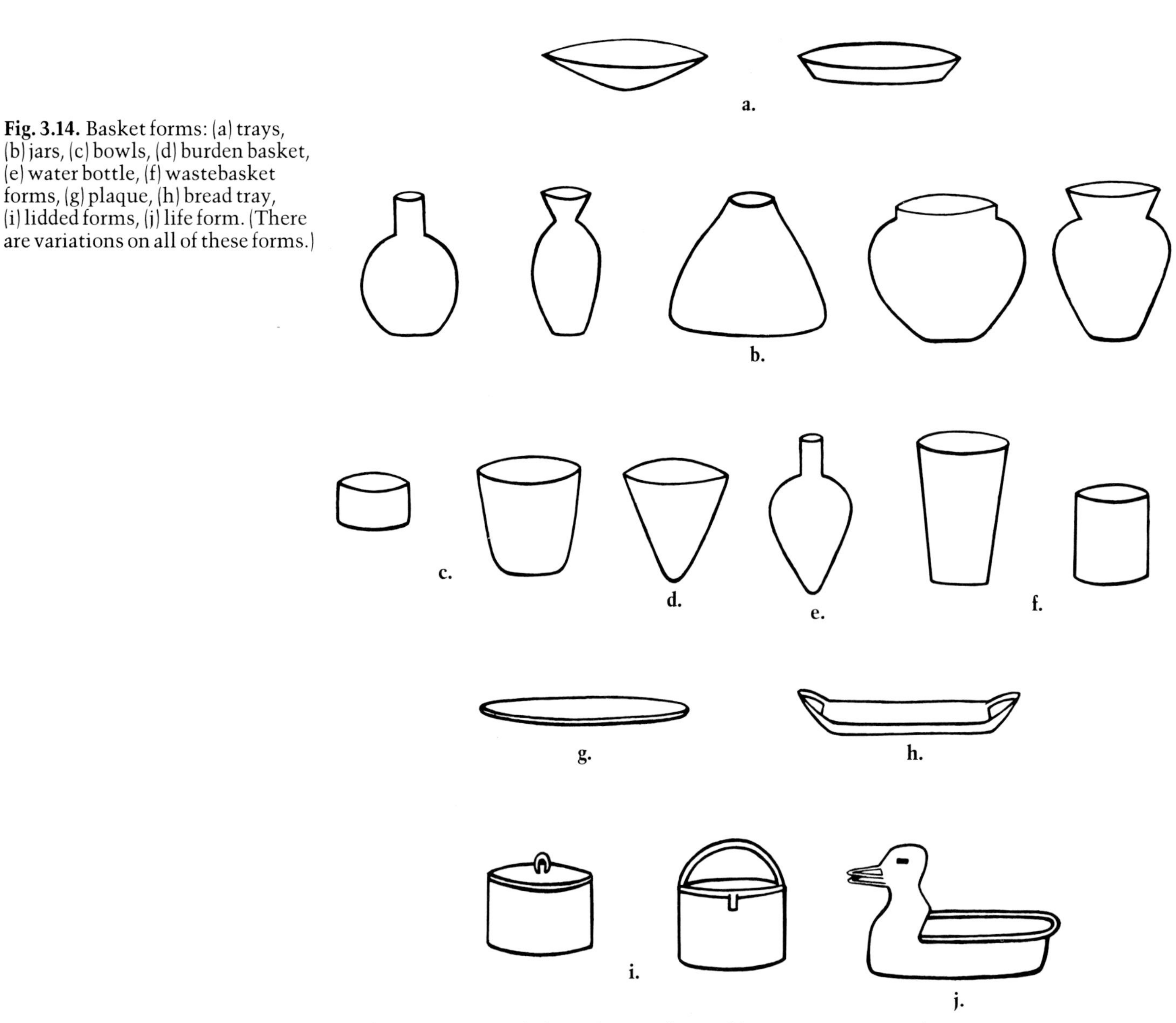

Fig. 3.14. Basket forms: (a) trays, (b) jars, (c) bowls, (d) burden basket, (e) water bottle, (f) wastebasket forms, (g) plaque, (h) bread tray, (i) lidded forms, (j) life form. (There are variations on all of these forms.)

the artist, with her desire for self-expression, or her response to tribal details of form. The wide mouth may have a longer or shorter neck; a slight outcurve, incurve, or straight line may be incorporated into its basic form. Vessel body can also be varied: it may be full and rounded, long and lean; it may have a distinct shoulder which can be high or low. The bottom of the jar may also reflect variety, for it can run the gamut from pointed to wide and flat or it may be rounded.

Trays represent the most abundant forms in the Southwest as a whole. They served many purposes, among others for gathering and winnowing seeds; for catching ground seeds or grains; for mixing and serving foods; and for washing. It would seem incredible that there could be variety in such a basket, but such is the case. Depth is variable, despite the fact that a wide, open mouth tapering to a small base is the rule. The wall of the tray can be gently sloping; it can take off in the vertical or nearly vertical, then slope downward and inward; the lip can be slightly outflaring, rarely inturned; and the body proper can be more or less rounded. Varied too is the base: it can be pointed or nearly so, it can be narrow or broad, it can be rounded or absolutely flat. Combining these varied details in a number of ways results in great diversity of tray forms.

Some tribes may express this diversity, such as the Apache,[22] while others may be more limited in this respect. Fewer variations in tray forms are to be noted in Pima and Papago collections, with the Papagos running first in this feature. The tray form is not common among the Hopis, although there is some difference in this matter in relation to time; one rarely sees a tray in later historic years which is not true in earlier times. The same generalizations here noted for trays in relation to several tribes would apply also to the jar form.

Bowl forms are generally less numerous than trays among most of the southwestern tribes. However, here, too, there is variation. Bowls are more common in later historic years among the Hopis; they are fairly abundant among Pimas and Papagos, and they are more limited among the Apaches. Frequently the two forms, trays and bowls, are illustrated together, with little or no clear-cut distinction between the two.[23]

A bowl is a deep and usually round form; however, there are oval shapes, particularly among the Apaches. Oval styles are not common anywhere, but they are widely distributed. The round bowl presents a variety in shape also, with the majority having straight sides and a flat or nearly flat bottom. Other variations would include those with sidewalls slightly bulging, an inward slant from rim to base, an inward-sloping rim, a slight outflare to the rim, or gentle rounding lines from the rim to a smaller base. Oval bowls tend to have less variety in shape, adhering primarily to a simpler and more straight-sided style.

Burden or carrying baskets were far more important to Southwest Indians in earlier years than they are today. However, a few Indians, such as some of the Western Apaches, still use this form. Conical and bucket-shaped burdens have remained popular through the years: Apaches still make and use the bucket style, and until very recent years the conical piece was used by several groups, among others, the Havasupais, Hualapais, Pimas, and Papagos.

Cylindrical forms may seem to be historic in style, and late historic at that. However, this form is also found rarely in prehistoric times. Whether native or introduced to the Jicarilla Apaches is unclear, but they have been producing this unusual shape in medium to quite large sizes for many years. About the turn of the century when the Papagos began to make more baskets for sale, and these of yucca, new forms came into focus. By the 1920s they were producing a cylindrical form, a deep straight-walled, flat bottomed, circular wastebasket. Prehistorically, this form seems to have been limited to ceremonial use; historically, it seems to have been made entirely for sale.

There is a large category of basketry forms made exclusively for commercial purposes. Not all of these fit into the true definition of a basket, for some serve more utilitarian purposes while others are strictly decorative or mere "gadgets." Among these commercial styles would be lidded pieces, usually circular, commonly used for sewing or for trinkets, purses, wood baskets, open-work baskets of various sorts, and a category of modeled animal, bird, human, and occasional other life forms. One odd type found prehistorically is called a trinket basket; it was a small bowl form with incurving lip; certainly some of the small and medium-sized, round and oval forms of today can be labeled the same. Sewing and work baskets are similar but usually larger in form and often with lids. Both the trinket and sewing-work shapes are rounded or straight in walls and flat-bottomed. Oval styles follow the same trends in walls and bottom.

Many and varied are the modeled life forms in southwestern Indian basketry. All are historic in time, for none has been reported from pre-Columbian sites. The majority of life forms belong to recent years, although a few began to appear about the 1900s. Modeled in the shape of the animal to be represented, and often identifiable as the same, the majority of these are today made by the Papago basket weavers, a few by other tribes. Quite popular are the cat and dog, with occasional humans. Owls, pigs, and ducks have been fairly popular as sales items. Sometimes the head of the cat or dog serves as a bottle "stopper"; quite generally they are modeled in the full round, insofar as this is possible in basketry. The duck's head alone is sometimes modeled on a round or oval bowl form. Whiskers are often added to the little cats; most of these pieces are small or miniature in size.

Plants should also be mentioned in conjunction with life forms in basketry. The saguaro cactus has been the most popular theme with Papago weavers, with small brush sometimes represented but not actually woven. Often a little scene is created by representing the saguaro in flat form and a full round figure of a woman with a stick in hand gathering red fruit from the tops of the cactus arms.

Work on most of the life forms is done in close or open coiled technique, for either of these is more adaptable to creating variety. If involved with a basket shape, as the duck's head on the bowl, that shape is also in the coiled weave. Much overstitching is employed to make eyes, mouths, and other details more realistic. Ears are often modeled in the weave. Feet are rather flat as a rule; so too are hands.

DESIGN ANALYSIS

Not surprisingly, design analysis for the basketry of all the tribes of the Southwest, each with its own distinct expressions in this art, can become quite complex. Parts of an analysis will be simpler in some groups, more elaborate in others.

Five major areas of analysis are to be considered, several of these with extensive divisions. These include area of decoration, layout, types of ornament, parts of design, and style. Before she starts to work, the weaver must first of all choose the area of decoration —that is, the particular part of the basket she wishes to decorate. At the same time, she must know just how she will arrange the pattern, which is layout. Parts of the design must be well organized mentally before the first stitch, and of course, she must know the type of ornament she will apply, for all materials must be prepared, especially colored elements, before she can properly start a basket. Style will come out as the basket weaver moves along, for it is in the putting together of these requisites that the basket becomes Apache, Navajo, or bears the style of whatever tribe the weaver represents.

Areas of Decoration

Area of decoration depends on many factors; in earlier years, the utility purpose of the basket would be basic to this choice. Water jars were seldom decorated, for the majority of them were heavily coated with piñon pitch, which meant that almost any design would be lost. Some burden baskets, reputedly, were not decorated at all on the side that would be next to the back; in prehistoric times, some baskets of this form had a much less significant and smaller design on this side. Often the walls of deep bowls and jars were chosen as the sole area of decoration of these two forms; however, the Apaches liked to decorate the bottoms of such forms, and thus the area of decoration for them was the entire vessel. Trays might be decorated all-over or restricted to a defined area. Whatever the form, and whatever its use, it was up to the weaver to make her decision relative to the above matters, but it was a decision which had to be made before the weaving process began, if the finished product was to have the desired unity and artistry.

Layouts

There are three basic general styles of layout: divided, undivided, and composite (Fig. 3.15). Under these are substyles: divided includes banded and half-banded; undivided includes centered, repeated, all-over, and organizational banded; the last category, composite, may include several of these types, such as banded-centered. Historic peoples not only used all layouts noted but developed a variety of ways of employing each one of them.

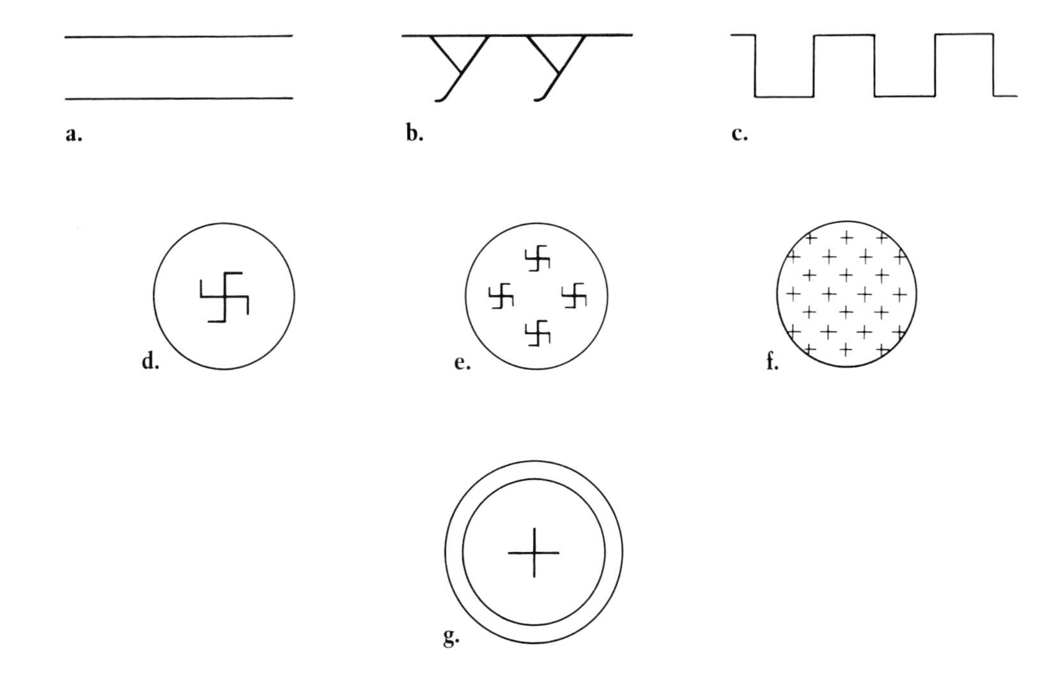

Fig. 3.15. Design layouts on basketry. Divided: (a) banded, (b) half-banded, (c) organizational banded. Undivided: (d) centered, (e) repeated, (f) all-over. Composite: (g) centered-banded.

Banded layouts are, properly speaking, designs enclosed between two lines. In basketry these lines are frequently woven as narrow enclosures; however, quite often the edge of a basket or the edge of a central solid colored circle might serve in place of an actual line.

The important thing to keep in mind is that a specific boundary was used by the weaver to contain the design, sometimes becoming a part of it. Rarely, one happens upon a basket where the weaver has changed her design plan along the way, and it is quite obvious.

When a band is used, the basket maker must also decide just how she is to apply design within this predetermined space. Her choices are numerous, controlled solely by custom and her ability. A running or a repeated design between the two lines represents the simplest choice; both styles are used by many basket weavers. Another utilization of the band is to divide it horizontally or vertically, confining specific designs to the resultant areas. The horizontal division is far more common than is the vertical; it is used by Apaches, Yavapais, and, occasionally, Pimas and Hopis. Far less common is the Chemehuevi use of the vertical band, generally with a single theme repeated in each division.

Half bands are also fairly common in basket designing. This means an element is suspended from a single line; often, as in Apache basketry, the black rim serves in this capacity. In the rim style, the half band can serve decoratively as few other layout styles can, for no other can fit so well at this point. Like many other layout styles, the half band is generally used in conjunction with some other style, although on certain basket forms or in certain weaves it may appear alone; this is true, for example, in Pai twined pieces and in Apache burden baskets. Simple geometrics are generally employed in half-band decoration, although on occasion more elaborate motifs may be so used.

The organizational band is one without benefit of bordering lines; however, the entire design is so used as to have an even edge on both top and bottom, or on each side if it is a vertical arrangement. A simple and regular fret would be a good example of this; many other geometrics and life forms have also been adapted to such bands. Organizational bands are featured by several tribes; for example, Apaches used this layout on jars, Papagos frequently apply it to modern trays and bowls, and Chemehuevis used it on small jars. It is not uncommon to find half bands, organizational bands, and true bands used in various combinations, two or all three together, on a single basket.

A *centered layout* is one in which the design is in the center of the basket, extending to a greater or lesser degree from there toward the rim. How far it should go to remain a centered theme is a matter of judgment; generally, this would be no more than three-fourths of the way out. By the same token, a centered theme can be small but seldom is; a small black circle in the center of a tray basket could be called a centered layout, but it is rare that so simple a theme is used alone. Centered layout can be made up of a simple or complex geometric design or of a single animal, two of them, or even a cluster of them. A mask on a Hopi plaque would serve as a good example of a centered layout. Centered layouts are much more frequently combined with other layouts to create complex ones.

Repeated layouts utilize the same or alternate themes which are spaced out around a bowl wall or that of a tray or plaque. The design element or motif is wider spaced than in an organizational band where they may be touching or continuous or are at least very close together. Generally they appear beyond center whether on a bowl or tray form. The designs in a repeated arrangement may be large or small, simple or complex. They may be repeated anywhere from two to a half dozen or more times, much depending on the size of the unit or motif itself and the size of the basket.

All-over layouts are commonly used by Southwest basket weavers, even where a tribal group tends to favor one or several other layouts. An all-over layout is exactly that: it covers practically all of the basket. Sometimes a little space is blank either at the very center or at the edge. There are more varieties of this layout than any other. The weaver can start with a theme in the center of the basket and carry it directly to the rim. She can make a continuous series of bands from center to edge. She can start with a black center, large or small, attach one or more motifs to this and carry it or them to the edge. She can place independent small or large elements, simple or complex in nature, all over the basket. The tray is perhaps the most common form where all-over layouts are utilized; bowls are often so ornamented; and, interestingly, Apache jars frequently are decorated with all-over layouts, for, as noted before, the base is always designed, and pattern often continues from the base to the rim.

Composite layouts represent the last style used by Southwest basket makers. This is a combination of two or more of the above described layouts. One common combination is centered and banded, with a definite space between the two. On the face of it, it might seem that there would be no difference between a composite and an all-over layout where the latter also has combined several other styles, but there is. In the latter case, all would be touching, or overlapping, or so close together that there could be no question of the intended style. On Hualapai and Havasupai twined burden baskets and bowls, there are frequent composite layouts consisting of half bands and true bands. A Hopi plaque may have a turtle in the center and an organizational band beyond it.

Parts of Design

Any given total design or pattern is usually made up of a number of parts. These parts include elements and/or units, and motifs, which produce the design itself (Fig. 3.16). Noteworthy is the fact that a given simple design can be each and every one of these. For example, if the only decoration on a basket is a central circle, then that circle is element, unit, motif, and design. If, on the other hand, the design is composed of a central black circle, a black encircling one-coil line about eight coils away, and six sets of four each of checkered diamonds attached to the line, then that pattern has to be broken down into its component parts. The elements are a circle, a line, and a square. Motifs include one which can be called primary, the stacked and checkered diamonds, and two which can be designated secondary, the line and circle.

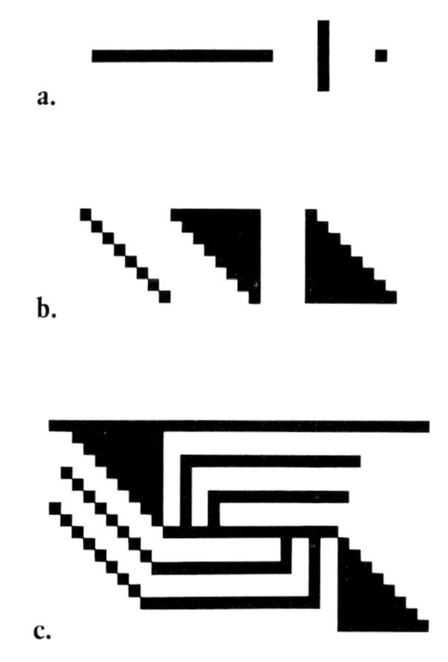

Fig. 3.16. Parts of design in basketry: (a) elements, (b) motifs, (c) the pattern or full design.

An element can be labeled the smallest part of a design, the basic part of a design. However, because there are many small parts of patterns which are not elements in the true sense of the word, the term unit is added. Perhaps good examples of this are the square and the triangle. Actually these parts of design are made up of four and three lines, respectively. However, the term element is applied frequently to both of these and to many more; thus, the word unit has been added here to accommodate to an already established terminology and to include other forms which are definitely used as elements. Many small life forms are used as elements, yet they are not such; quite properly they can be labeled units. A few simple and basic elements and units will be given here, and more will appear in each of the tribal discussions.

It is interesting that each tribe has developed through the years a pool of elements, units, motifs, and designs from which the weaver draws; basically, creativity is a matter of combining and recombining these to generate new patterns, or at least different ones; rarely, a new unit may be introduced. As in most of the craft arts, there is no out-and-out copying, and there is really little chance for originality; yet originality is present, for there are no two identical baskets unless so ordered, and that by a white man. Stars have been woven over and again by Apaches, yet differences appear in number of points, rounded or sharp points, outcurving or incurving sides, a narrow takeoff at the base from the inner circle or a wide or medium one, and any number of combinations and recombinations of these details, many with other units or motifs. The same variation in motifs, or even in units, for that matter, and an equally great number of variations in the ways in which all may be put together to form the design will explain in part why there is so much diversity in pattern in baskets of any given tribe.

Basic elements are the line and the dot, properly speaking. However, in this discussion, the terms element and unit will be used together; they are so designated on the accompanying chart (Fig. 3.17). Included, then, in elements and units for basketry are the dot, line, square, rectangle, triangle, diamond, circle, step, fret, and the simple life form. Actually life forms are sometimes so simple that they may be considered units, but for the most part, they are made up of lines, squares, and rectangles. Another important point to keep in mind is that the life form is frequently *used* as a unit; therefore, it is thought of as an independent entity or unit, whether it is complex or simple.

The line is surely the simplest form in the analysis of a design, and in basketry it varies with technology in several ways. To begin with, if used in plaited weave, it is broad, for the weaving elements are characteristically wide. In wicker it may be a stitch or more in width, while in coiled it can be a stitch or more or a coil or more in width. In this last weave will be found the finest lines, for in certain fine coiling the sewing element can be the smallest in any basket technique. In coiled basketry, lines can be straight, diagonal, perpendicular, or horizontal; they can encircle the basket and be curved. Lines are always straight in plaited weave; in wicker, if long, they are horizontal, but short ones may be horizontal, vertical, or diagonal. The curved line in coiled weave may be a complete circle or part of one. Curved diagonal lines are sometimes used to connect other elements or units of design. Straight or curved lines may form parts of or constitute whole bands; they may serve as the element of design, or as fillers in various geometric forms. Straight lines may be used to form geometrics, such as short, straight or diagonal units in bands, in either coiled or wicker weave; they are the basic elements in chevrons which are common in plaited weave.

Fig. 3.17. Design elements or units in basketry, showing some variations of each: (a) dot, (b) line, (c) square, (d) rectangle, (e) circle, (f) triangle, (g) diamond, (h) step, (i) fret and meander.

Squares are quite natural units of design in basketry, for the crossing of weaving elements at right angles readily produces this form. Squares can be in outline or solid in all three weaves. They can be concentric, with one, two, or more ever smaller squares within each, this particularly popular in plaited weave. The same is possible in coiled weave but is not used very often.

Size varies greatly in coiled squares: they may be very small or very large. The same is true of plaited, but in wicker, squares are usually small. One exception is in some Hopi baskets where the center square may well assume considerable proportions; otherwise the squares may be small. Squares are used stacked, joined, and to form checkers. In coiled weave, stacked squares are combined to build a variety of geometric forms.

Rectangles hold many possibilities comparable to the square, all as mentioned above, but they have several additional potentials. For example, inasmuch as the rectangle can be produced in different proportions, it can be built up in pyramid forms different from those made of squares. Because of its variability, many more modifications in the building of geometrics are possible, but, in general, the rectangle can be used as a solid, in outline form, in concentric arrangements, and stacked.

Triangles present an interesting unit in basket design, for the nature of technologies involved does not particularly invite this form; triangles, in fact, are one evidence of the inventiveness of the basket weaver. Actually, if a design does incorporate a triangle, the chances are that it will be in stepped or partially stepped form. Most triangles are so represented, yet the really fine craftsman was able to and did produce even and smooth-sided triangles. Like the preceding geometric forms, triangles can be solid or open; in addition, they can be right-angle, isosceles, or equilateral. Occasional other variations appear, sometimes quite by accident. Triangles, too, can be built up to create other forms, such as the hourglass, and often they are combined with other geometrics for the creation of even more elaborate patterns.

Much noted about triangles can be said for diamonds; for example, they are usually stepped but can be smooth-sided. Apaches made some interesting alterations in the basic shape of this geometric, the most common being the decrease in size and incurving of the lower half, and the increase in size and outward curving of the upper portion. No other name can be given to this form but diamond, or, better yet, Apache diamond. Many times the grace of these curving diamonds made up for distortions of the basic form; that it is a distortion is indicated in the earlier use of the plain diamond. Diamonds, like squares, were used in outline form, as solids, or one-half solid, one-half outline or solid with a negative pattern, or outline with a positive pattern within it, or stacked.

The circle is practically always related to the center of the basket, if it is used at all. Pimas and Papagos, when using willow, and Apaches employ a solid black center circle in practically all of their coiled baskets. This may be small or large, and frequently it may have one or more circular lines surrounding it. Often some immediate motif is associated with this central circle, not in any way interfering with its complete form. On the other hand, there are many designs which grow out of this center, becoming a part of it. Sometimes this remains a distinct motif in itself, but at others it becomes a part of the total basket design. The black material in all these baskets is martynia, which is fairly hard. Certainly in many cases the basket was started with this more sturdy material because the burden of wear was on the bottom.

Perhaps the most natural pattern in basketry is the step. All three techniques invited this form in the weaving process. In so many cases it becomes a part of such familiar forms as the square, diamond, and rectangle that it is neglected as a separate entity. And yet, time and again, it is used as a distinct design unit. For example, one of several stepped lines may proceed from the black center, or near it to the edge or close to it, in a tray form. There may be wide steps and short risers, or some other combination. The steps may be thick as made of a number of stitches, or narrow as composed of only two stitches.

Meandering lines and frets may also be considered as design units; further, they are to be found in all techniques of basket making. In general, they run the gamut from very simple to quite elaborate. They may be done in narrower or broader lines, independent of other themes or in combination with other units; they may be the sole decoration on a basket or become so involved with other patterns that they are lost. Many meanders or frets appear in horizontal arrangement, but it is not uncommon to find some running from center toward the edge of a basket, either in a straight or diagonal manner.

Another category of design units is the life form, including for the most part, quadrupeds, humans, birds, and butterflies. Snakes or other reptiles are less commonly portrayed, and when they are they tend to be more complex in form. Life units are made up of squares, rectangles, lines, and, rarely, other geometrics, but frequently they are used as units of design. Of course, in some instances, they are definitely motifs, or, for that matter, the total design. The latter can be demonstrated in late Papago work, where a lizard or Gila monster may be the only design on the basket, or on a Chemehuevi piece which has a snake for the sole decoration. Plant themes should also be mentioned, including bushes, flowers, trees, and cacti.

Types of Ornament

Technology and certain types of ornament are closely related, but in some styles of decoration there is little or no control of embellishment in technique used in producing the basic basket. There are at least a half dozen ways of decorating basketry, other than in the weave itself, which were or are used in the Southwest. These include painting on the finished basket; the addition of feathers, usually during the process of weaving; the addition of beads; and the addition of buckskin, tin tinklers, or other foreign material. The full modeling of life forms in basketry is late; it, however, is related to technology. Handles, loops for carrying baskets, and other such devices can be decorative; generally these may be tied to technology.

The woven design is, to be sure, the most common decorative device used in the Southwest at any time. Two basic colors have been mentioned, black and red, in this order of importance. The use of natural materials of other colors, plus the great variety of native dyes or introduced anilines, has already been discussed. The greater variety of colors surely invited some complexity of design, perhaps even new subject matter; technology and imagination were the only limiting factors here. The natural color of which most of the basket was woven tended to be on the light side, and, when bleached, as is yucca, is definitely white. Most of the light colors darken with age or even turn a slightly different color. The basic colors can usually be determined.

Painting is in no way related to the color in woven design, except where the native pool of elements, units, and motifs is concerned.

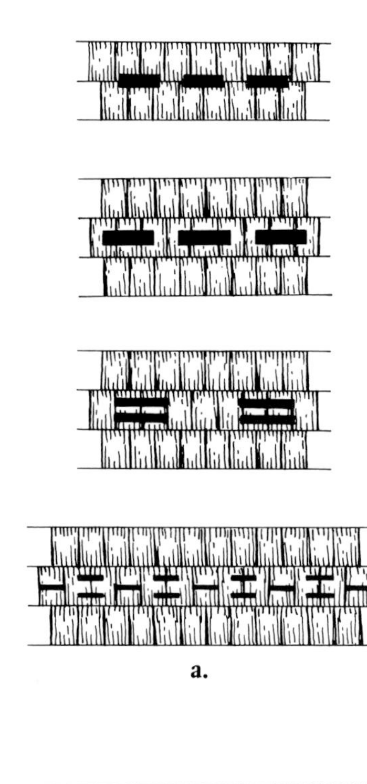

a.

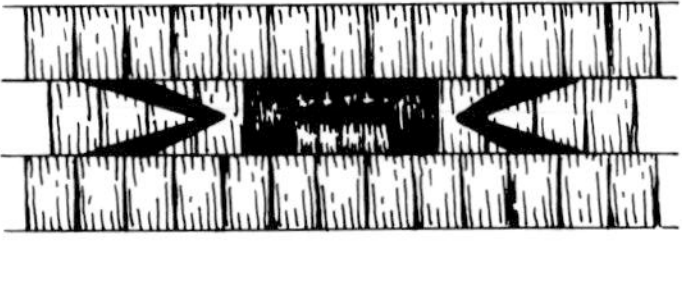

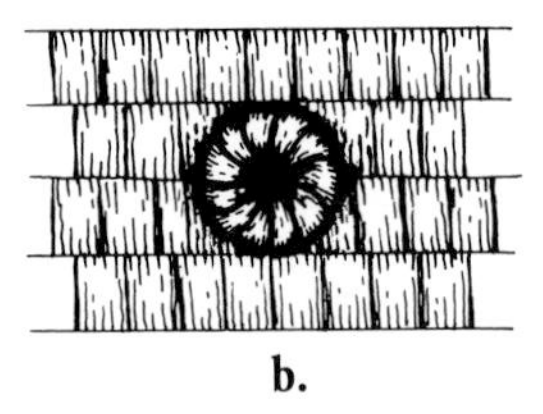

b.

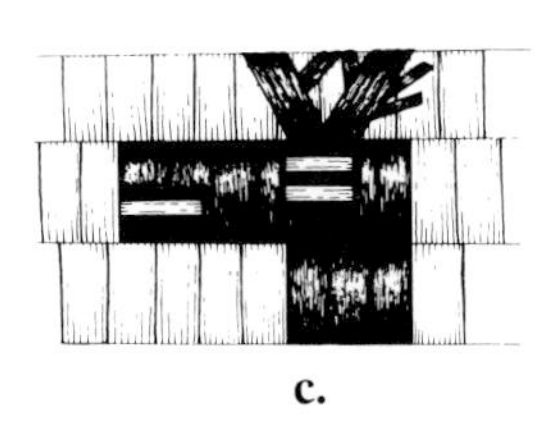

c.

Fig. 3.18. Types of overstitching: (a) horizontal, between and on coils, lighter or heavier; (b) diagonals, often combined with horizontals or circles; (c) more elaborate use of horizontal and diagonal lines, plus black and white overstitching.

Painting in the current geometric patterns has been practiced in a very limited manner in historic years, particularly by the Apaches and Pimas; for the most part, simple geometrics or bands were depicted. The impermanence of painted design invited no development of this technique; thus, it gained no favor. It is possible that this method of decorating was practiced more widely than is known, but the very fact that it did not last leaves this open to question.

Feathers which are added during the weaving process were used in a very limited manner historically. Generally, nothing but the hard center rib or quill remains to tell of their use, as in late historic Chemehuevi baskets. Otherwise, feathers have not been woven into baskets of other tribes, but on occasion they have been tied on pieces for ceremonial purposes. Beads appear at various times, largely around the turn of the century. Pimas, and rarely other tribeswomen, would attach larger or smaller blue trade beads around the rim of some of their baskets. Otherwise there has been very little use of beads in the Southwest, despite the fact that they were employed in abundance in parts of California.

Some types of relief work have been discussed under technology and are closely related thereto. They need to be referred to here again in relation to their importance in decoration. Actually, this would cover anything from the flat relief of a sewn element to represent an eye (Fig. 3.18) to modeled features on a jar cover. Hopis have long done oversewing to represent facial features, or details of a mask or costume. Colored filaments or natural ones on a colored area are used by Hopis, while most of the Papago oversewing threads are black or white. Modeling in the full round is also related to technology. Papagos in particular have expressed this unusual decorative technique, largely within the past thirty years. Of course, commercialization of basketry has been the great inspiration in this trend.

Foreign materials other than beads or feathers comprise one other area where decoration is involved. For years the Apaches used a rich red baize under a buckskin patch at the bottom of the burden basket. The cloth was often cut so that it would have a scalloped or v-shaped border around the edge of the buckskin. The buckskin itself was added for utility purposes, to protect the bottom of the vessel, but sometimes it too was cut so as to be more decorative. On these same baskets the Apaches often added four vertical bands of buckskin, usually along the area of the internal ribs mentioned above. These were more or less decorative as they were carefully (or carelessly) cut and attached to the basket side. Added to almost all of these bands, and sometimes also around the rim of the basket, were decorative thongs of the same soft materials, frequently with tin tinklers attached to their ends.

Style

Many factors pertaining to this craft are involved in the matter of style in basketry. Style reflects both the artist and his tribe; it involves all aspects of the expression of a given work of art, in this instance the total basket. It is concerned with details of form, with perfection of technology, with adapation of design to the shape involved. It relates to types of ornaments and their suitability to the specific basket in question. Reflective of style also are such aspects of design as repetition and rhythm, balance, positive and negative design, dynamic versus static decoration, curvilinear and rectilinear styles, geometric and life elements and units, symmetry and asymmetry.

Repetition and rhythm are very basic in most primitive art around the world, and particularly so in relation to any weaving crafts. The very nature of basket weaving would support this, for the evidence would indicate that weaving itself was perfected long before any attempts were made at the addition of design. Regularity and evenness of stitches in weaving were developed; perhaps there was evolved a system of counting or simple measuring which, when later applied to design, would invite repetition and rhythm. It is likely that song and dance had developed these two aspects of art, suggesting their use in other expressions. Thus there evolved in basketry of the plaited variety an over-two-under-two rhythm which in turn contributed to repetition in design. The better executed this repetition and rhythm, the better the design. Pride in workmanship carried over into pride in artistry. Certainly the lack of design in early prehistoric southwestern baskets, yet perfected method or technologies, would support this thesis.

Types of rhythmic repetition developed in all-over basketry design would include an a-a-a-a style (Fig. 3.19); in other words, the same element, say a dog, was repeated throughout the design, dog-dog-dog-dog. However, if the rhythm was a-b-a-b-, then the dog would alternate repetitively with another form, say a man; thus, man-dog-man-dog. Both of these repetitions are common in southwestern basketry. There are other and more elaborate types, for instance, a-b-c-b-a, this exemplified in an Apache basket where both color and form play parts: a mammal in a white triangle, a mammal in a red triangle, a man, mammal in a red triangle, mammal in a white triangle—or, as in the drawing, dog, man, bug, man, dog. Occasionally even more elaborate rhythmic repetitions occurred.

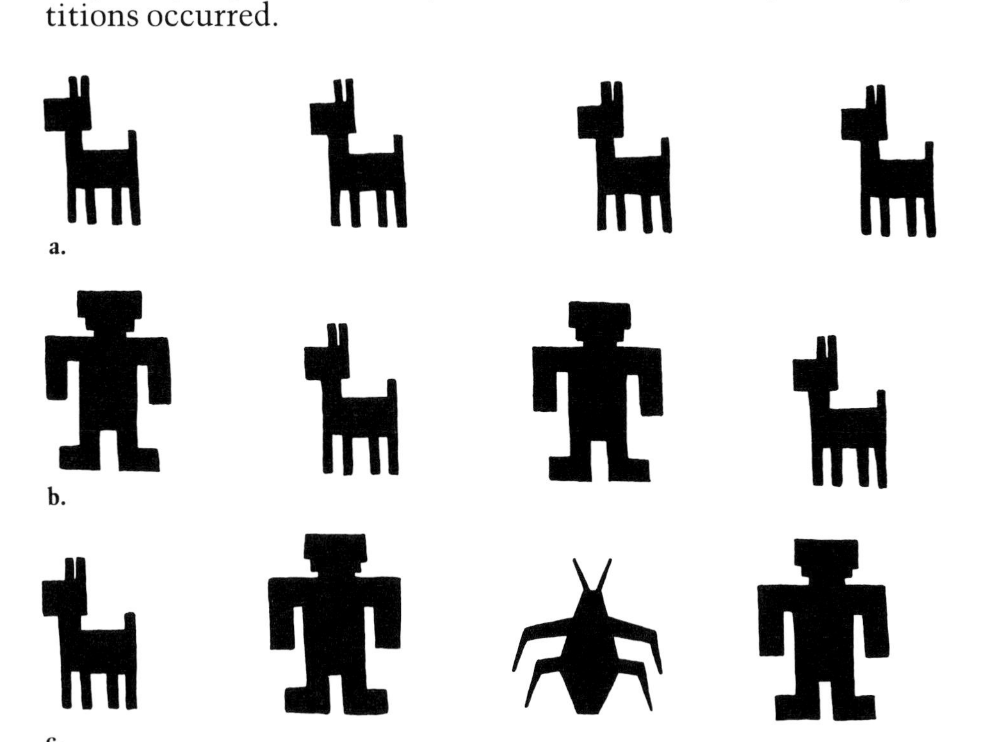

Fig. 3.19. Types of repetition in bands: (a) repetition of the same theme, a-a-a; (b) alternate repetition of two different themes, a-b-a-b; (c) three different motifs repeated in the order given, a-b-c-b-a.

Balance in design is closely related to rhythm and symmetry. Man is surrounded by balance in great abundance, beginning with himself. The halves of the human body are so obviously alike, as are many trees, a flower, all animals, and many another item with which man came in contact on frequent occasions. For millennia before he wove baskets, man made stone tools in which were developed beautiful symmetry and balance. Perhaps this contributed to the development of a balanced form in the basket itself; balance was also important to utility. This, then, was later applied to design. Many of these steps would be so slow that it may well have taken many hundreds, if not several thousands, of years of making baskets, perfecting technologies and forms, before man felt the necessary confidence to attempt design. But when he did, a few matters were so indelibly impressed on his mind, so well established in his fingers, that from the beginning there were symmetry and balance in basket designing.

Symmetry is most commonly left-right, as expressed in a triangle in Apache basketry; it appears in the left-right balance of each petal of the squash-blossom pattern in the Pima basket. Other life figures frequently express this principle—lizards and turtles, depicted as though one were looking down on the creatures, or a spread-wing bird which is balanced left-right throughout except for the head. Masks on Hopi pieces are usually presented in left-right symmetry. On Papago baskets, however, the woman picking saguaro fruit is usually in profile. Top-bottom symmetry is seldom used alone but is accompanied by left-right symmetry; a good example of this is the diamond, plain or elaborate. That this style with up-down balance was not as popular as the other, the left-right balance, is indicated in such matters as filling the upper half of a diamond while leaving the lower half plain or outlining the upper half and not the lower, thus breaking some of the up-down symmetry.

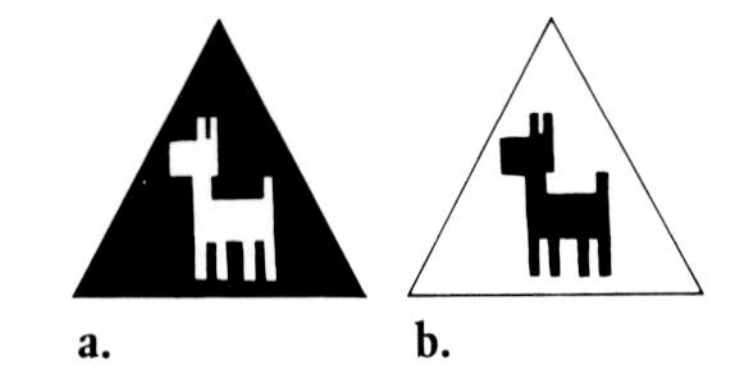

Fig. 3.20. Positive and negative designing: (a) a dog in light on dark, or negative patterning; (b) the common style is positive, as represented by a black dog on a white ground.

Positive and negative patterning were both developed by Southwest basket weavers (Fig. 3.20). Both styles were particularly popular with the Apaches, for frequently they would alternate a black element on a natural ground with a white one on a black ground. A great deal of leeway was expressed by this tribe in such matters, for sometimes they would alternate one positive theme with a totally different negative subject. Apparently positive design preceded negative by many centuries, for no negative patterns are found in the first baskets of early prehistoric times. Positive patterning has dominated throughout history in the Southwest; some tribes seem never to have developed the negative style, while others tended to use it frugally.

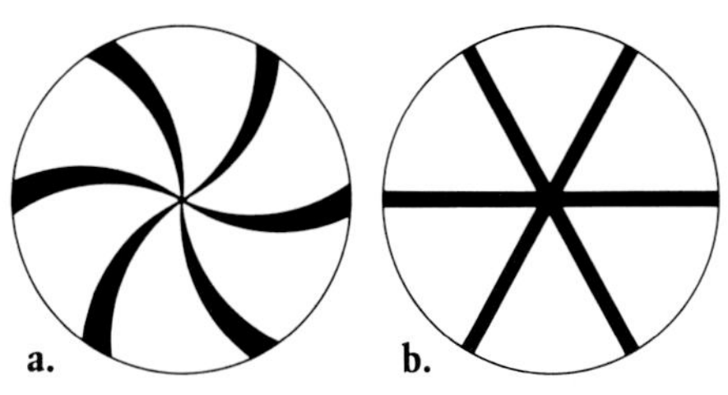

Fig. 3.21. Characteristics of the all-over design: (a) dynamic or moving; (b) straight out or static.

Dynamic versus static presents another interesting aspect of basketry decoration (Fig. 3.21). Almost all early prehistoric design was static, but by mid-prehistoric times dynamic patterning was well established; as far as historic tribes are concerned, there has been quite a difference in this expression from one tribe to another: both styles have been popular with the Apaches, as might be expected, while Hopis have favored static patterning, but dynamic styles do appear now and then, particularly in wicker baskets. Chemehuevi baskets are more apt to be decorated in controlled, static designing, and Pima is more dynamic than Papago.

Static patterns are those which do not move or express a feeling of motion, often because most lines are vertical and/or horizontal. Bands tend to be in this style, with designs within them either geometrics or life forms. When diagonals are introduced, either into the details of patterning or direction of the motifs, then the design often assumes a dynamic feeling. Motion can be varied in degree, from slight to exaggerated. A Pima maze pattern flows from center almost to the rim, thus demonstrating considerable dynamism. So too with an Apache swirl which takes off the center black circle and ends forty-five degrees or more at the rim. A pattern can be dynamic or static in small parts or in its entirety.

a.

b.

Fig. 3.22 Characteristics of designs: (a) rectilinear; (b) curvilinear.

Curvilinear and rectilinear patterning are both known to and used by Southwest tribes in the decoration of their baskets (Fig. 3.22). Unquestionably, the rectilinear prevails, for it is far easier to produce in all three techniques where weaving is a matter of one element crossing another at right angles. By the same token, in both coiled and wicker the direction of each line in the basket can be in a circling fashion. Particularly in the former does this have a tendency to create a circle from the center outward, for this is the nature of the coil itself; in both weaves separate encircling lines or bands can also be produced. In building up from one row of stitches to the next, the weaver can adjust the color so as to make for a curving line from inner to outer positions. According to the degree of this adjustment, the curve may be more or less exaggerated. Some weavers know and use this device, some know and avoid it; thus, designing is more or less curvilinear according to the whims of the weaver. Like all the other traits under consideration here, this feature often developed one way or the other as a tribal expression. For example, as mentioned above, old Papago baskets favored angular, rectilinear patterning while those of the Pimas featured curvilinear styles.

Geometric and life elements and units are often good measures of time or indicators of specific tribes. For example, few life forms were used by Pimas and Papagos prior to the late 1930s; thereafter, they became quite commonly used by the Papagos. Pimas still use few of them. In like manner, few or no life forms were woven into the baskets of the Apaches before the 1880s or 1890s; thereafter, they became quite common. Life forms are extremely rare in prehistoric baskets. In a sense, it is difficult to say that the life forms themselves are different from the geometric, for they *are* geometric. Men are made up of lines, squares, and rectangles, as are birds, butterflies, horses. It is in the arrangement of the several geometrics that the life forms are created, and there is no question but that they are life forms.

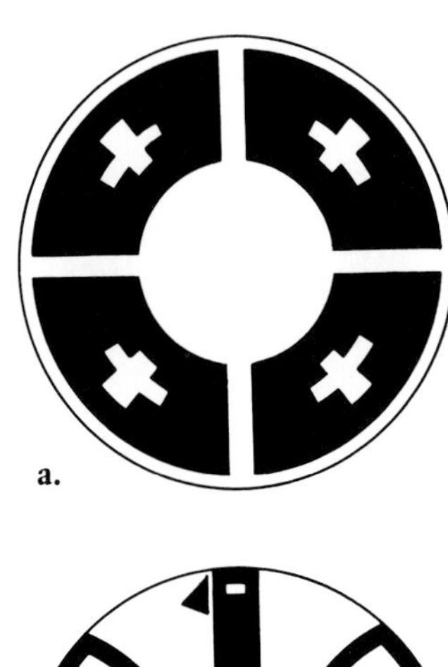
a.

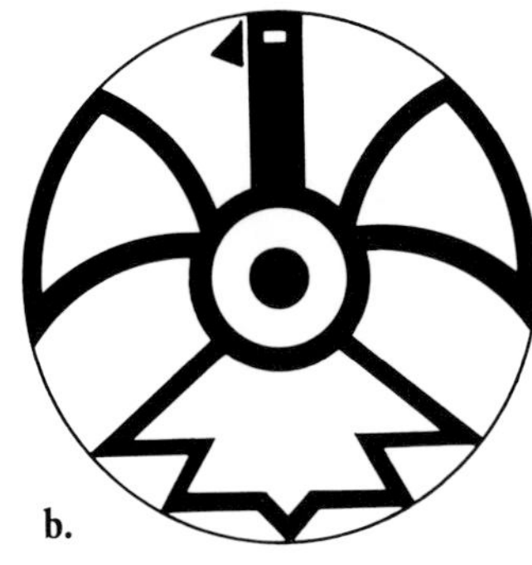
b.

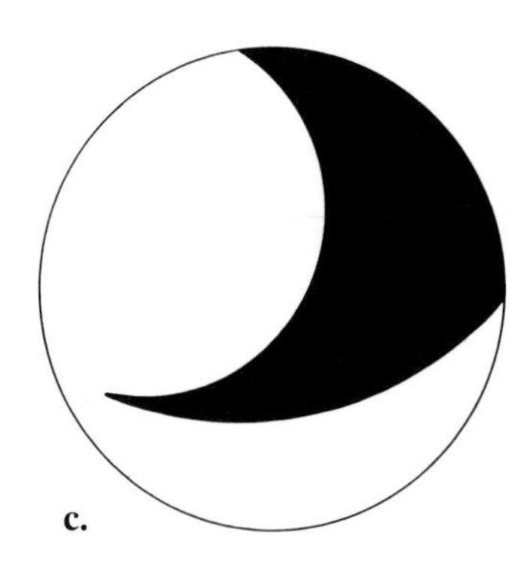
c.

Fig. 3.23 Symmetry in basket design: (a) symmetrical or balanced pattern; (b) asymmetry or lack of balance, slight; (c) more exaggerated asymmetry or lack of balance.

Symmetry predominates over asymmetry by a great deal in basketry design (Fig. 3.23). Again the motivating factor is technology, for it is easier by far to maintain symmetry in balanced repetitive elements and motifs than it is to break away and create an asymmetric pattern. Few tribes ventured in this direction, and the most prominent example is the Hopi—often and surprisingly in wicker weave. Here they excelled in producing a great swirl which starts with a broad base toward the center and moves out toward the edge, ending in an almost-point.

Design and form are closely related. An open tray invites a variety of designs while a straight-sided bowl with a flat bottom usually restricts pattern to the wall or at least divides it into wall and bottom. Jars almost always are not decorated on the base; however, an interesting exception has been noted in Apache jars where the base is practically always decorated. Otherwise all decoration of baskets is placed where it will be visible, where it can be seen and enjoyed.

One other feature might be mentioned in relation to style in basketry and that is the quality of the weave itself. This involves preparation of materials and quality of workmanship, as well as all of the above matters pertaining to style. Stitch and coil counts are very significant in relation to quality in coiled weave; around four stitches to the inch means that no fine designs can be created, that elements and units are large, as is the final pattern. Much detail can be expressed in a weave where the stitch count is sixteen to eighteen to the inch, as is to be noted in Chemehuevi and some of the better Apache pieces. The same general remarks apply to wicker, and, relatively, to plaited weave, but in both of these techniques there is less designing as a whole and therefore the problem is not quite as involved.

Style, then, is a composite of traits, a combination of many things well done. Creativity and imagination play a part, obviously, for the relatively limited pool of tribal themes would soon wear itself out if the weaver did not create as she went along from basket to basket. The weaver was well organized in her mind as to what form she was going to produce, what designs she was to use, and where she was to place each part of pattern. And, in addition, all of the matters just discussed—repetition and rhythm, whether the design is to be negative or positive, static or dynamic, curvilinear or whether it would be strictly angular geometric, whether there would be a few life forms added, whether there would be a flowing, dynamic, asymmetric theme or the usual symmetrical pattern—all of these matters and more would be well in mind before the weaver started the little coil for the basket beginning. Perhaps one of the greatest attributes of these craftsmen is their ability to visualize the finished product before they start to weave.

Chapter 4

Pueblo Basketry

Hopis have long been and still are the greatest puebloan basket producers. Whereas most pueblo women pursued one weave alone, Hopis practiced all three. Great variety characterized Hopi basket shapes and designs, but in both of these areas expressions were limited among other puebloans. Basketry has died out or is very limited among Rio Grande villages, but it is alive and progressing artistically among the Hopi Indians.

HOPI

Hopi Indian basketry probably has the longest continuous life of any in the Southwest today, for its heritage can be traced back 1500 years and possibly much more. Baskets are frequently seen about Hopi homes, either on walls or in practical or ceremonial use. The plaited ring basket serves as a sifter, coiled plaques or trays are significant in relation to weddings, other types are used as containers or decorations in the home. Vroman, who photographed the Hopis between 1895 and 1904, shows baskets hung around a fireplace and a row high above a shelf.[1] These may have been decorative, but many such baskets were used to bring produce in from the fields. Sifter baskets were employed to winnow seeds and grains. Baskets held parched corn, piki bread, cornmeal, corn, or other food stuffs.

Baskets are made for wedding presents; formerly, it was requisite for one to be given to a groom by his bride; when he died, it was buried with him as a necessary adjunct to his journey into the world beyond. Now a dozen or more are promised for the wedding occasion, to be exchanged between families. Baskets serve as containers for ceremonial events, for example, to be placed at altars or filled with meal or bean sprouts, often to be carried in the ceremonial dance. They are given as prizes at ceremonial races; they are the center of attention in the women's Basket Dance.

Baskets have always been an important trade item. Before any commercialization in relation to white man, Hopis traded baskets —or for baskets—with other tribes. Perhaps this may explain the appearance of the Navajo wedding basket design in a small piece carried in the Supai Dance by each masked man at the village of Hano (witnessed 1965). There was not only an exchange of baskets with other tribes but also between the Hopi villages. Certainly white man has been trading for Hopi baskets since the late 1800s, for there are considerable numbers of aniline-dyed pieces in museum and private collections dated before 1900.

Throughout the twentieth century Hopi baskets have been trade items to tourists who visit their villages and to traders both on and off their Reservation. The presence of Hopi basketry in larger or smaller quantities in competitive exhibits has encouraged not only their popularity, but also has increased their monetary value. The annual Hopi Craftsman Show at the Museum of Northern Arizona, Flagstaff, has been the greatest single factor in the development of the highest quality in this craft as a whole: throughout the year prior to this show members of the Museum staff visit the villages to offer encouragement to basket weavers. Results have been gratifying.

Reputedly, Hopi basketry degenerated with the use of aniline dyes in the late 1800s and very early 1900s. It is quite likely that this was true in some areas of basket weaving but not in all. For example, some coiled pieces utilized gross-sized coils, unattractive reds and greens, and designs that were less than commendable; on the other hand, some conservative coiled and wicker designing was very good in the use of both geometric and life motifs in good colors. With the shift of families from Old Oraibi to Hotevilla and a return to native dyes in 1906, certainly colors improved. About the same time large coils were still popular and they continued so for a while, but by the late 1920s and 1930s coils were reduced in size and designs were improved. It was noted that in 1931 about three hundred Hopi women were making good baskets for sale.[2] By the early 1960s great improvements had been made: Danson said in 1963 that better coiled work was being produced at that time than ever before.[3] By the late 1960s and throughout the 1970s another and still higher peak was reached, with the finest work in both coiled and wicker weaving and designing ever produced by this tribe. Many of the 1982 Hopi Show pieces (at Flagstaff) were superb. More elaborate designs characterized sifter baskets during these same years.

HOPI COILED BASKETRY

Traditionally, Hopi coiled basketry has been woven on Second Mesa only. It is, of course, one of the oldest forms of the craft arts among the Hopis, for their ancestors followed this technique as far back as they can be traced. Just when—and if—this craft became limited at an earlier date to Second Mesa is not known. However, it has been perpetuated in the villages of Mishongnovi, Shipaulovi, and Shungopovi of this Mesa since the later years of the nineteenth century. This weave is highly productive of design and, despite its large, fat coils, it has been most sensitive to the development of a variety of patterns. Too, interest in natural colors and native dyes has continued, despite the great popularity of aniline dyes among the wicker weavers. Forms have also remained primarily native, although a little license has been taken in this matter.

Materials

Materials in coiled baskets of Second Mesa are basically galetta grass and yucca.[4] Either of these materials may be split into very fine elements to form a firm and very round foundation. The Hopi woman is extremely clever in making additions to this foundation as she weaves, to keep the size even and regular throughout the entire basket. Yucca is always used for the sewing material. It too is kept the same size throughout the basket, despite the fact that the weaver prepares most of her material without any artificial aids. Sewing moves in a counterclockwise direction, and all stitches are non-interlocking.

Colton says that the white yucca used for background is from the core of the plant; occasionally, green or yellow may be substituted or at least used as a partial background. Green is from other leaves of the yucca, and yellow is simply the partially bleached leaf from the same plant.[5] Black and red or red-brown dyes (called "Indian red" by Colton) are produced from native plants, the black from sunflower seed (*Helianthus petiolaris*), piñon gum, and ocher, or from sumac (*Rhus trilobata*), and the red from one of several types of small grasses, *Thelesperma* sp.[6] The red dyed material is smoked, the black is not. There is some variation in all of these colors, darker or lighter shades of all of them to be noted in different baskets.

Hopi coiled baskets are begun by tightly wrapping a very small bundle, quickly turning it against itself, and starting the sewing into this circle. Very quickly the large coil is established. The Hopi woman sews so close together, and so tightly, that it is sometimes difficult to count the stitches. Hopi women split the yucca with an awl, and then use their teeth to split very fine and even splints. These prepared strips of yucca are kept in moist sand to make them flexible at Shungopovi, but at Mishongnovi and Shipaulovi the weaver runs the strips through her mouth.[7] A steel awl is used to pierce the coil below so as to accommodate the sewing strip. The Hopi woman is very cautious to pull the inserted thread tightly at this point, as well as when she is wrapping the coil. Each new stitch goes between two stitches below; again, this is done with the greatest of care.

Edges are generally finished in the regular stitch of the basket; quite commonly the design is carried into this rim coil. However, this is not always done and there may be a white or black edge coil. The end or tip of the last coil is usually rather abrupt.

Forms

Forms of Hopi coiled baskets are quite varied. Despite changes during the years, certain forms have remained popular for long periods of time. The flat plaque—and it is almost always flat in this weave—serves as a food tray; its life span is long, for it is found among pre-1900 baskets. Shallow trays are not uncommon. A small globular basket, which is used for seed storage, is similar to pieces of prehistoric times. Jars are also woven, more of them in earlier years than later. Deep forms, including the wastebasket (an obvious concession to white man), have also been popular for a long while; often they appear in older collections. On occasion, a very large basket may be woven by a Hopi woman, more or less in the wastebasket or jar form; several of these are over 5 feet in height.

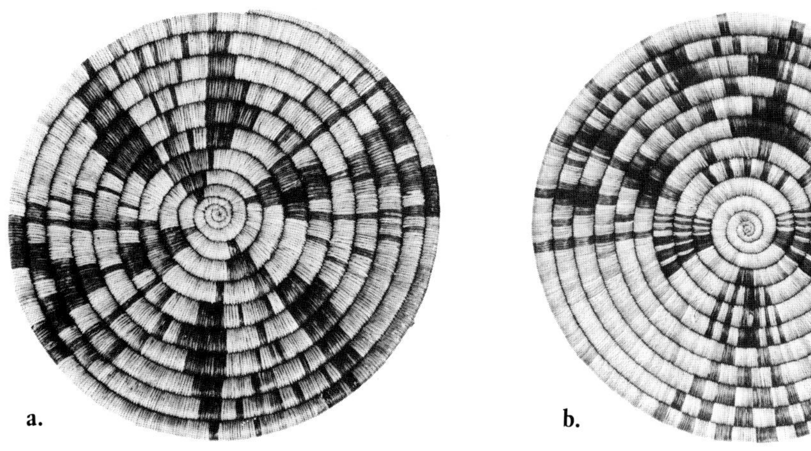

Fig. 4.1. Two early plaques featuring large coils and the use of red and green, the latter so badly faded it is hardly discernible. They are representative of the 1890–1930 period. (a) This is a good example of geometric pattern which radiated from near-center into the rim; (b) a simplified mask (*ASM 8207, 20670*).

Brief Historical Summary

During the years 1890–1930, coils were almost an inch in diameter; stitching, interestingly, was about the same then as now, averaging fourteen to the inch. Colors were predominantly white, bright red, and green, although there were other anilines plus natural colors. Design was rather generalized and less coordinated than in later years. Often there were lines from a real or imagined circle near the center which radiated into the rim (Fig. 4.1), and there were designs, usually simple, within or related to these lines. Common themes were clouds with or without rain (see drawings in margin) and usually in outline, elongated diamonds, and other geometrics which were often indefinite. Sometimes designs were almost all-over, for example, like a sunburst pattern with rays to the edge of the basket, or a large masked figure.

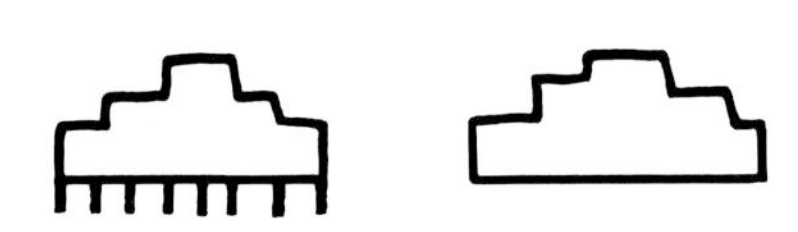

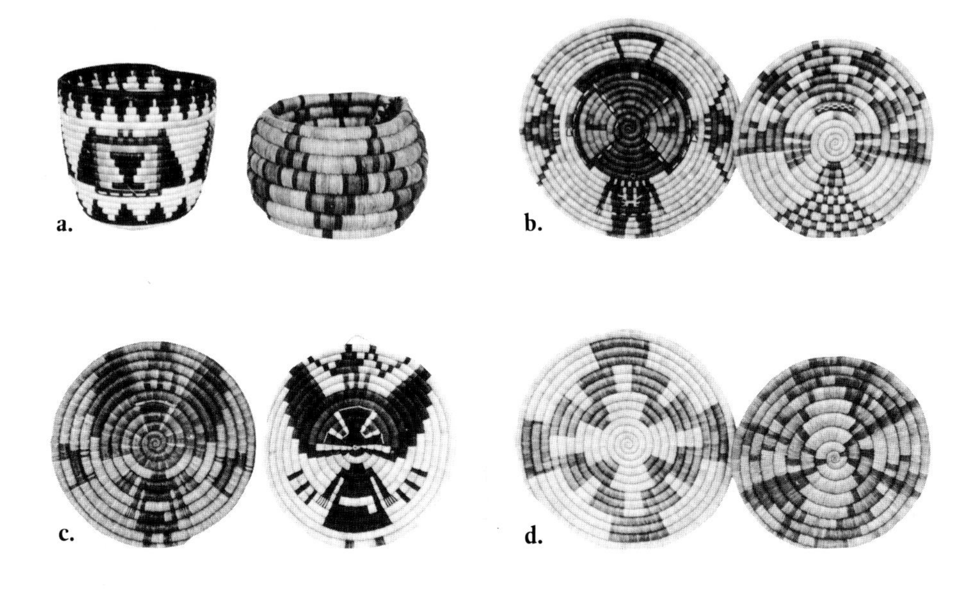

Fig. 4.2. Hopi coiled deep forms and plaques showing contrasting details in examples of the first period, 1890–1930, and one piece from the 1930–60 period. (a) Left, a deep basket, 1920, with Crow Mother mask in sharp outline and in excellent stitching; right, a jar with wide coils and design in red and green, probably about 1900 (*ASM 13050, 5456*). (b) Two plaques, one with large mask and a small body, the second a generalized mask, both before the 1930s (*ASM 12375A, E5877*). (c) Two Crow Mothers, the left figure early 1900s, the right collected in 1959 (*ASM E6789, E4011*). (d) Two plaques in geometric design; note large coils (1⅓ to the inch) in the right piece. Left plaque about 1930, right about 1900 (*ASM E10191, E1583*).

In the second period, 1930–60, designs became more elaborate, but often they were better planned and certainly more varied (Fig. 4.2). Negative or positive treatment may occur. Flower or starlike arrangements represent an advancement. Masks or full figures are now more popular, usually presented with left to right balance but not balanced above and below, a trait which had prevailed in the earlier geometric patterning. Wedding trays were well established, some with an encircling and distinctive design (see accompanying drawing), with a yellow center and black outline. Danson says that a starlike or almost circular-shaped pattern, in outline and repeated

twice, both black and with yellow between, is more typical of the wedding basket of the late 1950s and early 1960s.[8] The trays themselves are quite large, some of them 20 ½″ in diameter and 8¼″ in depth. In other baskets, there is a great deal of alternation of color, much more than in the early period, and not only in simpler color rhythms such as red-yellow-red-yellow but also in more complex rhythms such as white-red-yellow-red-yellow-white, then both of these repeated. There were some colored backgrounds. In this second period there were more horizontal layouts, as well as the early and popular vertical styles. Single or multiple bands had also become popular.

In the earlier period, designs usually went into the rim; in the second period they may do so or not, at the whim of the weaver. Rims were dominantly white in the early period; now they may be white, or black, or black and white.

As in earlier years, plaques continue to be the dominant form. Very popular also are round, shallow, straight, or sloping-sided bowls, some of them deep. A different shape is a bowl with square or rectangular top and round or oval bottom, some with two small handles. Decorating bowl walls are bands which may be continuous or broken, repeated or with alternate motifs. Masks are popular for bowl decoration, and deeper forms follow bowl treatment.

The 1960–80 period saw more changes than any other, with outside factors responsible for many of these. The American Indian had been "discovered," and baskets were selling at already high prices and were to climb even higher. Paved roads carried many tourists to the Hopi Reservation; a growing and great interest in Indian crafts was backed by tourists with full pockets. Basketry had been more quietly appreciated than some of the other crafts, but fully appreciated, nonetheless; many fine private collections attest to this fact.

Coiled basketry of this last period reached a peak in all respects. Forms were perfected; colors were the same but seem to have been sharper. Designs became greatly detailed, well balanced, regular in form—in other words, many pieces were perfect. Old design motifs prevailed, such as masks and kachinas, birds, turtles and other life forms, corn, and geometrics, many of these beautifully executed (Fig. 4.3).

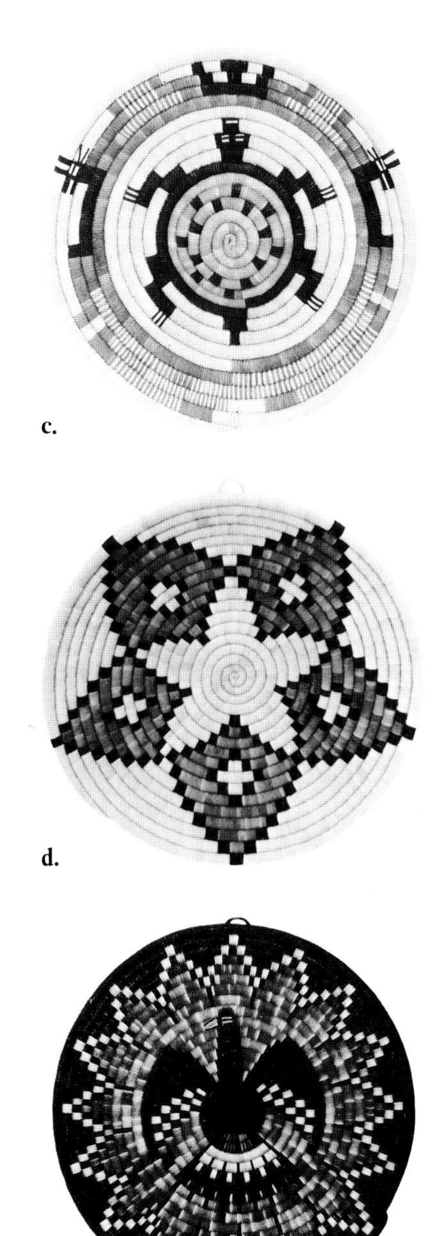

Fig. 4.3. Perfected coiled weaving, sharp colors, and details are expressed in the 1960s into the 1980s in a wide variety of subjects. (a) The old and familiar kachina *(MNA E3700)*; (b) the kachina with a large mask (left) continues, as do geometrics (right) *(ASM E2430, E8078)*. (c) More popular in this late period is the central, raised life form, here a turtle *(MNA)*. (d) A most pleasing treatment of the Apache diamond *(MNA E6995)*. Quite different are two 1982 Hopi Show pieces: (e) a bird on a mottled green background with a beautifully contrasting reddish border; (f) a kachina against a comparable background.

Plaques

Plaques are among the most abundant of all baskets in the coiled technique, and they present the greatest variety of designs. They are significant in relation to the overall history of coiled wares, for they were prominent in the 1880s and 1890s, as well as later. Plaques of the years just before and after the turn of the century were characterized by all traits mentioned above for this time. Designs were of such great simplicity that it is sometimes difficult to say what geometrics were attempted; many are meandering lines that seemed to create no particular form. Although simply presented, some masks are identifiable.

Designs in coiled plaques began to change in the second decade of the twentieth century. Indefiniteness was replaced with more specific geometrics. Kachinas or kachina masks, which came into prominence, were at first rather generalized but in time came to be quite detailed. The same is true of occasional other life forms which developed, such as birds, deer or deer heads, butterflies, and generalized floral types.

The greatest variety in design ever known in the history of Hopi plaques is to be noted in the late 1960s and 1970s. Geometrics were common, but more and more life forms were depicted. A wide variety of the ever popular kachinas and kachina masks were executed with many details; they appear in highly conventional presentations or in more realistic styles. Mudheads, kachinas with mudlike body covering and round knobs on their masks, were often woven into plaques either in full figure or in mask alone. Deer were presented in full figure, in "sitting" position (no legs shown), or in heads alone; many and varied birds were depicted, usually with outspread wings, full-spread tail, and head in profile. Frequently all of these are termed "eagles." Butterflies were colorfully portrayed, usually with outspread wings, antennae and head projecting in detailed manner. Floral and star themes are difficult to separate, but they are both popular.

Design layouts in plaques can be identified in later baskets, for they are not greatly different throughout the years; actually, there is a far greater difference in organization of designs than in layouts. The flat nature of the plaque invited all-over arrangements, and these were popular early and late (Fig. 4.4). One of the greatest differences was in the more diffuse nature of earlier patterning and the more concise, organized all-over designs of later times. In arrangement, designs or parts of designs may or may not go into the rim. Rims may be all white, black, or colored, or in some instances there may be a simple or slightly elaborate decorative theme around the rim, or part of the design, such as the rainbowlike headpiece of a kachina, might form part of the rim. Designs may be symmetrically repeated all the way around, or left and right balanced, or to the left-right may be added top-bottom symmetry.

The analysis of a group of thirty-two Hopi plaques dated from the end of the 1960s and the early 1970s will present a comprehensive picture of this late period of development. Sizes ranged from 7⅛″ to 15″ in diameter with more of them (nineteen) from 10″ to 13″ in diameter. Some earlier plaques were as much as 3 feet in diameter. Stitch count is varied, with thirteen stitches to the inch in four baskets, fourteen in six, fifteen in seven, sixteen in eight, and seventeen in seven. This shows a larger number of higher counts than in earlier years; for many decades the average was fourteen stitches to the inch with few over this count. Coils were also smaller, numbering from one and three-fourths (one) to four (one) per inch, with one counting three and one-half, five counting three, six with two, and eighteen counting two and one-half coils to the inch.

Colors in this selection were basically black, red, natural, and yellow. Sometimes green was added. Often three colors only were woven in, probably with black, red, and natural the most common; sometimes yellow was substituted for the red. The combination of black, natural, and green is pleasing. More colors were used in later years, and almost never were two colors used alone.

Of long standing was the oversewing of details, with an increase in this custom in later years. For example, in a plaque with a mudhead figure represented on it, the eyes, ears, top-of-the-head "blob," and an object in his hand are all oversewn in white.[9] In another figure of the mudhead, some black objects flying off the "blobs" are overstitched in white as are the rattle and whips in this figure's hands. Both black and white are used to overstitch the eyes and noses on red and black deer heads in other pieces. A rainbow above a mudhead has white overstitching on alternate coils of yellow, red, yellow, and black. At the sides of the face of a Butterfly Kachina are black squares with white overstitching. Green and white overstitching occurs on the body and feet of a relief turtle (see Figs. 4.3 and 4.4).

Certain types of design are indicated above for coiled plaques. Others, from a wide variety of collections, will further illustrate patterns. Certainly the mudhead figure, alone or in conjunction with other life forms, is typical. He may be presented in a simple or more ornate fashion, or, sometimes, in the head alone, complete with its three great mud blobs. The rich red-brown favored by these Hopi weavers is a natural for the mask and flesh of these figures, and black skirts appear on their full forms. Other kachina masks alone or full figures are favored by the plaque maker, such as Butterfly, Crow Mother, and Kachin Mana. About the shoulders of a Butterfly Kachina is a blanket with traditional black and red borders. The great black wings of Crow Mother make for a dramatic effect on a plaque with the head alone. Sometimes the full figure is equally dramatic with its white-belted black dress and with each of its outstretched arms terminating in four over-sized fingers—much of this detail is beautifully recorded.

Of other life forms, perhaps the most popular for plaques through the years have been deer and birds, particularly the eagle. Deer have been presented in many and diverse ways: in one basket, five heads of this animal appear along with a mudhead, in alternating red and black; in another instance four deer heads are represented with a turtle. Four red deer with upturned tails but without feet encircle another piece; fourteen deer heads in alternating black and red appear near the rim of one plaque, and another has heads in the rim coil.

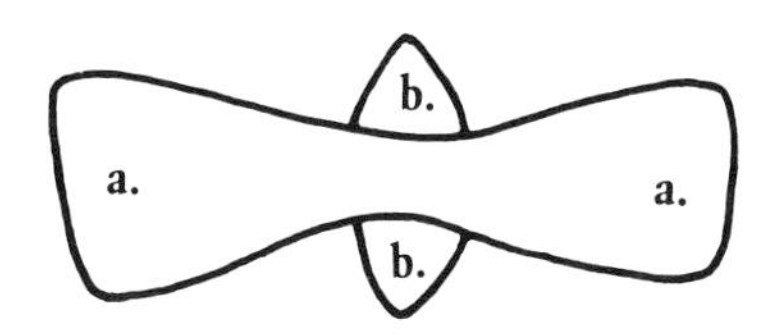

Geometrics in plaques are extremely varied. Reminiscent of the past are blocks built up in no specific geometric form; however, the majority of the later geometrics are definable. One favored style (see drawing) is characterized by a continuous major motif which is smaller in the center and expands toward the rim (a). A smaller motif nestles in the constricted central area (b). The larger theme

Fig. 4.4. Hopi coiled plaques of the 1960s and 1970s, beautifully woven. They illustrate the variety of designing in all-over layouts. (a) A highly conventionalized butterfly (left) shows the usual Hopi yellow, red, and black, and a subtle addition of pale green. The design to its right is labeled "pinwheel" *(MNA E6246, E6299).* (b) Quite elaborate is the Crow Mother (left), even to her fringed rain belt; quite different is the geometric (right) with the addition of clouds, rain, and lightning *(MNA E6245, E6305).* Additional plaques of the same period *(both photos by Ray Manley):* (c) a beautifully woven Butterfly Kachina with two ears of corn added at each side; (d) these three baskets feature corn and a mask.

may be in outline, in two colors, or it may have a thickened outline with a blank center or another motif within this central area. Another theme is a five-pointed star. Diamonds, too, are stepped, small and large. Larger, independent motifs may be repeated around the basket, in a-a-a-a or a-b-a-b alternation, with secondary or lesser motifs between these. Geometric themes may radiate from center to edge in the same or alternating motifs, or they may encircle the plaque in simple fretlike or cogwheel style.

Flower themes are popular for plaques. Some are four divisional and resemble the squash blossom; these are simple in outline. One has eight "petals" in heavy red and yellow outline, with a black center and black lines from this to the inner points of the petals. Another is like a daisy with eighteen delicately outlined yellow and long petals all coming out of a fairly small black center. A third piece has fourteen petals of alternating yellow and red outlined with black.

A combination of motifs is not uncommon, for example, a cloud theme with a Crow Mother–dominated plaque; here were a cloud above and two joined clouds at the sides, all complete with dripping rain and lightning. Most of the life subjects appear with geometrics.

Bowls

There are certain similarities between Hopi coiled bowls and jars, but there are also some differences (Fig. 4.5). Shape differs: bowls are

a.

b.

Fig. 4.5. (a) In the foreground, right, is a Hopi coiled piece which incurves slightly at the top, to resemble a jar. (b) In contrast are three typical Hopi bowls. To the left, one is decorated with two kinds of masks; to the right front is a small bowl ornamented with meandering steps; in back of the latter is a large piece with three large Crow Mother figures with alternating ears of corn. *(Photos by Ray Manley.)*

sometimes slightly incurved or frequently straight sided to the rim (Fig. 4.6), whereas jars definitely incurve at the rim or may even have a neck. Dimensions are similar in a few pieces, and in some instances it is difficult to distinguish between the two forms on this basis; however, when dimensions are quite the same, overall body

a.

b.

c.

Fig. 4.6. Three beautifully woven Hopi large coiled bowl baskets in the Museum of Northern Arizona's 1982 Hopi Show. (a) Full kachina figures alternating with ears of corn. (b) Black and yellow stepped diagonals repeated around the basket. (c) Two different masks alternate on this bowl's walls.

shape is a deciding factor. Often bowls are more shallow with such rim diameter-height ratios as 8½″ to 3¼″, 14½″ to 3⅛″, and 11¾″ to 8″. Some bowls, more like jars in measurements, are 9¼″ at the rim, 7″ height, or 16¼″ rim, 14¼″ height. Extremely shallow dimensions would also be representative of bowls, for example, one 14½″ at the rim and 2⅛″ in height.

Stitch and coil counts for bowls are about average for all coiled baskets. Six out of one group of fifteen baskets averaged fourteen stitches and two to two and one-half coils per inch. Five counts were fifteen stitches to the inch, three were sixteen to seventeen. Only one coil count was three to the inch, one was four, and the rest two to two and one-half.

Designs in this group of fifteen bowl baskets are quite representative for this form; color corresponds to that given for plaques. Five were decorated with kachina masks, one with mudheads. One with masks also had red deer heads, and two others had deer figures. One bowl added coyote tracks to the mask pattern; three of them had strictly geometric decoration alone, squares in one, steps in the second, and diamonds in a third piece. One piece was effectively ornamented with a row of nine ears of corn plus a second row of eighteen stepped motifs (Fig. 4.7).

Fig. 4.7. In this Hopi coiled bowl the variation in color of the ears of corn and contrasting colors of overstitchng on each are effective *(MNA E6209).*

In addition to these examples of designs on round baskets, a deep oblong bowl is of interest. It measures 15¾″ by 13″ at the rim, 9¼″ by 6¾″ at the base, and is 8 to 8½″ high. Stitching is irregular, ranging from fourteen to seventeen to the inch, and it averages two and one-third coils to the inch. The bowl base is variegated white and yellow but with no real design, while the wall design is elaborate. On the long sides are two opposed, full-figure kachinas, and each end is decorated with two opposed masks. To the right of the kachina figures is a black deer, to the left a red deer, both with heads turned back. There is much detail in all of the kachinas, with oversewing on eyes and mouths and on belts of the full figures, plus a rolled splint on the tops of their masks, details which provided colorful decoration.

A word might be said relative to overstitching on some of these Hopi bowls (see Fig. 4.7) as they are more complicated than the usual single-line style. On the oval bowl, several specific styles are employed: for eyes, there were three parallel black stitches; for the mouth there were two alternating vertical stitches, then one horizontal stitch. Slightly more elaborate stitching (see marginal drawing) occurred on a belt on several figures, white (a) upper and lower stitching, with black (b) spaced stitches between. The lower drawing depicts the arrangement, with each unit repeated six times, which appeared on the top of a mask.

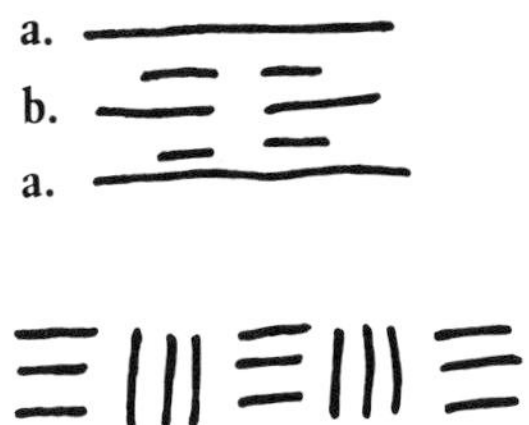

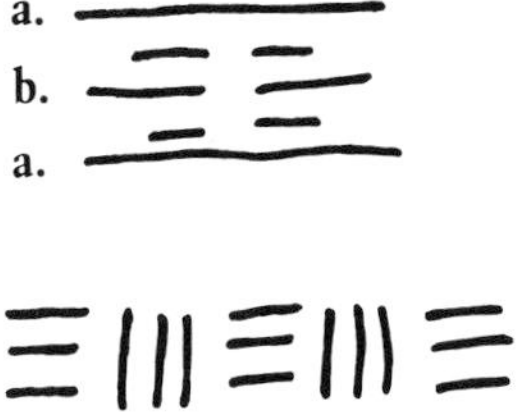

Jars

Although jars are fairly limited in numbers comparatively speaking, some Hopi examples of this shape and in coiled weave are among the most outstanding of Hopi basketry products. For example, one such piece is huge; its measurements are 40½″ height and 40″ rim diameter, with a slightly smaller base. The average jar, however, runs about 8½″ in rim diameter and 10″ in height, with a base about 2″ under the rim measurement. There are, of course, both larger (21⅝″ rim, 21¾″ height, 23½″ base) and smaller (6⅞″ rim and 6¼″ height) jars; proportions vary, with some heights less than diameters and some bases of greater dimension in contrast to a narrow mouth. Shapes, then, may be elongate, or tall and slender, or more squat, or like a round ball.

Most Hopi coiled jar shapes are simple, without benefit of any neck or with a very shallow one (Fig. 4.8). There is always an incurve from the wall to the rim, with more curvature than in bowls. The majority count about two to two and one-half coils and thirteen to fourteen stitches to the inch, with general qualities comparing favorably with other forms. Beginning coils are smaller than the rest; rims may be plain (black in one example), or the design may go into the rim. Bases may be undecorated or, not uncommonly, speckled with yellow and/or green, sometimes with these two colors plus black. Designs start at the turn onto the wall or a coil or two thereafter. Often the design which is lowest on the jar is geometric; equally often life forms are added, some of the latter going into the rim; or they may be bordered at the top with another geometric design.

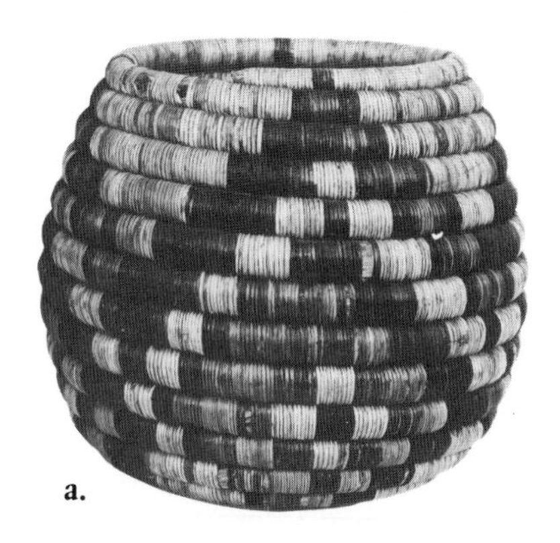

Fig. 4.8. (a) A typical Hopi coiled jar. An early piece, this type of geometric design was popular for many years *(ASM GP52641)*. (b) Frequently featured also is the Mudhead Kachina on this jar *(photo by Ray Manley)*.

As designs are arranged in a band between the rim and bottom turn, most of these jars have a feeling of a horizontal scheme. Once in a while a design in the same area has a feeling of verticality. Occasional designs on bases are to be noted. The very large basket mentioned above (with an acquisition date of 1935) is ornamented more or less all over the wall with Crow Mother figures, some kind of mammals (deer or mountain goat?), and a horned kachina. There is much oversewing, of eyes in particular. Other subjects in jar decoration would include birds, corn cobs, mudheads, masks, and several different kachinas. There are some jars decorated in geometrics alone; this seems to have been common practice in early years.

Jarlike baskets with handles or loops for handles are referred to as the "corn-planting" type (Fig. 4.9; also see Fig. 4.5); some have lids. One is 4¾" in rim diameter, 4" at the base, and 7½" high; it counts ten to thirteen stitches and one and one-fourth to one and three-fourths coils to the inch and is thus irregular in the last two traits. An elaborate stepped, horizontal zigzag is decorated in continuous yellow and alternate red and green, all outlined with black. Small wrapped coils with looped ends accommodated the handle which was about 10½" in all-over length. This basket was from the Voth collection which would make it late nineteenth century. A second corn-planting basket of the same diameter, but not so deep and similar in coil and stitch count, is dated "about 1915." Each of four designs resembles two cloud patterns joined at their bases. Two loops on the sides are identical to those on the other corn-planting jar basket.

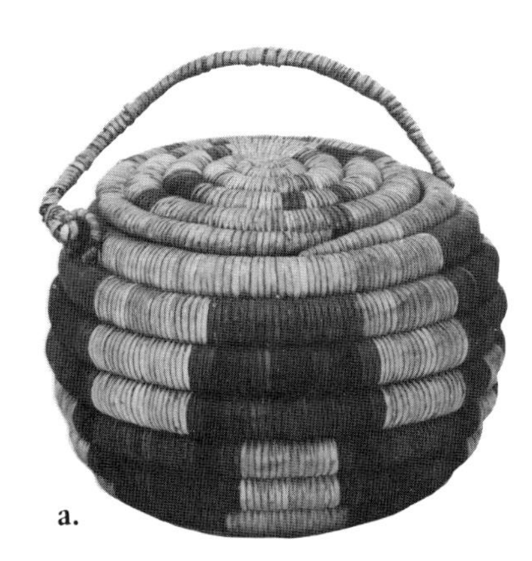

a.

b.

Fig. 4.9. (a) A small Hopi jar with a lid and loop handle; generally this is referred to as a "corn planting type" *(MNA 482)*. (b) This small jar with a handle has no lid *(ASM E3537)*.

Trays

Hopi trays are wider mouthed and more shallow than bowls. Because of these dimensions, all of the design can be seen at once; this invites patterning which tends to be different from that on bowls (Fig. 4.10), but more like that on plaques. In one group of fourteen baskets, nine did not have patterning into the rim while five did. As in plaques, there are more single masks, figures, and life forms rather than multiple arrangements, and these seem to be defined by a border in the form of a plain black, white, or two-color rim.

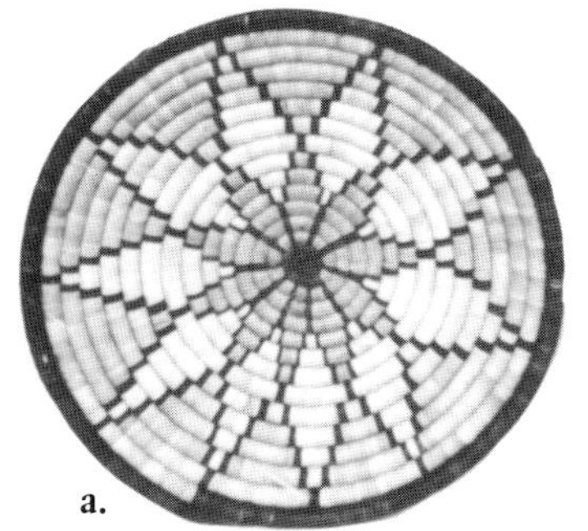

a.

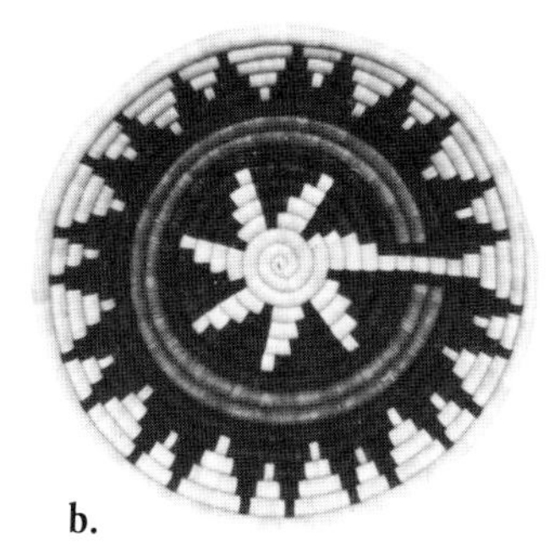

b.

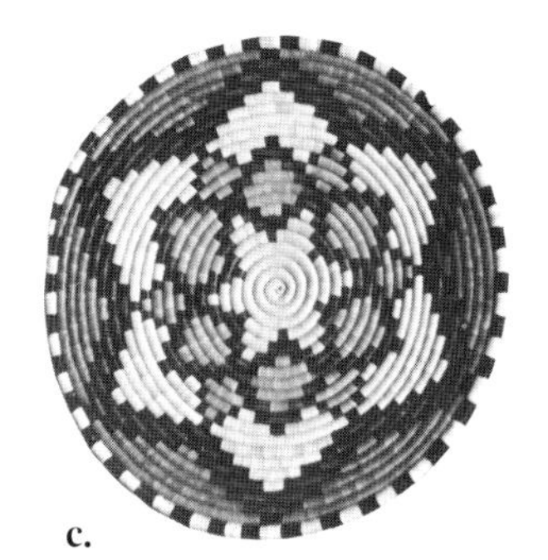

c.

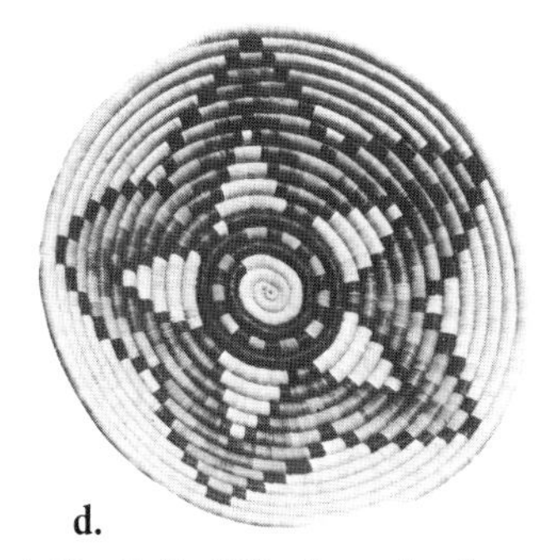

d.

Fig. 4.10. Coiled Hopi tray baskets. (a) A double floral pattern *(ASM E2429)*. (b) The Navajo ceremonial basket was the inspiration for this piece; however, note the paired stepped units on the outer edge of the motif *(ASM E6175)*. (c) An unusual treatment of the Apache diamond is the main motif in this piece *(private collection)*. (d) A not uncommon star theme in the usual Hopi yellow, red-brown, and black *(DHC)*.

In a selection of sixteen baskets, the largest diameter is 17¼", the greatest depth is 4". Half of these baskets were close to 12" in diameter and most of them were between 1½" and 2½" in depth. Stitch counts were varied in thirteen of these trays, running from fourteen to eighteen per inch, with eight in the sixteen to eighteen groups, and only five between fourteen and fifteen. Coil counts clustered around two and one-half to three and one-half per inch, with fourteen in this grouping, one example only with a count of two, and one of four.

In general, designs consisted of both life forms and geometrics. Life motifs included figures of a maiden with the native whorl hairdo, mudheads, birds (particularly the eagle), kachinas, deer, and the turtle. Geometric themes would include odd shapes such as the one depicted in the margin, or zigzags, rainbows, clouds, steps, stars, and corn ears. Some of these major themes appear alone, some in combination. Often there are several white coils in the center before the design begins. In any event, there is a pleasing layout in relation to the open space of the tray.

One tray has a raised turtle in the center; it is comparable to those on plaques, even to the oversewn eyes. One plain coil beyond the feet of this figure are nine coils in which appear eight black beetles with their heads toward the rim. Beyond them are red and green upside-down clouds. A solid black rim borders all. This is an exceptionally well-woven and pleasingly designed basket.

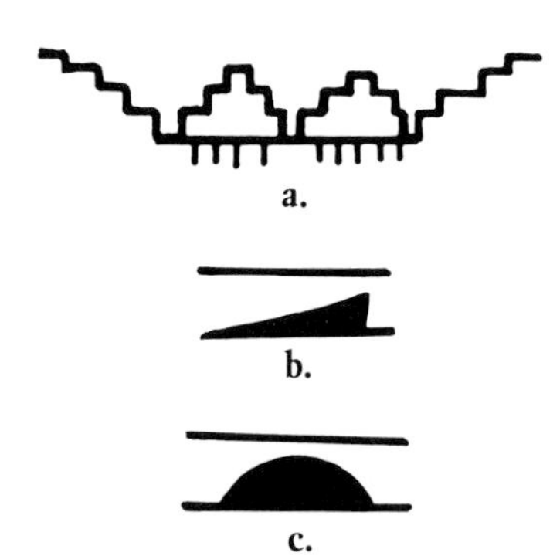

One of the most complex designs noted in trays is worked out from center to rim in the following sequence. First is a six-part, solid black stepped design, a white coil, then a nine-part, double-stepped zigzag, a white coil, and then a band containing three designs. The latter include, first, a double cloud (as in drawing a), one yellow, one red, both outlined with black and with lightning at the corners and rain dripping from them. Second is an unusual feature, an all-black eagle with a yellow beak that is tapered within one coil (see drawing b). Like his beak, a portion only of the eagle's head is in the rim coil (see drawing c). Frequently the Hopis resorted to this part-coil device for some small detail. Third is a deer with rather elaborate horns and with oversewn eyes and mouth.

Deep Forms

Coiled baskets which are very deep and straight-sided or nearly so (often sold as wastebaskets) are quite different from jars and deep bowls. First, they do not have the incurved rim so characteristic of jars and some deeper bowls (Fig. 4.11; see Fig. 4.2a, left). Usually they have a flat bottom, although some are rounded at the base. Some rim and base diameters are nearly the same, and other rims are more than twice that of the base. Rim and height measurements may be the same, or the former may exceed the latter, or, occasionally, the height may be greater than the rim diameter. On a sample of eleven deep baskets, stitch counts ranged from eleven to seventeen to the inch but cluster around thirteen to fourteen. Coils count two to the inch largely, with a very few under two, and only one deep basket with a coil count of three to the inch.

a.

b.

c.

Fig. 4.11. (a) A fine example of a Hopi coiled deep form. Traditional colors and cloud patterns with other geometrics are featured in this finely woven piece *(MNA E355)*. (b) A prize wastebasket with a woven kachina design with an added wrapped necklace, a rare feature *(photo by Ray Manley)*. (c) Alberta Susunkewa weaving a deep form *(photo by Ray Manley)*.

These deep forms are often decorated with kachinas or masks, mudheads, Crow Mother, or ears of corn. One old basket has a faded geometric design in black, natural, and yellow; the wall is built up of squares in these three colors and ends in eight cloudlike designs which terminate in the rim. Life forms and geometrics usually appear together on one basket; however, in such pieces the life form is the dominant motif while the geometrics are secondary in the design.

One deep piece with full kachina figures will be described in greater detail, for it is exceptionally large. It is 42¾" tall, 34¾" in diameter at the rim, and a little over 23" at the base. An article in 1969 states that the basket was over seventy-five years old at that time (probably not quite so old), that it took one and one-half years to weave, and that it was the "largest basket of its kind in the world."[10] Coils average almost two to the inch and stitches count thirteen to the inch. It has eight kachinas beneath an elaborate black, natural, and red zigzag. Figures represent varied kachinas with all costumes and body paint the same except on one, Crow Mother; masks, however, are detailed to the extent of suggesting different kachina types. Kilts are black and white, belts and upper-body paint red and yellow, and masks all four colors. Below the kachinas are three rows of zigzags, the top and bottom ones black-yellow-black and the center one black-natural-black.

Miniatures

Byron Harvey made a survey of Hopi coiled miniature baskets based on the following examples: about fifteen pieces out of a group of one hundred plus a few more, all collected by Byron Hunter in the Polacca area from 1963 to about 1967, and an additional one hundred or so "smaller, more finely woven baskets" collected by Harvey in 1967. "All of these baskets were woven by Hopi women from the Second Mesa village of Shungopovi, Arizona."[11] Objectives of the production of the miniatures seem to have been twofold: to test the skills of these weavers and to determine if any significant effects might result from the making of smaller pieces. The actual results demonstrated that the designs in miniatures were traditional, that there was a wide range of pattern, and that there was also some innovation.

The making of miniature baskets is uncommon among the Hopis. A piece about three inches in diameter is made for newborn babes and given to them by the kachinas. "Similar plaques are woven for ceremonial eagles which are fed and cared for as children"; further, Harvey maintains that these, and a few other small baskets, are not true miniatures, for the coils are as large as the central ones in regular baskets.[12]

Two basic forms are illustrated by Harvey, flat plaques and bowls. Thirteen of the plaques out of the thirty or so pictured have one small loop handle each; one has a snake in the center with its relief head projecting upward. Shapes of bowls differ a little: some are straight-sided, flat-bottomed; some have a gentle outcurve-incurve from base to rim, with the greatest diameter about center; one bowl curves gradually from rim to flat base. Bowls may be shallow or deeper; also, the majority of them have smooth rims and walls, and a few do have handles or other projections.

Fig. 4.12. An example of a Hopi miniature coiled bowl, made in 1973. About 1¼" in diameter and a bit over 1⅛" in depth, it is woven of the common materials for coiled baskets, shredded yucca for the foundation and strips of the same for sewing *(MNA E6264)*.

Miniature basket sizes in this group were all under 3" in width or height. In the Hunter collection the smallest plaque was 2½" in diameter, while all but one basket collected by Harvey were under 2" in diameter. The smallest Hunter example averaged six coils and nineteen stitches to the inch, but Harvey's pieces were finer, averaging eight coils and 23½ stitches to the inch. The finest in Harvey's collection had twenty-seven stitches to the inch.[13] Understandably, it took proportionately longer to make one of these miniatures.

Colors in miniatures follow the tradition to be noted in regular baskets. White, green, and yellow are basic, often with dyed black and red added (Fig. 4.12). All of this sewing material is of yucca, while the foundation for these small pieces is a bundle of grass, and hanging loops are "yucca strands, wrapped for strength."[14] Short lengths of yucca are wrapped, made into circles, and attached to a basket to form round and protruding eyes and a mouth, as in larger pieces.

Harvey divides his miniature designs into life forms, general geometrics, clouds, and kachinas. He maintains that some of the geometrics are meaningful. Black squares on a green base he labels tadpoles on a "green puddle background"; four squares taking off the corners of a central one, all red, represent antelope tracks; a black and white checkered band represents an anklet; proportionately large squares stacked into a diamond with a yellow cloud center he calls a summer cloud basket bowl, and the same design with a black center, in another example, he labels a "summer thunder cloud." In fact, there are several other variations on this cloud theme; for example, Harvey characterizes some as "clouds hanging down," "clouds in a circle, clouds hanging down just ready to rain."[15] There are other geometrics which are given names such as weaving comb, lightning, and rainbow. One basket has a woven belt design on it, another a dance wand. Usually a single theme appears on all of these miniatures, but one basket is decorated with two subjects, a rattle and a cloud design.

Other designs on these miniatures include life or related life forms, particularly a great number of kachina masks; to be sure, the weavers made an effort in the direction of variety. Most of the kachinas are very simply presented because of the small sizes of the pieces—in no way are they comparable to the more detailed masks on larger baskets. The same generalization applies to other life forms, although most of these are readily identifiable and some are fairly detailed.

On one of these miniatures the antelope is represented by four heads in a band, all turned in a counterclockwise motion. Forms of this animal with bodies but no legs are labeled "antelope sitting down." A butterfly figure more complete than most, is spread out over the greater part of the surface of a flat plaque. Well represented are two birds, an eagle and a red hawk, both, like the butterfly, consuming almost the entire surfaces of flat plaques. A spider leaves a bit more space between its form and the rim, but head and tail of a green horned toad touch the rim. The latter has red eyes and black body markings. The snake with its head raised in the center is a rattler; its yellow body has black markings and the tail rattles are realistic in alternate black and yellow. There are several plant forms represented, corn and sunflower in particular. Details in life forms are often depicted in color or overlay.

Perhaps the most recognizable masks are Koyemshi or Mudhead, Kokopel Mana, and Shalako, all on plaques. The Shalako mask is woven in black, red, yellow, and green on natural, with considerable detail in mask and chin decoration. White eyes and face stripe and whorl hairdo identify the Mana mask, and round red face and head knobs leave no question about the identity of the Mudhead. Most of the other masks appear on the side walls of bowls, each basket smaller in size than the plaques. As the designs are quite minute, this may account for their lack of detail.

The efforts of Hunter and Harvey to have miniatures made were fruitful in more ways than one. In addition to the one Hopi who wove these baskets for Hunter and the five who did them for Harvey, other women have taken up this new expression. Since all have found it economically profitable, the chances of its survival are good. Harvey believes that the "strong economic motive behind the production of these baskets was primarily responsible for the variety and innovation in design."[16] Perhaps most important, these tiny baskets adhere strictly to the Hopi world, without benefit of any outside influence except the inspiration to produce miniatures.

HOPI WICKER BASKETRY

Wicker basketry is produced on Third Mesa only; in 1963, a Hopi woman made the statement that Hotevilla only was producing this style.[17] However, all three Third Mesa villages and Moenkopi have made wicker baskets through the years. The Hopis have tried to encourage basket making by holding classes, and in 1974 they were successful in this venture. In fact this class was the first of several offered over a couple of years at Moenkopi. Appreciable price increases for baskets during the first half of the 1970s certainly was also an incentive to encourage such activities. Interestingly, in 1931 it was noted that wickerwork was particularly popular at Old Oraibi.[18]

Wicker as produced by the Hopis frequently has been termed the finest and the most artistic of this technique in the world. This has been true for many years, for even at the turn of the century the Hopis were producing a variety of geometric and life forms, particularly kachina masks, in this weave. Through the years quality of weaving and designing alike has improved. All of these areas of growth reached a peak in the 1970s, to result in some of the most outstanding craftsmanship ever accomplished in this technique. Again credit must be given for much of this superior attainment to the Museum of Northern Arizona, Flagstaff, for they worked for years to better the quality of this style of basket no less than the others.

Interestingly, materials have changed little through the years in wicker work. Sumac (*Rhus trilobata*)[19] for warps and several varieties of rabbit brush (*Chrysothamnus greenei, C. nauseosus*)[20] for wefts have been the basic materials for a long time. There is little deviation from this combination, although sometimes rabbit brush may be employed for both warps and wefts, while yucca (*Yucca valida*) is used for sewing the rim. Anilines replaced native colors before 1900 and remained popular for a few years thereafter, or until at least 1910.[21] Then they were abandoned in favor of native dyes; again, however, anilines came back into favor and they have remained so to this day. Despite the fact that colors derived from the two sources, vegetable and commercial, may appear in a single basket, the modern weavers are so experienced that it is difficult, at least sometimes, to tell one from the other.[22] Some anilines, however, can be too glaring in color to be mistaken.

More color was used in this wicker weave by Hopis than in any other basketry in the Southwest. In earlier pieces, colors are more positive and forceful; later, in many instances, they became more subtle. Rabbit brush was prepared for dyeing by scraping the stems with a piece of sandstone, then "the paint is put on the twigs with a bit of fur or a rabbit foot..."[23] Both Colton and Underhill credit the use of the navy bean (Colton says a black variety) for dark blue. Colton says that black is derived from sunflower seeds (*Helianthus petiolaris*) or from sumac, and adds, "Black basketry material is not smoked after dyeing."[24] Light blue, says Underhill, comes from larkspur, while Colton stresses dark blue from indigo. Colton credits sunflower seeds also for a fine purple and adds that carmine, pinks, and red-brown are derived from corn (*Zea mays amylacea*), which is not smoked.[25] Underhill lists both amaranth (*Amaranthus palmeri*) and cockscomb (probably *Amaranthus cruentus*) as sources of pink and says that various shades of carmine and lavender may also come from cockscomb.

Rabbit brush is the source of both yellow and green, the yellow flowers of this plant producing the first color and, according to Underhill, sometimes the bark was used for the latter. Yellow is also derived from a small native plant, *Pectis angustifolia.*[26] Orange-yellow can be obtained from saffron flowers (*Carthamus tinctorius*). Colton says that indigo might be combined with rabbit-brush yellow to make a green dye.[27] Red can be made from alder bark (*Alnus tenuifolia*), sumac berries, or cockscomb flowers, a red-brown from a grass (*Thelesperma megapotamicum*) which is boiled and strained and has alum added. Colton adds that both reds and browns for wicker and coiled baskets are derived from other grasses of the *Thelesperma* types.[28] A pure white color appears in some Hopi baskets in addition to the natural light color of rabbit brush after it has been peeled. The white is the result of bleaching the stems and "whitewashing them with clay."[29]

Obviously, many shades of all these colors can be had by using more dilute or heavier solutions of the colors; or different colors result from certain combinations of materials. The dyeing process involves placing the material in the proper solution, then much of it is "smoked in a closed container over burning white wool."[30] It must be kept in mind that there are some differences in the dyeing processes used by different Hopis.

Plaques

Plaques are the most common form of wicker basketry produced by Hopis today. A plaque is a flat or nearly flat, round piece—Hopi wicker plaques characteristically have the "hump" in the center from crossing wefts. Sometimes the plaque may be almost square or even oval in form.

In a group of fifty-two plaques, sizes varied from 9⅛″ to 21¼″ in diameters. Twenty-five of the baskets had rim widths between 12″ and 14″, sixteen were over 14″, and eleven were under 12″ in diameter. The crossed central element varied also, with the majority in a group of thirty-one pieces having three or four elements running each way, while in another collection they counted five and seven in four pieces each, nine in three, and eleven in one basket. Wefts per inch vary also: in one collection of twenty-three baskets, three counted twelve to thirteen per inch, twelve were between fourteen and sixteen, one had a count of sixteen to seventeen, six were between seventeen and eighteen, and one basket counted nineteen to twenty wefts to the inch.

In a private collection of finely woven plaques, wefts counted: two with sixteen per inch, two with seventeen, one with eighteen, and one with nineteen. Most of these figures represent only one area on the basket; however, counts are usually the same toward the center and toward the edge in a well-woven basket. It is meaningless to give warp counts, for they vary tremendously from center to edge and are usually not countable without destroying the basket.

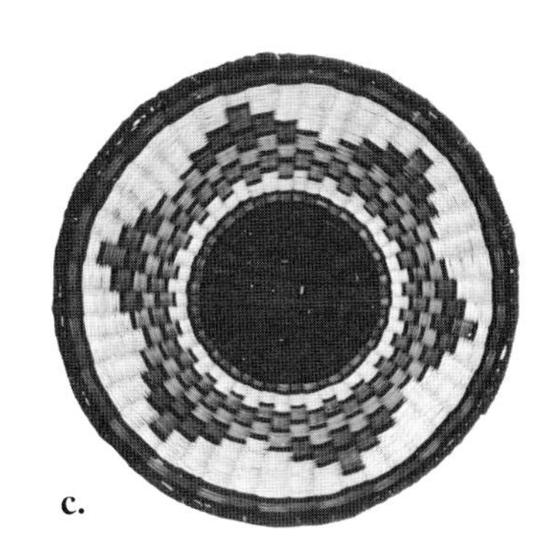

c.

a.

b.

d.

Fig. 4.13. Hopi wicker plaques which illustrate typical colors and geometric designs. (a) Two repeated motifs executed in a variety of colors *(MNA E5480, E5481)*. (b) Quite different are the volute themes in these two plaques, each woven in a variety of rich colors *(ASM E4410, E2422)*. (c) A pleasing geometric motif in muted colors against a white ground *(MNA E6202)*. (d) Four beautifully woven wicker plaques, two with volute designs, two with varied geometrics *(photo by Ray Manley)*.

Colors are extremely varied in wicker plaques (Fig. 4.13). Even the simplest has at least three or four or five different colors in a single piece, and the more elaborate ones have as many as seven different colors, often with two shades of one color. No matter how wild they sound, the majority are put together in such manner that there is little or nothing objectionable to them, neither in number of colors, nor in variety, nor in intensity. One basket employed this combination: red, green, black, natural, brown, orange, and dull green. Another was decorated in pink, orange, green, red, natural, yellow, blue, and black. A third featured natural, orange, green, gold, and white. Another colorful piece combined white, black, rust, chartreuse, pink, and yellow. A simple use of color in these plaques would be exemplifed in dark blue, white, yellow, black, and green, or in the use of black, natural, and yellow.

Plaques have the greatest variety in design of any wicker baskets. Two general styles of pattern were expressed, geometric and life forms. These might appear in combination or the life form might dominate the entire area. In geometrics there are bands both regular and organizational or, in addition, irregular arrangements which are almost bands. One banded piece, for example, has a dark blue-green round center, then successively and with white between, are bands of light red, blue-green and dark red, then the black rim. In several pieces noted, a round black center is balanced by one other design, a reproduction of the Hopi red belt complete with its black and green end-to-end small geometrics. One very modern piece has a version of a Navajo wedding basket design, complete with opening, on a yellow background.

Static rays, from a large or fairly large colored center, extend to the rim. These are quite varied, for they can be relatively simple or extremely complex. Dynamic and opposed volutes have always been popular; they may be single or double, short or long in each extension, simple in form and color or very complex. There is a great variety of diamonds used in these plaques, including Apache-like styles. Numerous other geometrics of varying shapes frequently appear in left-right balanced schemes; or not infrequently, two sets of geometrics may be arranged in an a-b-a-b fashion. Almost always there is a narrow beading in two alternating colors just under the black rim in plaques. Other geometrics would include triangles, short and long lines, squares and rectangles, and innumerable combinations of all of these.

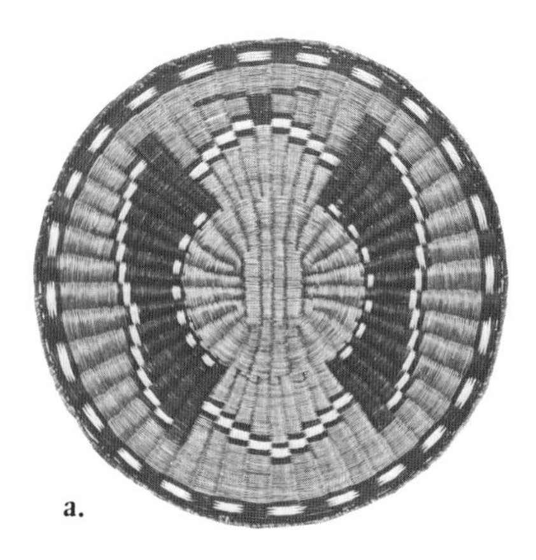
a.

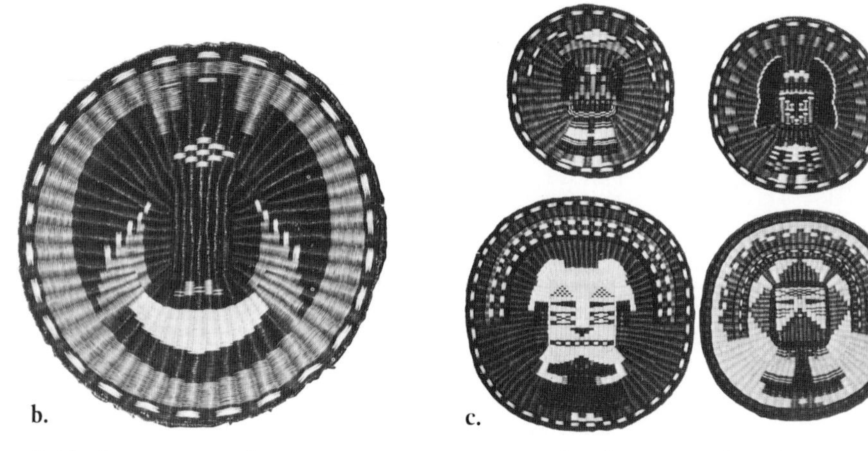
b. c.

Fig. 4.14. Several types of life forms commonly found in the Hopi wicker basket. (a) Butterflies may be conventional, as in this piece *(ASM E2424)*, or more realistic. (b) Favored among birds was the eagle, balanced left and right except for the head *(private collection)*. (c) The full kachina figure was often woven into these baskets, or sometimes the mask alone *(MNA 1982 Show)*.

Life forms on plaques concentrate on kachinas or kachina masks, birds, butterflies, or a Hopi girl with her hair in whorls at each side of her head. Kachinas usually offer the opportunity for the use of much color, an opportunity not neglected by the Hopi weaver of wicker baskets. Birds might be more or less colorful, but quite often this subject was all black except for a yellow beak and feet, and a bit of white on the tail (Fig. 4.14), or it might be much more detailed, with facial features plus wing and tail markings. The subject of the butterfly offered greater potentials for color. In fact, all life forms might be treated either in a generalized or in a more detailed manner. Kachina figures might include the details of decoration of the mask and of the garments worn by the mythical characters. Another favored subject is the koshare clown with great all-over white and black bands; or just this clown's face and neck decoration, and his "horn" hairdo sticking straight up from his head and presented in the same black and white bands.

These wicker plaque designs have prevailed for many years. Late nineteenth century examples show comparable geometrics, perhaps more haltingly expressed, certainly stiffer and larger in style, but much the same in detail. One example, dated about 1900, shows an eagle which is very much like those in the 1970s, except, perhaps, that his wings are more slender. There is a double whorl pattern which could have been produced at almost any time since 1900; it is solid color in one whorl and checkered in the other. Illustrations and examples of baskets of the 1920s also repeat these subjects: full kachina figures with the mask usually greatly over-sized (Fig. 4.15), birds, geometrics, and whorls.

Fig. 4.15. Two old wicker plaques made by Hopis. In this kachina figure (left) with a very large mask, the upturned wings on Crow Mother are quite different from other—and particularly later—treatments. Colors which almost melt together are featured in the geometric design to the right (*ASM GP26407, ASM 8181*).

Bowls

There is a definite distinction between the Hopi wicker bowl and the tray, although the two terms are used interchangeably (Fig. 4.16). The latter have more generous measurements at the rim and more gentle slope from rim to base; the bowl has a straighter side and a larger, flatter base. Often rim-depth proportions are different: bowls have a tendency to be deep; for example, dimensions are frequently 14″ or thereabouts in rim diameter and 4″ or 5″ in depth. Occasionally, however, they are proportionately still deeper, for instance, 13″ in rim diameter and 7″ in depth, or 13″ wide and 8⅝″ deep. In one group of nineteen bowls, one only was very deep; its dimensions were 14″ at the rim and 10½″ in depth. Trays are also much more shallow: two typical examples measured 13¾″ at their rims and were only 1¼″ deep, while a third was 11½″ at the rim and only 1″ in depth. Crossed elements at the basket beginning average about the same in these two forms, with three or four the more common numbers running each way. Weft counts also tend to average about the same, with twelve to fourteen per inch.

Color may sometimes be as varied in bowls as it is in plaques, but geometric designs prevail in the former (Fig. 4.17). In fact, it would seem that in decorating many bowls, perhaps because of the shape, the weaver felt limited in design potential and so took her artistic interest out in color. Some geometric designs start on the base of the bowl and continue up the side wall to the rim; so does color, with no neglect of the base. Confined to side walls are kachina masks, birds, and comparable themes.

= □ = □ = □ =

One bowl basket has a beltlike design of black and red woven on the side wall against a background of a variety of alternating colors. This pattern (see drawing) appears in several of these baskets and is varied by the use of much alternation and use of many colors, with the edging of each unit of the design in a contrasting color. In

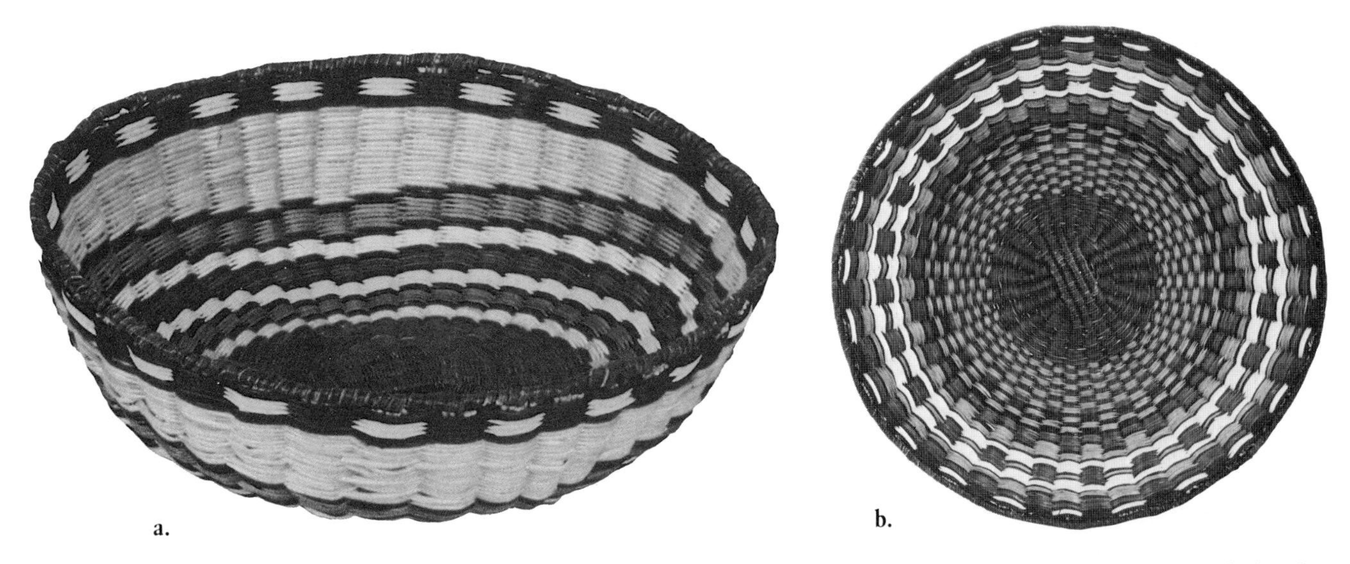

Fig. 4.16. (a) Hopi wicker oval bowl. Note the many colors used in this piece *(ASM E3518)*. (b) A round bowl with more muted colors *(MNA E6200)*.

another basket the bottom is checkered black and white while the side wall is ornamented with bands in a great variety of colors.

In wicker bowls, the center of the base varies as it does in plaques. Some are in one solid color, for instance, a 5½″ light blue circle, or a 4⅞″ tan circle. Some are varicolored; for example, one has a 5″ circle of alternate blocks of natural and light green, and another has a circle which is the same in diameter and is made up of an indefinite design but shows a subtle handling of natural, dark and light yellow, and orange.

Bowls, then, present quite a bit of variety in the combination of size, colors, and designs. Because of shape, design may be curtailed and major motifs are on walls, but little more could be done with geometric potentials known to the weaver than is expressed on these bowls.

Fig. 4.17. Hopi wicker bowls are dominantly decorated in banded patterns. Some projecting warps in the left example will be cut away, some bent to the left and sewed into the rim. Note bottom pattern in basket to right *(photo by Ray Manley)*.

Deep Forms

Hopi wicker deep baskets are very much like bowls; in fact, many are identified merely as "deep bowls." Actually their proportions are quite different and many have been sold as wastebaskets (Fig. 4.18), whereas the bowl is more apt to be used by the Hopis themselves. The rim tends to be wider than in the bowl; otherwise, there is a comparable gradual slant to the wall and relatively flat base. Or the form may be straight and flat-bottomed.

In one group of deep forms, height and rim diameter measurements ranged from 8″ to 23″ and 11½″ to 23″, respectively; the second dimension reflects the very wide mouth common to this form. This is a good sampling of size. Beginnings of deep baskets compare favorably with those of trays and bowls. Colors and designs are more like those in bowls; in fact, typical designs reiterate those on bowls. One piece has a blue center, then a succession of irregular bands, several of joined almost-triangles. A rare example of life design shows three eagle dancers between vertical, stacked diamonds; a geometric theme has a blue center and wall checkerboarding in black plus green, yellow, red, and cream. Other motifs include stripes, cogwheels, zigzags, and clouds.

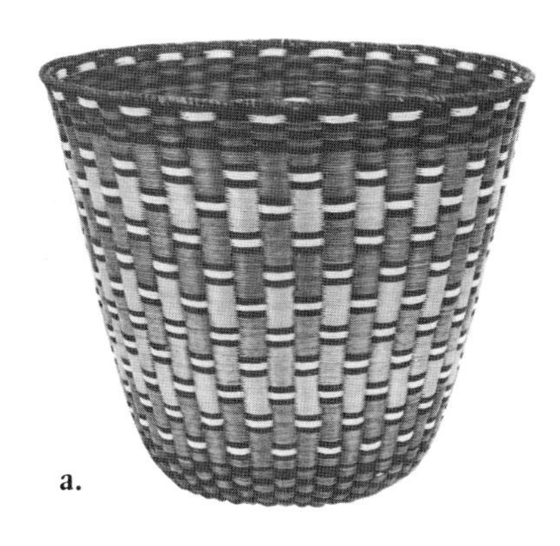

a.

b.

Fig. 4.18. (a) Hopi wicker deep form—a typical wastebasket style. Geometric designs prevail in the decoration of this form *(MNA E698)*. (b) A second deep form, also with characteristic banded pattern.

Trays

Wicker trays are not too abundantly woven, but some were observed in this survey. Calling it a bowl but illustrating a tray, Jeancon and Douglas said in 1931, "This is apparently a rather new shape."[31] As noted above, trays are wide-rimmed in proportion to depth. Their walls curve gracefully from rim to almost flat base —never are they straight-sided as in the bowl. Characteristically, they are shallow, as noted above in comparing them with bowls.

Because of the continuous line in the tray form and its consequent open nature, this basket was frequently decorated like the plaque, particularly in the treatment of life forms. Geometrics were handled as on many other forms; often they were continuous from center to rim. Layouts tended to be all-over, although some centered-banded styles were noted. Colors were as varied as in any form, sometimes more limited, often most abundant.

The double swirl appears in trays usually in two contrasting colors against natural or a third color; pointed or starlike motifs are fairly popular. In one tray are featured a light center circle and four almost-triangles slanted from the rim into the center. Bands are favored in many of these baskets. Another tray has a large yellow center of a slightly different shape (see drawing), almost a flower, and beyond it are successive bands involving the use of green, blue, yellow, a little orange, and of course black and white. A last geometric design has a central circle of orange with forty-eight narrow bands radiating from it to the rim. The bands are made up of orange, yellow, and green so arranged that there are alternations in every other band.

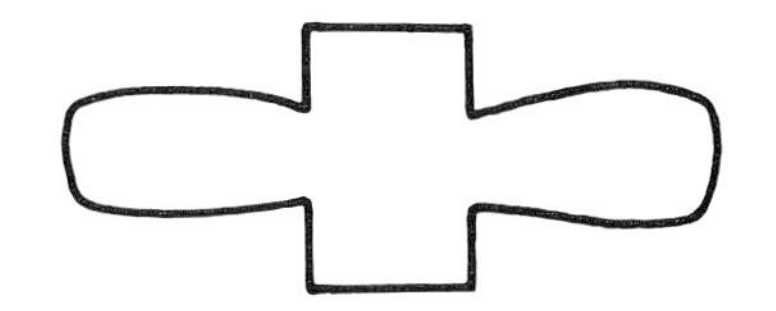

On wicker trays there appeared the usual Hopi motifs of birds, butterflies, and kachinas. One large tray, 15″ in diameter, had a thunderbird represented on it in the usual black and yellow. What was probably meant to be a butterfly was woven into a smaller tray

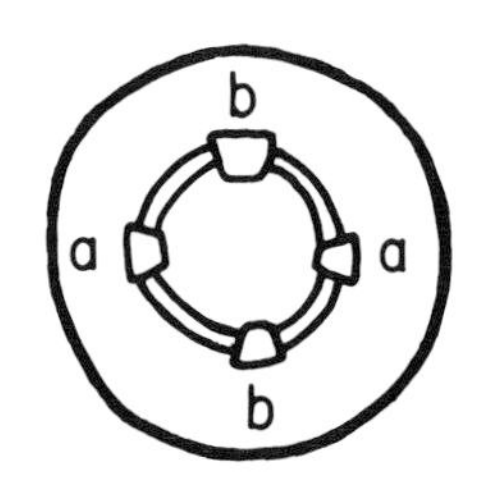

(9¼″ in diameter). Crow Mother is represented in the usual manner, stressing her great black wings and shoulder blanket. Another tray basket, woven in the late 1960s, is ornamented with a woman's costume, including her dress, shoulder blanket, and belt. This basket came from Hotevilla. The dress is depicted twice (see drawing) in opposed positions (a) and suggests in its dark colors the dark blue center and black borders of this piece. Shoulder blankets (b) are in natural color with red and black edge bands. The belt connecting these elements is predominantly red, as is the original. Several examples of this same general patterning were noted in this survey.

Peach Trays

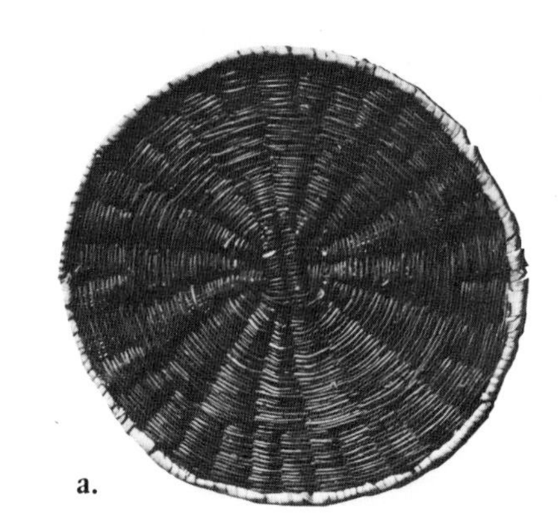

a.

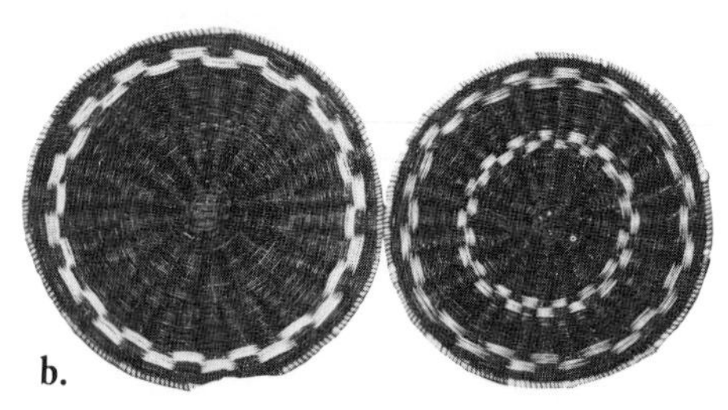

b.

Fig. 4.19. (a) A typical plain peach tray woven in the natural brown of the material *(private collection)*. (b) Two peach tray types exhibited at the 1982 Hopi Show; these differ from the usual basket in that they have simple encircling designs in light material against the dark.

Peach baskets, sometimes called trays, are not as common as piki trays. In some respects they are between the piki tray and the peach-gathering or -carrying basket—they are never as flat as the former nor proportionately as deep as the latter. Always they are woven in plain wicker weave, using single wefts over multiple warps (Fig. 4.19).

To start the basket, two groups of three of four warps are merely placed together with one set crossing the other, roughly in the manner of the usual wicker plaque or basket. The turn from base onto wall is gently curved; often the wall has a slight outflare at the rim. The whole or split element of the wild currant (sumac) may be used in these baskets; its soft brown tones are pleasing. Irregularities occur in all these matters of construction of the peach basket, for it did not receive the care at the hands of the weaver given to other wicker pieces.

One peach tray measured 18⅞″ in diameter and about 3½″ in depth. It was woven in quite open stitches. A second roughly circular example was 17⅞″ at the rim and 7¼″ in depth. A little above mid-point on the wall of the latter was a design created by twisting four wefts to form alternately four white squares, then four dark squares. These wefts were split elements obviously light on the inner side and dark on the bark side. Bundles of elements formed the rim, finished by wrapping as in all other wicker work done by the Hopis.

The peach tray basket is unique to the Hopi Indians. It never received any great amount of attention and was seldom decorated, possibly because it was used as a sifter for parched corn.[32] Perhaps the weaver was satisfied with the natural soft brown or sometimes black color in the material used, and with the simple lines of this utility basket. Into the 1930s this piece was popular, then it declined to the 1950s and into the early 1960s. However, by the late 1960s and into the early 1970s its popularity revived and the peach tray and a round flat version of the same workmanship were again produced. At the 1982 Hopi Show, Flagstaff, several of these trays woven in the dark material were decorated with encircling meanderlike designs in light or white material.

Piki Tray

A piki tray is a flat or nearly flat, rectangular piece of basketry which, as the name implies, is used for serving piki, the wafer-thin cornmeal bread made by Hopi women for ceremonial purposes.

The same general style, involving a plaited "mat" or center with a wicker edge, has been made for many years; differences are limited to quality of workmanship, the design in the portion within the border, and size (Fig. 4.20).

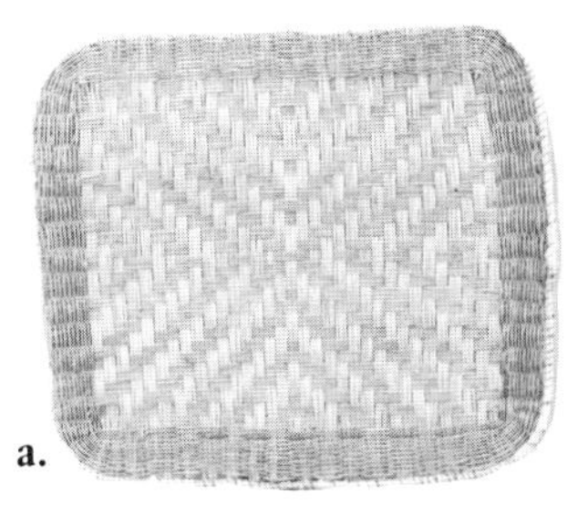

The plaited area of a piki tray is created by weaving bundles of split elements over other bundles of the same, often in units of four each way. Alternation can be over two such bundles, under two, or, to create a different pattern, it may be over and under one, two, or three such bundles of four each in a single basket. The material, wild currant, is split for the plaited area and, as for the peach tray, has a dark brown outer and a light inner surface; these contrasting shades are used to create design. For the wicker border, six, seven, or more whole rods are crossed by several bundles of split rods of three or four elements each continuing from the plaited section, the former serving as warps and the latter now forming the wefts of the wicker border. The edge of the tray is finished in the usual wrapping with yucca. Often all but one in a group of weft ends may be cut off, the single one usually bent to the left and incorporated into the rim unit.

The piki tray can be illustrated by one woven in the mid-1970s which measured 17¾" in length and 13½" in width. From the center and on each side of the plaited area were two nested chevrons and from the center onto the ends three of the same (for comparison, see Fig. 4.20a). This design was created by the plaited alternation of three elements over and under two groups of three each of the same, then the next three elements skipped one group of three but followed the scheme of over-two-groups-under-two-groups. All elements moving in one direction had the brown bark exposed while all going in the opposite direction had the light split side exposed, thus creating the design in color.

Further characteristics of piki trays are revealed in the following comments relative to thirteen examples, some from the Heard Museum in Phoenix, some from the Museum of Northern Arizona, Flagstaff, and a few from private collections. Sizes range from 13¼" by 13¾" to 29" by 27". Some were more oblong than these two; for example, one tray was 25" long and only 17½" wide, another was 22" by 14⅛". Several of the smallest borders were 1½" in width, the widest was 3". Units of weaving varied also; in place of the three in a group, four were common, or even six elements might form a unit. The over-under alternation varied to create different designs even in a single tray.

Designs are quite interesting in piki trays (see Fig. 4.20). In one which is dated 1928 and a second dated 1939 are nested chevrons. Two differences are apparent in the earlier piece: first, a large central X extending to each corner; second, more chevrons in each

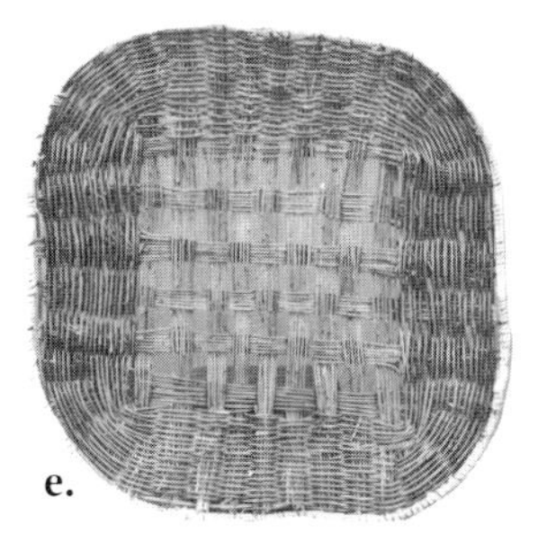

Fig. 4.20. Examples of Hopi piki trays. (a) A good example of the piece described in text except that it has more chevrons in each quarter section. The proportions in this piece are average, about 16⅛" by 17½" *(MNA 918)*. (b) A more elongate piki tray decorated with concentric diamonds from the interior to the edge *(MNA 2734A)*. (c) Quite large is this 30¼" by 27⅛" tray, neatly designed with all-over, concentric diamonds *(MNA 319)*. (d) Another large piki tray, this with diagonal bands over the entire plaited area *(MNA 4167)*. (e) An interesting 13" square example with a subtle, almost-checkered pattern *(MNA 1100)*. These pieces date from 1931 (b) to 1961 (d).

of the four areas, with two only in each area in the 1939 tray. Diamonds are popular in the piki tray: in two pieces, there are diagonal rows of them; in another there are two large concentric diamonds taking up most of the plaited area with line fillers at the corners. Thirteen plain diagonal lines fill the decorative surface on another tray. One other decorated piki tray had a most unusual pattern. Dated 1935, it has all-over, small stepped diamondlike figures, each with a dot in the center, and with nine rows of six-stepped diamonds in each row. Concentric large diamonds and diagonal lines fill the plaited area of two 1982 piki trays, these not so well woven as many of the above-cited examples.

Burden Basket

Fig. 4.21. Hopi wicker peach or burden basket, this one more nearly square. Four heavy strengthening ribs are woven into the corners. The deep-brown banded patterns are typical *(ASM 8100)*.

One piece of Hopi basketry which has received little attention through the years is the wicker burden basket (Fig. 4.21), often called a peach basket but not to be confused with the peach tray. This basket was made by the men and used by them, primarily for carrying peaches and corn. Underhill says they are also woven by the women. The same style of basket, although smaller in size, is used in the Bean Dance. About the Hopi and this basket, Underhill says, "Almost all of them made a carrying basket of wickerwork."[33] Of course, this is no longer true. One Hopi woman whose father made these baskets said in 1972 that he claimed that the men no longer knew how to weave these pieces. This is not entirely true either, for new wicker burden baskets were on display at the Hopi Guild in subsequent years, for example, in 1977. It may be concluded that these baskets are not so popular as formerly but they are still produced.

Whole rods of either sumac or barberry (*Berberis fendleri*) were woven over and under other rods of the same material in the making of this basket, generally with the weft passing over three, four, or five warps at a time. For a finer weave peeled twigs were used in a closer alternation; some of the coarser pieces were woven in more open manner. Often there were two heavy bent rods woven into or near the inside corners of the rectangular and deep basket. Also in some pieces a heavy rod was sewed to the rim to give a finished edge. Pieces of buckskin or other material in the form of bands were tied into the sides through the weaving so that the man could carry the basket on his back, with the strap across his forehead.

An interesting piece dated 1892 was the largest burden basket of this type observed. Its approximate measurements are 15″ in height, and 11¼″ in width, and its length (somewhat exaggerated through use) was 35″.[34] This piece had four or five elements in clusters serving as warps. Two heavy oak rods were used to support the form, as shown in the marginal drawing.

Another Hopi wicker burden basket made at Hotevilla in 1931 measured 17⅜″ high, 27½″ long, and 7⅞″ wide. Its base was 16⅞″ in length, which shows the usual smaller bottom. Each heavy rod toward the ends projected 4¾″ above the rim of the basket. Clusters of six elements served as warps in this piece. A similar piece, woven at Oraibi in 1923, measured 28¾″ in length and 16¼″ in height, but was only 3⅛″ wide. A Shungopovi-made burden basket, dated 1931, was labeled a "ceremonial carrying basket." It was small, as these ritual pieces usually are, measuring only 7½″ in height, 5⅞″ in length, and 5⅛″ in width (Fig. 4.22c). There were only two warp elements used in the bundles in this burden basket.

HOPI PLAITED BASKETS

Because of its continued use by the Hopi Indians, plaited basketry never wavered in production. The major changes which occurred with commercialization were accelerated production, more varied sizes, a greater variety of designs, and a few new forms. The same material, yucca, continued to be used, the same basic ring form prevailed, but the early square-based, round-topped piece was rarely woven after the 1920s. In 1963 they were weaving a few odd pieces, such as lamp shades and place mats.[35] The basic weave was twill plaited (see Fig. 3.3b, c, d); in this technique the ring basket was produced on all three Mesas.

The ring basket is illustrated by Vroman in his 1895–1904 photographs. One example is a much used, misshapen piece in the room where eight shots of a native hair-dressing series were taken.[36] Photo 18 in this book shows a twilled basket on the floor close to fireplace wood; the piece holds something, probably corn or cornmeal. In a scene in this same book showing a woman weaving a coiled piece, there is a large ring basket which has been propped up, thus showing its all-over decoration of parallel zigzags.[37] It is not possible to determine whether this last basket was woven in green (or yellow) and white or whether the light brought out the design in weave alone; but it tells that at an early date there were rather elaborately designed twilled ring baskets, and large ones.

It is mentioned in a 1931 publication that two patterns were produced in twilled weave, checkerboard, and diamonds, in the "work basket" (ring style).[38] Interestingly, a variety of shapes is mentioned in this article, including bottles, a belt weaver's harness, pottery rests or head rings, and cradle-head bows or hoods. The ring style persevered and was always the most important form. Other pieces were sporadically produced.

Not a great deal of change occurred in the plaited basket until the end of the 1950s and into the 1960s. Early in the latter decade designs were becoming more elaborate, as previously mentioned. Also more colors were added, such as orange, red, and magenta to the black, white, and probable green and yellow (Fig. 4.23). One 1982 piece featured a heavy all-over line pattern in green and purple. Another interesting change was in the shape, with oval and square forms added to the traditional round sifter-basket style shown in Figure 4.23.

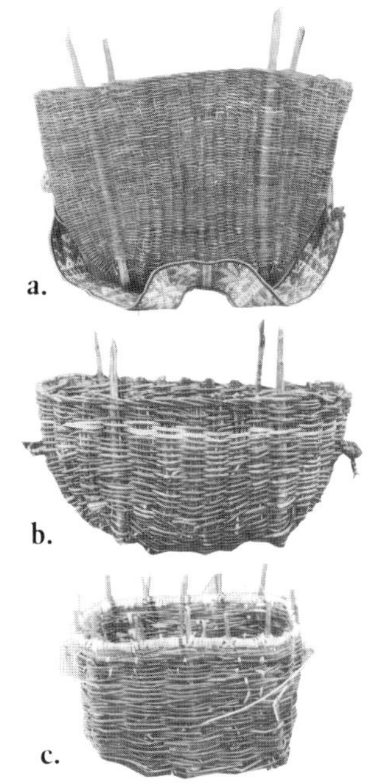

Fig. 4.22 (a) A large Hopi peach carrying basket. Although dated 1913, it was apparently used in the 1967 Bean Dance at Shungopovi and, when returned, had the attached blue, white, and red belt, possibly of South American or Mexican origin. Typically, it has the usual heavy rods near the two ends. Size is 28″ length, 8″ width, 17¾″ height *(MNA 2760).* (b) Hopi bean basket. Constructed in the same way as the peach or burden basket, this piece is usually smaller, 10″ long by 7″ wide and 7″ high; this one was carried in the Powamu ceremony of 1968 *(MNA 1097).* (c) A small burden basket, Hopi, labeled "Ceremonial, a child's size, Purchased—1931." Note the double warps projecting above the rim *(MNA 2771).*

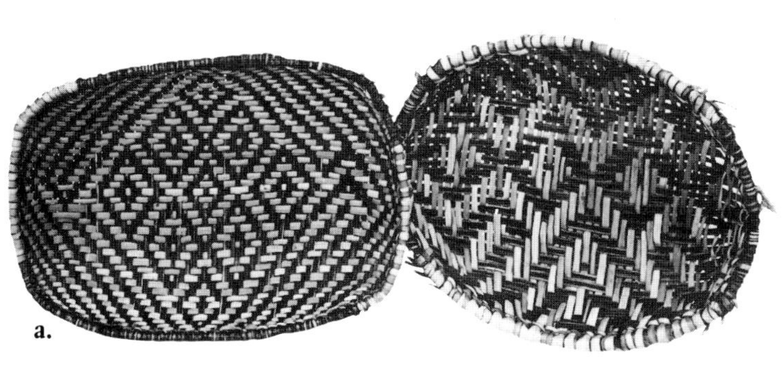

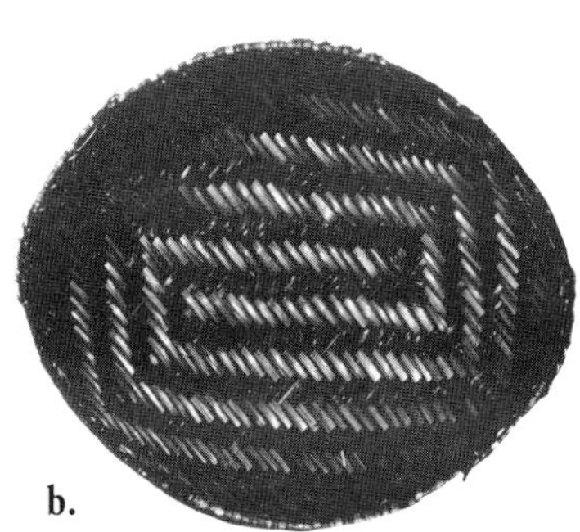

Fig. 4.23. (a) Two Hopi plaited baskets of odd shapes, the left *(ASM E6176)* decorated with a centered cluster of diamonds while the right piece *(ASM E3517)* illustrates the added use of black and orange. (b) These additional sifter baskets feature an unusual purple against natural green (left), and on the right, brown and red on bleached white yucca *(1982 Hopi Show).*

In the 1970s there was tremendous variety in ring-basket sizes. Obviously many of the smaller pieces, such as those ranging from 6″ to 10″ in diameter, were made to sell. Actually these would not have proved usable to the Hopis. Many of the smaller baskets were not too well woven, yet designs on these pieces were generally quite varied.

A miscellaneous selection of fourteen ring baskets will demonstrate typical features of this style. First, their diameters varied from 6¼″ to 18½″, with six of them from 13″ to 15″ across. One of these baskets had an almost square base 9″ by 9³⁄₁₆″. Two oval forms measured 13″ by 10″ and 16½″ by 10⁹⁄₁₆″. Depth is difficult to measure in the ring basket, particularly if the piece has been used, for this tends to make it lopsided; however, generally they run from 2″ to 4″. Diameter is more difficult to throw off, as the heavy ring tends to maintain the original dimension.

All of these sifter baskets had heavy wood rings at their tops; the two exceptions were fitted with heavy wire at their rims. All were sewed with a twined stitch just beneath the wood or metal ring, and were then clipped off about 1″ beneath the sewing.

Designs were created by way of clever manipulation of the relatively narrow yucca elements. In this group of fourteen, six baskets appeared bleached white, but when woven some of these could have been white, green, and/or yellow, with either or both of the latter two colors fading with time. Of the remaining baskets, two were green, three were white and yellow, and three were white and green.

Rhythm in weaving these plaited baskets varied a great deal. For example, one specimen had an over-one-under-one alternation in the small center of some diamonds, but then had 2-2-2, or 3-3-3, or 4-4-4 rhythms in the rest of the basket. Another basket had a 3-3-3 rhythm, and this was a common arrangement, as is a 2-2-2 alternation. Combinations of rhythms, as illustrated above, are usually employed for more elaborate patterning.

Designs in this selection of baskets included the following. In several pieces was an all-over cross which met in the center; this was outlined and within each outline was a set of concentric squares or diamonds. Another specimen had a set of five concentric diamonds covering the entire basket. A large diamond outlined the entire decorative area of one of these ring baskets, and within it were four sets of two concentric diamonds each; in another there is a central single diamond which is surrounded by concentric diamonds at the four corners. Many other arrangements of diamonds occurred, some with a play of color. Concentric squares or rectangles, working from center to edge, decorated other pieces.

Decorations in additional plaited baskets illustrate other patterns. One, in green and white, has a combination of diamonds and chevrons; one has an elaborate combination of double zigzags on each of its four sides plus outlined squares and rectangles and a centered group of concentric diamonds; others have varied arrangements of frets and zigzags. Many ring baskets have line patterns alone, some very complex. One has meandering lines all over the piece, these starting from a double-armed, fretlike center. Another has wandering, double-lined bands. All of these patterns continued into the 1980s, particularly lines and diamonds, plus crosses and others.

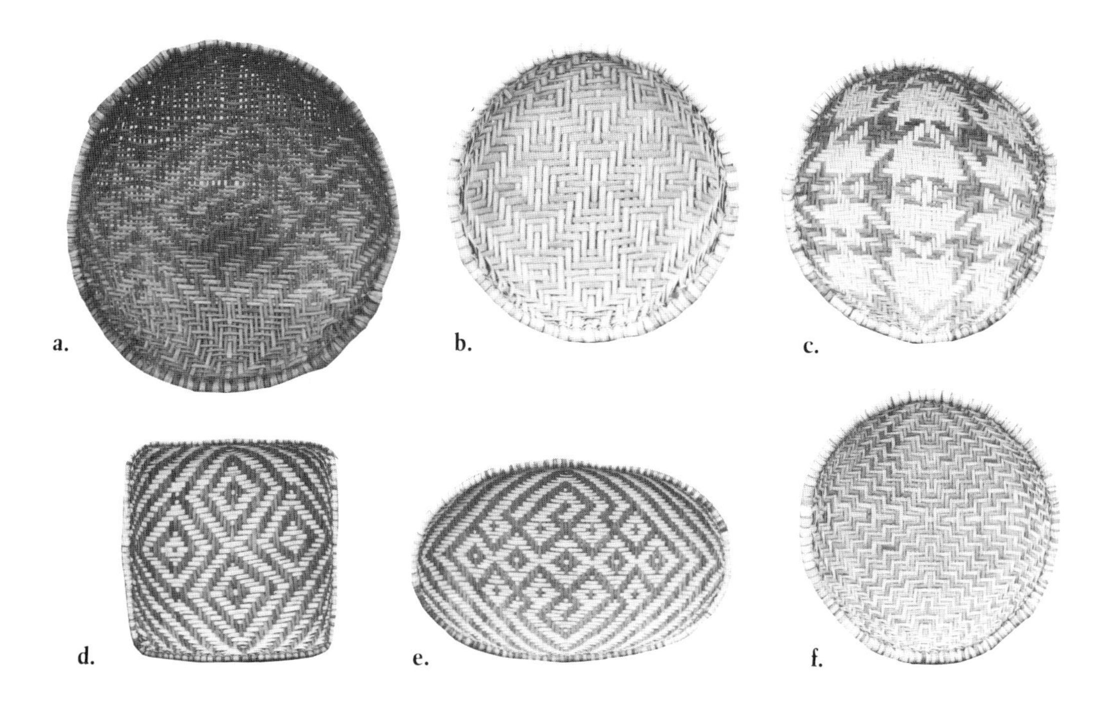

Fig. 4.24. Hopi plaited ring baskets. (a) Line pattern wanders from center to edge. This piece is about 16″ in diameter and 3¾″ deep. The outside fringe is ½″ to 1″ long *(MNA E8074)*. (b) A different arrangement of four internal stepped diamonds related to one large enclosing diamond. (c) Concentric diamonds in weave combined with a plaidlike pattern in color. (d) An excellent example of a square "ring" basket, also with a popular theme of four internal concentric diamonds surrounded by several more of the same *(MNA 2297)*. (e) An oval tray with another version of diamonds and lines. This tray is 10″ wide and 17″ long *(MNA E2215)*. (f) A most interesting four-part concentric stepped pattern, very neatly executed.

Certainly variety characterizes Hopi plaited basketry designs (Fig. 4.24). Even if the same motif is repeated, such as the diamond, there is no duplication. Combinations of several elements or motifs in a single piece would seem to be a feature of more recent Hopi plaited baskets, at least very popular during the 1960s and 1970s. The few early pieces examined revealed basically a single theme and certainly no more than two. Unquestionably the greatest variety in any period was to be noted in the 1965–75 decade.

In December 1976, a square-based, round-topped plaited deep basket was woven at Mishongnovi, on Second Mesa. The interior of the split leaf, which is white centered with narrow green edges, was kept on the inside of the basket, while the outside of the basket is the green of the outer part of the leaf. As explained by Wright a rather thick-leafed variety of yucca provided the material for this basket. In splitting the leaf with an awl (see diagram), the inner white is exposed. An over-three-under-three rhythm was used on the basket bottom, making large concentric squares over all of the base. On side walls an over-two-under-two alternation resulted in simple bands or almost-chevrons. It is of interest to see the revival of this old style in the midst of heavy production of ring baskets. Wright says that this deep style represented one-half of basket production from the 1870s to the 1920s.[39]

ZUÑI PUEBLO BASKETS

Baskets were important to the Zuñi Indians both for everyday use and for ceremonial occasions. Seemingly, most of the baskets, except the wicker peach-carrying style and possibly one or two other pieces plus the plaited ring basket, were obtained through trade. Early collectors of this craft at Zuñi seemed to be of two types: those who were unaware of the outside origin of many baskets used by Zuñians and claimed them to be made by this tribe, and those who knew they were not Zuñi-made and said so.

Although called peach-carrying baskets, this deep form was probably used to transport other food stuffs, as among the Hopis. Judd said that he had seen basket bowls (wicker, plaited, or coiled?) at Zuñi "filled with edibles of one sort or another—peaches in season, broiled mutton, bread, corn on the cob, shelled corn ready for grinding, and meal fresh from the milling stones." He also comments on the two-rod-and-bundle close-coiled baskets collected by Stevenson in 1881 at Zuñi: surely this was an import.[40] The above comments by Judd, then, reflect common usage of baskets at this village.

At Zuñi Shalako, Whitaker notes the use of baskets in several situations, but she does not say what kind of basket was so used. At one point a ceremonialist puts seeds and a fawn skin into a basket and a rabbit on top. "The basket is blessed by each of the gods and then raised to the six directions before being deposited before the altar." Later this basket and its contents are removed from the altar and passed down the line of seated gods where "each gives prayers for rain and good hunting and the basket is then returned to the altar." At one point in the ceremony, "the personators deposit seeds and a gift to the host in a basket beside the altar." And finally, during this dance, "The host carries a basket of food and sprinkles sacred cornmeal along the path of the dancers."[41]

In 1962 it was observed at the Zuñi Shalako ceremony that baskets were still being used for another purpose. Between the earlier evening kachina dances and the later Shalako performance, hosts in the home where these dancers were staying served coffee and breads of various sorts to all who had come to witness the ritual. The breads were in large pottery bowls, commercial pans, and coiled baskets.

There follows below a brief discussion of the two known types of Zuñi-made baskets, plaited and wicker. The likelihood of the weaving of coiled pieces in later historic years is dim, but probably they were produced at an earlier time. Certainly the vast majority, if not all, of the recorded coiled baskets were traded into Zuñi, made by other southwestern tribes. It is possible that the same is true of the wicker pieces.

Plaited Baskets

A picture in the Arizona Historical Society, Tucson, dated 1897, shows a Zuñi woman with several characteristic pots of her tribe and two plaited ring baskets (Fig. 4.25). Both look very coarsely woven; one shows the outside fringe, and it appears rather long. One basket definitely had concentric squares and the other seems to carry the same design, although the patterning is not as clear in the second piece. When Goddard wrote about Zuñi in 1931, he noted that the plaited yucca basket was still made at this pueblo.[42]

Wicker Baskets

When baskets were collected at Zuñi in 1879 by Stevenson, he refers to a number of wicker pieces and illustrates three of them.[43] He also illustrates a plaited ring or pot rest but does not illustrate or describe a plaited basket form. Further, he mentions baskets,

Fig. 4.25. Zuñi woman with two plaited baskets to her right. The upper piece has concentric squares as decoration; the lower basket has a fairly long fringe. These could be Zuñi, or possibly Hopi. The date on the picture is 1897 *(AHS 28454)*.

a.

b.

c.

Fig. 4.26. Several examples of Zuñi baskets. (a) Two wicker peach baskets, with four heavy ribs exposed on the bottom of each. The right basket has a series of brown horizontal bands from top to bottom. It is more than 12" tall. These two baskets are dated between 1900 and 1925 *(ASM E2698, E2705)*. (b) A tray and a deep form, the latter a small jar shape. The well-sewn tray is 15" in diameter, and it has several bands of red and green decoration. The deep form is about 8" high, is of fair weave, and also has red and green bands *(ASM E2710, 13964)*. (c) A peach tray and a bowl or small peach basket. Both baskets are brown except for white yucca rim sewing *(ASM 6110, E5096)*.

obviously coiled, made by Navajos and Apaches, as used by the Zuñians.

The three wicker types illustrated include trays, a shallow jar with a constricted neck, and deep forms, one with a handle (Fig. 4.26). The tray is very shallow and finely woven (Stevenson called it flat), and apparently it was undecorated. Three other trays are listed, but Stevenson notes that the one illustrated "shows the details sufficiently," and adds that all of them were used for winnowing small grain.[44] The beginning is like that described for Hopi trays, with three wrapped bundles going each way. Workmanship in this start is not as good as it usually is in Hopi pieces. Rim finish also compares with Hopi work; here it is fairly tight, but the sewing is not too regular.

Jar shapes are coarsely woven in a plain wicker which results in vertical lines in the weave. Neither of the two illustrated pieces is decorated; called peach baskets, both are referred to as used to gather this fruit. Certainly the shapes are different from the Hopi peach-carrying baskets. The shorter example is flat-bottomed, the taller more rounded on the base, and weaving is a little better in the latter. Rim sewing is better in the shorter basket, but it is quite spaced out in the deeper piece. Stevenson says these baskets are of willow. Twenty-one other baskets of this peach-carrying style are listed by Stevenson; "sizes and shapes somewhat similar," he says.

Stevenson also mentions several other styles of basketry, but they are not illustrated. One he describes as, "A globular-shaped water basket, with a small neck, about two inches long and three in diameter." He has this to say of a second piece: a "Double-lobed, canteen-shaped water basket, with both outer and inner surfaces coated with gum. The neck is about the size of that of the preceding basket. The center is compressed to about the size of the neck, the bottom flat."[45] It is herein suggested that this could be an Apache basket; this is supported by the fact that other Apache baskets are found at Zuñi, that it is an unusual but typical Apache form, and that otherwise the shape is rarely if ever found in this pueblo.

Next in time would be Mason's reference to Zuñi wicker work in 1904. He pictures a peach basket quite like the longer one described by Stevenson but of more open wicker work, with over-three-under-three rhythm, and with a much wider binding at the rim.[46] Finishing of edges on these Zuñi pieces is explained by Mason as follows: top weaving ends with three warps which are bent sharply to the left; these are wrapped. "They are then cut so that there will be always three of them included" in the sewing.[47]

Mason further pictures a number of wicker pieces from Zuñi, several obviously peach baskets.[48] Relative to this variety, he says, "The only work made by the Zuñi nowadays is their small, rough peach baskets, of twigs and wicker work, hardly worthy of notice except for their ugliness and simplicity. Those who are familiar with this interesting tribe of Indians say that trading is a passion with them, and that through their agricultural products and their refined loom work they are able to gratify this taste among the surrounding tribes for old basketry."[49] Thus it would seem that most of these pieces illustrated, with the possible exception of one, may be trade items.

In 1904 Matilda Coxe Stevenson noted that the Zuñis made coarse baskets of willow, dogwood, and rabbit brush. She adds that they made several forms, deep carrying baskets, a deep but smaller one for collecting grasshoppers, and winnowing baskets.[50] A deep carrying basket in the Arizona State Museum collected in 1926 and marked "probably Zuñi" will give some idea of the size of this piece. It measures 13″ in rim diameter and is 14″ in height. Several features might deny its Zuñi origin, namely, its fairly even weave and its decoration. From the rim is the following patterning: 3″ of light plain work, 1″ of dark, 3″ light, 1½″ of alternating light-dark, 3″ light, and a repeat of the light-dark motif. If not Zuñi, this basket is probably Hopi.

A last reference regarding basketry at Zuñi is from Underhill. She said in her 1944 *Pueblo Crafts* that the peach-carrying basket was "made at Zuñi until a short time ago," and added, "perhaps a few other pueblos weave them now and then."[51] This would mean then that Zuñis ceased to weave baskets in the late 1930s or early 1940s.

JÉMEZ PUEBLO BASKETS

Although little or no basketry is produced in the Rio Grande today, one pueblo in particular is not only currently active but apparently has been so for many decades, namely, Jémez. Perhaps trade as well as local use has kept this craft alive, despite the fact that few native women in this village pursue basket weaving. Men have produced baskets in some Rio Grande pueblos within the century.

Plaiting

At the pueblo of Jémez there has been carried on for a long time the tradition of plaited ring baskets, perhaps since prehistoric days (Fig. 4.27). In one instance a mother taught her ten-year-old daughter how to weave this piece; important as this craft is, this is not surprising. Williamson says that this basket was used for winnowing and washing wheat, for holding shelled corn, and for other purposes. Some women reputedly made these baskets rather readily, one making four or five "excellent baskets a week"; this "one" was the best weaver in Jémez in the 1930s.[52]

a. 

b. 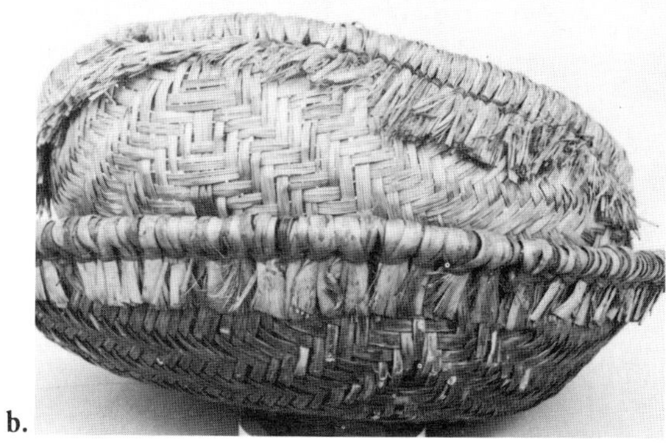

Fig. 4.27. Jémez plaited tray or sifter baskets. (a) Interior showing design of concentric diamonds *(ASM E4433)*. (b) Typical exterior of these baskets illustrating a heavy rim; in this second piece the rim sewing is of buckskin thongs rather than the usual yucca *(GP398)*. (c) Rose G. Valencia with raw yucca, a plaited mat, and finished baskets showing interiors and exteriors, at Pecos, New Mexico, 1982. (d) A woman washing wheat in Jémez in 1936, using Jémez plaited baskets. *(Museum of New Mexico)*.

c. 

d. 

The ring basket is made like that of the Hopi, in the form of a square mat which is then slipped into the wooden withe or ring and sewed into place. It is reported that these women weave these mats flat on the floor, "and, until well enough under way to retain their shape, are held in place by the weaver's feet."[53]

Yucca is the basic material used in the ring basket. It grows close to the village of Jémez and can be gathered any time of the year. Williamson notes that a woman with an ax can gather in one-half day enough material for fifteen or twenty mats for these ring baskets. Also along the nearby Jémez River grow clumps of sumac from which the long, sturdy stems are gathered. These are made into rings and secured in position with wire until they are dried. The "ends are matched, bound with yucca, and the ring is ready for use."[54] Williamson also notes that narrower yucca leaves are used for the making of smaller baskets while wider and longer ones are picked out for the weaving of larger pieces.

In weaving these mats for the ring basket, the Jémez woman crosses three units of elements by three others at right angles. Then continuing the over-three-under-three alternation, she prepares the mat. One of the most common results of such alternation is the diamond, and it is the characteristic design of this Jémez ring basket (Fig. 4.28). In fact, Williamson says, "There is no variation from this, nor is a two-color pattern ever attempted."[55] Almost all of the mats are woven in squares which means that most of the baskets are round. All Jémez baskets observed were of this shape, although Williamson does say that occasionally a rectangular mat is woven which means that a few oval baskets are produced.

Fig. 4.28. A Jémez yucca ring basket maker plus the raw materials: (weaving yucca, to right, sumac for rings and rings leaning against the wall), the woven mats in foreground, and finished baskets of many sizes in background (from *El Palacio,* Vol XLII, Nos. 7, 8, 9, 1937; *Museum of New Mexico photo*).

When the mat is completed, it "is sprinkled with water and pounded upon a flat stone to soften it before the ring is placed." Usually the weaver has a collection of rings she has made beforehand, and she chooses one suitable to the size of her mat. Then "standing in the center [she] pulls the ring up until only the ends of the yucca extend above it. These protruding ends are bent around the squawbush ring and are bound to themselves with strands of split yucca leaf, kept pliable in a bucket of water."[56]

A simple twined stitch is used in sewing the ends of the mat into position. These ends are then cut all around on the basket exterior, with an effort made to keep them even. Frequently they are not regular in size; however, one of the features distinguishing the Jémez from the Hopi ring basket is that the fringe on the Jémez basket is longer than that on the Hopi piece.

Jémez ring baskets range in size from 3″ to more than 30″ in diameter. The very large pieces were made for wood baskets. Average sizes were 19″ to 26″. The same range in these basket sizes was observed at the Pueblo Indian Arts and Crafts Market at Albuquerque in 1941, and in still later examples of this piece. A picture of a Jémez weaver and her baskets shows Anna Maria Toya, the great weaver at this village at that time, and a number of her baskets large and small, several varisized rings, the long withes for making rings, and yucca for weaving the baskets.[57] (See Fig. 4.28.)

One example of a specific Jémez ring basket will suffice, for there is significant variation in size only. This piece is 13½″ in diameter and 5½″ in depth. It is all in natural green of a rather dark shade. In the weaving process, two elements are used as one, another diagnostic of the Jémez basket, for Hopis use a single element in this plaited weaving. The over-three-under-three rhythm produced four concentric diamonds in this piece. Fringe is irregular, measuring 1½″ to 1¾″ long; the rim rod is large and heavy, and is ½″ in diameter. Withal, this piece is well woven, another characteristic feature of the Jémez ring basket.

OTHER RIO GRANDE PUEBLO BASKETRY

Rio Grande puebloans probably never developed basketry to any degree in historic years. As a matter of fact, basket making declined in pre-Columbian days as pottery developed. By full prehistoric Pueblo times, technology had reached a peak but production and design had retrogressed. Less is known about the days immediately preceding Spanish arrival in 1540, but the supposition is that basketry had not picked up to any extent. Equally little is known of this craft among the puebloans from the opening of this historic period in 1540 to the last quarter of the nineteenth century which "saw the almost complete disappearance of coiled basket making." Ellis and Walpole also make this comment: "No notes on Pueblo basketmakers of the modern period (except for Hopi) then existed in the literature [circa 1941], and not more than a score of "Old Pueblo" baskets had been reported."[58]

Photographs of various pueblo rooms of the late nineteenth and early twentieth centuries do show baskets on their walls. In some instances these pieces are not pueblo made; for example, Havasupai-Hualapai coiled baskets are among those noted. Apache baskets seem to have been widely traded also, for they have been identified in old collections from such places as Zuñi as well as Rio Grande pueblos, and further as illustrated on the walls of pueblo rooms. It seems that during dances at the pueblos, Jicarilla Apache guests often left baskets in response to staying several days with pueblo friends.[59] Hough, in 1918, said essentially the same: "Mention should be made of the baskets acquired by the Hopi from other neighboring tribes. At the time of the explorations of Major J. W. Powell in Tusayan [Hopi country], great numbers of these baskets were collected and at first thought to be representative of the Hopi basket art.... They consist of twined pack baskets and pitched water bottles of the Utes and Apaches; strong fine coiled bowls and twined pitched water bottles of the Havasupai; coiled bowls of the Ute-Navajo and water bottles probably from the Mohave [probably not]. There were also rod and splint baskets, evidently very old, whose origin is unsettled but which were found also at Zuñi and in the Rio Grande pueblos."[60]

Plaited

Ellis and Walpole credit the Rio Grande puebloans with three types of baskets, coiled, plaited, and a wicker style. Many of the coiled pieces they illustrate could well be of Apache or even Navajo origins —or inspiration, when and if made by a puebloan. The plaited ring basket, described under Jémez, was, of course, still woven by these villagers and at "San Felipe and some of the other pueblos" in 1959 according to the above two authors.[61] Bahti also notes that plaited yucca baskets from Laguna "are identical to those of the Jémez."[62] San Juan Pueblo examples are illustrated in a Curtis book[63] in a photograph of two women washing wheat. Each has a ring basket in hand, and one piece seems to have been decorated with wide-banded, concentric diamonds.

Wicker

The next technique, wicker, is comparable in some respects to that used in three Hopi baskets, the piki tray, the peach tray basket, and the carrying basket, all described above. But in the Rio Grande the shape is often different: it is a round or oval and usually fairly deep bowl.

This wicker piece, the bowl, is made by the San Juan, Laguna, San Felipe, and Santo Domingo puebloans[64]; formerly it was made in many Rio Grande Indian villages by men. Ellis and Walpole have this to say regarding possible origins of this piece: "Whether the idea was introduced by 'Mexicans' as stated in Jeancon's field notes, or was native, as is suggested by the somewhat similar old Hopi piki trays and burden baskets, is unknown."[65] Actually the piece is so different (Fig. 4.29) from those Hopi baskets that one would be

Fig. 4.29. A type of wicker bowl made by several Puebloan groups in the Rio Grande. Usually it is woven of unpeeled willow rods, hence the lovely dark brown color. Lower parts of the basket are woven close together, but above, the weaver spreads out the elements to create openwork, often with scalloped edges *(Pecos, New Mexico)*.

tempted to follow the first suggestion, or, perhaps, add the possibility of Anglo-American influences. They resemble the piki tray or peach burden basket only in that all three often used dark elements which were woven in multiple units. The Rio Grande basket had a fairly closely woven bottom and lower wall, but the rest of the wall was in wide-spaced bundles of elements. When these bundles reached the rim, they were woven in graceful curves, giving a scalloped effect to the rim. Seemingly the most common material was and is unpeeled willow rods, although there is some variation, for example, in peeled and even in dyed elements.

One of these pieces observed in 1963 is about 12½" in diameter at the scalloped rim; its base is 7" in diameter and depth is 4". Both light and dark elements, apparently both peeled and dyed and unpeeled willow, were used. Near the edge at the base and at the turn were a red band and a single white line. The openwork then started with a lacing of two white and three dark elements into the scalloped rim. In another piece, six dark elements in bundles were used in this same loose, openwork wicker weave. All in all, these baskets are very graceful.

In an article dated 1936 is illustrated a San Juan man holding a very flare-rimmed, openwork basket of this type. The center bottom is in close wicker with a very dark round center and with a cogwheel edge on a light ground. Off this is the wide, openwork band done in clusters of elements and with a scalloped edge. According to the article, the material is peeled and unpeeled willow. It is suggested that this openwork flaring form is "probably of European derivation." The article also notes that four boys were being trained in willow weaving, "and in obtaining the red dye from the plum root to combine with the peeled white."[66]

Coiled

Coiled baskets, whether made by the Rio Grande puebloans or acquired by trade from other tribesmen, were used for "serving bread at mealtime, holding ground corn meal, briefly storing fresh and dried fruits and seed corn, and in religious context as small containers for the corn meal carried by women in certain dances and as receptacles for family fetishes (with or without accompanying corn meal). They occasionally appeared in the altar equipment of religious societies, and sometimes were used to support the base of a vessel while the potter coiled up the sides and smoothed the surface."[67] Regarding this last usage, in the December 1945 *El Palacio*, there is a picture of a pueblo woman making pottery; the vessel on which she is working sits in a basket, and in a second and larger basket close by is what looks like a mass of clay.[68]

Ellis and Walpole attribute decrease in production of coiled baskets in the Rio Grande partially to the disappearance of materials in the river valleys close to the villages, but the same materials were available in the nearby mountains. Nonetheless, baskets continued to appear on the walls and ceilings of their homes, or they were used under ceremonial or other conditions as indicated above. Some were in storage rooms; for example, in one Zía home were sixteen stored pieces: "Four were Ute, six were Jicarilla, one appeared to be old Navajo, and two were known to have been made by a Navajo woman friend of the owner's wife and presented as gifts. Two more had been made by the Zía owner himself, years earlier";[69] as this event was dated 1956, it would seem that it represented a situation typical of pueblo acquisition of baskets for years and years.[70]

Several incidents pertaining to the making of coiled baskets by men from the pueblos of Zía and Jémez, with much earlier possible examples from Santa Ana and San Juan, would indicate a lingering production of this craft in these pueblos. A few of the baskets illustrated from Zía are distinctly Navajo in design: for instance, one is very like an early Navajo piece in which there is a wide, wavy-edged, red band with a thin black border, and with a ceremonial break at one point through the entire band. This piece could be either Navajo or Pueblo from the standpoint of stitch-coil counts, which are eleven and four, respectively. The maker is unknown.

A second piece, also attributed to Zía,[71] has a row of nine large, full crosses in red outlined in black with tiny designs at each corner. This motif is Navajo but the total design is not, for Navajos did not seem to employ so much repetition in a single basket. Also several small details would seem to differ from the more typical Navajo style; for example, the decoration at the top corners appears to be steps rather than squares, short zigzags, say the authors,[72] and, although the basket is in poor condition, it would seem that there are no designs at all on the corners of the lower halves of these crosses. This second piece is less likely of Navajo origin than is the first basket. The five coils per inch would favor the pueblo, but the eleven stitches could well be Navajo or Zía. Perhaps it was a Navajo inspired, pueblo-made piece.

On the other hand, typically Navajo in general arrangement and design motif is the basket illustrated by these two authors,[73] in which there are three very large crosses of this same heavy type, again in red outlined with a thin black line. Slight differences occur in detail of this design: tops of the crosses are not outlined, nor are there tiny squares at the top corners. Too, the little squares seem not to have been woven at the bottoms of the crosses; however, most of the basket is worn and design is indistinct at these points. Thus, this piece which is credited to Santa Ana, might have been woven in this pueblo, perhaps with inspiration from a Navajo basket for the motif. At the same time, it must be stressed that it could have been Navajo-made, for through the years these weavers have expressed slight variations of certain details of standardized patterns.

As a matter of fact, it is rather more logical that the less sedentary Navajos should have made and traded more baskets than the puebloans, for as Ellis and Walpole say: "The Pueblos probably never used as much coiled basketry, whether made by themselves or obtained in trade, as they did pottery. For generations their cooking and major storage was done in pottery vessels specifically designed for these purposes, and practical for sedentary life." A few uses for baskets survived, and certainly "Traded or homemade baskets served equally well, and lasted for many years."[74] For obvious reasons the plaited basket continued to be made, for no substitute was available. Perhaps also the puebloan may have woven the ceremonial meal basket; this would have depended on attitudes toward accepting trade pieces or not, which may well have varied from village to village.

Some authors have used the varieties of techniques employed by the Navajos in basket making, and particularly the earlier one-rod and the presumed later three-rod or two-rod-and-bundle foundations, as evidence of pueblo influence on this tribe.[75] Incidentally, if the Navajos acquired some of their basketry from others, possibly puebloans, how can the one-rod coiled piece dated 1775 and described by Vivian, be so finally accepted as Navajo by those authorities? Perhaps this was an early trade item from the pueblos. If "Trade with Jicarilla Apaches goes far back into Pueblo history," why could not trade with Navajos do the same thing? In fact, these authors refer to pueblo trade with Navajos for pottery and blankets and particularly for their "pointed-bottomed cooking-pots, which were prized by Pueblo sheep-herders because they settled down into the embers of the camp-fire, and hence heated more quickly than did the round-bottomed Pueblo cooking-vessels."[76] It is possible that Navajo basket weaving dwindled after Bosque Redondo (a four-year period, 1864–68, of captivity of all Navajos who could be rounded up by the U.S. government, under Kit Carson), except for the piece which then was or later became ceremonially important. Having been basket weavers themselves, it seems highly improbable that they would have borrowed such a piece from another tribe, at least until developed tabu wiped out their production of the basket. Until then the likelihood is just as great that Navajo basketry found its way into pueblo homes, and that their designs may also have influenced basketry produced by the puebloans.

Mason supports Zía origins for several jar baskets which he illustrates.[77] These he labels "Sía Ancient Coiled Baskets," and says they are made of willow or *Rhus*. One has a wide, outflaring rim, a rather straight-lined body, a wide lower diameter, and a rounded base. The second piece is straight-necked but has more rounded lines in the body and a wider diameter but a very flat base. Rims are described as single-strand plaited.

Ellis and Walpole discuss and illustrate baskets from Zía, Santa Ana, San Felipe, Nambé, and Jémez; they also have something to say of Santa Clara and Acoma basketry.[78] These Rio Grande baskets show the use of sumac and sometimes willow for both foundation rods and sewing material. Yucca was also used for foundation bundles. Foundations were varied, including one-rod, two-rod-and-bundle, three-rod, five-rod, and several odd ones such as two-rod and four-rod-and-slat. The majority of the weaving was close coil and counterclockwise. Both light and heavy walls appear, the latter like Navajo–Jicarilla Apache, but some definitely pueblo-made. The tray form was most common, and some of these, for example at Jémez, were small-bottomed and had deeply flaring side-walls, again a Navajo–Jicarilla Apache trait. These Rio Grande trays measured largely from 11½" to 15½" in diameter, with two small meal trays 5¾" and 6½" in diameter. Depths ranged from 2" to 5" in the larger baskets, but were only 1¼" in both small pieces. Descriptions of Santa Clara baskets noted some to be as much as 2½ feet in diameter.

Rims were in both the regular sewing of the basket and in braiding, with either the terminal inch or the entire rim in this herringbone stitch. Coil counts were largely low, running generally from two and one-fourth to three and one-half per inch, but with one finely woven piece with seven coils to the inch. Stitches also tended to be on the low side, with several counting seven and eight to the inch; however, here again there were two baskets with high counts, one seventeen to the inch, and a second with fifteen to the inch.

Designs were absent on some baskets, particularly the prayer-meal type. Otherwise patterning was dominantly simple, with two basic colors used, black and a dull red, both of these native dyes and woven in. At least one red and green decoration was noted. In speaking of one Jémez basket it is said, "Dyes from the trading post are used to color these elements to be used in the design, but shades are more muted than in the colored designs of Jicarilla baskets,"[79] but what those colors are is not mentioned.

Basic patterns include large crosses, diamonds, bands with wavy and stepped edges, and triangles. Crosses may be very large and three or four in number or smaller and more numerous in count. One Jémez piece has six large triangles and six smaller ones between the larger ones, all pendant from the second coil from the rim. Many of the designs are in large areas of red outlined with fine black lines; several are in black alone. Small black squares or two-square steps are added to patterns or motifs here and there.

Certainly there are many similarities in both technology and design between some of these Rio Grande and Navajo–Jicarilla Apache styles. Without more knowledge of the many wide gaps between earlier pieces and those of this century, little can really be concluded as to whether it is a matter of Rio Grande pueblo influences on these two non-pueblo tribes or the other way around, or both. Except for the Jémez plaited ring basket, there was little in the way of basketry production in the Rio Grande pueblos in the late 1970s.

Chapter 5

Basketry of the Apaches

Apache basketry presents a very broad picture, for there are four distinct Apachean cultural groups speaking a basic common language in the Southwest. These include the Jicarillas of northwestern New Mexico, the Mescaleros of south-central New Mexico, and the two Western Apache groups: the Fort Apache in the northern part of east-central Arizona and the San Carlos adjoining them to the south. As the Apaches were wandering peoples, several tribes or representatives were settled together on reservations in these different locations.

Coiled baskets were made by all of these tribes, but there are many differences which will be discussed below. In fact, some are so very different that it is difficult to believe that they were made by members of the same Apachean-speaking peoples.

Among the Western Apaches, the San Carlos and Fort Apache groups, and the Mescaleros, wicker basketry of several types has been found. No plaited work was made by any of these tribes. Interestingly, coiled basketry is made today largely for sale among the Jicarillas while wicker basketry, particularly in the burden style, has remained popular among the Western Apaches for their own use and for sale. With few exceptions, basketry of any sort is almost non-existent among the Mescaleros today, but in the early 1960s the Jicarillas started a definite comeback in the making of coiled work. Western Apaches are now doing a little coiled but perhaps more wicker.

MESCALERO APACHE BASKETS

In his book, *An Apache Life Way*, Opler describes some of the uses of the basket by the Chiricahua Apaches who lived on the Mescalero Reservation. The coiled basket is required for the girls' puberty rite. At the end of the first day of this ceremony, the attendant and the initiate have placed before them a deer skin, and on this the girl kneels. "Before her the attendant places a coiled basket tray, made of the unicorn plant, filled with bags of pollen and with ritual objects."[1] On the fourth and last morning, at sunrise, "The singer faces the east with the basket before him and sings four songs. Everything is taken out of the basket except white clay. Then the singer faces the girl, and puts pollen first on his own face and head and then on her head.

Meanwhile the attendant has mixed water with the white clay in the basket. After another song, the singer paints a line of white and red on the girl's face."[2] This is followed by the medicine man painting various parts of the girl's body with the white clay. At this point, ritual objects are put back into the basket; it is placed twenty-five or thirty "paces to the east" and the girl runs around it clockwise. It is then placed the same distance to the west, north, and south, and the girl encircles it in each of these directions.

In curing rites the tray basket is used to hold ritual materials such as pollen, paint, and eagle feathers. The tray basket was also employed by the Chiricahuas to winnow certain grass seeds, and they used their burden baskets to gather sunflower seeds. Tray baskets were employed as containers for foods and for parching seeds, plus other purposes.

According to Opler, the early Mescalero coiled tray basket was woven of sumac stems (*Rhus trilobata*) for the foundation and yucca (*Yucca baccata* and *torreyi*) for sewing. Then, as later, they used yellow, green, and white yucca (*Yucca* sp.), devil's claw for black, and root of the narrow-leafed yucca (*Yucca baccata*) for a reddish color. For their large burden baskets, he says, withes of sumac or mulberry (*Morus* sp.) provided the proper materials. Elements for designs were dyed with the juice of fresh walnuts for dark brown, boiled root and bark of mountain mahogany (*Cercocarpus parvifolius*) for red, and "algerita root" or yellow ocher for yellow. Water jars were made of sumac or less often of mulberry. Opler says that "Jars for tiswin are usually larger than those for carrying or holding water."[3] These jars are sometimes covered with red ocher, then always with piñon (*Pinus edulis*) pitch, always on the inside, sometimes on the outside also. The pitch is poured into the basket when it is hot, stones are added, and the stuff is rolled around until the

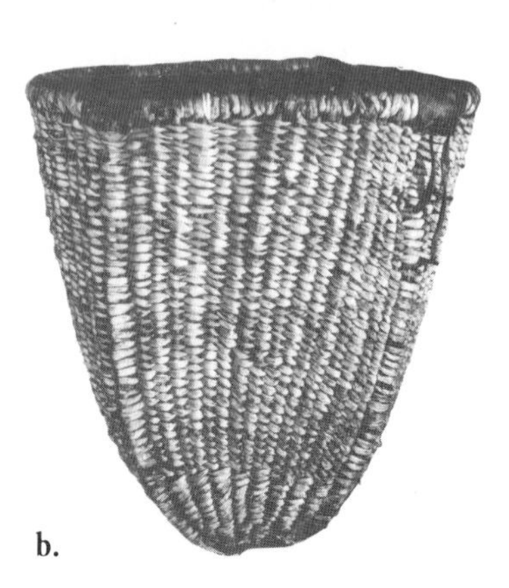

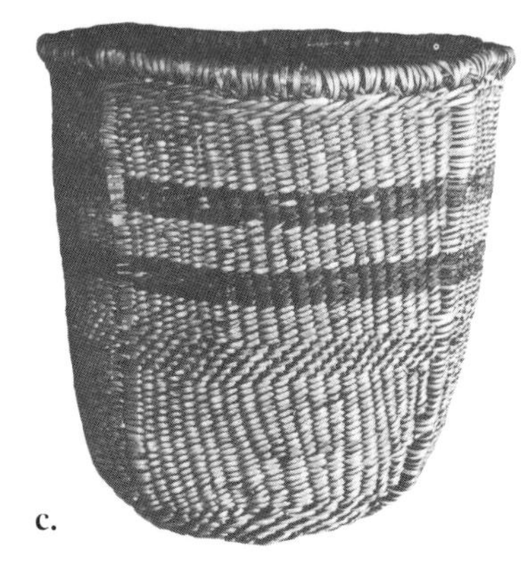

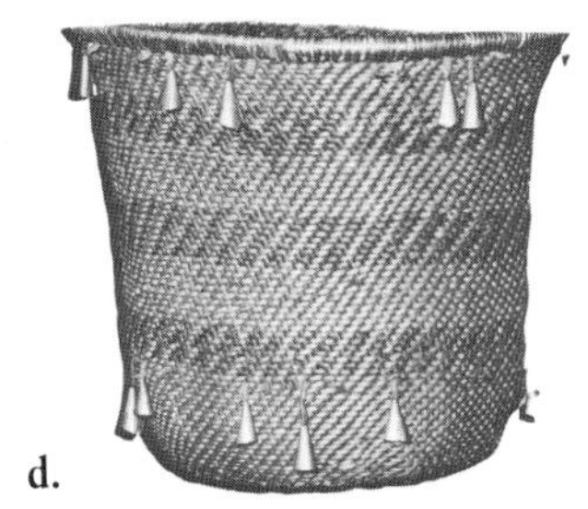

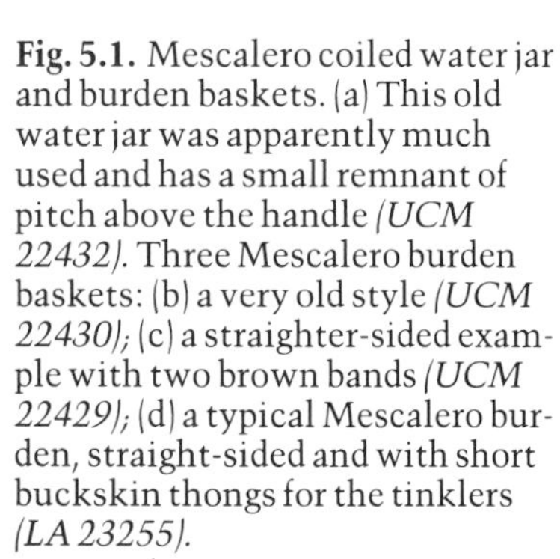

Fig. 5.1. Mescalero coiled water jar and burden baskets. (a) This old water jar was apparently much used and has a small remnant of pitch above the handle *(UCM 22432)*. Three Mescalero burden baskets: (b) a very old style *(UCM 22430)*; (c) a straighter-sided example with two brown bands *(UCM 22429)*; (d) a typical Mescalero burden, straight-sided and with short buckskin thongs for the tinklers *(LA 23255)*.

inside of the vessel is covered. A stick with a buckskin on the end is used for pitching the jar exterior. Hide or wooden handles are added on the two sides of the water jar.

Burden baskets of the Mescalero were bucket-shaped (Fig. 5.1). Twining was the weave; usually design was the result of slight variation in this technique but sometimes it was in color. Opler says that these patterns were seldom more than bands of color woven with strands that have been soaked in dyes.[4] Rarely, natural-colored yucca was used.[5] He also notes that the bases of these pieces may be covered with buckskin or rawhide and may also have fringes hanging from them.

Mescalero coiled baskets are thin-walled and flexible. Weavers start with a circle, splay it out, and often leave it rough; then they sew counterclockwise to the rim, which is in the regular sewing stitch and usually in one color, although sometimes rims are in alternating white and yellow, or design goes into the rim. The foundation is stacked, of two or more rods or slats one above the other, plus a withe or several elements above these two.

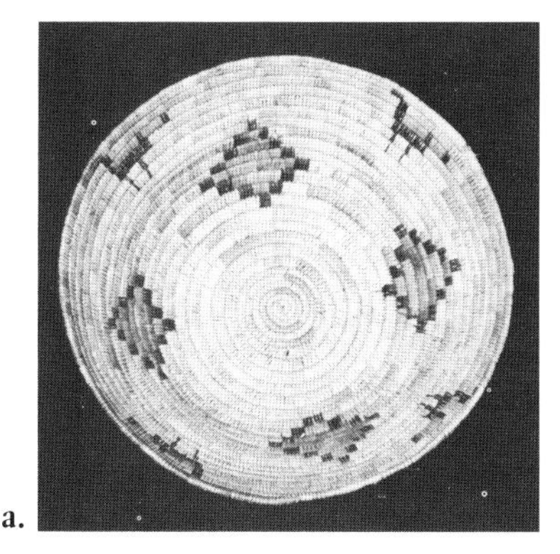
a.

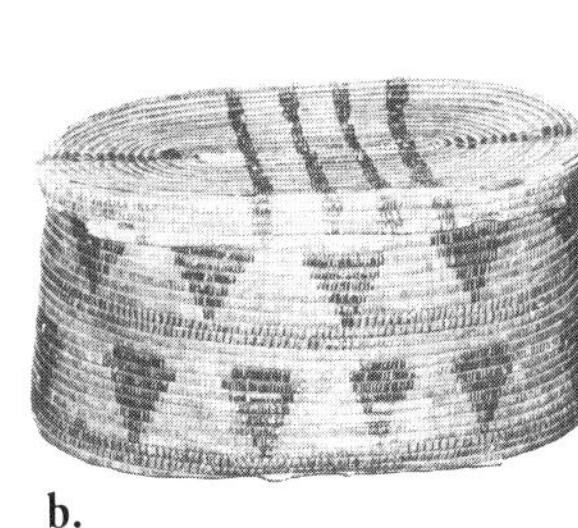
b.

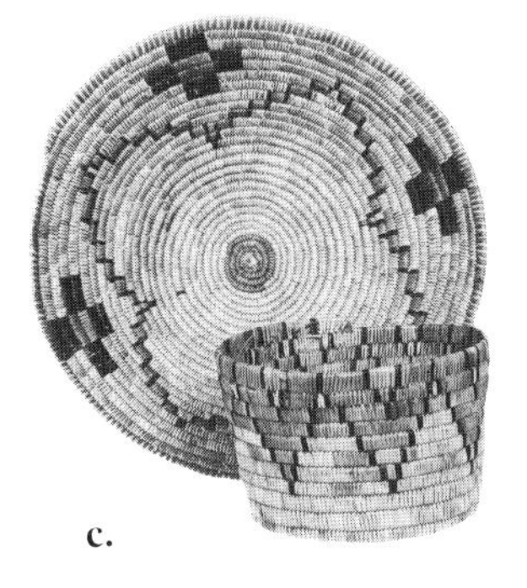
c.

Fig. 5.2. Mescalero Apache coiled tray and bowl forms. (a) The tray has a typical stepped diamond in yellow outlined in red-brown, and a less obvious animal (or bird?) at the rim *(LA 31088).* (b) The oval bowl, lidded, features spaced-out triangles, with heavy lines on the lid *(LA 1117a–b).* (c) Typical tray and bowl forms in the usual Mescalero colors of yellow and red-brown *(ASM E6, ASM GP4282).*

Trays, deep forms, and bowls were made by Mescalero Apache Indians in coiled weave; trays are better known, and deep forms and bowls are seldom seen (Fig. 5.2). One bowl had a lid; it was oval in form, measuring 6½″ by 11″, and it was 5″ deep. The sidewall of the piece was decorated with an eight-pointed zigzag which encircled the basket; double-stepped outlines formed the zigzag. The lid had a comparable design, but it was a solid band. Another shallow bowl had a four-pointed star (or flower) in a stepped pattern, and between the points (or petals) were elaborate units of four-stepped motifs. All designs were yellow outlined in narrow, dark red-brown. Two other bowls were decorated with the same central motif, the star.

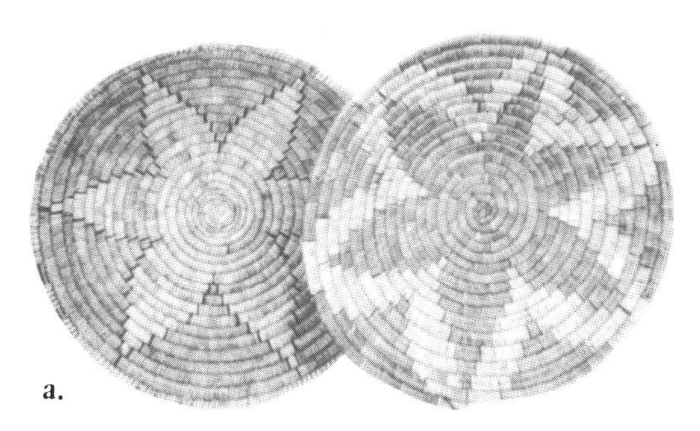
a.

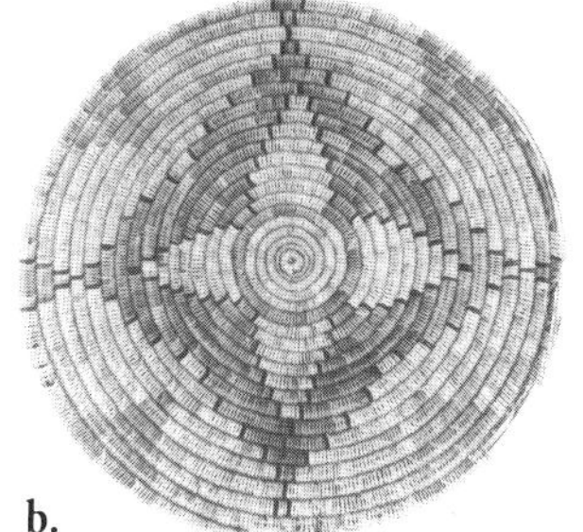
b.

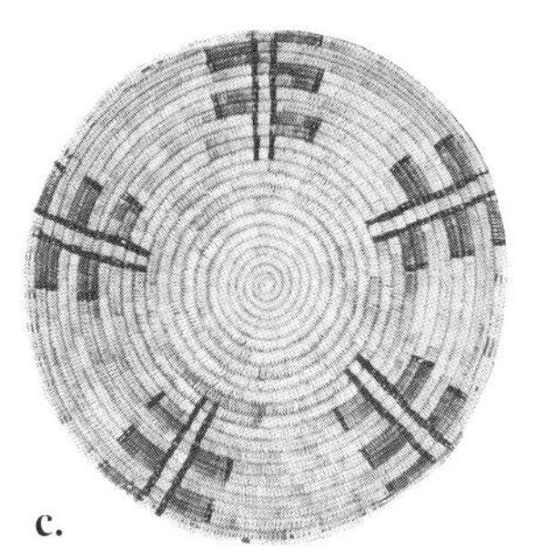
c.

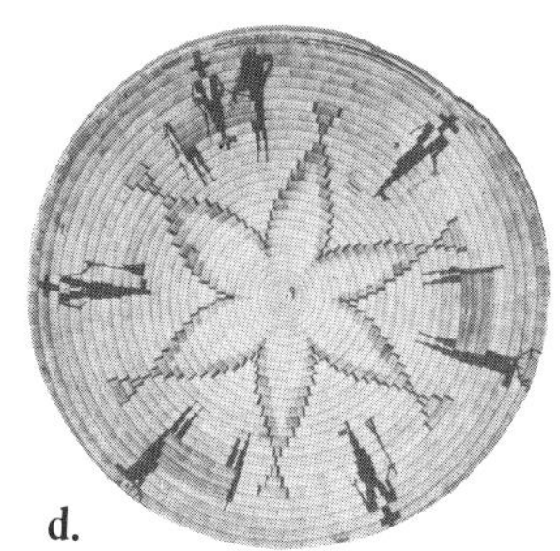
d.

Fig. 5.3. Mescalero Apache coiled tray baskets. (a) Two old-style pieces: left, a negative flower *(ASM GP52649);* right, the same in positive style *(ASM E2592).* (b) A four-petaled flower in yellow outlined in brown *(ASM GP4280).* (c) Parallel lines with yellow projecting rectangles on each side, tipped with red-brown lines *(LA 31095).* (d) An unusual portrayal of alternating men and deer and a man on horseback *(Rex Arrowsmith, Santa Fe).*

Coiled trays varied in size, but many were large. In a group of seventeen in the Southwest Museum, Los Angeles, the range was around 12″ to 19″ in diameter and most of the pieces were 2½″ to 3½″ deep; coils were under two to three to the inch and stitches counted eight to ten per inch. Most of the designs were geometric, but there were also life forms. Large outline stars or flowers were most common; most of them were in yellow, and some were outlined in red-brown or in black. Various other patterns were used on trays (Fig. 5.3). One basket was decorated with yellow outline diamonds with an edging in brown. Sixteen alternating groups of vertical, stepped triangles joined by a line, with some pointing up, some down, encircled the wall of another shallow tray. Stepped-outline chevrons decorated one piece, all done in a brownish or red-brown color. Several combinations appeared of a large yellow star edged in narrow brown, with a stepped motif more or less outlining the star. Rather unusual were four keystone figures pendant from the rim of a tray; they were yellow outlined with narrow red at the bottom and along the two sides; this type of outlining is typical of Mescalero Apache designs. One other geometric design in this collection involved a large central Maltese cross with the top of each arm decorated with a large slender triangle, and with coyote tracks between these motifs. The only life forms in this selection included the figures of two men and two women, all woven in yellow and outlined in red-brown.

Fig. 5.4. A Mescalero coiled-basketry deep form tapers slightly outward from base to the rim. Triangles pendant from rim and up from the base create negative diamonds which in turn have positive diamonds within them, all details stepped *(LA 36734)*.

In a private collection of six Mescalero baskets, several trays are of interest. One is 15″ in diameter, 3½″ or over in depth, and with an average of eight stitches and three coils to the inch. The rim is alternately brown and white stitching; in brown also are six vertically arranged motifs each comprised of a stepped chevron and a coyote track, then a repeat of the two units. A second tray is 17″ in diameter, 3½″ in depth, with seven to nine stitches and two coils to the inch. The main motif is made up of four yellow diamonds outlined in red steps, while other design elements included squares, rectangles, bands, and lines.

Several deep, straight-sided Mescalero Apache coiled baskets were observed (Fig. 5.4). One was 11″ high and the same in rim diameter; stitch count was nine, and coil one and one-half to the inch. Apparently there had been a design on the bottom, but it was not clear. On the sidewall there were large concentric, stepped zigzags with stepped triangles above and in the deep areas, and a single tiny one tucked in under the high points. Pleasing balance results from the placement of these secondary themes.

Fig. 5.5. A Mescalero coiled jar which became a pitcher with the addition of a handle. This typical coiled-jar form was decorated (now faded) on body and neck *(UCM 22431)*.

A coiled jar is illustrated by Mason.[6] It has a short neck, very flat shoulder joining the neck, and a gently sloping sidewall to a flat base. On the major part of the wall are two horizontal zigzags, a lower wide one and an upper narrow one, both stepped. Partly on the rim and partly touching the wall are two more zigzags, the lower one narrow and the upper one broader. About the base of the neck are two yellow coils, the rest are white, and all of the zigzags are yellow. Simple or no patterning is characteristic of these jars (Fig. 5.5).

JICARILLA APACHE BASKETS

Jicarilla Apache basket weavers employed sumac, which was pale and glossy brown, or willow (*Salix* sp.) both for foundation rods and for sewing splints in coiled weave. Three or five rods were arranged in a mass, thus creating a small or a large and round coil, both contributing to a rigid wall. Sewing was good in a number of these baskets, and designing was characterized by massive simplicity until late years, when it became more elaborate and of smaller units. Forms included deep trays, oval bowls often with two handles, and deep cylindrical forms frequently with lids (hampers), deep bucket forms, full-bodied water bottles, and some odd shapes.

Designs were executed primarily in native dyes and included red from mountain mahogany bark, yellow from barberry root (*Berberis repens*), plus black and purple. The few earlier aniline dyes were basically red and green, but from the late 1950s on they included a wide variety of red, purples, turquoise, brown, black, yellows, greens, oranges, blues, and others.

Geometric, animal, and plant designs have been used through the years, particularly since the revival of basketry. This revival took place at the end of the 1950s and into the early 1960s; it saw an increased production and much interest in the colors mentioned above.

Jicarilla basketry is a good example of the influence of the trader on native crafts. It was a trader who entered a number of the baskets from this tribe in the Gallup Ceremonials in the early 1960s, where they won a first prize. This served as an impetus for more of the women to weave.[7] Increase in tribal activities, plus the paving of a road onto the Reservation which brought in more people, also helped to stimulate interest in this tribal craft.

A few other general characteristics of Jicarilla baskets should be mentioned. Often they have handles. The majority of them have braided rims; this braid is not "flat" on top as in some of the Navajo pieces but gently falls over the sides. Coils are counterclockwise.

Specific shapes in Jicarilla baskets are quite varied (Fig. 5.6). Trays run the gamut from fairly shallow and wide-rimmed to quite deep and almost conical in outline. Bowls tend to have wide and flatter bases and are usually deeper; some are oval in form. One such piece in the Southwest Museum had a scalloped rim; some have end handles. Some traylike or bowl-like pieces are footed; one bowl is like a large cup with a single handle on one side. A few jars are woven. One very odd piece is a pitcher, complete with spout and a woven handle; hampers were woven in earlier years. At one time a few fishing creels were also produced, a relatively small, oval, plain piece with an attached lid.

Sizes of Jicarilla pieces varied a great deal. In earlier years many baskets were larger in size for utility purposes. Surprisingly, quite a few remained large through the years, for white men also found some use value in a great many of these baskets; this is particularly true of the hamper. In a group of seven trays, one each measured 12″, 14″, 15″, and 17″, and three are 16″ in diameter. One tray is 3″ deep, and there are three each of 4″ and 5″, thus indicating a greater depth for this Jicarilla form. Bowls varied in size from 7½″ to 17″ in diameter and from 2″ to 9″ in depth, with most of them around 13″ to 14″ in diameter and 2″ to 3″ in depth; there was a general trend for depth to respond to rim width. Very few coiled jars were observed and these were in small sizes, around 10″ in height. Straight-sided deep forms ranged from 8¼″ to 36″ in height, and these had rim diameters from 9½″ to 16″.

Stitch and coil counts were less varied than in most basket types. The majority were between seven to eight stitches to the inch, with a few counting six, and several counting nine. With a few exceptions coil counts were two and one-half to three to the inch with some both under and over these measurements.

Decoration of Jicarilla basketry has gone through some interesting stages. Simple, massive designs prevailed in earlier years (Fig. 5.7), many of them not unlike Mescalero styles such as the star theme on trays. One such tray, with a handle on each side made by extending and wrapping the rim coil, was ornamented in two large purplish stars made of bands, one inside the other, and each four-pointed. Faded red and brownish colors were both common on old trays, as in a zigzag-decorated tray with handles (Fig. 5.8).

Several old pieces from the Western Archeological Center, Tucson, present some interesting colors and designs.[8] One has

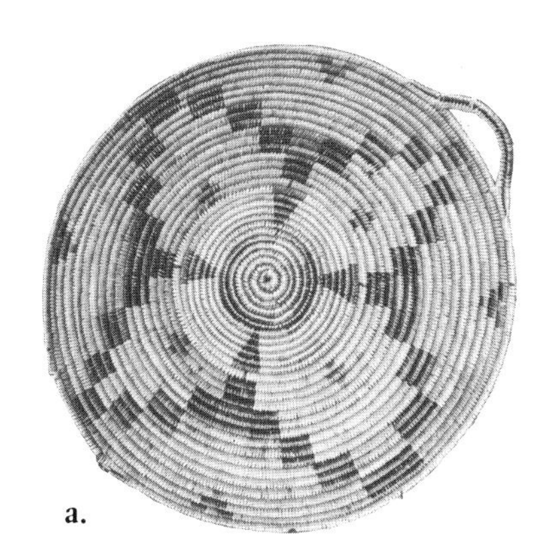

a.

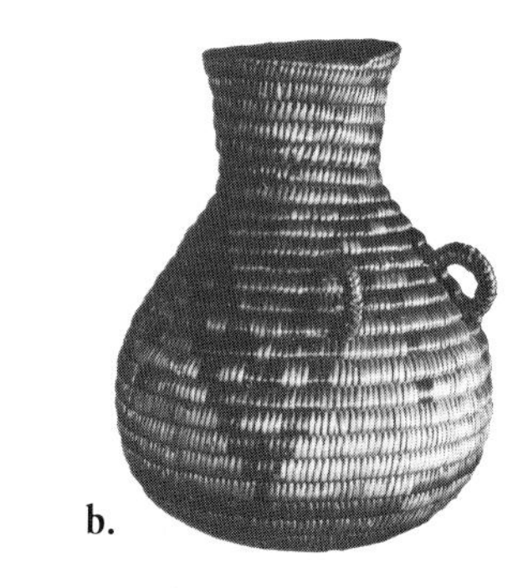

b.

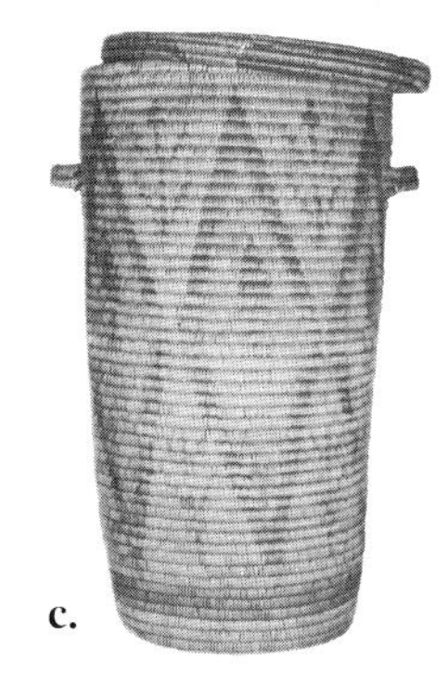

c.

d.

e.

Fig. 5.6 Jicarilla Apache shapes of coiled basketry vessels: (a) tray *(LA 23435)*, (b) jar *(UCM 19551)*, (c) hamper *(Wyoming State Archives, Museum and History Dept. 5332AB)*, (d) creel *(Rex Arrowsmith, Santa Fe)*, and (e) a bowl wih handles *(UCM 19953)*.

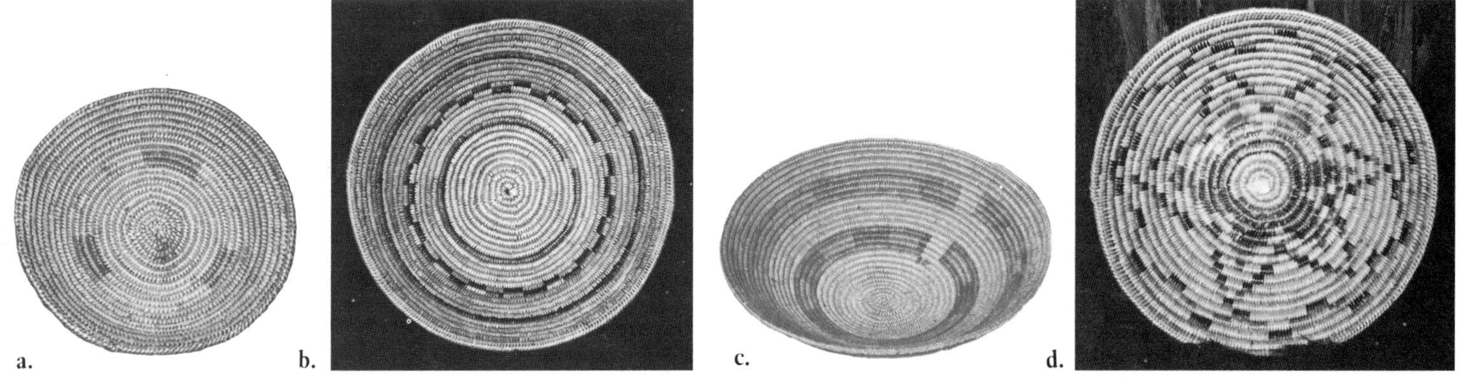

Fig. 5.7. Designs on old Jicarilla Apache coiled trays which range from (a) very simple rectangles *(UCM 18070)* to (b) light lines *(LA 23509),* to (c) heavier bands *(SAR B71),* to (d) a star motif *(Kiva Shop, Santa Fe).* Note the openings in pattern in (b) and (c); also the colors in (d), now faded, include natural, red, green, and purple.

stepped diamondlike patterns with a lower line extension, and their interiors are bluish in color and exteriors are tan. There are also pink coils in this piece. Another basket is ornamented with a repeated fat T, but several colors make this quite varied—dark and light greens, red, yellow, and tan all combined for the inside and for outlining. Five poorly spaced large diamonds decorate another tray; they are largely in that favored old color, a blue-purple and red-outlined. One other piece, definitely with a five-rod foundation, has a

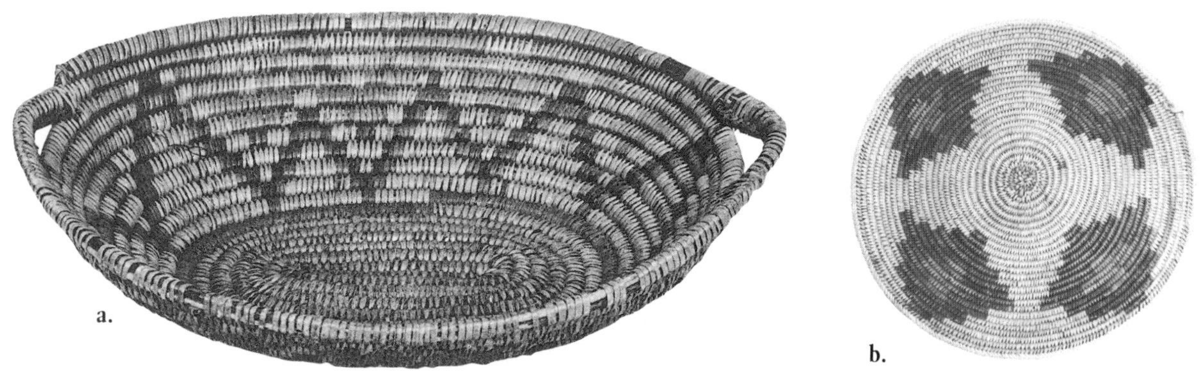

Fig. 5.8. (a) An old Jicarilla Apache coiled tray basket with handles. The zigzag pattern is made up of combined red and now almost blue-gray, the latter probably green in its original state *(ASM E5187).* (b) An old-style tray with four stepped diamonds with light centers *(ASM 56978).*

four-part design featuring a keystone with stepped edges. Colors are largely red and green, but there are touches of purplish blue. Green triangles are pendant from the rim. One tray has reddish leaves for a decorative motif, another a double circle open at one point.

A very simply decorated tray has four red and green double coyote-track patterns repeated around the tray wall (see marginal drawing). All outer squares are red, inner ones are green, and the central one is white. On other basket trays simple geometrics in red alone or red and green are repeated, usually four or eight times. One large tray, 21″ in diameter and 8″ deep, was ornamented with an elaborate meander of almost-zigzags, which combined the usual red and green and had a bit of orange added. Used in the Jicarilla puberty rite was a tray about 20″ in diameter; the design always included

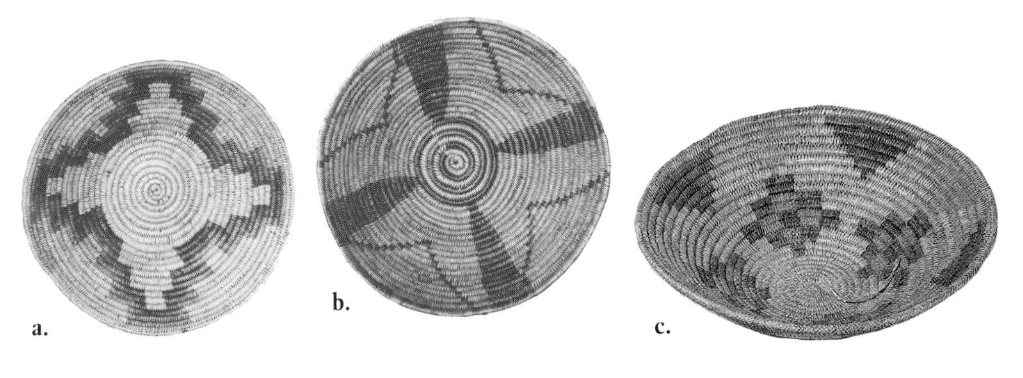

Fig. 5.9. Additional Jicarilla trays reveal (a) a typical stepped star or floral theme in red, green, and orange outlines *(LA 23461);* (b) another but lighter-line floral motif enclosing a heavy red elongate triangle outlined in green *(LA 23486);* and (c) an all-over patterning of triangles and heavily stepped diamonds, this a late piece *(SAR B287).*

Fig. 5.10. Jicarilla coiled bowls are often like trays but deeper and with flatter bottoms. Many old Jicarilla trays have four opposed deep-red triangles which touch tips. In this later piece a red-outlined green diamond touches a red triangle, with a repeat of the red-outlined green diamond tipped by a coyote track between the pairs *(SAR B363)*.

butterfly and mountain (zigzags) motifs. The basket is turned upside down and beaten as a drum.[9] One other popular old design on trays was a cross with a tiny square on the tips of each arm. Could this be related to the same on Navajo baskets? Certainly there was variety in Jicarilla tray designs (Fig. 5.9).

One bowl which was 19½″ by 14¼″ and 6″ deep, was decorated in red and green with joined, odd-shaped geometrics, all forming an organizational band. An oval, flat-bottomed basket was decorated with a zigzag along the walls; this design had a green center with red on either side. Another observed oval bowl was plain; one was simply decorated with large coyote tracks on the sidewalls and with squares at the corners (Fig. 5.10). A large bowl decoration consisted of two four-pointed stars on the wall, and between the points of the outer ones a figure of a horse-like creature. All designing was in red.

Often hampers were ornamented with zigzags (Fig. 5.11); one large piece had two such themes facing each other so as to create almost-diamonds (the zigzags never really touched). Another older piece in faded purple had outlines of two large diamonds which were topped by a red and green, fat T-shaped affair, with green center and red wings at the top; between the diamonds were two other diamonds, one blue outlined with a red center and one red filled with a yellow center. This piece was smaller in size, measuring only 8¼″ in height and 9¾″ at the rim.

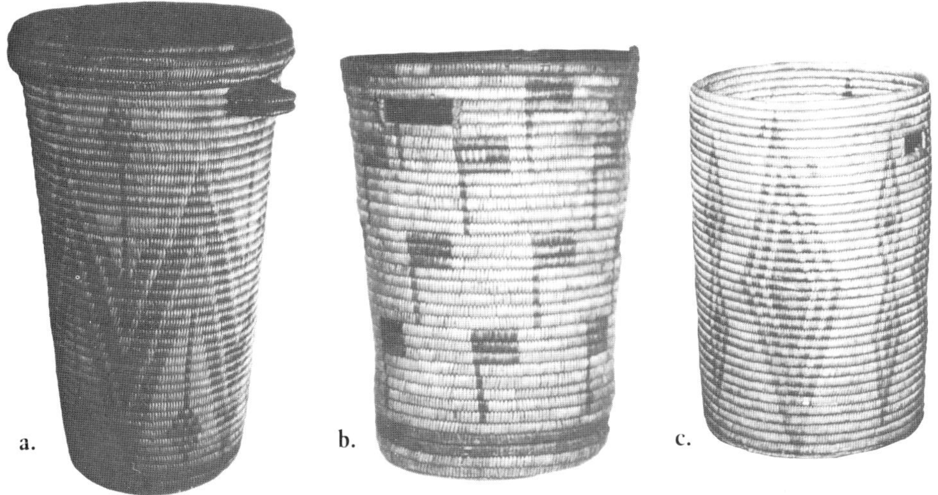

Fig. 5.11. Jicarilla Apache coiled hampers. (a) A deep red and green zigzag encircles the basket. Note projecting handle *(UCM 19550)*. (b) A flaglike motif appears all over this piece *(Wyoming State Archives, Museum and History Dept. 67-130-2638)*. (c) Not uncommon is an elongate diamond, here in red and green and alternating with a simpler double diamond around the hamper wall *(LA 23538a)*.

Two old hampers in a private collection had lids. The rim of one is braided; the other is finished in regular sewing. On the smaller hamper are vertical ladderlike designs done in red and green with the "rungs" bent upward in the center, and with short red extensions on the sides of the "poles." The larger, straight-sided basket is ornamented with the following from the bottom up: two meanders,

Fig. 5.12. Jicarilla Apache undecorated coiled basketry jar. Note braided rim on the narrow neck. On the rounded body are two horsehair handles through which a heavy buckskin carrying strap has been tied *(UCM 22104)*.

the lower one brown, the upper one double and of red and green; flattened, stepped diamonds in narrow outlines of brown and with an inner cross in green, the diamonds flanked by coyote tracks; and a top design like the first but reversed. The lid to this latter piece was more simply decorated but used these same motifs. A very large hamper, 27¼" high and 16" in diameter, had handles made by leaving openings in the weave near the rim. Decoration featured plain and alternating red, green, and white coils at top and bottom and between them elaborate zigzags and diamonds in the same colors.

Coiled jars were also made by the Jicarilla Apaches (Fig. 5.12). One jar had a braided handle over the top and a lid. In shape it was fairly short, and had a medium-wide neck and a rounded body. The jar was undecorated, but the lid had alternating red and white coils. A second plain piece had a neck which was different; it was small at the base, had a straight side and a wider rim. Another coiled jar had a longer, medium-wide neck and a more squat but gracefully rounded body. The weaver completely enclosed the preceding coil for one stitch at wide intervals so as to create spaced lines from base to rim.

To update coiled Jicarilla baskets, mention will be made of several trays, the dominant form, plus other pieces, and the aniline colors used in these examples, which is also known as Revival Style (Fig. 5.13). One rather deep piece is 14" in diameter and about 7" in depth, and has a braided rim. It is decorated with four large triangles alternating with four stepped almost-triangles. The former used red, green, yellow, and black, while the second motif has a red center, then a green and a purple outline. This basket was displayed at the 1975 Gallup Ceremonials. An earlier display, the 1966 Ceremonials, showed the continued use of not only the tray but also deep forms (smaller than the older ones) and oval bowls. There are many of the same motifs on these baskets, such as stars, V-shaped themes, stacked triangles, more diamonds and zigzags, plus simple floral themes such as the one depicted in the margin, in green with yellow flowers.

A 1963 collection of Jicarilla tribal baskets reveals much of the same wide range of colors and designs.[10] In addition to all of the above, there are figures of horses standing on solid-colored squares and of deer standing on curved red lines and between elaborate floral themes. On one of these baskets, a small deep tray, are three very simplified American flags in red, white, and blue.

Fig. 5.13. A Revival-Style Jicarilla basket, with small all-over patterning. The very small central star is not typical of earlier weaving, but there is a carry-over from early to later times in the several colors in each triangle *(Kiva Shop, Santa Fe)*.

Jars reveal the same characteristics as do trays, with a good representation of them in the 1971 Gallup Ceremonials. Jars appeared with and without necks, plain and decorated. Plain pieces were like old ones in shape, but decorated pieces might be rounded or more straight-sided. The full range of colors and designs appears on jars as on trays: red, purple, green, orange, blue; featured were diamonds, crosses, lines, checkers, and other geometrics. As on trays, more design units appeared on a single piece than in earlier years, and more colors in a single basket. For example, a motif might be green on the outside, with a thin purple outline, and red, yellow, orange, and green inside! This resulted in the lack of any distillation of distinct patterns in some decoration. In earlier years, the one color, or at most two-color crosses, diamonds, zigzags, and other themes stood out distinctly. In these late pieces it is often necessary to look several times before motifs or units are obvious.

In comparing the Jicarilla-Mescalero designs in coiled basketry, it can be said that in earlier pieces they are similar in their simplicity, but later Jicarilla pieces tend to be heavier and more ornate either in the individual motif or in the addition of a secondary one. Too, the Mescaleros seem not to have been affected by any of the aniline dye ventures, and certainly not by the latest one.

WESTERN APACHE BASKETRY

When it comes to attempting to establish the age of Western Apache baskets, it seems as futile as it does with most other tribal pieces of this nature. However, in a number of old photographs, some of them dated, at least a beginning of time differences can be suggested. Rarely is a private collection dated, and the same tends to be true of many museum collections.

In one photo dated in the 1880s, an Apache woman sits beside a tus and holds a coiled tray on her lap. The center of the basket cannot be seen, but it appears that a black coil serves as a base out of which come double, wide-stepped designs, apparently four of them. Much of the basketry area is undecorated, a feature characteristic of other baskets of known earlier age. An 1880 photo shows a basket with a black center, two black coils alternating with white ones, and a simple six-pointed starlike pattern. The main difference between this piece and late ones is that there are no additional patterns; the simple main motif stands alone. A jar dated about 1900 has organizational bands from base into neck. Simple joined diamonds form the first row, then, in succession, joined coyote tracks with squares above, a row of zigzags; on the shoulder are open and very simple checkers, and on the neck a double row of arrow points. There are no additional small patterns on this piece; again, it has a certain simplicity not generally found later. An 1890s photo of a large jar shows a full, bulbous form and a large neck. On the body, onto the neck, and into the rim are great zigzags made of quadruple, stepped lines.

A basket from a private collection is of interest as it has the date "1902" woven into it twice. To be sure, the date could have been copied at a later time, but often these dates were woven in the year indicated. This piece has a tiny black center plus a large, loose, four-petaled outline flower tipped with triangles which go to the rim. Dogs, men, and crosses are scattered inside and outside the flower, in black except for one dog, one date, three men, and the lower parts of a fourth man, all woven in red. Two other men wear red kiltlike affairs. The men are represented with both arms down or up, or one up and one down. Two or three fingers are represented on the hands.

Materials

Because the baskets of San Carlos and Fort Apache (White Mountains) Indians have so many similarities in materials and techniques, and in the overall matters of sizes, stitch and coil counts, forms, layouts, and decoration in general, they will be discussed together here.

With an abundance of rivers or creeks and other water resources in the Western Apache area, and particularly in the White Mountains, it is not surprising to find many and varied plant resources available to these weavers—and they exploited a great number of them. Somewhere in most of this area are found a variety of sumac, and squawberry or squaw huckleberry (*Vaccinium*), both used for water jars. Sumac may also be used for burden baskets, as may willow (*Salix lasiandra*), mulberry in earlier years, and cottonwood (*Populus fremontii*). The last three were also used in coiled baskets, with sumac rarely added in this technique. Apparently there were several varieties of willow (*Salix* sp.) sought by the Apaches. Cottonwood is whiter than willow, although both turn a golden color with age; both were used for foundation and sewing material. Devil's-claw (*Martynia louisiana* or *Proboscidea louisiana*) which was abundant in Apache territory, was employed for decoration in almost all of the coiled basketry. A little red was used in later coiled work; its source is the bark of the root of yucca, either *elata* or *baccata*.

Other materials were used by Western Apaches in the making of their baskets. Various commercial dyes appear in the burden basket designs, either in woven elements or as painted on the finished piece. Often before pitching the water bottle, these Indians rubbed red ocher onto the surface; the pitch itself might also impart some character to the finished surface. Various additions were made to some of the baskets, such as handles on the water jars, or rings of wood or metal in the rim tops of these and burden baskets, and further ornamentation on both. Handles might be made of bent sticks or horsehair, or even of old rags.

Occasional ornamentation on the water jar or tus, as it is commonly called, was in the form of a simple geometric usually on the shoulder, made with the tip of the finger after it was dipped in ground charcoal. In addition to color decoration on the burden basket there was often a buckskin patch on the base, sometimes with colorful cloth exposed at the edges; four buckskin bands vertically placed on the basket walls; and buckskin thongs added at the rim, or down these bands, or around the edge of the bottom patch, or in all these places. In later years chamois was substituted for the buckskin. Pieces of cloth often found on the bases of tray baskets were not placed there for decorative purposes—rather were they patches for worn-out or weakened bottoms. However, heavy cloth patches early attached to the burden baskets were sometimes for protection against wear.

Techniques

Several methods are involved in starting a twined burden basket. Two, four, or six warp strands may be placed at right angles to two, four, or six others. These may be carelessly or more carefully bound together. As Roberts says, "the bottom is a hodge-podge of labyrinthine weaving by which the desired end was accomplished, the method being only dimly discernible."[11] Twined weaving begins at the edges of the crossings, with additional elements put in if needed, "but without any mathematical regularity," in spoke-like fashion from the circular beginning. After a turn is made into the sidewall, no further warp elements need be added unless there is to be an expansion of the wall size. With an exaggerated diminution of size, say to the rim, a number of warps will be cut out.

The weave in burden baskets may involve two wefts and a single warp or two wefts and two warps. Twining is done in the first instance with each weft alternating over and under each warp and crossing between warps, thus giving the effect of vertical ribs. In the second case, the same thing is done but over two warps at a time and moving one ahead each two, thus resulting in diagonal lines on the basket surface. This latter weave, the twill twine, is used in making the Apache water bottle and some burdens. A three-ply weft may be used at points of turning in the tus to strengthen the vessel; or not uncommonly this may be used on the water jar and burden basket for designing. Weaving in burden baskets is often very good, but in water bottles it is apt to be careless. The rim of the burden basket is made by cutting off some of the warps and bending others to the left, then adding one or two wooden withes, wrapping and sewing them onto the body of the basket. Rim sewing may be in the same material as the weft or it may be of buckskin. The rim of the water bottle may vary from a bundle of grasses to three rods; it may be sewed with regular overcasting or with a false braid, usually not too well done.

In coiled baskets the beginning is the three-rod foundation wrapped a short distance, turned on itself to form a ring, sewing into this ring, and continuing in a counterclockwise fashion. In these baskets a remarkable evenness of coil size is maintained throughout the entire piece, but it may vary according to the size of the basket. The rim is finished in the regular sewing, usually in black, although there is some variation such as alternate black and white stitches or wider areas of the same. In rare cases double coiling is found; that is, a moving coil is split and divided into two separate coils which continue to the rim. Roberts reports that in one large jar basket the coil was split at the turn from base to sidewall and continued to the rim where the coils end on opposite sides.[12]

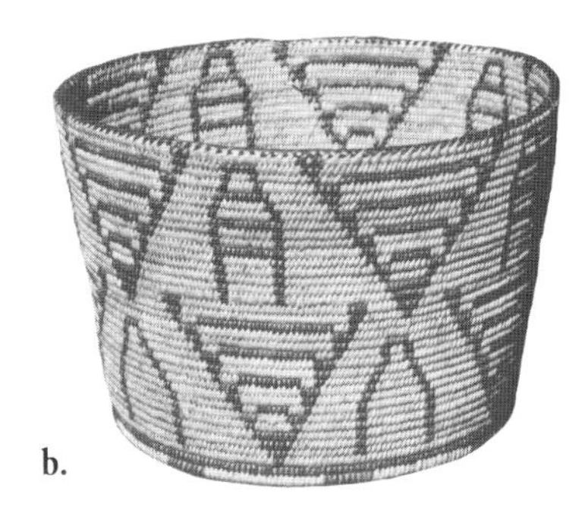

Fig. 5.14. Western Apache basketry forms. (a) Trays were always the most common form *(SAR B174)*. (b) The bowl was seldom made *(private collection)*. (c) Burden baskets were and still are woven in abundance *(UCM 10359)*. (d) The water jar, however, has lost its popularity *(ASM E2797)*. (e) The coiled basket jar is often beautifully decorated.

Forms

Roberts identifies form on a basis of three fundamental needs of the Apache Indians: one, "the securing and storage of water"; two, "securing food, carrying it home from a distance, together with fuel, which must be sought far and near"; and, three, "household utensils—for holding meal, winnowing grain, parching corn, boiling food, mashing berries, mixing doughs, serving stews, and holding water for cooking, washing, and laundry."[13] These three basic needs were served, respectively, by the water jar or tus, the burden basket, and the tray and bowl (Fig. 5.14). Trays also served ceremonial needs, such as to hold sacred meal in the girl's puberty rite, to hold the white paint with which to paint her, and to hold "the seed corn which is sprinkled over them" or the pollen to sprinkle over the girl and her godmother. Apparently the latter baskets are not sacred; they become the property of the women assisting in the ceremonies, who used them about their homes as they needed them.[14]

a.

b.

Fig. 5.15. The Western Apache tus or water bottle is varied in shape but rarely does it have any decoration. Forms include (a) flaring rim tus *(DHC)* and (b) a distinct shouldered style *(private collection)*.

Roberts pictures certain types of baskets and discusses some others in her text. In one photograph[15] are illustrated three basic water jar or tus forms and three varieties of one of them. First is a bilobed jar with the continuation of the upper lobe into a fairly long neck. The constriction between the two lobes serves to accommodate a cord for suspension. The second tus form has a fairly rounded body, a medium mouth, and a flat bottom, with two handles on the sidewall. Variations in both body and mouth-neck sizes and forms characterize the third style; basically, it has a similar but more definitive shape than the second style, often with a wider mouth, a shoulder, and a flat bottom. All water jars of this third form have two or three handles or lugs. Although she does not illustrate one, Roberts does refer to a pointed-bottom style "evidently intended to be carried about, like canteens."[16] In a survey of Apache baskets in the Arizona State Museum, Tucson, all these basic styles of the tus were noted, with many variations of each form (Fig. 5.15).[17]

Roberts notes a variety of lugs. Certainly there were both symmetrical and attractive leather straps fastened by "sewing splints which pass back and forth through holes perforated with an awl"; or they may be produced by using short bent sticks "sewed to the walls of the basket with withes, and held fast by great lumps of pitch"; or made of split sticks; or of horsehair, "braided and drawn through holes made by an awl in the walls of the basket." She also notes that some lugs were made of "twisted bark, reinforced with copper wire."[18]

For the burden basket, those illustrated in a photograph by Roberts show variations from a slightly smaller-based, wide-mouthed style to a type with a base only slightly smaller than the rim.[19] Not a great deal of variety is illustrated. In examples from the Arizona State Museum Collection a great range in form is obvious, from cone-shaped pieces to examples with virtually vertical sides (Fig. 5.16). There are deeper and shallower pieces, there are baskets as wide as they are deep, there are slender straight-sided examples.

a.

b.

Fig. 5.16. Western Apache burden baskets. (a) A typical old style burden basket of bucket shape with buckskin thongs, and with the usual type of banded decoration in black and red *(SAR B392)*. (b) An Apache girl holding a modern style burden of more conical form, with dark brown bands of decoration and with long brown chamois thongs *(photo by Ray Manley)*.

A few of the burden baskets have an abrupt outcurve at the rim. Some are true bucket shape, smaller at the base than the rim; some are fat, straight-sided pieces; and a few are wider than they are deep. There is one style which is parallel-sided more than halfway down, then it turns abruptly into a conical base. Like the tus, there are many in-between styles.

Bowls are illustrated in drawn examples of "old" and "new" types by Roberts.[20] She does not distinguish a tray form, but rather includes what are probably the two forms in one general style, bowls. The "old styles" have, as a whole, wider bases in relation to rims and straighter sides. The major exception to this, a pointed-bottom shallow piece, is a probable trade basket. In the later pieces there are more curving lines in sidewalls, and smaller, flat bases.

In her "old forms" there are three only which might be designated as bowls: one has slightly wider rim proportions, but all three are deep and flat-bottomed, and two have severely straight sides. Of the new forms, again three might be called bowls; they are deeper than the rest, two so deep there can be no question, and the third with the characteristic straight wall to the wide flat bottom (Fig. 5.17).

As to trays, there are so many variations in this Western Apache form that but a few can be mentioned (Fig. 5.18).[21] Again, Roberts shows quite a few of these. There are extremely shallow trays with almost straight sides meeting a flat bottom which may be wide, narrow, or anything in between. The same can be said for curved walls on very shallow trays, although a continuous curved line from rim to center bottom is usually found in less shallow pieces. Deep trays may have all of the characteristics of the shallow form; then, there is every conceivable combination in between. There are also outcurved walls on trays, there is definitely one with a flare in the upper wall to the rim. The Apache missed none of these possibilities in tray forms.

One form not covered in Roberts's discussion relative to fundamental needs of the Apache is the coiled jar; she lists this as one of a few "old forms" made for white men. Apparently these jars or ollas were first made in the late 1800s, for this is when tourist traffic was recognized by this tribe. In her photographs of eight such pieces, she notes that they are "Modern Un-pitched San Carlos Coiled Ollas."[22] These, of course, always with designs woven into them, never served the natives as did the tus; surely they were never pitched!

a.

b.

Fig. 5.17. (a) A Western Apache bowl. Its high, out-sloping walls are covered with life figures and geometrics. The headpieces worn by some men may represent gans dancers. Some of the animals are black, as are all the men, but others are red *(SAR B304)*. (b) A well-made Apache bowl *(Hoel's, Sedona)*.

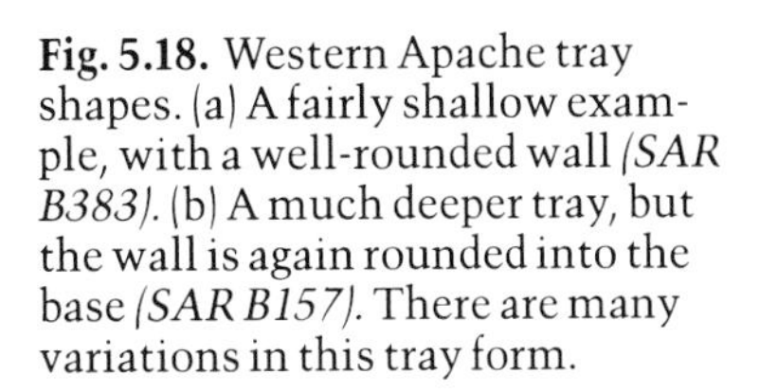

Fig. 5.18. Western Apache tray shapes. (a) A fairly shallow example, with a well-rounded wall *(SAR B383)*. (b) A much deeper tray, but the wall is again rounded into the base *(SAR B157)*. There are many variations in this tray form.

a.

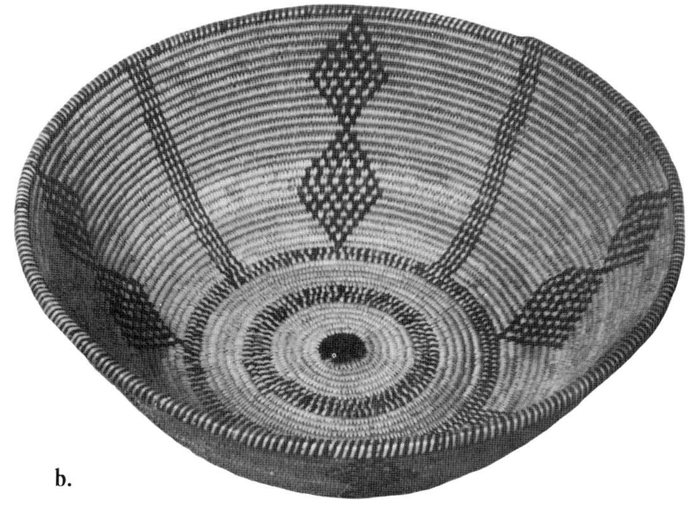

b.

Three general forms of the San Carlos coiled jar are pictured in Roberts's illustrations. One has a wide outflaring mouth which ends abruptly at the high flat shoulder of the fairly straight body wall; the bottom is flat. Seven examples of a second style include a jar with a medium to wide mouth, short to long neck, and a gentle wall slope to the widest diameter which is high, and a more or less sloping wall line to a flat base. Her illustration of Fort Apache Reservation jars reveals three very different types.[23] One style is similar to the above in its wide mouth and almost flat high shoulder, but it is more squat in proportions. An unusual style has the same features plus a curving depression toward the center of the otherwise straight sidewall. A third is a bilobed piece, much more regular in form than the tus examples of this style.

Variations on these basic coiled olla forms, plus others, are well represented in the Arizona State Museum Collection, except for the bilobed jar (Fig. 5.19).[24] In the wide-mouthed type with rounded

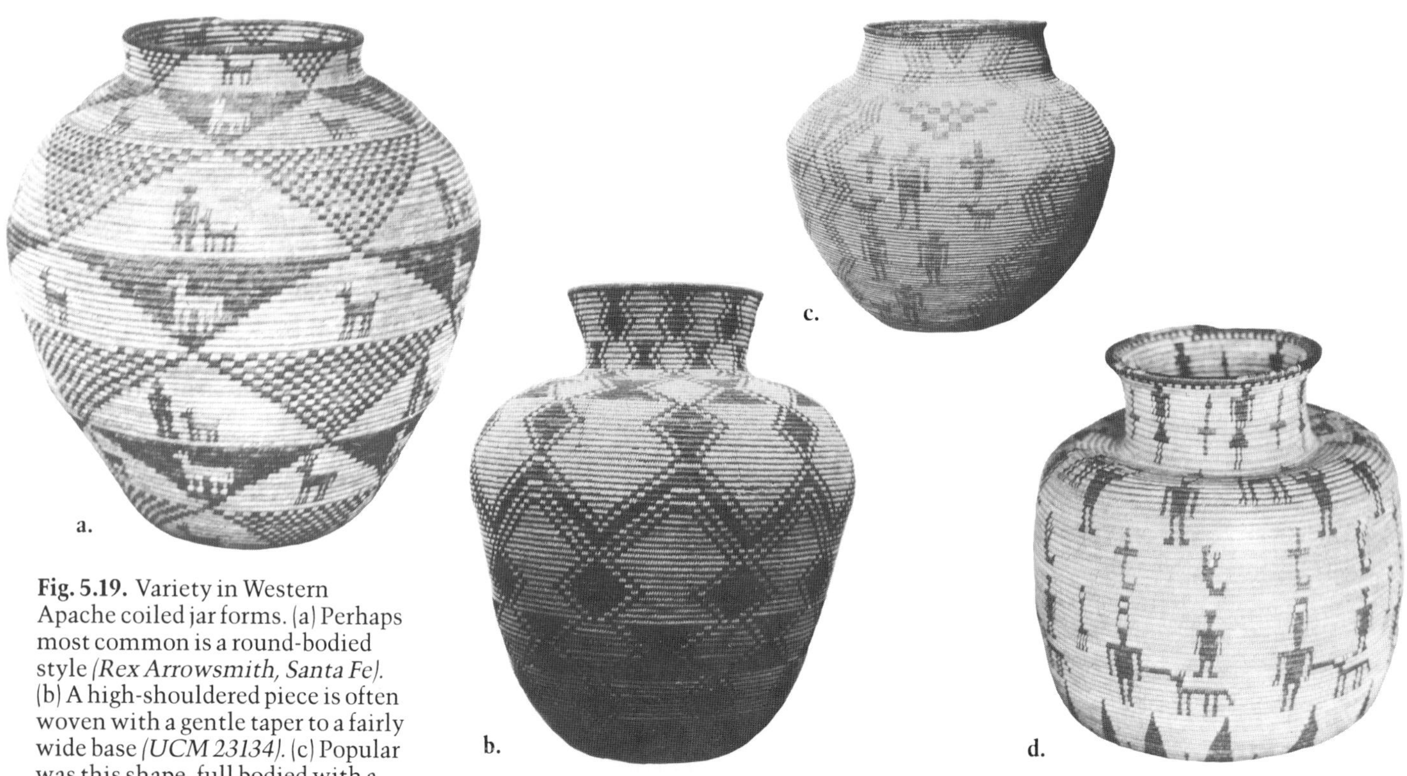

Fig. 5.19. Variety in Western Apache coiled jar forms. (a) Perhaps most common is a round-bodied style *(Rex Arrowsmith, Santa Fe)*. (b) A high-shouldered piece is often woven with a gentle taper to a fairly wide base *(UCM 23134)*. (c) Popular was this shape, full bodied with a medium-height shoulder *(private collection)*. (d) A depressed shoulder-neck and straight body to which design is aptly adapted *(private collection)*.

body, necks may be smaller or larger in diameter, short or tall; bodies may be more slender and longer or more bulbous and shorter, the latter usually with a wider base. Flat-shouldered types are, in some cases, almost depressed where neck and body meet, and the flat or nearly flat shoulder may merge into most delicately curving wall lines to a fairly small base. High, round-shouldered types with graceful body lines are also well represented in this collection. Variations on this style would be in wider or narrower and higher or lower necks, in fluctuations in placement of the shoulder and in its diameter relative to total jar body width, in the degree of slope in the body wall from shoulder to base, and in smaller or larger bases.

In relation to Fort Apache styles there is also some additional variety. The wide-necked, more squat form has some representatives with more rounded bodies, and the straight-sided form with a depression about midway has a variation in one piece with more slender proportions.

The Apache weavers did not seem interested in variety of shapes beyond potentials within the basic utility forms. The coiled olla would be one exception to this statement. Roberts also mentions oval forms, some with lids, plus a straight-sided, wastebasket type. To this can be added flat plaques (only three noted) and a cup and saucer (one only). Miniatures perhaps should not be included under miscellaneous forms as Roberts says, "In fact, miniatures of all forms of utensils are made for the children who play at attending to all the duties which occupy their mothers."[25] No doubt many of these were merely small copies, not miniatures. In succeeding years and in varying sizes, some true miniatures, other, simply small copies of the tus and other jars and burden baskets, have also had popular appeal.

Decoration Aspects

Design layouts in Western Apache baskets present four basic styles: banded, all-over, composite, and centered. Of banded layouts, two types were common: regular banded with woven even-line edges and organizational banded without these lines; there are also half-bands. All-over layouts are very common and quite varied, often leaving little undecorated space. Composite styles are also abundant; favored types include centered-banded, centered-half-banded, and centered-organizational banded (Fig. 5.20). True centered layouts are quite rare in this basketry, perhaps because the Apache decorator could not resist putting in designs all the way to the basket edge.

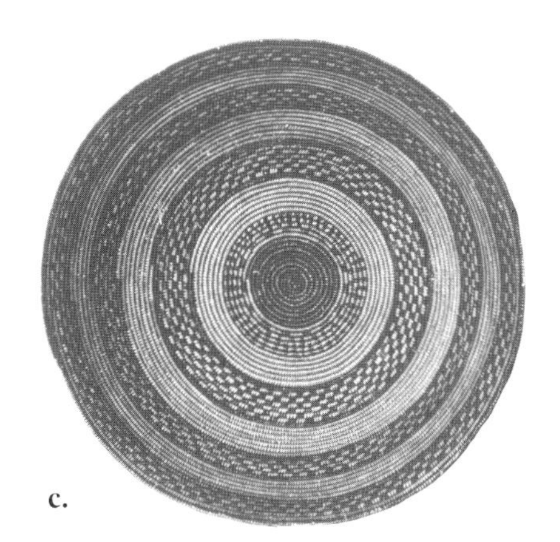

c.

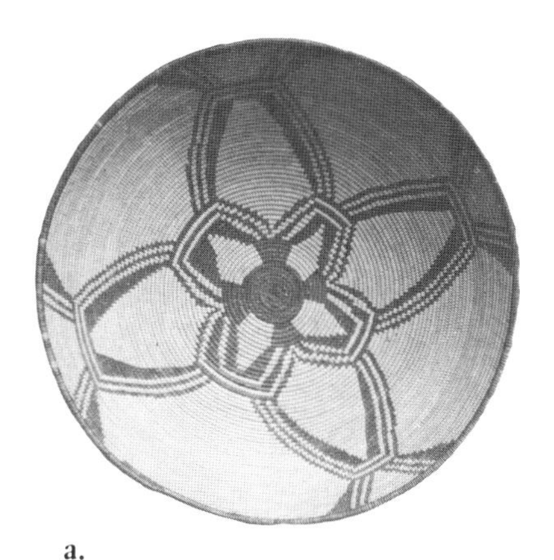

a.

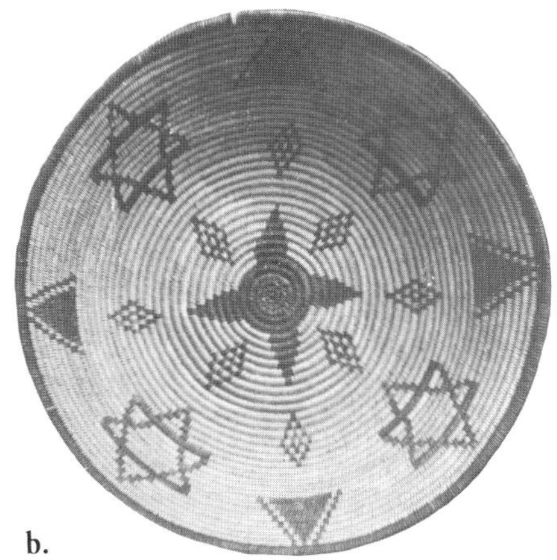

b.

d.

Fig. 5.20. Examples of several different layout styles in Western Apache baskets. (a) All-over, a most common style *(ASM E2821)*. (b) Repeated *(ASM E5882)*. (c) Banded, regular *(Duffield collection)*. (d) Composite, centered and organizational-banded *(Rex Arrowsmith, Santa Fe)*.

Units and motifs in Western Apache design do not differ essentially from most basketry, but they are applied in highly individual ways. Their use is limited by the same elements employed by all basket makers: the line, square, rectangle, and triangle. With this beginning, creativity takes over and Apache design becomes different from the patterning of many other tribes which use the same elements and technology. Most of these comments apply to coiled basketry. Twined wicker weave limits the decorator, of course, to the extent that she is unable to branch out beyond a few simple themes confined to relatively narrow bands; even here, however, the Apache expressed variety beyond belief with so few potentials.

First, some of the twined wicker elements and motifs will be discussed in a few words.[26] Again, these are drawn primarily from the collection of the Arizona State Museum Apache baskets but are supported by many other pieces. Basically most of the patterns are involved with alternation of colored stitches, but a few go beyond this. For example, there are crosses of several varieties; diamonds, usually continuous and connected; triangles which are generally balanced in opposing colors; zigzags which may take a sharp or expanded form in varying numbers of stitches and therefore are fat or thin; coyote tracks, usually joined; and parallel vertical or horizontal arrangements in a variety of simple geometric designs. There are also chevrons, diagonal lines, or just simple line motifs.

Designs in coiled weave go far beyond the twined themes, with variety that can be attributed to imagination only. There are variations in the basic elements themselves, to say nothing of how they are combined and recombined to the whims of the weaver.[27] A cross section of this subject can be well illustrated, again from the Arizona State Museum Collection.

First, the line. It may be used as a single unit, double, triple, or multiple. It may be narrow or broad, long or short. It is commonly used to form various geometrics, and it is often combined with various other geometrics to form a variety of motifs. It may be extended from a corner of another motif, with no particular reason except to be there. And it is often involved with life forms, as a part of the total creation.

The Apaches exhausted the possibilities in the use of squares and rectangles, for they used these two elements in the creation of a tremendous variety of motifs and designs. They appear in single or double outlines, as solids, or made up of bars or lines in horizontal or vertical arrangements, and in occasional other ways. Rectangles may be shorter or longer, depending upon the needs of their adaptation to a specific situation. Either squares or rectangles, or both, may be combined to make a great variety of geometrics or life forms, or they may be used as parts of either. Some of these life designs are made up of solids, or they may have parts such as feet or the head made of squares or rectangles.

Triangles are perhaps next most common in Western Apache designing. Constantly they are used as elements or units or, with attachments, as motifs. Generally they are solid, rarely they are in outline; they appear alone or attached to other units or with occasional small additions. They may be checkered or they may contain inside, if solid, a negative pattern such as a cross, dog, or coyote tracks; if in outline, they may enclose a positive pattern. They can be presented alone, in vertical stacks, or horizontally in a variety of ways such as in alternating positions with one above and two below. All three sides of a triangle may be smooth, or the top or bottom may be smooth and the two sides stepped. In outline they may be single or in the form of two concentric triangles. Not infrequently there may be some small addition to the top of a triangle, such as a square off one corner. Generally triangles are equilateral or as nearly so as the weaver can make them, or they may be isosceles in form. Right-angle forms seem to be, frequently, the result of an error on the part of the weaver. Generally the point of the triangle is down, although some are up.

Diamonds are perhaps next in significance in Western Apache basketry; they appear in proper geometric form, balanced above and below, solid or in outline, the latter single or concentric. The outline diamond may also have positive designs within it, such as coyote tracks or crosses, or the solid form may enclose negative patterns. Often the solid diamond has beyond it a single or double or triple outline, of squares and stepped. Diamonds often take most unusual forms, outcurving in their upper sides and incurving and of smaller proportions in their lower sides—they become most artistic in their many moods; these will be referred to as "Apache diamonds." Vertical or horizontal, simple or complex netlike arrangements of diamonds are common motifs. Diamonds may also be very slim or squat in form.

The cross is another basic unit of design used in Apache basketry decoration. It is frequently used alone, or it may be a part of another unit or motif. It may be of even-armed form or of the Latin style, or may have multiple horizontal arms. Sometimes it is solid; sometimes it is made up of short lines for each extension. Usually it is of medium thickness, but on occasion it is thick-armed; one such piece has eyes, a nose, and a mouth represented in negative in the black cross. In one representation, the cross seems to be on a chain. Occasionally something rests on one corner of an arm of the cross (such as three short lines) or at the bottom of the center piece (such as a square or a coyote track). Despite these additions, the cross remains a unit of design in its usage in all these cases.

The swastika is used as a design unit. It may be solid or in outline; its bent arms may point to right or to left. Occasionally an arm on the end of it may be missing or something may be perched on an arm, or ends may point in different directions.

Chevrons are equally simple design units. They may be solid, or they may be constructed of squares or rectangles. They may face up or open to right or to left; they may be deep or wide in form. In these baskets they appear singly or in double or triple form, or, for that matter, in a long concentric row. More solid chevrons which are stepped may be outlined with steps of simple or complex nature.

Coyote tracks are commonly used in coiled basketry. The Apache chose to throw this unit of design in at a whim or to incorporate it in the total pattern. It might be made of four simple squares or rectangles about an open square. Often it was single and alone, or it might be double or multiple, usually stacked vertically.

A category of miscellaneous design elements would include such things as the date 1902, the letters H, F, T, and P, and the arrow point. The saguaro is simply presented with its central stalk, several branches, and either flowers or fruits. Letters and dates are obviously simple and complete units within themselves. The arrow point is simple, pointing either up or down; some are slender, some fat. Roberts says the arrow point is diagnostic of San Carlos Apache designs. The name of a weaver, Albertine B., is woven five times into a tray basket.[28]

In Western Apache coiled basket patterning, these motifs are used extensively and take on the feel of elements: zigzags, stepped themes, meanders, the arch, and center motifs. All involve the basic elements of design but these are combined into motifs of far greater complexity.

Meanders might take a vertical or horizontal alignment; they might be single, double, triple, or even quadruple. On occasion meanders could wind themselves into other geometrics; they could be perfect in form and balanced, or they could be most irregular. Vertical meanders were often opposed, and they might be plain or they might have animals, humans, or geometrics scattered between them.

Stepped themes were a natural in coiled basketry design, for the crossing of weaving elements at right angles creates such units or motifs. The angular step in itself is simple but it, too, has many variations; often it becomes a motif. It could be simple in equal-sized risers and horizontals, or these two could be diverse, the latter a simple line, the former a square. Simple or complex stepped themes might be single, double, triple, or quadruple, again becoming motifs. Such themes might encircle a basket, usually at a greatly slanting angle and from lower left to upper right. Zigzags function quite like steps and meanders: they might move straight out, or they might curve from center to edge. They too were single, double, triple, or quadruple in form and were often made up of small squares. Like meanders, they might enclose crosses, animals, or other units of design.

Arches are commonly seen in Western Apache basketry. They, too, are made up of squares, often with a rectangle in the center top. They may consist of one, two, three, or four rows, and some have heavy centers with outlines of steps. Some are tight and sharp, while others are wide and loose. Most are curvilinear, but some are more angular in form. Usually the arches encircle the basket in single or multiple fashion.

One last geometric should be discussed: the center black circle. When alone, surely it is a unit of design. Frequently, however, the Apache ingeniously embellished the circle, thus making it a motif. She left it free but placed units of design about it in such manner that there could be no mistaking their close relationship: simplest would be a ring or two rings about the black circle. Other simple geometrics might be placed close to the center circle so as to associate them directly with it; or four men might surround the black center, their feet but one coil removed from it.

Then there were many attachments directly to the center circle which definitely unify it into a different motif; often these set the pace for the entire basket decoration. Stars or flowerlike projections emanating from the black circle are very common; they may have three to six or more points. Often they are solid, but some are merely outlined in light or heavy lines, or tips above are solid, and most are stepped. Other units taking off the black center would include straight or stepped lines, few or many, long or short; checkers, from two to five rows of them and the first row touching the black circle; triangles with their tips also touching the center unit; rays or cogwheel projections. Life forms are also related to this black center, for example, men standing on a pedestal which rests on the circle, and dogs standing on the ends of arms of crosses, the latter on the tips of each petal of a flower coming out of the center.

Many life forms appear in Apache basketry, often directly associated with other elements or units, or simply sprinkled here and there throughout the total design. There are five categories of life forms: humans, animals, birds, and, rarely, plants and reptiles. Both men and women are represented, usually in the same manner with arms to the sides or a bit out from the shoulders, body a simple rectangle, and legs straight down, usually with the feet out to right and left. Heads are generally a small block, rarely with a hat added or sometimes with strange projections across the top (a crown?) or two projections, possibly feathers. Hands are nonexistent or have two or three huge fingers. Occasionally both arms are up, or one may be; often in these cases they are disproportionate. Men are sometimes presented as though wearing kilts, while women wear long and full skirts. Most human figures are static, although a few seem to have a bit of life to them.

Dogs, horses, and deer are the usual animals; one figure looks like a bobcat. Bodies may be long or short and they, plus head, necks, and tails, may be stepped. Heads are usually forward, but some are turned all the way back. Ears appear on horses and dogs, deer have great horns, and usually all of these creatures have four legs although in some instances there are only two; legs are placed quite close together at each end, or they are all equally spaced. Tails may be short or long, up or down, fat or thin. Some of these creatures have great muzzles. Often men and horses or dogs are portrayed together; rarely, a man is riding a horse, but he is more apt to be standing on it!

Birds are not commonly presented but now and again there appear great spread-wing eagles. Rarely buglike creatures are woven along with other motifs, and there are some lizards. The only recognizable plant form is the saguaro.

Design Analysis in Wicker Baskets

The Western Apache tus served these people for many years in several capacities. Larger sizes were significant in collecting and storing water; smaller ones were important to sling on the back when one was on the warpath, out gathering foods, or traveling for any purpose. Of the three types mentioned previously, the round-bodied, sharp-shouldered, and bilobed, the first two were the more commonly made. A picturesque sight in the 1930s and 1940s was the Apache woman filling the tus at a creek, pulling a bundle of greens to use as a stopper, then placing the jar on her head to carry it back to her wickiup.

In a group of fourteen of these water bottles, the range in size is from 7″ to 18″ high. Most rim diameters are from 5″ to 9″, with a few over the latter measurement, one 12½″ and one very wide outflaring rim 15″ in diameter; the height of the latter jar is only 14″. It may be added that in some of the bilobed styles, the mouths are but several inches across. More specifically, shapes in the round-bodied include an outflaring and 2″ high neck on one piece, and a second piece with a 4″ wide and more graceful neck. Another variation on this form is a jar with a more squat body and a wider flat base which measures 8″, while the total height is only 3⅜″ and the wide mouth is 5⅛″ in diameter. One shouldered type has a 9½″ mouth diameter and the neck is 4¼″ high. Another is 14″ tall and 8½″ at the shoulder, and the neck is 4″ tall. There is one bilobed tus in the group, with a smaller upper lobe, a sharp constriction, and a small neck. Total height is about 11½″, the neck 2″. Most of the bases on water jars are concave.

Handles or lugs appear on most of these water jars. They are of the types discussed above, bent wooden handles, wide leather straps which were stitched on a shouldered piece and on a round-bodied basket from San Carlos; from Whiteriver are handles made of four braids of coarse hair (horse hair?). One piece from Whiteriver had handles made of twisted devil's-claw strips. On some baskets the handle area was too heavily pitched to determine the method of attachment.

The technique used on the water jars in this selection is largely plain two-ply twine with three-element twine on some of them for decoration or for added strength at a turn into the wall.[29] One small tus had the three-ply twine at the sharp shoulder and neck turns, but also on the shoulder proper where it was strictly decorative. On this jar there were dim black designs, a zigzag just below the shoulder and parallel short diagonals on the shoulder. A round-bodied tus was in plain weave and had the decorative stitch at the neck and at three points on the body proper, at the base turn, and at the beginning of the concavity on the bottom.

The most elaborately decorated tus in this group was from Whiteriver; it had three bands of various alternations of black and red stitching in short diagonals which is much more in the tradition of the burden basket than the tus. This piece was unpitched; this fact and the elaborate decoration may indicate that it was made strictly for sale. On a bilobed jar there was a black band on the top of the lower lobe, and there appeared to be double twining above and below the band but the pitch was too heavy to be sure of this. Another Whiteriver piece, 8¾″ tall, had decorative diagonal twining in four bands, one high on the neck and three rather evenly distributed on the body.

Fig. 5.21. Decoration on Western Apache water jars. Very little decoration appears on this form, ranging from simple black lines on the shoulder, as on this example *(DHC)*, to a few geometrics placed in a similar position.

It would appear from the above examples that the Whiteriver pieces were more decorative than water jars from other areas. There seems to be little difference, however, in quality of weaving, for most of these baskets were rather poorly woven as a whole. This is a characteristic of almost all water jars, for crushed juniper or other leaves were to be rubbed into the interstices, red ocher smoothed over the surface, and then a layer or so of pitch, often thick, swabbed over the entire basket, all leaving little evidence of quality of weaving. The black design, usually of soot put on with the finger, often did not show too well. As these bottles saw hard wear, they were typically undecorated or designed in a very limited way (Fig. 5.21).

Through the years, the materials used by the Western Apache in making burden baskets included sumac, willow, cottonwood, and, earlier, mulberry, as noted above. White Mountain Apaches used the last material extensively, as is to be noted in the grayish coloring of sewing elements of many of the baskets from this more northerly area. The bark was left on sumac sewing splints in particular; it could be twisted and thus employed for the decoration. Other decorative materials were used, including native and aniline dyes and paint. Rather unattractive commercial dyes of red and green were employed from time to time, the former color more commonly than the latter.

Sometimes two heavy withes are crossed on the burden basket interior (rarely exterior) and woven in as the basket develops; these help to strengthen the construction. Frequently, they are covered on the exterior by the vertical, decorative bands of buckskin and are not noticeable except from the interior.

In a group of thirty-seven Western Apache burden baskets, the size range was from 6½″ to 15½″ for height and from 7″ to 25″ in rim diameter. There is a general correlation in height-rim measurements, but now and again there are wider-mouthed but shorter examples in these baskets, or there are taller, narrower pieces. Twenty-one of the baskets in this large group clustered around 11″ to 15″ in rim diameter, while twenty-four of them measured 10″ to 14″ in height. Warps ranged from two to five per inch with three examples counting two to the inch, five counting three, and four each counting four and five to the inch. Wefts ran higher per inch with four each counting five and six, and seven with eight wefts to the inch.

Use of buckskin included thongs around the rim, often in eight clusters or in a continuous row. The clusters at rims and halfway down the four bands had three to four thongs in each; rarely they might number up to eight. The buckskin patches applied on the burden-basket base were cut into scalloped or pointed edges. In one case the edge was cut off square across the top (as shown in the drawing) and had holes beneath these flat tops. Often beneath the patches and showing a bit beyond the cut edges was a piece of cloth, usually a rich red or, in one instance, blue material. Thongs appeared at intervals or close together around the base patch.

Buckskin bands down the basket sides were of different widths, and frequently they were irregularly cut. The same applies to thongs; they were wide or narrow. It was common practice for the Western Apaches to attach cones cut from tin cans to the ends of these thongs. On the older pieces in this selection the cones—or even the buckskin—might be missing; however, enough cones remained to show that they might be longer or shorter. These make a pleasing sound as the Apache woman moves along with the burden basket on her back.

Decoration on burden baskets (Fig. 5.22) in woven and colored designs included plain black or brown on natural with red frequently added to the black. One piece utilized brown and yellow on

a.

c.

b.

Fig. 5.22. (a) Two fine, old Western Apache wicker burden baskets: left *(ASM 1611)*, bucket-shaped basket has three bands of decoration all stresssing diagonal patterning, with a few simple geometrics—the cross, lines—thrown in between. The right *(ASM E4327)* is squatter and broader in form and has alternating plain red stripes with wide bands of checkers between them. (b) Two typical modern pieces, the left with wide brown bands alternating with bands of black and white joined coyote tracks *(photo by Ray Manley)*. (c) A 1983 piece at O'odham Tash, Casa Grande, Arizona, illustrating the modern use of life forms.

natural. In one of these baskets, woven design was in black on natural, with both red and green paint added for further decorative effect. Occasionally an orange shade is also used; these were the only colors noted in the baskets of this collection.

Practically all designs were banded, with variety vested in the nature of these bands: how many, whether narrow or broad, what details are used, how these small details in each band are put together, and what colors are employed. In one piece, top and bottom bands are the same with six rows of alternating red, brown, and yellow, then with three rows of yellow between. Quite frequently there is a repetition of the same band several times; one such instance involved three bands of alternate black and white stitches. Another basket was decorated similarly but had a very different appearance with its four bands of alternating heavy black and narrow natural diagonals.

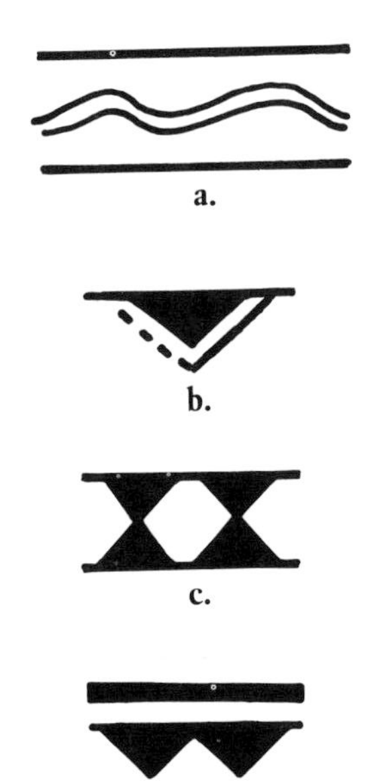

Some baskets have as many as nine rows of alternating natural and designed areas. Occasionally there is a combination of bands of design woven in and other patterns painted on the exterior of the basket. One painted basket has four rows of wide-spaced diagonals: the two center bands are the same except for pea-green paint between every two diagonals. And, of course, there are bands of natural between the colored ones.

Other variations in pattern occur in bands of burden baskets. One example has alternating black and natural squares so arranged in three rows as to create checkers. Another has a row of alternating black-white vertical lines, but they are broken in the center with red stitches; a second black band has an undulating narrow red band within it (see drawing a). Unusual is a black triangle with a black line on one side and alternate black-white stitches on the other (drawing b), with coyote tracks on this same basket. Opposed triangles (drawing c) decorate still another piece. Featured in one burden basket is a heavy line and below it, separated by two natural rows, joined black triangles (drawing d); other motifs appeared on this same piece.

A very large burden basket from San Carlos was entered in the 1975 Gallup Ceremonials and was woven within this year (Fig. 5.23). It measured 25″ to 26″ in height and was 35½″ in diameter at the rim. Obviously this piece was a novelty; its decoration as well as its size support this idea. From top to bottom it was decorated as follows: a band of yellow-red-yellow lines; a row of diamonds with upper yellow and lower red halves; repeat of second band; another repeat of second band; an elaborate band of cogwheels in successive rows of red, greenish yellow, orange, white, orange, greenish yellow, and red; two repeats of second row, joined reddish coyote tracks, and again two repeats of second row. White bands were between each of these colored areas.

Fig. 5.23. Another Western Apache burden basket. Its proportions can be deduced from the size of the person holding it. Despite its largeness, it is well woven and has a repeated pattern in each band *(Rick Rosenthal)*.

In summary, it can be said of Western Apache burden baskets that older pieces generally have simpler designs. Repetition of the same motif two or three times was common. Seldom were there more than two motifs, and often these were used in this way: one above and below and a second in between. Black and red predominate in older pieces, often one color alone used in a single basket.

In the later burden basket, from the 1930s and 1940s on, there was a tendency to use more colors in a single piece, black, natural, and red perhaps the most common combination. But, as already noted, yellow was fairly frequently added, or blue-green, or green. More rows of designing were common in the later burden basket, with four decorated rows not unusual, and sometimes more. Too, the variety of motifs in a single basket is frequently greater in the later piece. Quite generally bands are more elaborate, often achieved by using larger elements or by employing three colors within a single band, or by using alternating double stitches of contrasting colors. There is more solid work in later baskets, more line or light patterning in the older pieces. However, in later years, even in the 1970s, some White Mountain burdens stress older styles. In comparing the two styles in general, it can be noted that the same design elements are used by both San Carlos and White Mountain weavers: diagonals, triangles in bands, checkers, parallel horizontal lines and bands, diamonds, and zigzags. The same colors were popular, red and black, with less use of other colors in the White Mountain pieces.

One last point regarding the burden basket concerns the small one, 6″ to 8″ in height, the ones made earlier for the Apache girl, later for sale. In form and size they resemble larger pieces, particularly in that the rim diameter usually exceeded the height of the piece. Generally designs are of the same elements and motifs and often as elaborate in total patterning as in the large utility baskets. In other words, they are small versions of the larger burden baskets. From 1981, life motifs are not uncommon on the burden basket, particularly on small pieces.

Design Analysis of Coiled Baskets

Trays represent the most abundant coiled form produced by the Western Apaches. When made for their own uses, they tend toward medium and large sizes; smaller trays became popular with commercialization. Up to about the end of the nineteenth century, trays were quite simply decorated, but at this time a great quantity of design became popular, particularly with the addition of life forms. Certainly one of the peaks in decoration was reached at this time, just before and after 1900. Apaches continued to produce trays for their own use after this time and into the 1940s, but thereafter fewer of these pieces were made and used. Today not many trays are woven and these few largely for sale.

A study was made of many of these trays and a selection of 112 chosen for analysis. These are taken from a wide variety of collections, both private and museum, and conclusions are supported by many other baskets. Thus, it is thought that this selection will give a comprehensive summary of Apache tray baskets.

In size, these pieces range from 8″ to 29″ in diameter. There are, of course, both smaller and larger individual examples, but the major range is well represented in this selection. Baskets of 10″ to 16″ in diameter were the most common sizes. Coils counted from two to nine to the inch with thirty-five counting five and thirty-three counting six to the inch; stitches were from eight to nineteen to the inch with twenty-one baskets with thirteen to the inch, twenty pieces with a count of fourteen, and with most of the remaining with lower counts and a few higher. All in all, Western Apache basket trays are well woven.

A great many Western Apache coiled trays are all-over or composite in design layout. With the black center, large or small though it may be, these styles were natural, particularly with this Indian's penchant for filling all available space with design. There are, of course, other layouts, such as centered; varied are the composite layouts, for example, centered-banded.

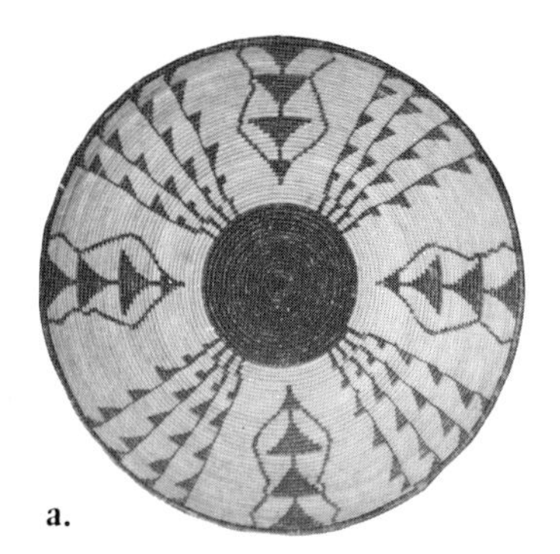
a.

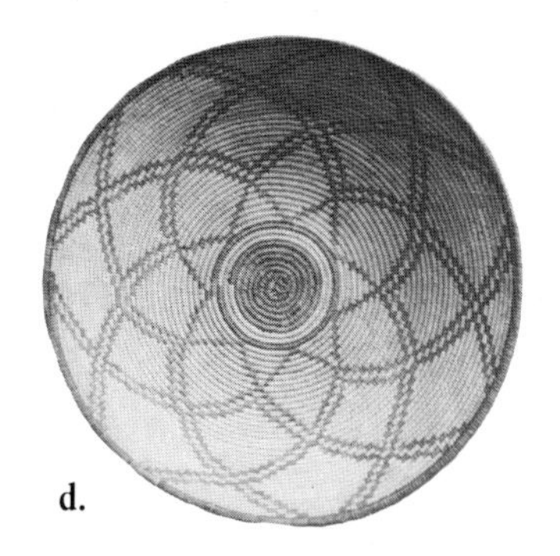
d.

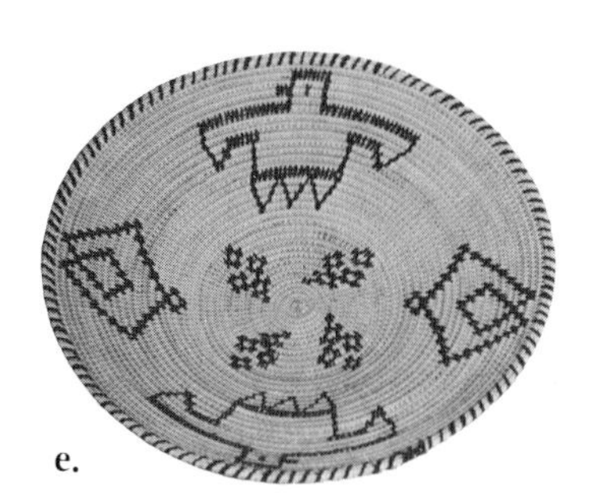
e.

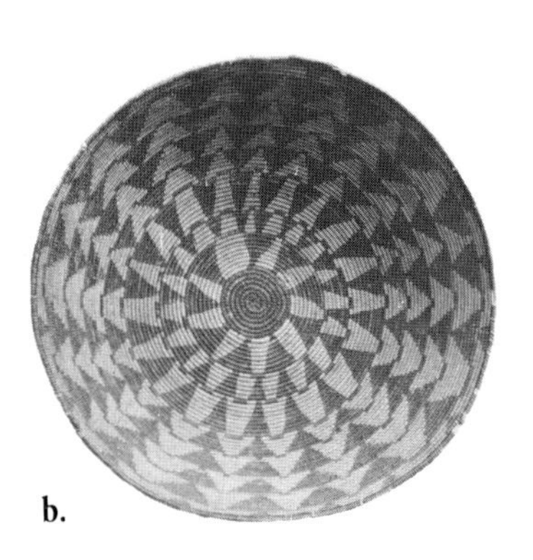
b.

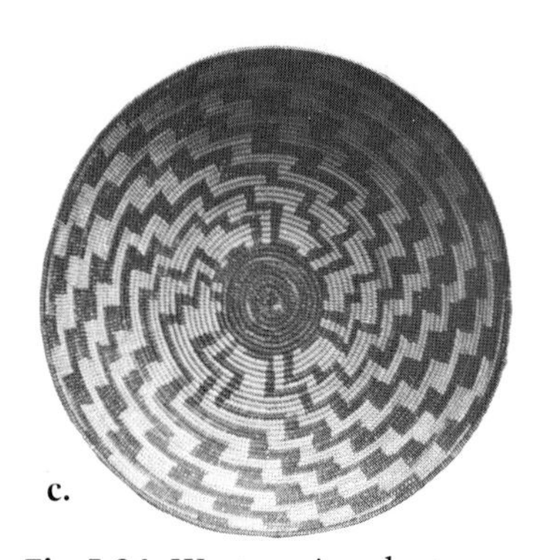
c.

Fig. 5.24. Western Apache trays decorated with static and dynamic patterns. (a) Despite a few zigzags in this pattern, it moves straight out from the center circle to the rim *(Hoel's, Sedona).* (b) Rows of stacked triangles move in static manner to the rim *(ASM E3254).* (c) Most dynamic are steps which curve their way to the rim *(ASM 1599).* (d) Less vigorous but still moving are the graceful curves of flower petals *(ASM E1551).* (e) A 1982 basket which shows the return to static patterning and extreme simplicity of Apache coiled work of these later years *(SAR 1982-5-1).*

All-over patterns with either static or dynamic radiate arrangements present some variety (Fig. 5.24). Center motifs may be a circle, a star, or a combination of the two, and the design may take off directly from the central theme, or it may be removed by a coil or two. Stacked triangles, small or large, plain or outlined, may move out in a straight line to create a static arrangement. One basket has a combination of longer rows of triangles with shorter rows of nested chevrons between them; an interesting and spectacular piece has concentric outline stars also moving outward, and superimposed over these are small stacked red diamonds in very heavy outlines. Both of these baskets are good examples of static radiate treatment of design.

Radiating themes may be small or large, far apart or close together, four, five, or more in numbers. Motion may be slight or great; in one basket each moving motif goes almost 360° around the basket. These dynamic elements include fairly narrow and stepped curving lines of squares, stepped zigzags, double and very wide steps, triple small steps, wide curving bands, or very wide thick steps made of rectangles. Most of these themes are sufficient unto themselves, but now and again a number of small elements will be thrown in between them. One basket has human figures added with careless plan between double lines. In earlier pieces the radiate themes were frequently far apart; later they may be the same or, more often, extremely close together.

All-over banded patterns are as varied as any. Here again they run the gamut from simple to complex (Fig. 5.25). They may be made up of a black center and two or more discrete bands, or a center star and a single organizational band, or they may consist of rows of tiny meanders, say five of them. There are also many variations on the regular or closed band; one basket has two, each filled with checkers.

From here on bands elaborate. A first step is represented in a small black center with a four-unit double meander beyond it, then a second six-unit meander close to the rim; this pattern is clean and uncluttered. Another step in growing complexity is represented by a center star with its tips touching a checkered band, a band of joined red triangles, and three white coils beyond, a second checkered band which touches the rim.

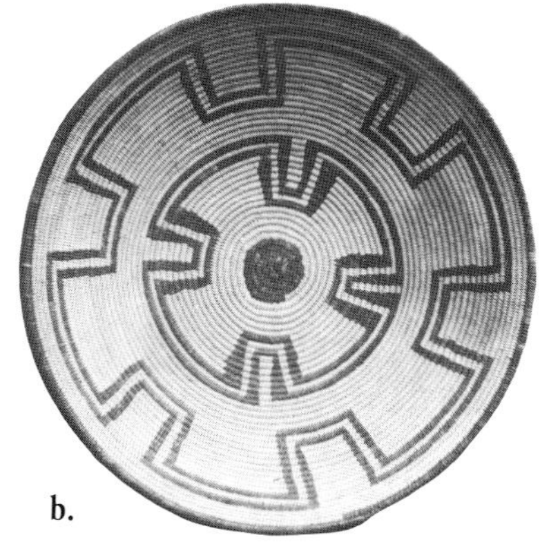

Fig. 5.25. Banded patterns in Western Apache baskets. (a) A regular band scheme, with two bands of checkers and stepped zigzags between them, center to rim *(ASM 9809)*. (b) Pattern is made up of two wide organizational bands *(ASM E2825)*.

Continuous bands from center to edge might be made up of alternating white and checkered rectangles. One of the Apache weaver's favorite motifs, the curved-line triangle (see drawing), plain or outlined, is frequently presented, either in simple or complex bands. One interesting version of this has a row of six such triangles with the tips of their single outlines touching the black center circle, then a second row of six larger triangles, double outlined, and between this row and the rim the following woven in, in good letters and numbers: "Phoenix, Ariz. 1916."

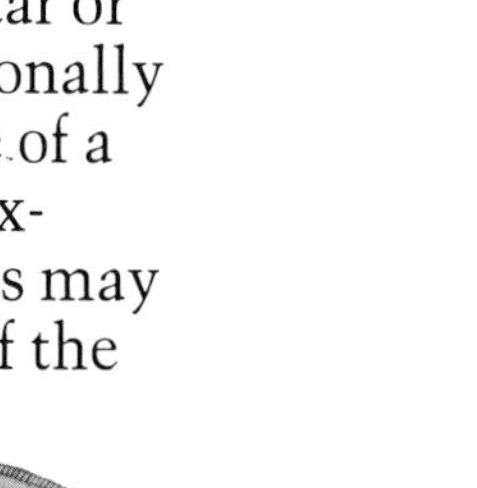

A category of tray patterns which might well be labeled star or floral is frequently all-over in every sense (Fig. 5.26). Occasionally there is a star center and a very large double or triple outline of a flower beyond and to the rim, both motifs four- or five- or six-pointed. From here on they become more complicated. Lines may be plain, but there will be more and more rows of "petals" of the

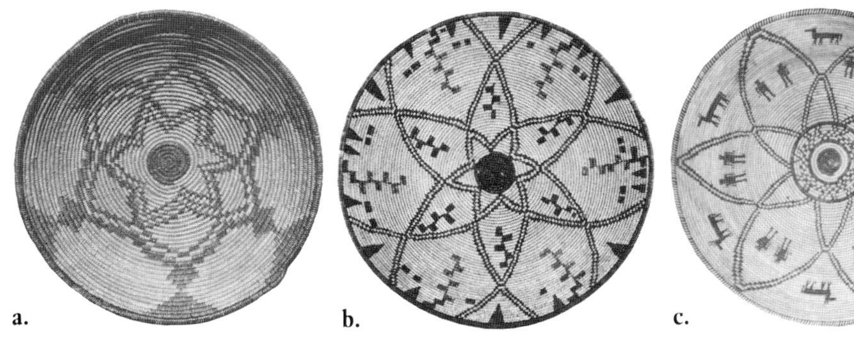

Fig. 5.26. Star motifs in Western Apache baskets. (a) An early piece with a double star theme with limited attached geometrics *(private collection)*. (b) Triple rows of stars are heavily adorned with different geometrics *(ASM 2363)*. (c) Another floral all-over patterning with life forms within and between petals *(Hoel's, Sedona)*.

flower, or the petals may be overlapping, and usually they go to the rim. One basket has a tiny, solid, black, four-petaled flower in the center, then a huge heavy-lined four-petaled flower to the rim, and four additional smaller petals between and attached to the larger ones. Thrown inside the petal outlines are men, dogs, coyote tracks, and swastikas with confused arms, and at the rim and between petal tips the element depicted in the margin.

Another interesting all-over pattern is centererd in meandering lines, usually in facing pairs of meanders which may be in single, double, or triple lines. This, too, may be repeated four, five, or six times. The units may be so close together that they are difficult to see as separate entities or they may be rather far apart.

Apache coiled jars represent a basket with great variation in form, as previously noted. In one large selection the round-bodied form varies in proportions but quite generally has a gentle outcurving and incurving body line from neck to base; some are more squat than others. In the second form, the elongate style, body proportions definitely contrast with the first form: basically they are narrower; in fact, some are almost "skinny." The third style, the shouldered type, is often quite distinctive, as the shoulder is almost always high and frequently sharp. Perhaps one of the most graceful of all Apache jar shapes is this shouldered type with gentle curves throughout and with emphasis on quite slender proportions.

That the Apache coiled jar was developed as a result of contact may explain the great variety in forms and sizes. The latter vary from 4½" to over 5 feet in height. As in other forms, such variation denies utility value, at least for the extremes. Further, the Apaches seldom, if ever, used this jar about the native wickiup.[30]

In a selection of forty-six coiled jars, height ranged from 6" to 35½". There is no clustering; instead, there is quite a scattering of heights. There are no more than four baskets of any single height measurement in this grouping. There is not the range in rim diameters, nor should equal variation be expected in this measurement because of the relative smallness of neck. The range is 3" to 18", with only one example each of 3", 4", 17", and 18" diameters. There are seven, six, seven, and five examples of the 7", 8", 9", and 10" diameters, respectively, and not over three examples of those above and below these measurements.

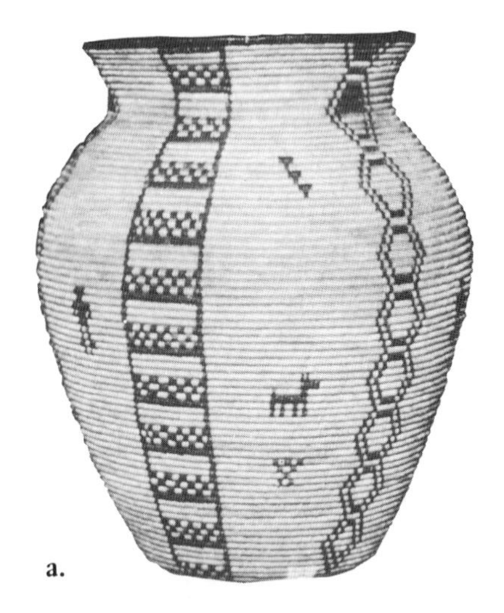

a.

b.

Fig. 5.27. Western Apache jars with vertical and horizontal arrangements. (a) Clean design on a graceful jar is composed of two alternating vertical designs, narrow rows of checkers enclosed by vertical lines and joined diamonds *(LA 23301)*. (b) Horizontal bands of geometrics and life forms on a sharp-shouldered, wide-mouthed old Apache basket *(Hoel's, Sedona)*.

In stitch and coil counts many of the baskets in this jar selection are high. Clustering does occur in this feature, for thirteen baskets have a stitch count of twelve, and eleven pieces have a count of thirteen per inch. Coils are four and five per inch, with fourteen examples of the first and twelve pieces with the second count. Interestingly, there is often a consistent count of stitches and coils on body and neck alike, although occasionally coils on the neck are a little larger than those on the body. Out of thirty-seven jars in this group, twenty-five rims were all black, ten had alternate black and white stitches, and two featured larger areas of alternate black and white. All rims were in regular sewing, all but one ending in the same regular stitch, the one exception having a ¾" termination in braiding, a rare feature in Apache baskets.

Principal colors used in Western Apache coiled jars were black and natural, although an appreciable amount of red-brown was also used. Red is both natural and dyed; the former tends to be darker, while the dyed is often lighter but may be of various shades and tends to wear away, thereby giving different tones to the dyed material in a single basket. Rarely is any other color used in the coiled jar.

Designing is usually abundant in this Apache jar, literally from the bottom up; in fact, no jar was observed that did not have a pattern on the base, some simple to be sure, but many quite elaborate. It must have been esthetic satisfaction to the weaver to decorate the base, for it was not visible. Designs ranged from the black center circle, sometimes so large that it came up onto the wall, to a star, to a circle plus other geometric and even life forms, although the latter are rather rare.

One of the most common of these base designs is a flowerlike or star theme in the usual variations of the Apache basket weaver; another interesting theme is a zigzag. In several examples these continue from the bottom of the basket all the way up the sidewall; in one case, it stopped at the beginning of the neck, in another it went to the rim. In the first instance, there were four stepped sets of double zigzags, in the second five sets of three zigzags each. Then, of course, there are the many simple geometrics found throughout Apache baskets, crosses, coyote tracks, odd shapes made up of squares, two vertical lines with a top cross bar, various forms made of checkers, simple lines, stepped lines and bands, checkered as well as solid diamonds, and stepped triangles.

Wall patterns in Western Apache coiled jars are almost always quite vital and dynamic, whether the designs are arranged vertically or horizontally (Fig. 5.27), whether the patterns are geometric or life forms. Designs are pleasingly arranged according to shape of the vessel on which they appear, so much so, in fact, that it would seem that the weavers concentrated on this matter—perhaps the weavers were competing for a limited market in those early days (Fig. 5.28).

A tall, elongate-bodied jar features two large, horizontal zigzags on the wall, with dogs and men tucked here and there under the peaks of the zigzags. On the upper side of the "downs" of the zigzags there are proportionately large arrow points; as previously noted by Roberts, these design elements would make this a San Carlos piece. A third smaller zigzag is on the upper part of the body and flows onto the neck; arrow points appear in the neck area, and pendant from the rim are triangles. This is a pleasingly synchronized pattern.

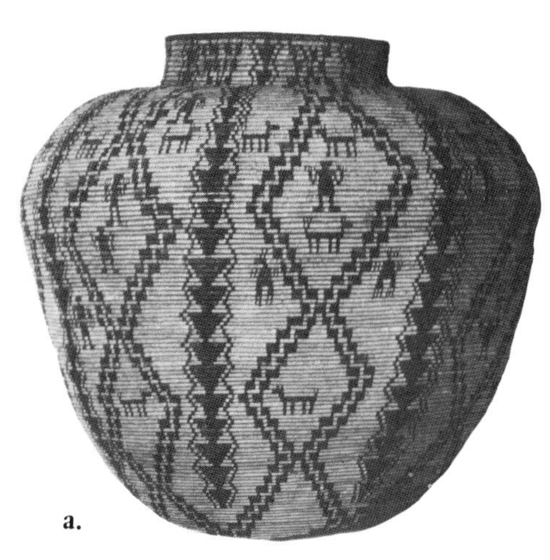

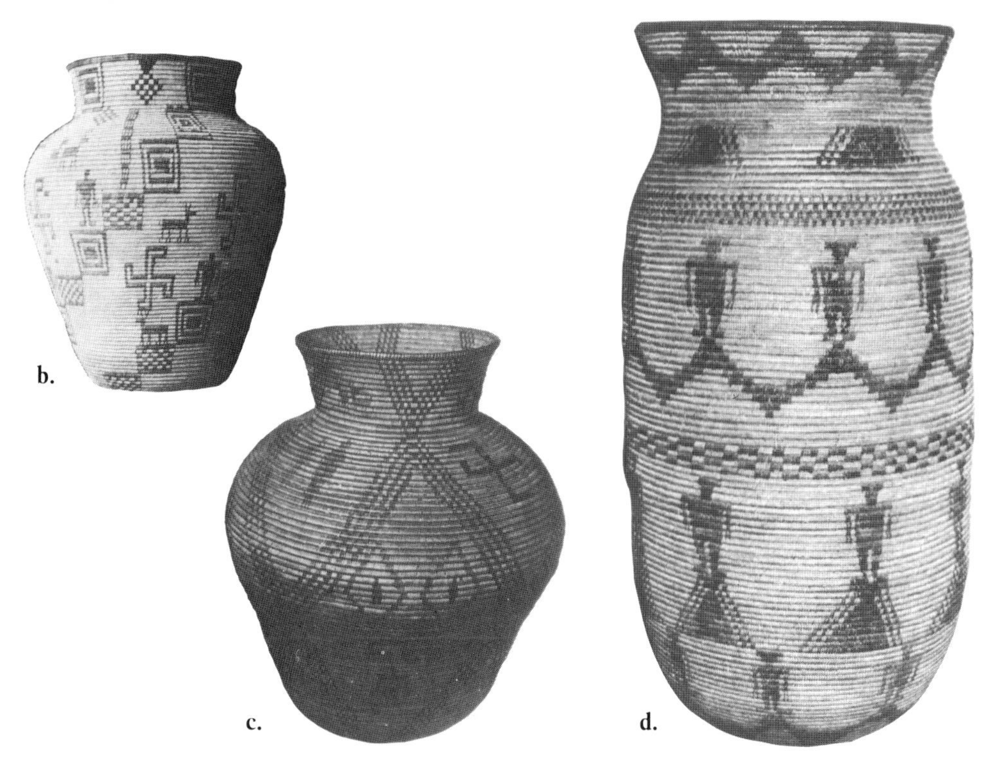

Fig. 5.28. Adaptation of decoration on Western Apache jars of different shapes. (a) A high, wide-shouldered piece is effectively decorated with vertical patterning *(SAR B301)*. (b) A high but more gently rounded shoulder responds to diagonal patterning *(Hoel's, Sedona)*. (c) An allover netlike division with varied designs in each resulting diamond on this more rounded form *(Hoel's, Sedona)*. (d) Long slender lines of this old basket are made attractive with horizontal patterning of varied subjects *(Garland's, Sedona)*.

A straight-sided jar is decorated in a most interesting fashion in alternate horizontal rows of checkers and black bands, with negative figures of dogs and men in the latter. A beautiful piece from San Carlos features vertical arrangements of three rows of connected diamonds, with alternating solid and open diamonds within them. Between rows of diamonds are scattered figures of a human wearing a fringed skirt (gans dancer?), plus a saguaro, a horse, and a stepped-edge diamond. Vertical arrangements of diamonds or a stepped pattern occur on a number of baskets of this elongate shape.

The second shape of jars, the rounded style, presents some comparable patterning. For example, one such piece has two pairs of three-line vertical zigzags which alternate with vertical arrangements of triangles and diamonds. Between these are other vertical arrangements of individual crosses and dogs. All designs move into the neck and to the rim.

In shouldered jars there are repeats of many of the types of design already described. One of the chief differences, however, lies in the utilization of the shoulder in the placement of certain parts of pattern, particularly if the shoulder is pronounced. In one such case, the wall of the jar is covered with a large network formed by touching stepped zigzags. Within the diamonds so created are figures of men standing on small quadrupeds for two rows, then a row of men with headpieces who again could represent the gans dancers. Below the shoulder and very slightly onto it are black diamonds with white crosses in them; the neck has a separate design, two rows of small black and opposing diamonds. Another basket with a shoulder, but a rounded one, has seventeen ghostlike figures on and above the turn. Below is a checkered band, beneath this are spaced-out rectangles with different elements in them; for example, one is black and has an A-like figure topped by a triangle, which in turn is topped by a cross in white (see drawing). A bit of the base pattern, a flower, shows at the very bottom of the wall. Above the "ghosts" are triangles joined to a band of checkers, and on the neck is a series of spaced-out joined triangles, the lower larger, and the upper ones smaller.

Another beautifully shaped piece has three exaggerated zigzags arranged horizontally on the wall of the basket, and a smaller repeat of the same at both base and top of the shoulder. Both above and below this main theme are numerous figures, with 133 life and other forms in the various sections created by these divisions, including men, horses, dogs, men on horseback, and others.

Thus, there is great variety in jar decoration, for the weavers utilized all typical Apache designs. They do adapt them to the form of the jar, and they are clever in the application of all possible elements and motifs. The Western Apache weaver seems not to have been daunted by new and different shapes.

Coiled bowls are not too abundant in Western Apache basketry but some were woven, particularly shortly before and after 1900. Two types prevailed, a round form and an oval shape; these two will be treated separately, for the starts differ and design is frequently adapted to these beginnings.

For the most part, the round bowl has straight or almost straight sidewalls. Some are shallow, some very deep. In a group of thirty-seven bowls, there was a range in size from 6⅜" to 18½" in diameter, with fifteen of these pieces measuring 11" to 13" in rim width. Depths ranged from just under 2" to 10", with eight bowls 2" deep, seven 3", eleven of them 4", and five 5" in depth. In a small selection of seventeen representative bowl baskets, stitches had a range of ten to twenty, with either two or three examples each counting from eleven to fifteen stitches to the inch. Coils were more clustered, with six baskets having four to the inch, five with five coils, and three with six coils per inch. There were a few both above and below these stitch and coil counts; in particular should be mentioned one basket with a stitch count of twenty and a coil count of seven.

Fig. 5.29. Bowl decoration of Western Apaches. This round vessel is heavily decorated with vertical bands of joined black diamonds with negative geometric patterns within them, and one positive animal (dog?) in one only of the white areas between. Vertical design stresses the bowl depth *(ASM 56936)*.

Designs on round bowls are varied (Fig. 5.29). One bowl has four unevenly spaced groups of four dynamic steps swirling from a small black center to the rim. In the bottom of a straight-sided bowl is a five-point flower, step outlined, with double coyote tracks at each tip. Tucked in between wall arrow points, and close to the rim, are pendant triangles, all solid except that four pairs have negative figures of quadrupeds in them while single triangles between the pairs do not. Pattern is pleasingly adapted to the bowl wall.

A very deep bowl has no bottom design, but has two organizational bands on the generous wall. In the lower one are large quadrupeds, small men, and odd geometrics (see drawing), the last directly above the animals. The upper band has a row of complex geometrics, with small and large humans sandwiched in between them. A very straight-walled, flat-bottomed, deep bowl has a continuous pattern from the base onto the sidewalls and to the rim. Seven stepped triangles take off the black center circle and end at the rim, with a deer and a geometric motif between every two of them.

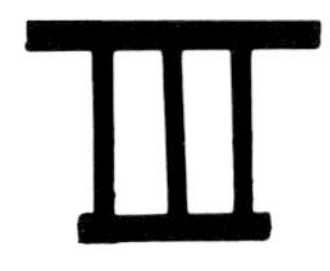

These several examples suffice to demonstrate that typical Apache design layouts and designs appear on bowl forms. They feature all-over and banded layouts; they combine humans, animals, and geometrics in the typical manner of this tribe. There are the usual Apache elements, squares, rectangles, triangles, diamonds, frets, steps, floral or star units, arches, and so on. Many of these designs might well be taken for tray decoration, but they are pleasingly adapted, as well, to the large flat bottom and straight sidewalls of the bowl form.

Oval bowls are not very common in Western Apache basketry. Some believe that they are a later development; certainly designs noted in all baskets of this form would bear this out. Generally sewing is counterclockwise on the outside and better on this side; this would seem to indicate that the weaver considered the exterior the "right side."

In a group of nine oval baskets, sizes ranged from one 10″ by 7⅝″ and 2¾″ deep to another 18⅜″ by 13¾″ and 3¼″ deep. These are typical sizes for this piece. Generally length is from 3″ to 5″ greater than width, although once in a while it is less than 3″. Depth is seldom over 5″ and in a majority of these pieces is between 3″ and 5″. Stitch count in these nine baskets runs from twelve to eighteen, with five of them fourteen to the inch; coil counts run from four to six, with four of the baskets counting six coils to the inch. It can be said, then, that oval baskets are rather high in both stitch and coil counts. All rims are in regular sewing, most of them in all-black, but with several each in all-white and alternate black and white stitches. One was finished in larger areas of alternating black and white, all of this part of the design. Quite naturally all of these baskets began with a long wrapped coil.

Oval bowls are designed in a manner suitable to the form of this piece (Fig. 5.30). In a sense, this is not greatly different from the tray style. However, in place of the tray's circular black center, there is usually a narrow and long oval black central area corresponding to the wrapped beginning, plus some black coils beyond it. Frequently there are no more than one or two black coils beyond the wrapped starter, occasionally as many as four, and sometimes there is a white center. Alternate black and white stitching may also border the black wrapped center.

a.

b.

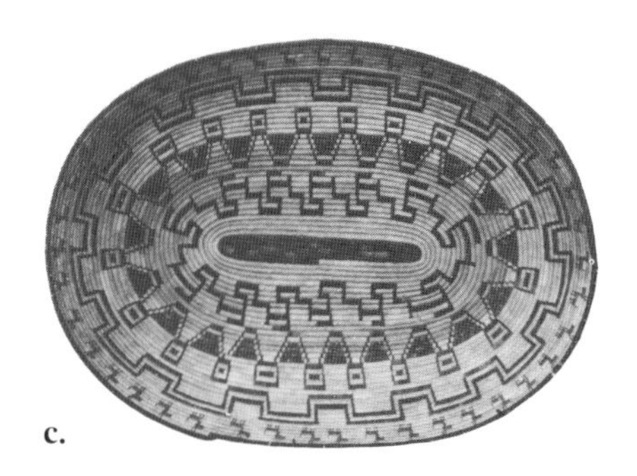
c.

Fig. 5.30. Designs on oval bowls, Western Apache baskets. (a) Frets emanate along the sides from a black center, with a simple triangle at each end *(private collection).* (b) A separate center and banded wall designs decorate this piece *(Hoel's, Sedona).* (c) Varied bands of different small geometrics or life elements decorate this basket from close to center to rim *(Rex Arrowsmith, Santa Fe).*

In the main, patterning on oval bowls flows from the center to the rim whether wall lines are more abrupt or more gentle. Two basic layouts appear, multiple banded or all-over; the first style may involve two or three bands, or other combinations such as a half-band plus a regular band plus an organizational band. In all-over layouts, the patterning is tied into the central black oblong and continues close to or to the rim.

Both geometric and life elements appear on these bowl baskets. In the main they are comparable to those on trays including line themes, squares, rectangles, diamonds, triangles, crosses, coyote tracks, checkers, arrows, steps, men, and dogs (or horses?). Most of this patterning is in black although a little red occurs, either within motifs or to form them. In one of these bowls there are two coils of blue-green between the major motifs.

One oval piece has quite a long center, then one coil of alternate black and white stitches, a white coil, and a black coil with an attached coil of black and white stitching. The main design takes off the latter: first a row of nineteen arrow points, a black coil, a row of nineteen points with longer stems, a five-coil row of checkers bordered on each side by a black coil, and a row of nineteen crosses extended into a black-white-black coil alternation, the last forming the rim.

One of the most interesting pieces in this group of nine oval baskets has a narrow and long black center bordered by three rows of alternate black-white stitching. Four white coils separate this from a six-coil band of black and white checkering on which stand a dozen strange-appearing men. They have tiny heads, wide bodies with arms extending straight out from shoulders, then downward, terminating in huge hands with two, three, or four fingers to a hand. Beyond the men are thirteen outline triangles pendant from a black rim.

As noted above, not many odd shapes were woven by the Apache basket maker. Seemingly these women wove baskets for their own uses basically, and were not concerned with basket weaving for sales' purposes in any styles except those which they had always produced: the tray, the tus, and the burden basket. The one probable exception was the woven jar and they did a magnificent job on this, in variety of form and decoration.

The cup-saucer and flat plaque need no more than passing mention. On the other hand, the straight-sided piece is of interest as it is one of several of this shape. It was collected early in the 1900s. It is 7¼″ high and 11″ wide at the mouth. Stitches are long and slender. Like coiled jars, it has a pattern on the base, simpler than most: a black center and one black coil. On walls are vertical and wide black zigzags which have negative patterns in them, including in each a cross, a solid square outlined with a line square, two joined coyote tracks, and several parallel lines. The interesting feature here is the pleasing adaptation of design to a foreign shape.

Miniatures

In the proper sense of the word the Apaches have not made many miniatures. Most of their baskets which might be so-called are just cut down a bit from the small-sized pieces made for the children. Many such small baskets were also made at a much later stage and for sale. The majority of true miniatures, under 5″ in height or diameter, have been made during the late 1970s and 1980s in addition to the small copies which are 6″ or 7″ or slightly larger in size.

Of the very few Apache miniatures observed, forms included trays, burden baskets, rare examples of the tus, and coiled jars. One tus and several examples of each of these other forms will be discussed individually, thus indicating such matters as shapes, measurements, stitch and coil counts, and decoration.

The tus has a wide mouth, long neck, and gently rounded body. At the rim it measures 2″, the base is 1¾″, and the total height was 3¼″. It is woven in a diagonal twine. As is typical of the water jar, the base is concave, and the entire basket is covered with pitch. The piece is true to type even to two small loops attached at the sides for the carrying strap.

Of two miniature coiled jars, one is 2½″ high, the other 2¾″, and rim measurements are about the same. The smaller jar has fourteen to fifteen stitches and five coils to the inch. The larger piece has a very simple decoration, two horizontal bands of repeated vertically standing rectangles in brown. More elaborate motifs decorate the smaller basket. On this jar wall are three vertical double zigzags; between these a dog, and above it a pair of legs (see drawing), then two more dogs, and the legs again.

Trays are very much like their large counterparts, even to quite elaborate designs. Two have fairly flat bases and fairly straight sides, a third has a gently curved wall emerging from a smaller flat base. These three measure 4¼″, 4½″, and 4¾″ in diameter and 1⅛″,

1½″, and 1½″ in height. The smallest piece counts nineteen to twenty-one stitches and eight coils to the inch, the middle piece twelve stitches and six coils, and the largest, which is a little more irregular, counts fourteen to sixteen stitches and six to seven coils to the inch. Alternate black and white stitches are used on the rim of two pieces, but the largest is finished in all black.

Decoration on the smallest miniature tray is all-over: seven stepped triangles attached to a fairly large black center serve as a springboard for graceful arches which touch the rim coil. It is a pleasing, well-balanced, well-executed design. Similar in general theme is the decoration on the middle-sized miniature tray. There is a smaller black circle, a white coil, and a black coil on which rest seven arches. From the tips of these, seven slightly larger arches develop, and then again from the tips of the second group seven more and also slightly larger arches move to the black rim. Simpler by far is the pattern in the third and largest tray. A central star is the dominant motif, and there are rectangles between this and the rim.

A fourth miniature tray basket has quite straight sides which slope from base to rim. It measures 5″ in diameter and is 1″ deep. The base is 2½″ wide. Stitches count twenty-two to twenty-three to the inch, coils six. An all-over layout features a great, five-pointed star or flower, the tips of which reach out to small arrow points pendant from the rim. Between the latter are coyote tracks also touching the rim, and below the tracks are five more arrow points. All of the arrow points are in alternate black and white stitches. Although rather thick walled, this miniature is well made and the design pleasingly balanced.

Three small burden baskets are rather typical of their larger counterparts, but a fourth is totally different. The first two measure 3¼″ and 4½″ in height, 3½″ and 4⅝″ in rim diameter. Both are in twined wicker weave. One of these (see drawing a) is decorated with a band of alternate black and natural, each three wefts wide. The second piece (see drawing b) is more elaborately decorated: three natural wefts from the black rim is a pattern comprised of a red weft line, then alternating red-black-yellow stitches, then a red weft line. Five natural wefts away is a repeat of the colored group, again five natural wefts, a repeat of the colored ones, and five wefts of natural to the buckskin covering on the base. Both baskets have four tiny vertical straps like the large originals, two sets of tiny thongs, one at the rim, the second lower on the strap, and thongs around the bottom patch. All are buckskin on the larger basket but chamois on the smaller piece. The smaller piece is very well made.

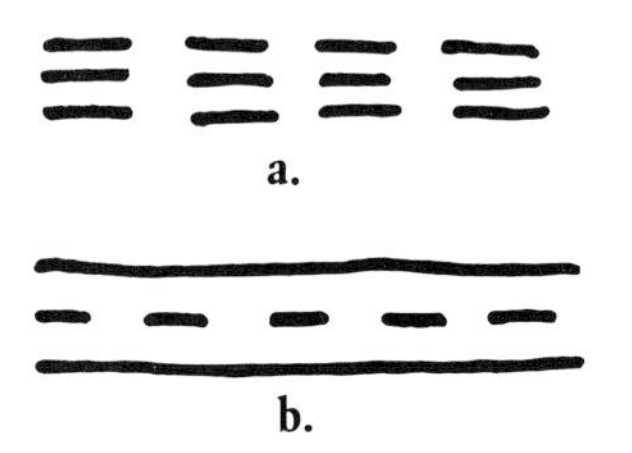

The third and fourth miniature burden baskets, known to be White Mountain, are both 3″ high. Both have single rims. The first has an alternation of decorative bands in natural and red. A red rim starts the color in the second piece and is followed by three natural wefts, two red (formed by the back of the sewing element), three natural, two to three red, then natural to the base. This piece is not too well woven.

A fifth burden basket is obviously a piece made to sell, for it is covered with beads, a most unusual situation in Western Apache basket weaving. It measures 1¾″ in height, 1¾″ in rim diameter. The typical burden basket features in this beaded piece are the bucket shape, a buckskin patch on the bottom, a "carrying strap" which is beaded, of course, and "dangles" of beads near the basket top and almost halfway down, and around the buckskin patch, these simulating, obviously, the buckskin thongs. All these beads are blue and white. A bit of decoration on the upper part of the basket shows two touching zigzags, one blue, one red.

Thus it can be said, despite so little in the way of miniatures, that when the Western Apaches made such baskets, they did an excellent job. Perhaps the making of small baskets which duplicated the larger ones through the years for their little girls made possible the weaving of finer miniatures.

VERSATILITY AND SYMMETRY

This survey of Apache baskets will indicate the versatility of the weavers of this tribe. It will show that for their own purposes they adhered to a limited number of forms but varied these, and added a few along the way in response to white man's desires. Despite limitations on form, surely there was no curtailment of design. The Apaches branched out early in their basketry decoration and came to enjoy fully the whims of the moment as they added miscellaneous and extra elements or units to the basic pattern. It may have been no more than one upraised arm on one figure of a dozen, but there it was and it was typically Apache!

All in all, Western Apache basketry is by far the most vital, the most varied, the most abundant of any weaving by all of these tribes. Part of this can be attributed to contact and the possibilities of selling these products but more is due to the creativity of the Indian woman herself. These women adhered to the basic forms which they used in daily tasks, and they developed design elements and units into ever more interesting creations.

There is much asymmetry in large or small details, but there is also pleasing symmetry in Western Apache basketry. There is great creativity in shapes, with much variety in San Carlos pieces in particular. Balanced repetition is typical, but this is frequently broken by the addition or shift in position of some small figure. Frequently the latter would seem to be more intentional whimsy than poor weaving and more characteristic of San Carlos than of White Mountain weavers.

Chapter 6

Basketry of Piman Tribes

Papago and Pima Indians made baskets which were very much alike in earlier years. Both used willow, the Papagos making treks to the River Pima lands where this material was available. Both also employed martynia for a decorative material. At a general glance the baskets of the two tribes might seem the same, but more careful scrutiny shows that there are many differences. Then, of course, at a later date the Papagos used yucca which the Pimas never did, and the former branched out into totally new and different forms and styles of patterning.

PAPAGO BASKETRY

Papago coiled baskets have been produced since the late 1970s in the greatest quantities of any Southwest tribe. This trend started shortly after, if not shortly before, the turn of the century; and although there have been periods of limited manufacture, surely the total trend has been upward. Traders, individual weavers, and the Papago Guild in Sells have variously influenced both quality and quantity, as well as the price structure of Papago coiled weaving in recent years. Many individual weavers have taken their pieces to traders both off and on the Reservation, have sold them to visitors to their homes, occasionally to institutions, at state and other fairs, and at various exhibitions. All in all, a growing interest in Papago basketry has been developed, and in the 1980s prices have exceeded any expectations of earlier years.

PAPAGO COILED BASKETRY

As used by the Papagos, the coiled technique needs to be divided into several categories based on the individual method involved. Crudest of all is that called "bird's nest"; next is crude coil or a space-stitch style, often simply expressed; third is regular close coiling; and last is split stitch. Coiling was productive of most Papago baskets through the years and of all of them today.

Techniques

Bird's nest is done without benefit of true warp and weft elements; because it consists of one element only, Shreve chooses to call it pseudocoiling which is, indeed, a properly descriptive term. Spaced stitch is exactly this: on large pieces, the stitches may be an inch or so apart, whereas in small baskets they are closer together but never touch. Close coiling is a technique in which stitches touch or nearly touch; it is productive of the greatest variety of Papago shapes and is the longest lived of their techniques. Split stitch, wherein the stitches are splayed apart, although known for many years, has been in particular favor for a variety of pieces since 1940 and doubly favored since 1960 or 1965.

Kissell reports the popular use of open-stitch coil, first in "crude coiling" for the making of large granaries, and secondly as coarse coiling which was also used in the making of granaries. In crude coiling or bird's nest, twigs with smaller twigs and leaves attached are used as the sole "element." One such stem is inserted in the growing wall, first on the inside, then on the outside; the stem end of the twig is securely inserted into the previous round of twigs and the "leaf end secures itself by winding about the previous twig."[1]

Coarse coiling is very different from crude coiling. First, the former has a proper foundation and a weft, is "sewed" in the manner of all coiled work, and is done in a counterclockwise fashion. Kissell calls the method involved here "spiral coiling" or open coil, the latter because the sewing elements are spread out, revealing the foundation. The work is much more substantial than that in bird's nest coiling as is indicated in the two-year life span of this work as against eight or ten years for the coarse coiled storage basket. Very large pieces are globular in form, some as much as 6 feet high, but smaller ones (1½ to 3½ feet high) are barrel-shaped. These bins are covered with a specially made lid or with a worn-out basket bottom. Often they are sealed with mud, "in fact, the whole bin may be completely covered."[2] These storage bins were made in the house or in the storage hut where they were to remain permanently. Often the weaver climbed inside to make the larger baskets.

Sewing in crude coiling is rather simple, usually with stitching alternating from row to row, or one directly above the other, but with irregular coil and stitch sizes. There were some variation in these matters, to be sure, but compared to Pima work the surfaces were more irregular, uneven, cruder.

Shreve reported that no granary or salt baskets had been "made for about forty years." Salt baskets she represents as a full-bodied, wide-mouthed jar shape, grain baskets of more rounded body and smaller neck. She also illustrates stitches both alternating and directly above each other and touching,[3] and presents quite well-made Papago salt and storage baskets. One of the latter is more like a large deep, straight-sided bowl.

"Women in Kohatk say that they have always made round, or oval spaced-stitch baskets for tortillas and bread." Then they made them for sale and "people liked them"; as they could be woven quickly, they continued to make them. Perhaps this is the connecting link between the past and present in what will now be called open-stitch coiling, this not to be confused with crude and coarse coiling. Shreve believes it goes back to the 1890s,[4] but Kissell neglects to mention this technique. Shreve illustrates two well-formed "spaced-stitch baskets" which are dated 1890 which could easily compete with some regular open stitch in shape and workmanship of later times. Thus this technique may well be older than is generally thought to be the case.

Later came split stitch, perhaps not before 1943[5]; although Shreve heard reports of work earlier than this date, she never saw any. Certainly, the technique was well established by this time and remained popular for a long time to come. Wheat stitch, which was first developed in the 1960s, was well established by 1966; thereafter and into the 1970s, there was much in the way of combinations of open stitch, split stitch, wheat stitch, and regular close coil. To add to the complexity of the situation, the terms "split" and "open" stitch are used synonymously, to the confusion of all. For that matter, both split and wheat stitch are open stitches, and so, understandably, there is reason for some confusion in the use of terminology.

Perhaps wheat stitch should be defined. Basically it is a split stitch with an extra stitch to one side. However, "flurries" have occurred; the extra stitch originally appeared to the right, now it may be to the right or to the left. Originally it was a single additional stitch, now it may be one, two, or three, or a combination of longer—or very long—and shorter stitches. Methods of combining different wheat stitches, or wheat with other stitches, will be discussed below in specific examples.

Plain or close coiling is most common among the Papagos and needs no further comment here than to say that it is started with a circle or a knot and/or a small plaited area. Plaiting is not only employed here but formerly was important in producing several utility pieces. Both plain (over-one-under-one) and twill plaiting were used, the latter in common over-two or three and under-two or three alternations, rarely others.

Materials

Materials used by the Papagos in the making of their baskets would include a wide variety of desert plants. Technique is often the dictator as to what materials are to be used, or what parts of what materials; for example, whole yucca leaves were used in plaiting, split leaves for wefts in coiling.

For the three rigid supports in the coiled-without-foundation burden basket, the Papago used the ribs of the saguaro (*Cereus giganteus* Engelm); fibers for cordage for the basket proper came from agave (*Agave deserti* Engelm)[6], and the ring was made of cat's-claw (*Acacia gregii*).[7] In making heavy- and coarse-coiled storage baskets, they would use, rarely, wheat straw (*Triticum vulgare*), or, more commonly, bear grass (*Nolina microcarpa*), and ocotillo (*Fouquieria splendens*) for foundation materials, and yucca or mesquite bark (*Prosopis velutina*) was the source of weft or sewing material. For crude "bird's nest" basket granaries the Pimas employed arrow bush (*Plucca borealis* or *Plucca sericea*); the fresh and pliant stems with the leaves on served as their sole material according to Russell, but Shreve adds that greasewood (*Larrea divaricata*) might also be used by the Papagos.[8] In the majority of early Papago close-coiled baskets, sewing material was obtained from the Pimas and was usually willow (*Salix nigra*) or cottonwood (*Populis fremontii*); from about 1900, they added yucca for the weft. Quite commonly, the basic foundation material, early and late, was bear grass, although sometimes cattail (*Tyrha angustifolia L.*) was used for foundations. Decorative black was from devil's-claw (*Proboscidea parviflora*), and the inner bark of the root of the Spanish bayonet (*Yucca arizonica*) or rarely manzanita (*Jatropha cardiophylla*) provided a reddish material for limited designing. In plaited work, the Papagos used sotol (*Dasylirium wheeleri*).

An interesting point might be mentioned here. During the years 1974–75, there was a drought so serious that frequently martynia either did not come up on the desert or did not produce desirable pods. As a consequence, very little black was used in baskets woven in 1974; a little more but still not much was used in 1975. Green yucca alone appeared in many baskets observed at Sells during these two years. Designs were more open; black was used particularly for outlining motifs, with much less of it in solid work.

a.

b.

c.

Fig. 6.1. Basic forms of Papago baskets in old styles: (a) the tray, (b) the bowl, and (c) the jar *(AHS)*, this last dated 1898.

Forms

Forms in Papago coiled basketry today present the greatest variety of any southwestern native pieces. This has not long been true, for in 1916 Kissell illustrated but seven forms, three full-bodied bowls and four shallower tray styles (Fig. 6.1). Shreve, in 1943, illustrated twenty forms plus novelty shapes which would include "candle sticks, vases, hats, purses, cups and saucers, sahuaro cacti, and even animals."[9] Most of the general forms now have many variations within them, further multiplying diversity.

In a general classification, their basic shapes are trays, bowls, jars, wastebaskets and related deep styles, plaques, life forms, coasters, and a wide variety of miscellaneous forms including all of Shreve's plus more (Fig. 6.2). Trays are large and small, shallow and deep. Bowls are straight-sided or rounded, large and deep like the wine basket, very small, with or without lids, and with other variations. Jars are massive as in the storage piece or medium-sized; they are more rounded or straighter in body form; they have longer or shorter, wider or narrower necks. The wastebasket, a form developed for white man, is characteristically deep and straight-sided, although some slope gently inward to a flat base. Plaques are typically flat, but a few curve gently upward at the outside; coasters are flat-based with a tiny, straight edge. Life forms are greatly varied, from owls and dogs to humans and cats, while in the miscellaneous group are many variations from purses to gadgets. In the category of miniatures, practically all forms appear; there is not, however, as much variety in each as in the full-sized forms.

Design Analysis

Design layouts are as varied in Papago baskets as in any others of the Southwest, and more varied than most. Both divided and undivided styles are represented. Divided styles are favored for deep forms such as jars, deep bowls, and wastebaskets, with banded styles very common and with repeated layouts fairly so. Trays, plaques, and sometimes very shallow bowls may use centered,

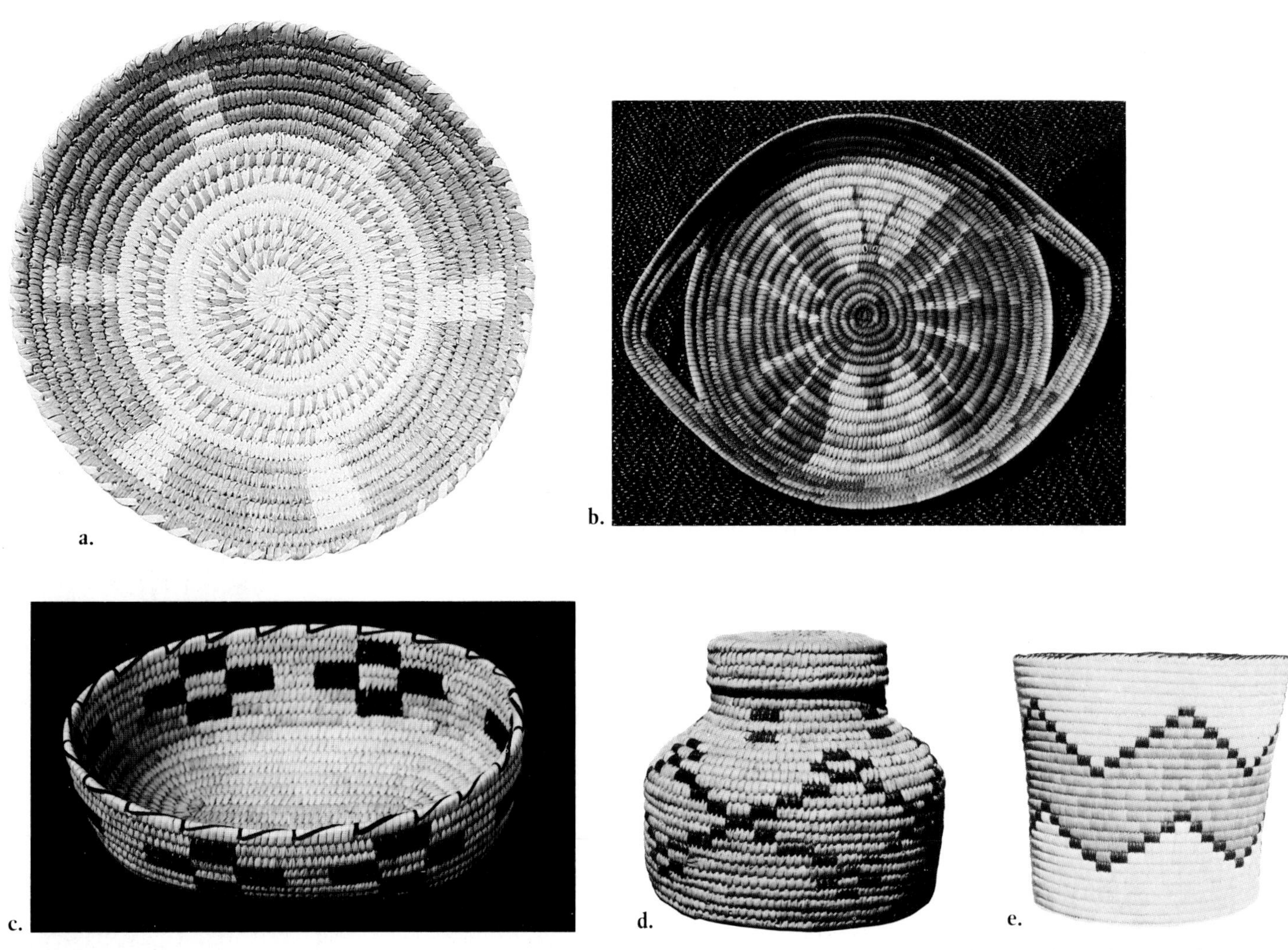

Fig. 6.2. Later Papago shapes became quite varied: (a) a tyical tray; (b) flat-bottomed tray with short, straight sides, this example with handles; (c) oval bowl; (d) a lidded jar; (e) wastebasket *(Gallup Ceremonials, 1975)*.

repeated, all-over, regular or organizational banded, and complex styles; in the last, and particularly in tray forms, the following are used: double- or multiple-banded, centered-banded, and both of these with organizational-banded.

Repetition is, of course, a typical characteristic of Papago design, either in an a-a-a-a or a-b-a-b style. In the older willow pieces, the first repetition shares with the second in popularity. In earlier yucca pieces there was more in the way of a-a-a-a repetition; this lingers into the 1970s in a great many baskets, and particularly do smaller ones exhibit a preference for this style.

In referring to the number of times a motif is repeated, or in number of parts of a motif (for example, a five-pointed star), there is again some correlation of late work with early styles. In old pieces a four-times repeated or four-part motif dominated; in the 1970s, the number four still is popular but not to the same degree: in one group of thirty-six baskets, eleven were four-part or four repeats, eight were three, and six pieces had five repeats. Growing popularity is to be noted for the single motif, for there were ten of them among the thirty-six baskets.

Designs as a whole are much too complex to be summarized in a few words; nonetheless, general trends can be indicated. Life forms are conspicuous by their absence or rarity in the early and pre-1900s, but by the 1970s they were common or even outnumbered geometric styles in some collections. Undoubtedly this is a reflection of commercialization, with a steady increase of plant and animal motifs through the years. Kissell pictures no real life forms in her old Papago baskets, and only one piece has the very geometric turtle shell design. Yet of nine of her "modern" pieces, one each has saguaros, turtles, humans, and quadrupeds. Of the thirty-six in the above-mentioned collection, six have simple geometric designs, one each was decorated with complex coyote tracks and turtle-shell patterns; and decorated in life themes were twelve baskets: one butterfly, two snakes, one bug, one human and lizards, a turtle, five each of birds, and man in the maze. Ten baskets were ornamented with floral themes and two with the old-style squash blossom.

Trays

Trays were and are the most useful form of basket made by the Papagos, basically for service within the house (Fig. 6.3). Kissell noted, regarding the tray, "Only on ceremonial occasions is it employed at the present time, as an eating dish, when the small watertight tray of the Papago medicineman is called into service, both as a drinking cup and a piñole dish, when on expeditions to the sea for sacred salt, and when curing the sick."[10] Otherwise it was "the most frequently used basket of these tribes," the Pima and Papago, for it served in the preparation of vegetables, meats, seeds, berries, fruits—whatever food was being readied. It served for winnowing wheat and for catching the fine flour after it was ground on the stone metate with a stone mano. It served for mixing foods, for making bread. It was both "supply" and "receiving" basket when mesquite beans, an important food of the Papagos, were pounded in a wooden mortar with a stone pestle. In parching wheat with live coals, Kissell notes that the Papago used an old basket.

Shreve reported in 1943 that trays made entirely of devil's-claw "were used for parching corn and some other seed." Martynia, she says, will not burn except at a very high temperature. She also says that this tray is about 3″ in depth and 13¾″ in diameter as used by the natives, but says that smaller ones were made for sale.[11] Kissell indicates other uses for the basket tray such as a lid for large grain baskets and for clay ollas, as a drum (by turning the piece upside down and beating it with the hand or a stick), and for sale. For the last purpose they were made of yucca, while for all other uses at this earlier time, they were woven of willow or cottonwood.

Kissell illustrated only four variations in the form of the tray. All are sloping-sided and flat or nearly flat-bottomed, varying basically in depth. Shreve's outlines of forms are a bit too sketchy to establish distinct variations, but there would be four or five different tray forms, including oval ones. As long as the Papago used this basket, its basic shape did not vary much; but as they developed it more and more for commercial purposes, tribal styles become less distinctive and trays in general were more varied.

Perhaps it might be said of the tray today that its shape is more frequently planned with the idea in mind of decorating it in a particular way. Certainly, the great variety of forms does allow for diversity in decoration. Practically no baskets are made now that are not decorated, for, again, the piece made to sell must be ornamented.

In one selection of something over 140 baskets, quite a range can be noted in size, shape, proportions, start, rim finish, colors, and designs. This group dates largely within the 1970s, with perhaps a few

a.

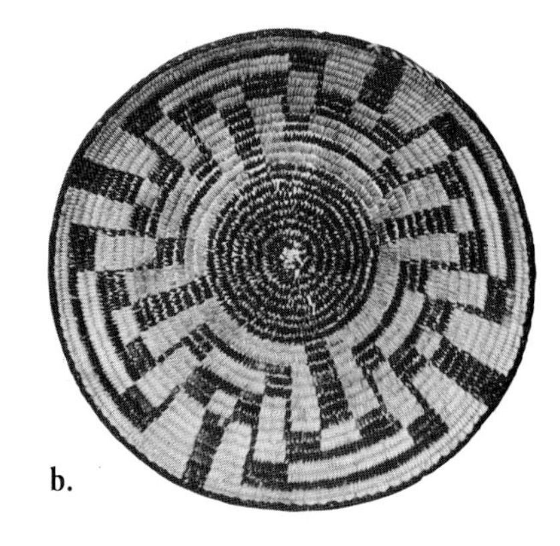

b.

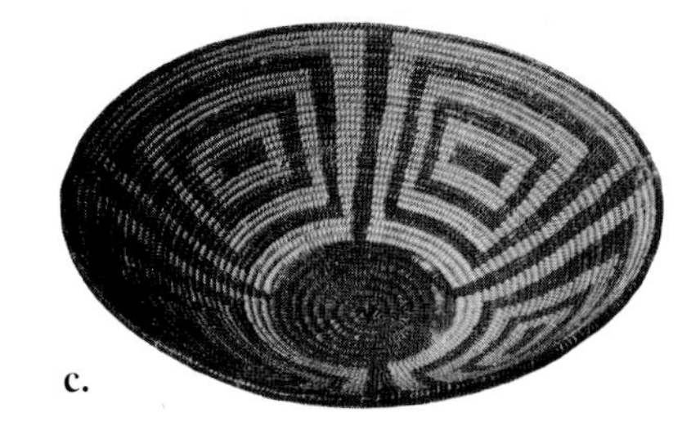

c.

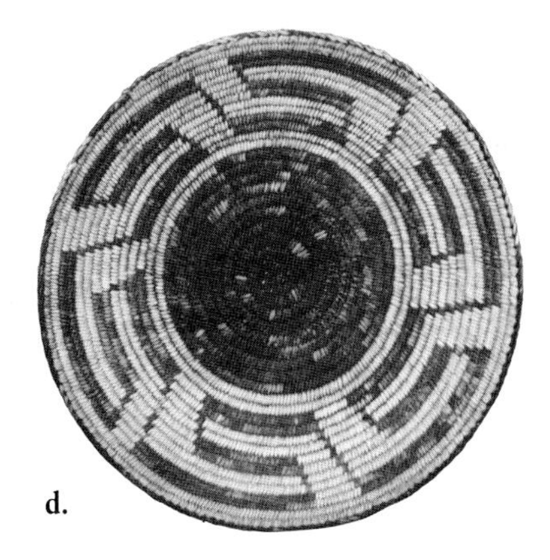

d.

Fig. 6.3. Papago tray forms of early years in willow. (a) Some were deeper, had all-over integrated designs *(ASM E6009)*. (b) Squash blossom patterns were early, this one heavy and angular. (c) "Tortoise shell" is the name of this design *(ASM 5568)*. (d) A large black center is typical of many old pieces *(ASM 4681)*.

which might be a little older. Emphasis in discussion of this selection will be placed on the more recent pieces.

In size these baskets ranged from miniature, 4⅝", to as much as 23" in diameter. In between were all possible measurements. The largest group in this selection, twenty-two baskets, measured 8" or a little over in diameter; 10" bowls counted next highest, numbering nineteen; and 12" pieces were next, seventeen in number. As trays increased in size, they became fewer in number in this group. Those with 11" diameters numbered sixteen, 14" styles were twelve in number, and there were ten measuring 15". From here on there was a sharp decline, particularly as size increased, with only one or two examples each of trays with diameters from 16" to 23".

There is some correlation between tray diameter and depth in the 1970s, which reflects a greater shallowness than in earlier pieces. The vast majority of trays under 14" in diameter have a depth of 2¾" or less, even down to 1". Out of some eighty-three pieces under 12" in diameter, only seven were 3" or slightly more in depth; a few were 2¾" deep, the majority less than this. In the remaining fifty-seven trays, greater depth is in proportion to greater diameters. Of this number but a dozen measure 4" or more deep—only three trays are 5" or 5½" deep, eight are between 4" and 5", and the remainder are under 4" in depth. One 16½" diameter tray is 1" deep; an 18¾" one is 2¾" deep.

As to stitch and coil counts in trays, there is such great inconsistency that little can be concluded regarding this matter. In this varied collection there seems to be a series of very fine small baskets; therefore, the stitch and coil counts on this end of the spectrum tend to be unusually high. For instance, in nine baskets in the 4" and 5" brackets, and several in the 6" diameter group, stitch counts run from ten to eighteen, whereas this is true of limited instances only in larger baskets. Some coil counts are higher, four, six, seven, and eight to the inch, with the remaining five counting three and one-half to five to the inch, which is better than the average of larger baskets. These figures are doubly interesting in that these nine trays are from varied sources, not from a single superior collection. In the remaining 131 baskets, the highest coil count per inch is six, and there are only two examples of this; then there are twelve trays with coil counts of five, and all the rest count under five. Many pieces in the larger part of this collection count two, two and one-half, and three coils to the inch.

Start and rim finish in these 140 baskets present a typical 1970 situation. At least seventy-nine of these trays were started with a knot, and possibly more, for in several situations it is impossible to tell for sure what the beginning really is. At least eleven baskets were started with plaiting, while no less than twenty-three specimens combined plaiting and a knot in the beginning of each. Interestingly, the knot appears on the interior of some trays, and the plaiting on the exterior, while the reverse is true in other pieces. There are five examples of coiled beginnings; as is typical for Papago baskets in general, this start is not a common one.

As to the rim finish (see Figs. 3.13a–e, h) the typical Papago styles of some years are to be noted in this group of trays. Most popular is black oversewing on the final natural coil; occasional other colors are involved, and a variety of stitching is to be noted. Plain white rims numbered fifteen, plain black seventeen. Two examples of yellow final coils were noted, as were two examples of braiding, both in black. Alternate black and white stitching appeared in five trays, and an unusual combination of alternate white and yellow was observed in one piece. There were irregular numbers of black and white stitches, and these were usually involved in designs into the rim; in one of three baskets so finished, there was the head of a man in the maze as the only black in an otherwise white rim. The predominant rim finish was slanting black stitches over a white coil, from lower left to upper right, this style appearing in thirty-seven trays. There is variety in this seemingly simple decoration, for stitches were long or short, and widely spaced or close, sometimes so close they were overlapping. Comparable stitching leaning from lower right to upper left appeared in six baskets only. In one instance such stitching had a definite curve to it.

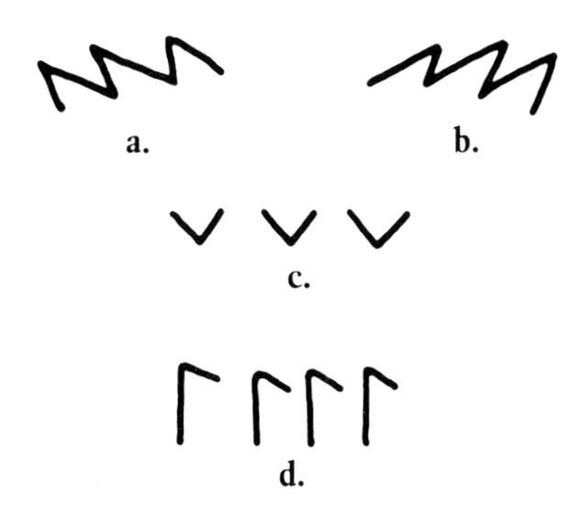

There was quite a bit of variety in other types of over-stitching, usually in black but occasionally in red (see Fig. 3.13f, g). Major types included the following: plain cross-stitching appeared in seven baskets, double cross-stitching in three pieces, and cross-stitching to create diamonds occurred in eight trays. Two other styles (drawings a and b) also occurred in eight and four instances, respectively; rim finishes in drawings c and d ornamented one basket each. Such examples show the versatility expressed in so simple a matter as rim decoration.

Designs in trays present a great deal of creativity on the part of the basket weaver (Fig. 6.4). Trays offered the opportunity of different surfaces for decoration, the open bottom of a flat-based, low-walled style, the gently curving wall of a shallow form, and the extra area of an outflaring rim. Despite the fact that many of these shapes were not traditional, the decorator approached them with the expertise so characteristic of the primitive artist. Simplicity

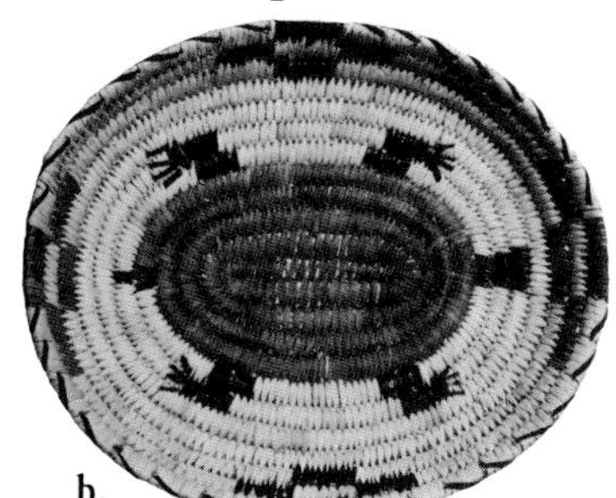

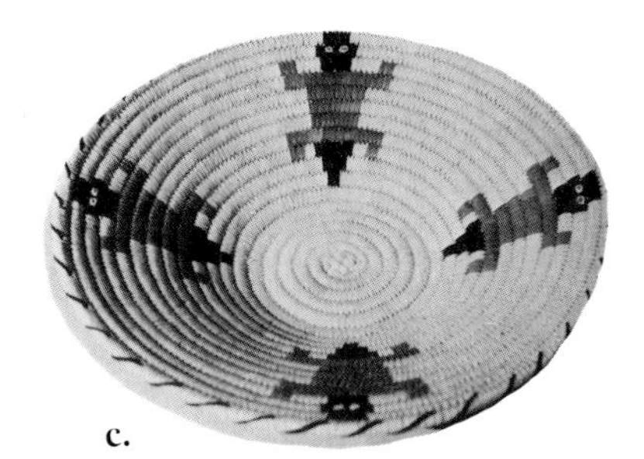

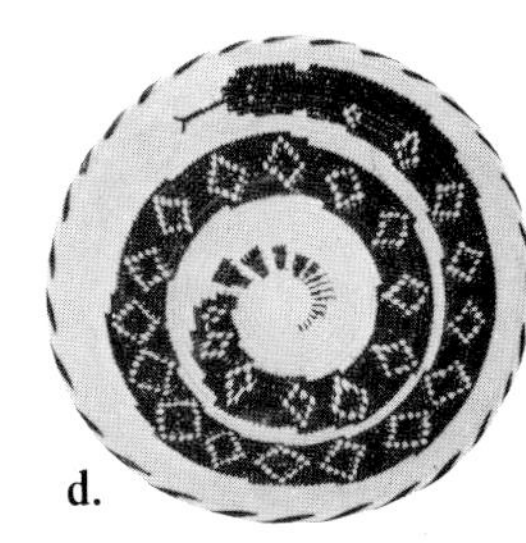

Fig. 6.4. Later styles of Papago yucca trays. (a) These pieces show the continuation of geometrics, minus a black center, using natural green yucca, and with simplified pattern *(ASM E5452, E7477)*. (b) An elongate form (turtle?) is here adapted to an oval bowl *(DHC)*. (c) Pleasing placement of four creatures on the sidewall of a tray, clean and clearcut *(DHC)*. (d) In late years, the snake (here a diamond-back rattler) has become a popular motif *(DHC)*.

dominated in many decorative schemes, but complexity was not unknown in innumerable examples. The following representative pieces from the above 140 baskets, plus a few others, will support the ingenuity of the Papago weavers.

In one small tray basket, three simple meanders take off a black center to curve upward and widely to the right, each terminating at the base of three black coils at the rim. One shallow tray is decorated with a single figure of an eagle in red, wings outspread and taking up most of the space in the small piece. A very popular design is found in several of these trays, a five-petal flower in solid black, or a star of six points (or flower of six petals) in black against the white of the bleached yucca. Sometimes the floral theme is outlined with an angular but undulating line frame. A pattern of long-standing in Papago basketry remains a favorite: a solid stepped black triangle with an intricate line fret taking off its tip, this composite repeated several times on the wall of a shallow tray.

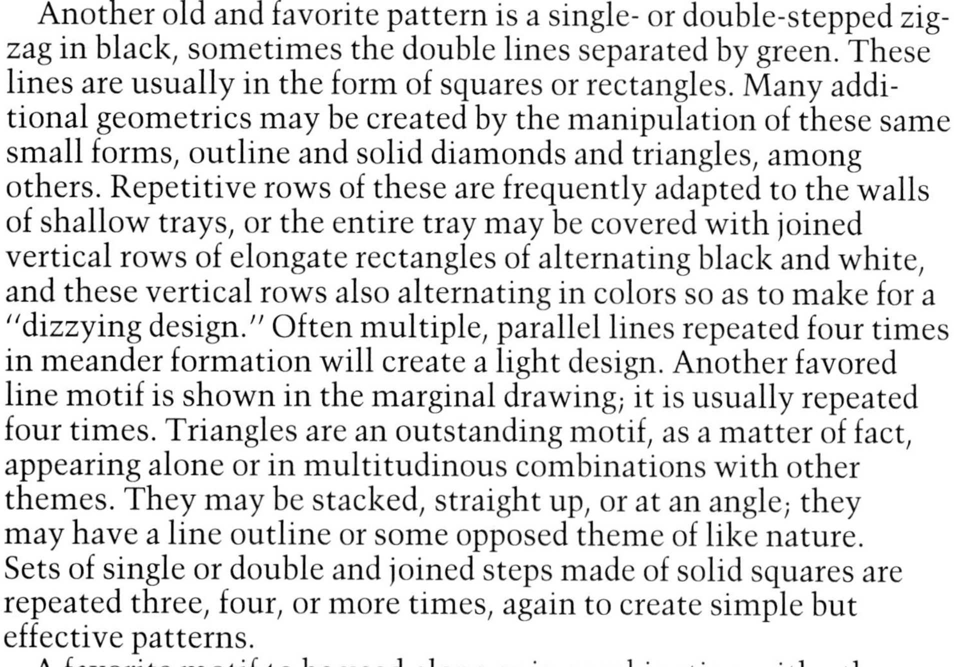

Another old and favorite pattern is a single- or double-stepped zigzag in black, sometimes the double lines separated by green. These lines are usually in the form of squares or rectangles. Many additional geometrics may be created by the manipulation of these same small forms, outline and solid diamonds and triangles, among others. Repetitive rows of these are frequently adapted to the walls of shallow trays, or the entire tray may be covered with joined vertical rows of elongate rectangles of alternating black and white, and these vertical rows also alternating in colors so as to make for a "dizzying design." Often multiple, parallel lines repeated four times in meander formation will create a light design. Another favored line motif is shown in the marginal drawing; it is usually repeated four times. Triangles are an outstanding motif, as a matter of fact, appearing alone or in multitudinous combinations with other themes. They may be stacked, straight up, or at an angle; they may have a line outline or some opposed theme of like nature. Sets of single or double and joined steps made of solid squares are repeated three, four, or more times, again to create simple but effective patterns.

A favorite motif to be used alone or in combination with other themes is the coyote track (see drawing). Several large ones may be the sole decoration on a tray, or there may be two rows of four each. They are used alone, or stacked, the last two or more being one above the other. Sometimes this detail is built up in such complex forms that it is believably a "non-coyote track." A Maltese-like cross is used, generally in outline alone, or to outline some other theme, or as the central motif with a second motif near the edge, such as a small, solid black duck swimming near the rim of the basket.

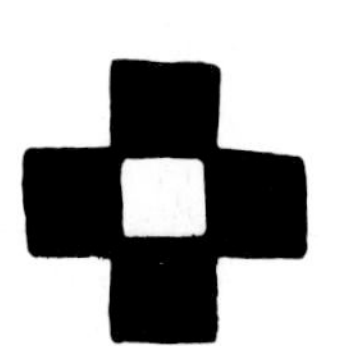

Plants have become fairly common as used by the Papago; in one instance a delicate bushlike affair is created from irregularly shaped, nested chevrons, with attached "dots." Five of these are spaced out to ornament a very thin-walled, open tray. So too is the squash-blossom design or some version of it, sometimes very simplified, sometimes in its usual complete complexity.

Oval trays present another unusual aspect of Papago basketry. This form was quite generally not made aboriginally, but a few such forms were produced now and then after contact by various southwestern tribes. Most of them produced by the Papagos can be called trays, and, like this form in general, there was some variation in details of shape. Some were longer in proportion to width, some had more gracefully sloping sides while others were flat-bottomed and had shallow and straight sides.

Inasmuch as this new form of oval tray did find a use among the Papagos, for bread and tortillas, they tend to be larger in size than the average round tray. Some are smaller, about 8″ in greater length, but many are 16″, 17″, and 18″ in this same dimension. In one grouping of ten oval trays from miscellaneous sources this size variation is illustrated, the smallest piece being 8½″ by 6″ by 1¼″, while the largest observed measured 19″ by 13″ and was 1¼″ deep. In most instances the rim diameter is slightly greater than that of the base. Coil and stitch counts vary little from those of regular trays, and the same is true of rim finishes.

Design in oval baskets of the Papago may have a slightly different emphasis in some pieces, while others conform to the usual scheme of the round tray. For example, elongate subjects, such as a lizard, may be featured alone; in one of these, the green body took up the major central part of the basket while the black feet, tail, and head were woven into the extremities of the oval. Gila monsters and turtles were similarly adapted to this form. One other life form was a large black scorpion with his head at one end and curled tail in the other. A snake, on the other hand, had its rattles and body start at one end, the major part of the body continued along one side and the opposite end, then the head with a tiny mouse in front of it occupied about one-half of the other side. Geometrics are not uncommon in these pieces.

Handles appear on both round and oval trays, although they are more common on the oval. Occasional handles from one edge to the opposite side and over the top will appear on both forms. Common at either side are small handles, which are extensions of one or more coils which are wrapped for a short distance, then again join the main part of the basket. As in bowls these may appear just below or at the rim.

Bowls

Bowls represent a form which changed as time moved along (Fig. 6.5). They were quite limited in variety of shape in earlier years: Kissell defines the bowl as "Broad, globular, flat based." However, in the later yucca product, straight-sidedness, lids, or handles, or other details distinguish this form. A majority of bowls are worked from the outside, whereas all trays are sewn from the inside.

a.

b.

c.

d.

Fig. 6.5. Several Papago bowls which illustrate styles from earlier types to modern ones. (a) An old-style, sloping-sided, flat-bottomed example with black center and sidewall triangles with fairly heavy long and short lines, all integrated *(private collection)*. (b) A classic swastika decorates this willow basket, also an older piece *(ASM 7894)*. (c) Two modern, simply decorated yucca deep bowls, with a dancing man and a repeated diagonal geometric *(ASM E8472, E3963)*. (d) A late piece, wide-mouthed, with handles, and a wide yellow zigzag outlined in black *(ASM E3959)*.

Use value played a large part in bowl shapes at the turn of the century. For example, Kissell notes that the "primary function of the basket bowl is that of transportation, its secondary use that of a temporary receptacle."[12] Carried in it were cactus fruits, vegetables, small seeds, and occasional other products, while still earlier it was used for watering horses. In special situations it was used as an eating bowl. Deep bowls were used for wine-making and drinking.

Many of the bowls were water-tight. Walls of these old bowls are solid, heavy, thick, and hard. Sewing was generally fair but always tight, despite the fact that often stitches were no more than eight and coils no more than four to the inch. These early pieces measured from about 15¾″ to 19½″ in diameter and about 7″ to 8½″ in depth, with some smaller, some larger. All of these early bowls followed the same general shape and size range as given here, and certainly they did not have handles, lids, or other such additions.

The wine bowl is one of the most interesting forms produced by the early Papago weaver (Fig. 6.6). Very deep and generous in its proportions, it frequently measured around 14″ at its rim diameter and 10″ or more in depth. Although dimensions are not recorded,

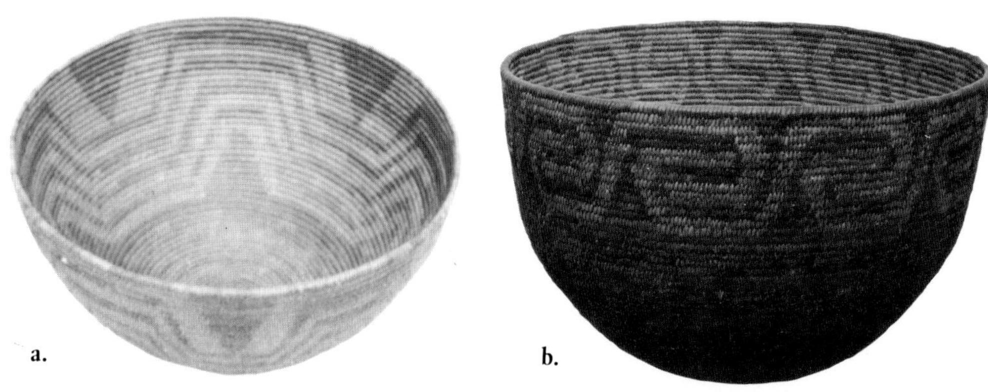

Fig. 6.6. Papago wine bowls. (a) This one is 16″ wide at the rim and 8″ deep. It has a simple pattern which comes off a large black center and involves triangles and lines *(ASM E2239)*. (b) A comparable large, black center circle onto the wall, and out of it grows a meander pattern high on the wall *(James S. Griffith)*.

one example pictured by Lumholtz is but a fraction wider at the rim than in its height dimension. This piece has a heavy wall design made up of the unit shown in drawing a; these were arranged in diagonal rows from base to rim. Another Papago wine basket in a private collection measured 14½″ in diameter and was 9½″ high; it had four coils and ten stitches to the inch. The black base extends up the wall to within 3¼″ of the rim, and within the remaining narrow band is the motif shown in drawing b, repeated twelve times and in such a way as to give a negative effect. A third wine bowl was noted as carried on the head of a Papago woman in a parade in 1973. The design was a typical old one, six repeated, double, obliquely placed triangles joined by horizontal and oblique lines (see drawing c). The rim in this piece was white.

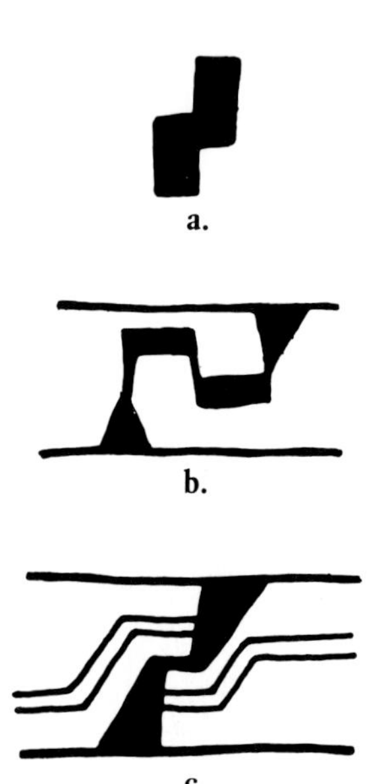

In some ways the wine bowl was like other large pieces of this type; in other respects it was different. It tended to be wider, deeper, more tightly made, for its major use was to hold liquids, and its decoration tended toward more severe treatment: often its black base came up high onto the sidewall, and the wall pattern was often more limited and simpler.

Most of the other early bowl designs were simple also, but tended to be in wide bands, thus covering the greater part of the sidewall. Frequently the center bottom was a smaller black circle (sometimes larger), and the wall pattern started shortly after the upturn from the flat base. In some instances there would be a projection off the black center, such as an elongate but heavy triangle, with bands and smaller solids (usually another one at the rim) associated with it by attachment to outlines around the solids. In some baskets wide lines take off the tip of a large triangle to form a swastika, as in trays. Other patterns include rays, squash blossom, turtle shell, and coyote tracks.

Kissell illustrates several deep bowl forms which she labels "modern," and indeed they are very different from the wine or any other old bowls. Their straight sides and abruptly flat bottoms lack the beauty of the generous, rounded curves of the old pieces. They seldom have black centers (only two out of nine pieces do); their designs are spotty, spread out, and not "one of a piece" as in the older basket forms. Repeated single elements prevail in each of seven pieces, and two baskets have life forms for decoration. Already, then, in 1916, changes can be discerned in the "modern" pieces as contrasted with the old-style willow baskets.

Natively, and as early as Kissell's time among the Papagos, these Indians would not use the yucca substitute basket unless there was nothing else around. And, by the same token, occasional willow pieces were woven into the 1980s but usually with simpler designs and for routine use as well as for sale.

Shreve notes many of the changes which had occurred in bowl baskets by the early 1940s. Some baskets remained from earlier years, particularly bowls and trays, for domestic use and for gifts. However, no longer was the bowl used for carrying produce, although it still served as a receptacle about the Papago home. She also notes that the wine basket (called "large basket" by the Papagos) was still used for collecting the saguaro fruit and preparing the wine which was made for the still important rain ceremony, and that the basket was also "used the rest of the year for storing corn and other produce."[13] The wine basket has long since been dropped from use to any degree among these Indians.

In 1943 Shreve reported the continued use of willow baskets and said that two or three were to be seen in every home. She pictured six baskets "bought by the Papago Arts and Crafts Board," four of them domestic food baskets and two gift pieces. Three of the first group are in old-style designs, and in continuous patterns, one a dynamic whirl of squares moving to the upper right off the black center and connected with horizontal fine lines; and the second of two alternated rows of paired triangles with negative bands between them; and third, a five-pointed floral theme taking off the black center with each petal outlined with stepped triangles. The fourth food basket was more in the contemporary style, with a solid black, eight-petaled flower, with a stepped band beyond it touching the black rim. The two gift basket designs[14] were also in the old tradition, one a four-pointed squash-blossom pattern, and the second a small central black circle with four tiny projecting triangles, then ten fine lines outlining this, and with four tiny black triangles pendant from the rim.

Two willow baskets (Fig. 6.7) from the southwestern corner of the Papago Reservation, purchased in the early 1940s,[15] are quite similar to these last two gift baskets pictured by Shreve. The first piece differs from the gift basket in that it has but three petals to its squash-blossom design. It is 16½" in diameter while the piece in Shreve's thesis is about 6½" in diameter. The other is like Shreve's second described gift piece except that it has thirteen parallel encircling lines instead of ten. It is 14½" in diameter while the Shreve example measured 7½" in diameter. These two pieces averaged fifteen stitches and six coils per inch. Shreve does not give the stitch-coil counts for her two gift baskets, but she does note that "the fine coil was used in aboriginal times for the gift basket"; the finest counts she gives are nine to eighteen coils and as high as twenty-two stitches to the inch in the best willow weaving.

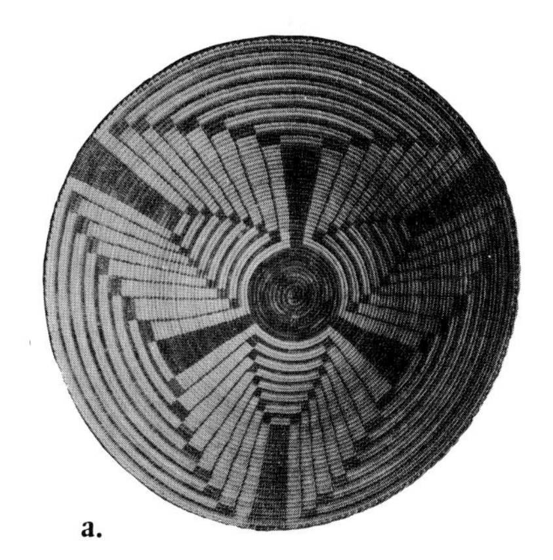

a.

b.

Fig. 6.7. Two Papago deep basket trays from the southwestern corner of the Reservation. They are beautifully woven; (a) uses the age-old squash-blossom design (16¼" diameter), whereas (b) has multiple, delicately repeated encircling lines creating a blossom, and a diameter of 14¼" *(private collection).*

Shreve pictures other bowls in this early 1940s period made of yucca. A well-made piece has a lid with a knob on top and three part-spirals of stepped black-yellow-black. The sidewall of the bowl is decorated in like manner but with more lengthy spirals. This bowl had a straight wall and flat bottom; along with more rounded- and pointed-bottomed pieces, it was one of the three favored bowl shapes of these mid-years. Additional designs on the straight-sided style pictured by Shreve[16] include three large coyote tracks within a band bound by one black coil above and below, a row of very conventional turkeys, a large simple fret, and a zigzag made up of horizontal rectangles and squares on the diagonal. All four of these designs take up the larger part of the bowl wall.

In the years to follow, many of the above changes, which started in Kissell's time and continued into the 1940s, were perpetuated in the bowl basket. Size was extremely varied, running the gamut from miniatures to as much as 14" and 15" in diameter. Form fluctuated perhaps more than at any other time, with straight, outcurving, incurving, globular, and other walls, rounded and flat bottoms, sometimes with lids or handles (Fig. 6.8) or with scalloped edges. Design, although basically simple, was varied in units and motifs, from simple to slightly complex geometrics to a wide variety of life forms. In willow baskets, centers were always black, in yucca bowls they were predominantly white; the willow piece rims were braided, closely overcast, or terminated in regular sewing, all of this usually in black; in the yucca basket the white rim was frequently overstitched in black.

Fig. 6.8. Papago bowls, some with lids or handles, or both. From left to right: an oval form (8¼" by 5¾", 4½" deep) with a man and a woman on the ends and a mule-like creature on each side and on the lid *(ASM E3947a)*; a square bowl with double coyote tracks on the sides and single ones on the lid, plus a loop handle *(ASM E3958a)*; a simply decorated lidless form with a large handle *(ASM E4381A)*; a simple meander ornaments the lid of the right bowl, while a more complex one is to be noted on the sidewalls *(ASM E7479B)*.

A few designs in a group of thirty bowl baskets will show the variety in the mid-1970s. Some weavers dipped back into the past for pattern inspiration; some let their imaginations and creativity have full play. These pieces varied in size from small to medium; craftsmanship also varied, for some pieces are beautifully woven, others are rather poorly done. Many of these thirty bowls begin with white centers; some have large black circles out of which the design springs. Edges, too, run the gamut from plain black to plain white, close and overlapping to spread-out overcasting, half–cross-stitching to cross-stitching. Basic colors are black and white.

The simplest patterns are banded. In one piece a black circle about halfway out emits three solid, slightly curved triangles which reach to the black rim. Another simple but effective theme is joined coyote tracks; two rows of these, plus black triangles pendant from a black rim, ornament a second piece. Some baskets have floral themes; squash blossoms appear in three of them, one each with four, five, and ten petals. Several bowls feature the old-style elongate triangles with lines off their tips evolving into swastikas.

Two bowls are ornamented with life forms. One has an elaborate presentation of three massive butterflies, done largely in black outlines with black details on yellow bodies. The other features five figures of some creature, possibly a Gila monster. Feet (or toes) and bodies are in lines, while heads, tails, and legs are solid.

That all of the pieces in this collection of thirty bowls are modern is demonstrated in various ways. Coils are large in a majority of them, and sewing not very good except in two or three baskets. Designs were "old style" in a majority of examples in that they are joined or continuous, four only having spaced-out or repeated themes. This feature does not make the baskets "old," however, for white centers and rims, the use of yucca, quality of weaving, and large coils would all deny this. Thus this collection is an interesting mixture of the past and the present, showing a common trend in basketry in the 1970s in which the weaver dipped back into the past for inspiration in designing.

A sampling of designs will indicate the nature of the decoration of the oval bowl. Perhaps the most unusual employs much martynia, both in the bowl proper and in the lid. One lid has a large centered star in negative, plus a negative fret pattern on the bowl. A second lidded piece has a heavy black meander on both lid and bowl. Other oval bowl designs include stepped squares, a great, heavy U-shaped design with stepped edges, stepped triangles, simple zigzags of stepped rectangles encircling the body of a bowl, and more complex meanders.

Jars

Jars are quite varied as produced by the Papagos (Fig. 6.9); they range in size from the great storage jars to miniatures. They are narrow and wide, short- or long-necked, they have thin or fat bodies, they are lidless or have lids simple or complex. With the exception of storage jars, this form was not made in earlier years, for abundant ceramic pieces served for the same uses. Kissell pictures no jars except the granaries; she dismisses the subject by saying that ollas and wastebaskets are made to sell. On the other hand, Shreve includes at least four different jar forms, although several bowls seem to be more jarlike than anything else. Russell illustrates the Pima coiled jar and classified it as a form produced for the white man.

a.

b.

c.

d.

Fig. 6.9. Papago jars. (a) A 1940 piece which has a flaring neck and rounded body. A zigzag on the rounded body and diamonds on the lower part are created in parallel rows of joined squares *(DHC)*. Two new jars which are more slender: (b) decorated with a row of dancing men and women; (c) scattered birds, butterflies, a bat (?), a dog, and geometrics (b and c, *Gallup Ceremonials, 1975*). (d) A tall jar featuring horizontal design arrangement *(Rick Rosenthal)*.

Kissell says that Papago crude-coiled granaries are used for storage of corn, wheat, and mesquite beans. They are built on the ground, raised above the dirt by boards or stones, and are barrel-shaped with a slight in-curve at the top.[17] She notes further that they have a coiled base and are more carefully woven of willow, cottonwood, or bear grass; the wall is built of arrowbush. Sometimes this basket will reach to a man's shoulder,[18] but more often they are not so large.

Shreve gives four basket forms which she calls "olla" shapes. In contradiction of Kissell, she says, "In aboriginal times these shapes were used for water bottles and salt baskets."[19] Further, she notes that "olla shaped baskets were apparently one of the early shapes adapted to commercial baskets." These olla forms have straight necks or necks with outflaring rims, and either rounded bodies, top and bottom; or rounded with a flat base and of narrower or wider diameter; or with outflaring neck and almost pointed bottom. These baskets were tightly woven and further waterproofed with pitch, possibly from the mesquite tree. Shreve claims that the olla-shaped piece was much more popular between 1905 and 1925 than it was in 1943. Certainly in the 1970s it was greatly outnumbered by other forms.

Other jar forms were developed through the years. The olla form with medium and straight neck remained popular; so did the outflaring rim with rounded body but flat base. Later there were both straight necks and rims, and outflaring rims with more elongate bodies. Short and long, narrow and wide, straight and outflaring necks were also found, usually on round-bodied baskets. Jars without necks, high shoulders, and rounded lines were produced but were not common; the same neckless style with outflaring and rounded lines to a flat base is occasionally to be noted. In a large number of jars one square example was noted. One very awkward shape had a medium neck, outcurving body which sharply incurved about two-thirds of the way down, then moved in an almost straight line to a flat base.

Lids were noted on sixteen of a group of thirty-seven pieces. Lids varied almost as much as the shapes of the baskets. Some were flat with a lower projection to fit into the mouth of the jar, and with a rounded knob on top, or with a braided loop handle, or the loop may be made of one or several wrapped coils. Knobs and loops may rise 1" or more or less above the flat part of the lid. One loop handle was 1" wide. A new basket with an unusual lid was observed in 1963: the lid is shaped like the rounded jar itself and is smaller in diameter, but it is almost as high as the jar and has a small loop handle on the very top.

Quite frequently lids are decorated; sometimes the decoration is synchronized with the jar patterns. For example, on the large lid of the last type mentioned are multiple, vertical coyote tracks, with the same type found on the jar, but fewer of them. In another case the jar has an elaborate pattern on it while the lid is ornamented with simple concentric lines. Another lid has but a single black line near the edge. On one of these baskets there is a three-line fret; on the lid is a two-line and simpler fret. On one interesting small jar done in split stitch, five flowers are sewn over the stitching on both the main body and the lid of the piece. Five birds decorate the wall of another jar, while three different birds appear on the lid. Needless to say, the majority of lids are plain or, at most, very simply decorated.

Papago jars are somewhat more difficult to make than other forms; therefore, they are, on the average, better made than bowls, plaques, and other simpler shapes. Perhaps only the better weaver will attempt such forms. Of the group of thirty-seven baskets mentioned above, few fell below a stitch count of six, although coil counts are varied from one and one-fourth to five to the inch. One piece in this group counted twelve stitches to the inch but only three coils. In fact, the latter is average for these jars.

Designs on jars are varied. One piece of the thirty-seven was all black, the rest were designed in black on the natural yucca, with two adding red. Design runs the gamut from steps to triangles, lines, diamonds, frets, coyote tracks, plus chevrons, zigzags, and checkers. Life forms include bats, turkeys, eagles, deer or deer heads, butterflies, centipedes, dogs, and men and women; one piece has four running, two-humped camels[20] on it (Fig. 6.10). Quality of design varies greatly; some of it is symmetrical and pleasantly arranged, or it may be haphazardly ill-spaced. There are no designs on jar bases.

Fig. 6.10. Papago yucca jar decorated with two-humped camels and men. (The camel bell was found on a ranch in California about 1880.) The basket was purchased in 1928 in Casa Grande, Arizona *(collection of and photo by W. L. Bowers, Colorado Springs, Colorado).*

An old Papago jar in the Arizona Historical Society collection is dated 1899 (see Fig. 6.9). It is a low-necked, gently rounded-bodied, flat-based piece, and is ornamented with all-black figures. A row of men, not touching, appears two coils below the rim's edge; below them are alternating men and horses. At the bottom and to the turn onto the base are what appear to be legs or pants alternating with horses. All figures are generalized, with no details. An effort was made to represent a hand and maybe fingers, with the result that the two stitches used in the latter result in a clawlike appearance. It is of interest to note these life figures at such an early date.

Certainly the wide variety of subjects for decoration on jars, and particularly with emphasis on life motifs, would indicate that this form was made primarily for sale. This is true from the beginning, as indicated in the piece cited above and dated just before 1900. Kissell mentions but does not develop the statement that raising and transporting water was done "in the old time water-tight well buckets and bottle baskets." Then she says that "the olla and waste-basket forms seen in curio shops are trade baskets made for white man's use and not for the Indian's." Certainly all the jars studied in this survey would fit into the commercial category.[21]

Plaques

Among the Papagos, as with other tribes, flat plaques are conspicuous by their rarity in early years; actually, there could be little or no native use for this form. As a matter of fact, the plaque was of little significance to the white man until it became adapted as a hot plate or, more commonly, as a decorative piece made with a loop to hang on the wall. Serving in these capacities, it came to be a favored piece, and, for many years, has been made in considerable abundance.

Sizes are extremely varied in plaques. In a miscellaneous group of twenty-eight pieces the range was from 5″ to 23″ in diameter, with fourteen of these between 5″ and 9″. There was one each 21″, 22″, and 23″ across, plus a few smaller and some "in between" sizes. Since small sizes sell better than larger ones, this is not surprising at all. There is quite a range in coil and stitch count, as might be expected, for most weavers try a plaque sooner or later. Coils count from two to ten per inch, with fewer coils in most pieces. There is a wider range in stitch count, from six to twenty-eight per inch. There were three each with six and seven stitches per inch, eight with eight per inch, then no more than two or three examples of higher counts of nine to thirteen, and then a big jump to two plaques with a stitch count of twenty-eight each.

Designs vary greatly in the Papago coiled plaque (Fig. 6.11). Some are simple, some more complex. In layout they are centered, repeated, or all-over. The shape, of course, allows for almost any type of layout.

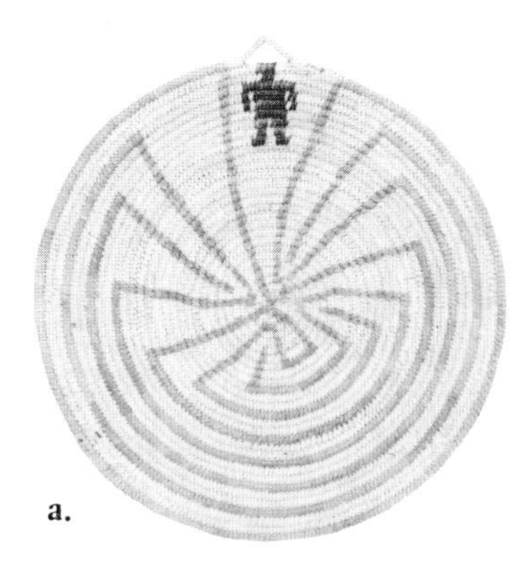

Fig. 6.11. Papago coiled plaques showing some variety in design. (a) Largest (14″ diameter), the man in the maze is a favored theme; here the maze is in green and the man in black *(ASM 5567)*. Life forms were very common in this shape: (b) a bird *(ASM E7518)*; (c) lizards in the plaque at left *(ASM E3336)*, and the piece at right indicates the continued popularity of geometrics, with single and double coyote tracks in this example *(ASM E3948)*. (d) Papago plaques show the colors commonly used today—white, green, yellow, and black—and geometrics which remain popular. Note the negative white flower on a green base *(ASM E7477, 10126, E226)*.

In the above-mentioned group of twenty-eight plaques, the following designs were used: seven geometric, twelve man in the maze, two reptilian, one saguaro, two birds, and four star or flower themes. Geometrics include the usual steps, lines, bands, meanders, and cogwheels, while life themes incorporate flying ducks, Gila monsters, humans, saguaros, and man in the maze (in one plaque a black maze, a red man). Frequently eyes are oversewn. The star-flower motif is varied from three- to twelve-pointed, with five-pointed or petaled styles most favored, for there were four plaques decorated with this style and one each with three, four, and twelve points. One of the five-pointed themes was in negative; the points of two others go into the rim, and thus there is alternate black and white at the edges.

Wastebaskets

Wastebaskets are mentioned by Kissell as made solely for white man; Shreve mentions their popularity in the 1940s. Forms would include small straight-sided, flat-bottomed pieces, plus one that is wider at the top and smaller based. In addition to these two main shapes, there are a few variations such as one with a slight pinching about halfway down on an otherwise straight side.

Dimensions of the wastebaskets vary considerably, but this form is also made in sizes which could not have served this purpose. For example, there are straight-sided, flat-bottomed pieces which are no more than three, four, or five inches in height. In a miscellaneous group of thirty-seven baskets of this form, three were under 5″ in height and all the rest were over 8″ in this dimension. Six were 13″ and six 14″, fifteen ranged between 8″ and 11″, and there was one each 15″, 16″, 17″, 18″, and 20″ in height. The majority of the baskets were taller than they measured in rim diameter; in fact, twice as many in this selection had heights greater than rim diameters; a few were equal in these two measurements. In practically all instances, the base of the wastebasket is smaller than the rim, but in a few cases so very little less as to be negligible.

Bases are dominantly all white in these wastebaskets but a few were ornamented. One was solid green, and five had some kind of decoration on the bottom proper. One base was ornamented with alternate white and green coils; one had the outline of a simple four-petal flower. A two-coil black center begs the question of decoration. One base had on it a large green star outlined in black, while a fifth base featured a large green circle with five elements taking off it. Then there were two baskets in which the wall pattern started on the botton; in both instances a simple fret begins several coils before the turn-up for the wall.

a.

b.

c.

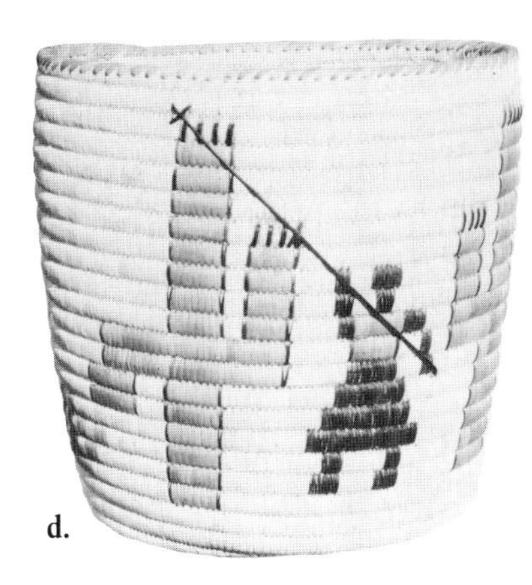

d.

Fig. 6.12. Papago coiled wastebaskets present variation in shape on this generally deep, straight-sided, flat-bottomed form. (a) The tallest (14″) is also the oldest of those shown here; it was collected about 1922. Note its smaller base and variety of life forms, including a man wearing an ornate head piece, birds, and deer *(ASM E4018)*. (b) This piece was collected about a decade later; it features great Gila monsters and birds *(ASM E5326)*. (c) Dating from 1975, this wastebasket is more carefully ornamented with two meandering bands. (d) A favorite theme for some of these forms is a Papago woman collecting cactus fruit (c and d, *Gallup Ceremonials, 1975*).

Wall designs are, of course, the center of interest on wastebaskets (Fig. 6.12). Surprisingly, there is quite a variety, although the layouts tend to be organizational-banded and repeated, with occasional other styles, such as half-band. In some cases design covers all the wall, but again, this is usually a banded style of organization. Designs include a great variety of geometrics and life subjects, all adjusted in form and arrangement to this deep shape.

One large piece has five saguaros with three triangular arms on each, from just above the base to the rim, plus a turkeylike bird about midway up the basket wall, all in black. A basket with a fairly small base has a thick organizational band made up of two joined broad zigzags in green with black stepped outlines on each edge and one joining the bands. The wall of another piece has three sets of seven nested and diagonally arranged chevrons. An open stitch on another piece is so arranged as to form all-over small diamonds. Very attractive is a piece with a green base which continues about two-thirds of the way up the wall where a deep zigzag occurs—the green is outlined in black squares, thus creating white triangles at the rim. One well-proportioned wastebasket is ornamented with two black deer and two large saguaros in green, tipped with black fruit. In addition, the following many themes were used in vertical placement to accommodate to the tall walls of these pieces: the saguaro was a particular favorite, with women picking the fruit, plus other subjects such as the Maltese cross and such life forms as scorpions, frogs, birds in flight, dogs, and horses.

Life Form Baskets

Although long made in clay for children, life forms were not woven in basketry techniques in early years. Kissell reports none, but Shreve refers to quite a number of them including plants, animals, and humans. The saguaro cactus seems to have been the popular plant then as now, and it was woven in the early 1940s in somewhat the same way, with a small plaque base and with main branch and arms woven of loops which were then sewed together in flat fashion. Among the animals she pictures are a fairly flat Gila monster with black head and black-and-white transverse stripes; a rather flat-legged turtle; a quite formless, fat owl; and birds of more realistic shapes. Some birds were presented as a rounded basket with added fat legs, a slight superstructure for the head, with a questionable mouth, and added projections from the basket rim for wing feathers. Dogs, deer, and horses are also made. Humans are usually full-skirted women, with loose blouses; Shreve reports two holding parasols, and several each with plaited purses and pottery jars. Details such as eyes and hair were represented in overstitching. Seemingly, then as now, there was little or no areal variation in these forms.

a.

b.

Continued popularity characterizes life forms in modeled Papago coiled basketry (Fig. 6.13). Humans, owls, ducks and other birds, turtles, dogs, cats, and occasional other pieces such as pigs were still popular in the mid-1970s. Most of the figures are done in regular coiled work, although occasional other weaves, such as open coil, might be involved in a small way. Black martynia was the major color added to the white yucca, although touches of yellow or green yucca were occasionally used for detail; other materials such as horsehair for cats' whiskers might also be added.

One owl is 7½″ tall, with a 5¼″ base; wings extend a little beyond the latter measurement. The major part of the figure is in open stitch except for such details as long wrapped areas for wing beginnings and oversewing for the round eye. In a 1975 owl the whole head is woven as a separate piece which can be removed like a stopper from the jar body. Some owls are woven in open stitch;

there was the usual overstitching for facial details. Another owl was woven in open and split stitch throughout, a common method in later years.

Quite commonly represented is the duck. One is about 4½″ long, 2¾″ wide, and 4″ tall. Stitch count is about eight, and coils are about four to the inch. Both wings and eyes combine black and white, and the beak is made by extending coils, to a greater degree for the upper part and to a lesser extent for the lower. A second, slightly smaller duck has a removable head; wings and a three-part tail are merely extensions of coils, with black overstitching to stress details.

Dogs are quite common figures in coiled weave, usually presented in a sitting posture. Of three examples, one is 4¾″, one 5½″, and the third is 8″ in height in this sitting position. The smallest was 4¼″ from feet to tip of tail, the largest 7¾″ in the same measurement; in the latter there were two and one-half coils and six stitches to the inch; eyes, nose, and mouth were oversewn in black, and ears, nose, legs, and tail were all extended coils. An elaborated coyote track appeared as decoration on each side, front, and back in this largest dog. In all three dogs the head served as a stopper, for it was coiled as a separate piece. One little dog is different in that it stands on all fours. His barrel-round body has an odd geometric woven on each side and his tail stands straight up!

c.

Turtles were popular in later years. Usually they were made in two separate pieces: the lower included the main body, head, feet, and tail; the upper piece, a mere lid, served as back. In general, the lid and rest of the upper body were checkered to make them more realistic. Tail and legs were usually coiled loops, often black; the head might be made of three coils, with additional wrapping; and eyes were in white oversewing on the black head. Of four examples, heights are from 3″ to 7″, while in length they are 9″ to 12¾″. These are about average in size. As early as 1964 a turtle "piggy bank" was observed: it had green rectangles all over the body, and a slit in the center of the back. Two more of these same turtle banks were observed at the Arizona State Fair in 1968.

Two less common later forms are pigs and rabbits. One sitting rabbit was 8¼″ tall, to his ear tips. Rather well woven, most stitches counted eight to the inch; however, in the same piece there were counts of three or four to the inch, these understandably irregular as they responded to irregularities in body form. Legs of the rabbit were bent coils, ears of four coils, eyes and mouth were oversewn, and the head was made to serve as a separate piece or stopper. The one observed pig was in a standing position, and it measured 3½″ high and 4¾″ long from his tiny curled tail to his snout. Body was in open stitch, legs and ears were extensions of coils, the snout was in two rows of black, close coil, and the tail was a twist of martynia.

d.

Fig. 6.13. Various Papago figures "modeled" in basketry. (a) A lady with braided hair, and a saguaro complete with buds (or fruit?) on top *(ASM E8168, E4693a)*. (b) Another lady, this one complete from her hat to her sandaled feet, and with a tiny basket in one hand and a basket purse in the other *(DHC)*. (c) A sitting dog and one standing on all fours *(DHC)*. (d) A pert owl with "handles" for ears, separate plaque-like pieces sewed on for wings, and oversewing for eyes *(DHC)*. All figures are woven in yucca.

Human figures are usually women. One simple example is 7″ tall, with the body in open split stitch; the head is regular coil, and arms are in wrapped coil. Eyes, nose, and mouth are all sewed on in black, and regular black coils represent the bobbed hair. These are typical features and an average size for many of these female figurines. Another doll is made of an upper, rounded basket shape and a lower sloping-sided style which typifies a full skirt decorated, in this figure, with a fret design. One arm is upraised; all features are like those described above.

Another figurine differs in several details: the skirt is elaborately ornamented in a squash-blossom-like pattern, and there is an eagle design on the "blouse"; the arms are simple double coils sewed to the upper part of the body, and black braided hair is represented with a white band around the head, all designs in the weaving. No feet are represented in this piece. One figurine differs in its yellow spiral skirt and large black diamond blouse decorations, and there is a distinct scowl on her face! One of the most elaborate of this type is a 19″ figure which has feet, a deeply scalloped dark green design on the skirt, a removable open-coil basket hat, and two elaborate basket purses, one in each five-fingered hand. Both of the purses are in open stitch.

Although plant forms in some small variety are woven into baskets, very few are "modeled" in some type of coiling. Now and again a bit of grass is "growing" at the base of a large saguaro cactus. In one such case, the base is an open-stitch plaque which has the bunches of grass around the centered saguaro. The latter is a single round plant with no arms; it is woven in open stitch and has a cluster of red fruit on its top. Some representations of this plant have one or more arms projecting from the center growth and are woven frequently in close coil stitching.

Miscellaneous Coiled Baskets

An unusual form of basket woven by the Papagos today on rare occasions is a so-called "cradle," a reflection of another lost tradition, for in much earlier years cradles were common. This piece is nothing more than a large oval basket; of three observed, one has three handles, and one a handle or "hanger" and a hood. The first is 32″ long, 20″ wide, and 9¾″ high, with a 3″ extended-coil handle at each end. A third handle appears several inches from one end; it may have been woven for the purpose of holding a net or such covering above the baby. The second cradle is 23½″ long, 13½″ wide, and 6½″ high all around except the hood area, which is 13″ high. The "hanger" extends 5″ beyond the basket.

The larger of these two cradle baskets was ornamented with a wide green zigzagging band which was outlined with black rectangles forming steps, and the rim was outlined in slanted and touching overstitching. This large cradle counted one and one-third to one and one-half coils and six stitches to the inch.

The third and very fancy cradle is 22¾″ long, 11½″ wide, and 6¾″ high. It has both an outward-projecting top edge of about 2″ and a scalloped rim sewed with black cross-stitching. On the wall are three large frets on each side and one at each end, all in green, and continuous, for they are joined at the top; there are four vertically stacked, black coyote tracks between the frets.

Another odd shape woven by Papagos is a "mail" basket. This is a rounded piece made of two separate shallow tray shapes sewed together around the edges but leaving the top open. On the back piece is an extra, double-pointed projection, with a handle extending from this so that it can be hung. On this mail basket, on the other side, is a central design of a long turtle (or short Gila monster?), with four coyote tracks toward the "corners." A second mail basket is woven of two pieces, has a wide slit at the top, and an additional woven loop for hanging.

One of the unusual forms (Fig. 6.14) made by Papagos over a fairly long period of time is the coaster; these were quite popular in the late 1930s and into the 1940s. They are woven as any other piece, usually starting with a knot. Stitch and coil counts are about average, with one set of six with five coils and ten stitches to the inch; each in this set measured 3¼″ in diameter. A second set of six was a little cruder; each piece measured 3½″ in diameter and had six coils and eight stitches to the inch. The coasters have perfectly flat bases and very low vertical rims measuring just under ½″ in one set and ⅜″ in the other. Characteristically, the rim coil is about twice the width of the other coils.

In one set of coasters there was a coiled black rattlesnake on the flat surface of each piece, complete with rattles done in black and white stitches. Eyes are oversewn in white. In this set, five white rims were overcast in black cross-stitching with the remaining one done in a zigzag stitch. Another set was ornamented with the figure of a black owl in the center of each coaster; there is much rhythm in the very round-edged wings of these little figures. Again the eyes are oversewn. The weaver of this set of coasters managed to carefully overstitch the edges of all pieces. A third design is extremely simple, with but three concentric circles of black in each coaster.

For want of a better term, several woven pieces will be called "bags" or "purses." That they are to be carried is indicated in fairly high woven handles; that they are purses is evidenced in the fastening of the lids on one side so that they can be opened; that they may be kept closed a braided loop fits over a "woven" button. One of these purses is 6″ high, 6½″ wide, and 10″ long, and it has a 6″ high handle. This purse averages three coils and eight stitches to the inch. The basket rim is ornamented with cross-stitching in black; the handle, which is three coils wide, has plain line overstitching on each edge. On the basket proper are three vertical, double rows of diamonds created with stepped squares. A second bag is 6″ high with a plain flat lid; the handle is 4½″ high; the lid is decorated with double coyote tracks, and the body of the basket with four flying ducks on each side. A third basket is oval; it is decorated with green butterflies outlined in black on the basket proper, and on the lid is just a green encircling band.

"Coin purse" is the name applied to a small piece which has two slightly rounded baskets, each about 3¼″ in diameter, braided together except for a single small slit. One such piece is quite finely woven, having twelve to fourteen stitches and about eight coils to the inch. For decoration there is a turtle on one side and an eagle standing on an apparently split arrow on the other side.

One very unusual woven piece is barrette-like, for the hair. These are circular in form, with a short slit woven into each so that the "bar" can be slipped through them. Two barrettes are about 1⅝″ in diameter. One counts fourteen stitches, five coils, and the other fifteen stitches and five coils to the inch; they are very thin-walled. Both are made of white yucca with a design in red from yucca root. On one barrette four white coils form an eagle's body; then the head, great wings, and tail which extend beyond the body are in red. The second piece has a stepped outline star, then a second comparable star taking off from the tips of the first, both in red.

A rarely seen piece woven by Papago basketmakers is a cup. One of these is 3″ wide at the rim, more or less, and 1⅞″ tall. There is a

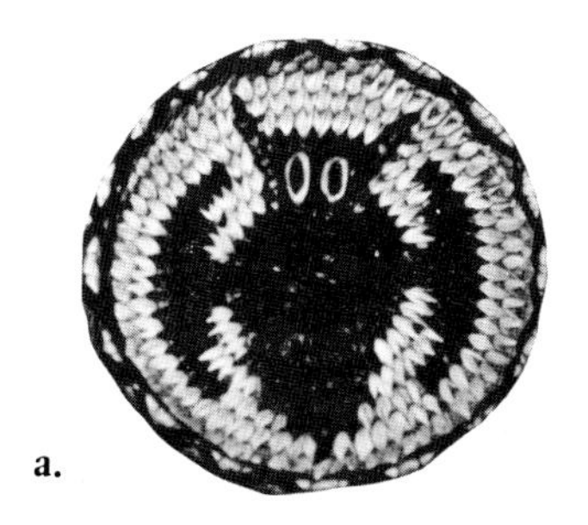

a.

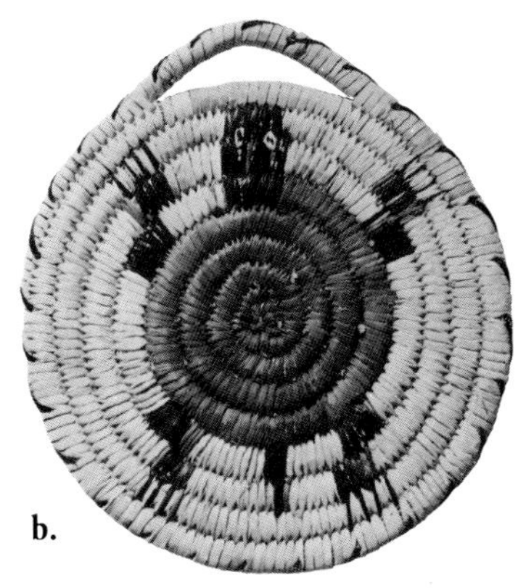

b.

Fig. 6.14. Papago pieces obviously made for sale. (a) A coaster style of the late 1930s, woven with an owl covering the better part of the 3½″ base *(private collection)*. (b) Frequently a plaque had a coil extended into a loop so that it could be hung *(DHC)*.

smaller foot at the bottom like a regular cup. It has a two-coil handle which is sewed on; its count is nine stitches and five coils to the inch. From the rim down, this cup is decorated as follows: one white coil, a coil of alternate black and white stitches, one white coil, two coils with squares in black, and five white coils to the base. Another cup has no handle but it does have an attached saucer.

Then there are footed "goblets"; one of these is 2" high and 4¾" in diameter at the rim. A second is like this but with a smaller foot and with a lid and a strap handle over the top. A third goblet is shallow and wide-footed; another is 10" wide at the rim, 4¾" at the base, and its total height is 3¾". It has a handle which is a wrapped single coil, and decoration on the "cup" portion consists of a complex coyote track. Still another goblet is 5½" in rim diameter, 2¾" high in the cup part, and 1¾" in the foot; on the cup are joined diamonds, on the lower part a zigzag line.

A small woven candlestick is 3½" in diameter but undecorated.

Hats appear now and then in Papago basket collections; one is quite well made, with very sturdy walls and a scalloped brim. The top is 5½" in diameter, the brim 2¾" to the base of scallops or 3¼" to the outer edge of them; the total height is 4⅜". This basket hat is fairly well woven, counting seven stitches and four coils to the inch. Scallops are made by pulling out the last coil and wrapping it. A bit of decoration appears near the bottom of the crown, consisting of alternate black and white stitches forming a three-coil band.

Miniature Coiled Baskets

Papago miniatures are relatively recent in development; they are not mentioned in earlier reports on this tribe. They begin to appear in sporadic instances in the 1930s but really became well established in later decades, particularly into the 1960s and 1970s. Although some are well made, the majority of the earlier ones tend to be poor or mediocre in quality; later they are better. The majority are made of yucca; but finer pieces are made of horsehair.

Yucca was used in miniatures in bleached white, with green and yellow or the black of martynia added for decoration. In horsehair both black and white were used in weaving these small pieces and for decoration (Fig. 6.15). There is tremendous variety in shape, with most of the large forms duplicated, from flat plaques, shallow bowls, lidded vessels, oval to straight-sided pieces, to life forms, particularly cats. Sizes tend to be under 4¼" in diameter or height; some of the smallest measure ¼" in height or ⅜" in diameter.

As a whole, decoration in Papago miniatures tends to be relatively simple, yet it follows the general styles of larger pieces. Many of the smallest baskets have some simple geometric theme, really a part only of a larger design. These might include a single, repeated square or rectangle, or the same in various simple arrangements, such as two of these touching at the corners. Encircling coils of green or black are popular, or a simple black center may be the only design. Occasionally lines may become frets, or stars or flowerlike themes, or a relatively simple life form may be woven into a miniature basket. Even the maze occurs now and again.

Two collections of Papago miniatures will be discussed to illustrate all of these aspects. The first is represented by thirty-five baskets, the second by over ninety pieces. These two collections are representative of most of the miniatures produced by this tribe; both collections consist of baskets made during the years 1964–67.

Of the first collection of thirty-five baskets, twenty-six were woven in yucca, nine in horsehair. Sizes varied: diameters at the rim range from 3/8″ to 2 5/8″, with some bases the same, particularly in straight-sided pieces, or a little smaller, with the greatest variation in one piece measuring 1 1/2″ on the base and 2 1/2″ at the rim. Heights were even less varied; the smallest in this dimension was 1/4″ high and the largest was 1 1/8″ high.

a.

b.

c.

Fig. 6.15. Miniature baskets and figures woven by Papagos. (a) A white horsehair cat. (b) Black horsehair is the chief material in these tiny baskets. (c) Black and white horsehair is combined in several of these miniatures. *(All from DHC.)*

Stitch and coil counts are very difficult to make in such baskets; thus, the following figures must be taken for counts made as close as possible. Yucca coils measured from six to seventeen per inch with nine baskets counting seven, five with eight coils to the inch, ten with ten, and five with twelve. Stitches range from four to eighteen per inch. In some of the horsehair baskets stitches were so close or, even, so fused, that it was impossible to count them; however, those counted in this material were about average; for example, in two of these baskets there were only seven to eight stitches to the inch, and the two highest counted ten to the inch. In the yucca pieces the range was from four to eighteen stitches per inch, with most examples (eighteen) clustering around ten to twelve stitches per inch. In general, it can be said that both stitch and coil counts were much higher than in regular-sized baskets made during the same years.

To start the miniature the Papago women usually tied a simple and small knot; in some examples it is impossible to tell what the beginning was like. Either martynia or yucca might be used for this beginning, or black or white horsehair. Rims were plain white or black, that is, of the regular coil; or there was overstitching, usually in black on the white edge coil. Even in the horsehair pieces the same was attempted, largely in cross-stitching, while other baskets in this material ended in a plain black or a silvery white coil. Two designs appear in rim stitching, a diagonal style and cross-stitching, with thirteen examples of the former and five of the latter in this first collection.

Designs in general included single-coil bands on the side of a straight-walled piece or a bowl, sometimes with a black rim coil. Or this band might have two, four, or five rectangles placed on it at regular intervals. A black center appears on a bowl form. The simple geometrics referred to above include the following, among others: angular Z-, L-, or S-shapes, or two rectangles one above the other, touching at the tips in one basket and overlapping slightly in a second. One basket has an encircling black, stepped zigzag placed about center of the straight-sided piece, and coyote tracks in positive or negative occur on several pieces. One interesting design was on a tiny flat plaque, all black except the rim coil which was white and flattened out at two points to form a cat's ears. On the black were oversewn white eyes and mouth, plus added white whiskers. A single piece has a flowerlike design in negative yellow and black; another piece is woven in an open and split stitch.

One well-made horsehair piece is woven in the shape of a hat, with a "band" and the edge in cross-stitching. There is a chin strap for this piece, complete with a "slide." A horsehair bowl basket is done in an open stitch, with black sewing on a black foundation. Sewing is done with two horsehairs at a time. The sewing of some coils in black, then some in white is all that is attempted in the way of design in several of these horsehair pieces; not much more attractive is an attempted checkerboarding in black and white in another of these pieces. Rather better results were obtained in a white six-petaled floral design on an almost flat tray. Perhaps the most attractive piece in this group is a low bowl with a foundation of light and dark (reddish) hair, a center circle sewed in dark hair, then the rest of the coils to the rim in an open stitching in forty-one or forty-two white or silvery "rays" to the edge.

Handles were added to several pieces, formed of an extension of the coil in several instances and in the form of two added loops of martynia in another. On one lid, the handle is a regular foundation wrapped with martynia. The use of black and white is well balanced in most of these pieces. As in regular-sized baskets, both open and close coiled work is done, both regular and split stitches are used, and sewing is counterclockwise.

The collection of over ninety Papago miniatures was analyzed by C. Joanna Bowser (Fig. 6.16). Her comments and analysis, plus additional notes on the illustration of the baskets, are herein given. These baskets were produced during the mid-1960s.[22]

The same materials were used in these miniatures as in larger baskets, bear grass for the foundation, yucca for sewing, and devil's-claw for designs. Tiny beads were added to some basket rims for additional decoration and for the eyes on one cat's face. The maker of these pieces did not weave larger baskets nor did she make any horsehair miniatures. These yucca pieces, she said, "were quick to make and easier to sell."

These baskets are true miniatures, for in size they range from ½" to 3¾" in diameter for trays and ½" to ¾" for the little bowls and deeper forms. Stitches averaged about eighteen to the inch with a range of twelve to twenty-two per inch. Coils counted no less than four to the inch and in the majority of pieces about fourteen to the inch. Designs included both geometric and life forms, many of them inspired by Pima-Papago patterns in a book the weaver borrowed from the Tribal Meeting House at Sells, the Papago Reservation center.

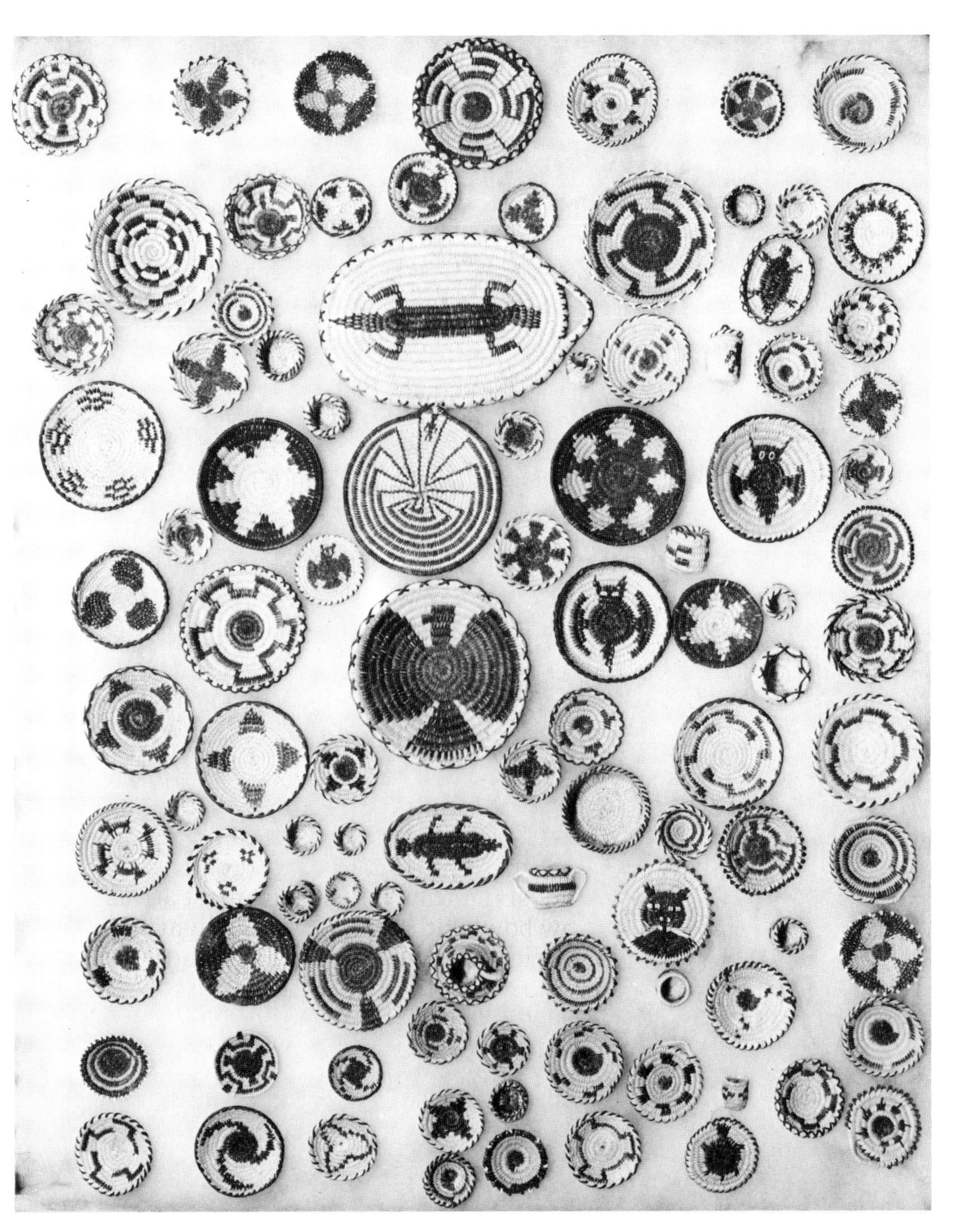

Fig. 6.16. An assortment of Papago yucca and martynia miniatures. Many of the designs represented in these baskets are common to both Papagos and Pimas, in geometrics and life forms alike *(Bowser Collection)*.

Geometric designs included stars or flowerlike themes which were three-, four-, five-, or six-pointed, and they were in both positive and negative. Coyote tracks appear in single or double style, and alone or in combination with other simple designs. Stepped triangles are woven most commonly in groups of four. Some very small pieces had nothing but a black center and rim, or bands of one black coil alternating with one of white. Wide-stepped lines dynamically emanate from a black center or just appear without benefit of the black area. One of the largest baskets has the maze pattern, complete with a tiny figure of a man at the opening.

In life forms there is considerable variety. The owl seems popular, appearing in at least three baskets, and possibly several others (quite small pieces and indistinct patterns). The largest plaque in the collection is decorated with a spread-wing eagle which takes up most of the space to the rim coil. A turtle appears on a very small basket, a cat's head on a larger piece. Three oval baskets are ornamented with elongate creatures, one definitely a lizard, another perhaps the same, and the third more like a beetle.

Certainly the Papago who wove these miniatures made an effort in the direction of originality, for there are no two pieces exactly alike.

Open-Stitch Coiling

In open coiling, as indicated above, several different types were produced and used by the Papagos. Great storage jars were woven in years gone by; few survive into recent times (Fig. 6.17). Stitches in these were often as much as an inch apart, yet sometimes they were evenly spaced.

a.

b.

Fig. 6.17. (a) A large open-stitch storage jar woven by a Papago woman. This piece is quite regular in shape, even in its diagonal stitching. (b) Two additional storage jars of Pima origin for comparison *(Rick Rosenthal)*.

As pieces became smaller in size, this space stitching remained popular. Forms in which it was used included trays, both round and oval, bowls, jars, lidded pieces, wastebaskets, and a few others. Added to or taking the place of plain space stitching was plain split stitch, or, later, wheat stitch, styles expressed in the same forms just listed. Most commonly used materials in all three weaves were bear grass and yucca; color does not often appear earlier in these baskets—seemingly decorative effect was vested solely in the weave itself, even for more recent pieces.

A group of fifteen trays which involve open stitch will indicate general situations relative to the types of weave. In size, the trays range from 6⅞″ to 10¼″ in diameters. All baskets except one were under 2″ high; all were circular except two which were oval. Bear grass and yucca were the two materials used, the former showing through as green and the latter white in all baskets except one in which some green was used to change band color. Except for the two oval pieces which were wrapped, discernible beginnings included five plaited inside with a knot on the outside and five with a knot alone. Rims varied as in other Papago basketry.

A few descriptions of specific pieces will show variations of combinations of weaves (Fig. 6.18). All of the baskets started with one to three close stitch coils. Open stitches go straight out from this point to the rim, or they may curve to the right or to the left. Very dynamic is a tray with seventeen rows of long split stitching arranged at an angle. Seven baskets were done in wheat stitch; some move in a straight line to the rim, some curve up to the right. In several there are fourteen to sixteen rows of wheat stitching. In one basket the stitching increases in size from the innermost to the rim coil.

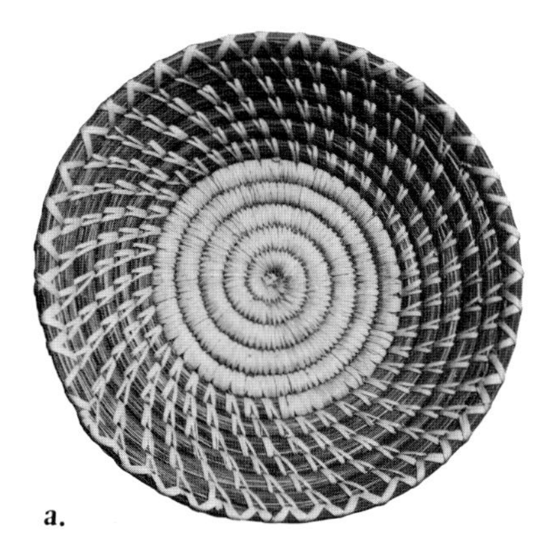
a.

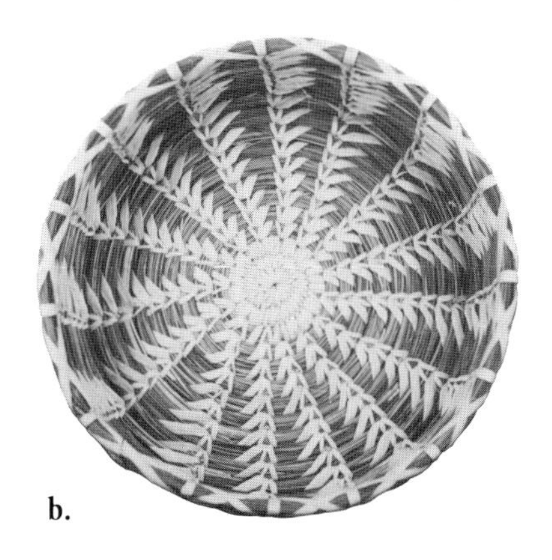
b.

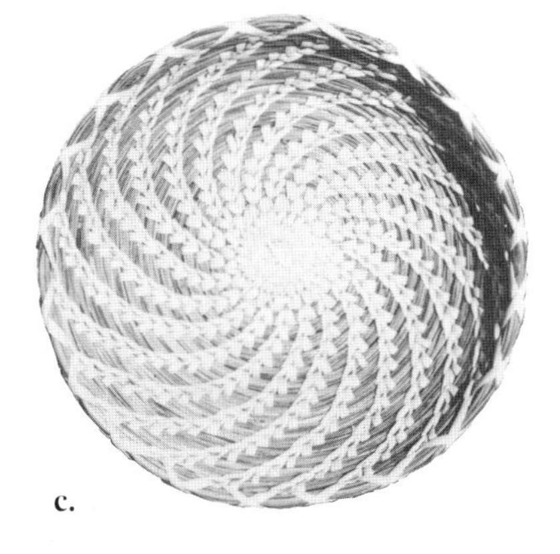
c.

Basketry in other collections shows greater versatility of stitch combinations. One small oval covered basket, 1½″ high and 4¼″ long by 3″ wide and with a lid, is covered with split stitch from center bottom to top of the lid. Rim top is finished in a plain spaced overcasting. A flat round plaque has quite curved split stitches from center to rim, the rim sewed with a zigzag effect. Similar to this is an oval plaque with several rows of regular coiling, then curving wheat stitches to the rim (see Fig. 6.18).

Trays are much the same in size as those in regular stitching but with fewer of the larger pieces. Most of them begin with regular coiling. There are both straight-out static plus curved dynamic stitching, with variations in degree of curving. Very delicate and attractive is the work in one tray which has three rows of plain coil, five of open split stitch, two plain coils, and five rows of split stitch to the rim. Another variation in stitching is exhibited in an extra wheat stitch on the right which is of varying lengths. Light brown wheat stitching is used on the wall of another tray, with several rows each of white ground, dark ground, and white ground to the rim. Very delicate also is a tray with four plain coils at the center, off which is a seven-petaled flower with single row wheat stitch dividers which merge into split stitch, the latter arranged so as to outline the plain, unsewn petals.

Open stitch forms fit well within the range of regular coiled bowls; however, the range is not as great. In decoration, the walls of bowls often resemble the patterning on trays. One unusual piece, has, successively, four rows of black wheat stitching, one close coil, three rows of white wheat stitches, two rows of the same in black, and a last two rows of white wheat stitching. A very deep bowl has a brown base, a band of white split stitch, two brown close coils, a band of white split stitches, and a single regular coil in brown.

This same banded effect has been very popular for wastebaskets in alternating green and white. One piece has regular coils at the turn onto the wall, a wide green band of split stitch, two regular coils, and this alternation repeated three more times. A very lovely wastebasket with quite a thin wall has this arrangement after the turn from the bottom: six rows wheat, two close coil, fourteen wheat, two close coil, fourteen wheat, two close coil, six wheat, and the two rim coils in close stitch. Fine weaving adds to its attractiveness.

Jars with or without lids are quite often produced in open stitching. A tall, lidded jar has banded effects on its wall like those described above for wastebaskets. Perhaps the most dramatic open-stitch jar is one with two constrictions in its wall between base and

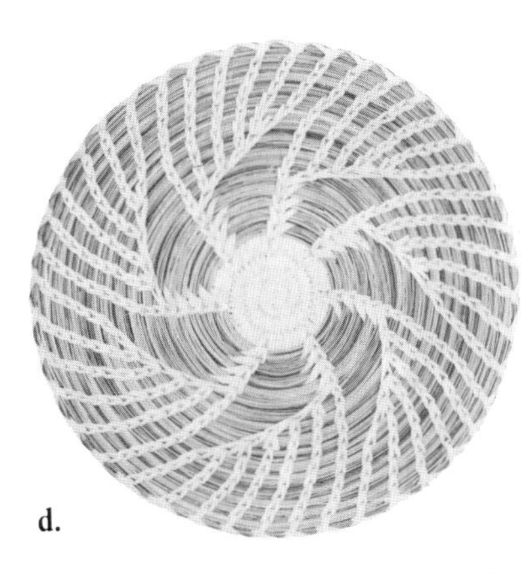
d.

Fig. 6.18. Papago trays sewed with split and wheat stitches. (a) A lacy effect is attained by spiraling a simple, close split stitch in this tray *(DHC)*. (b) Even and close wheat-stitch sewing straight out from a plain coil center to the rim in white yucca over the green beargrass foundation gives a striking result *(DHC)*. (c) In this small tray a short wheat-stitch gives a pleasing effect *(DHC)*. (d) Spacing the stitches in this piece created a floral pattern *(DHC)*.

lip (Fig. 6.19). A vertical zigzag line is followed from bottom to top, in wheat stitch, this design exaggerating the basic form of the jar.

A few life forms have been woven in open stitch, or open stitch may be used partially in weaving a basket figure. An owl has a body like a vase, with constriction low on the form, and diagonal split stitching on the body. Two ovals made entirely of split stitch are merely sewed onto the body as wings. A separate head is straight-sided and has an almost flat piece for a top, this projecting beyond the lower part, and all done in split stitch. Oversewn eyes are black rings with black centers.

a.

b.

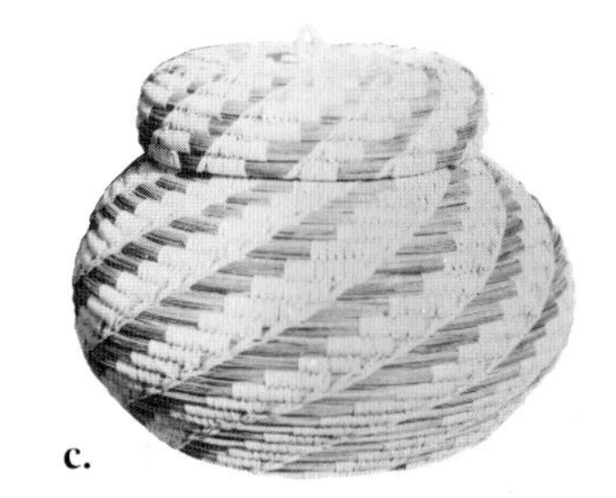
c.

d.

Fig. 6.19. Examples of split and wheat-stitch Papago jars or lidded pieces. (a) A fairly large oval form with plain and close split stitching *(DHC)*. (b) A pleasingly formed piece with vertical wheat stitching *(DHC)*. (c) Spiraling, multiple wheat stitches add to the attractiveness of this piece *(Gallup Ceremonials, 1975)*. (d) Most unusual is the shape of this jar, as are the zigzag wheat stitches *(DHC)*.

PAPAGO PLAITING

Plaiting is a technique formerly used by the Papagos and Pimas for a limited variety of utility items. As these domestic uses disappeared, so too did the technique and its products. Apparently all forms known to have been made by these two tribes were still in use when Kissell made her study in 1910–11; not all had disappeared when Shreve made her study, but production of plaiting had decreased from 50 percent of all basketry to less than 1 percent in 1943. Part of this was due to an increase in coiling for commercial reasons. All of the plaiting done by both tribes was twilled and in over-three-under-three or over-two-under-two or, rarely, over-four-under-four rhythms. Two of these rhythms might be combined in a single piece, particularly one in the base and the other in the wall of the same basket.

The sotol leaves used by the Papagos for all plaiting are referred to by Kissell as "Palmea"; this plant is also popularly known as "spoon cactus." Formerly, the leaves were knocked off with a long stick or, according to Shreve, a long-handled knife might be used.[23] The sharp edges were cut off; the leaves were split lengthwise down the center and put in the sun to dry. Kissell reports that when the weaving was to be done, the dried leaves were "buried in a hole in the ground, water poured over them, and then left in the damp earth through the night."[24] Later, Shreve says, the dried strips were "re-dampened by sprinkling with water and wrapping in a towel."[25]

Forms in plaiting were very limited. Two pieces, a headband and a back mat, were woven to be attached to the kiaha or burden basket, and a ring which supported pottery jars (or other burdens) either on the floor or on the head of a woman as she carried the piece or other objects. Then there were three baskets produced in the plaited weave: a strainer, a general purpose piece, and a medicine man's pouch (Fig. 6.20).

The two pieces made for the burden basket disappeared with the kiaha itself, for they were specialized for use with this form alone. On the other hand, the small bit of weaving in this technique, the basketry headring, continued to be made as long as women thought of no substitutes. Natively it was adapted to the shapes of pottery jars and baskets, both with rounded bases. The small twilled ring was placed on top of the head to support the burden. Kissell adds: "A woman so laden is a pretty sight as she steps along with easy gait and erect carriage, balancing, without the aid of her hands, the great weight upon her well-poised head, for it is this practice of transporting burdens upon the head which has given her that grace of bearing which well befits a queen."[26] I saw Papago women on the streets of Tucson carrying burdens on their heads in the late 1920s and early

a.

b.

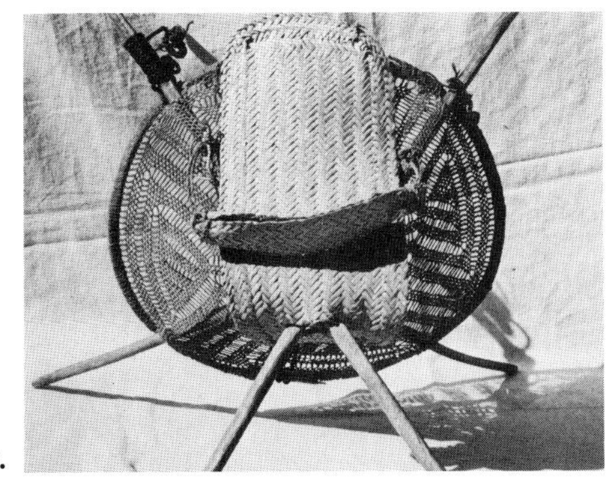

c.

1930s, the burden often consisting of pottery and basketry wrapped in a large cloth which they had brought into town to sell, and the "ring" by now a bundle of cloth tied into a circle.

Fig. 6.20. The two most commonly woven plaited baskets made by the Papago are (a) a round-topped, square-based bowl basket and (b) an elongate, rectangular pouch with a top or lid, used by the medicine man. The first piece is 10" in diameter, 4¾" high *(ASM E66)*, while the pouch is 18" long and about 5" wide *(ASM E2379A)*. (c) The protective back mat on the Papago burden basket was also plaited *(ASM)*.

The three types of plaited baskets noted above were produced in the twill weave. The pouch was lidded and rectangular, and was used by the medicine man for his treasures; the low circular bowl of more open weave served as a sifter;[27] and a piece comparable to the latter but deeper, square-based and round-rimmed, and often with a lid, served for general household use, mainly to hold various items such as trinkets, seeds, sewing articles, and so on. An over-three-under-three rhythm dominated in the making of these baskets, although some slight variation might occur, particularly in the beginning of the basket construction.

Two types of bases were common in starting either the strainer or the deeper form. In one, an over-three-under-three rhythm resulted in the creation of concentric squares on the base, while the second involved a combination of the same with an over-two-under-two alternation which produced a large cross on the bottom. A square turn into the wall characterized both of these baskets, and from there on the basket became circular or near-circular in form. Walls of both of these base types have horizontal, parallel bands of touching chevrons (or zigzags); sometimes the base with the cross may continue its pattern beyond the base so that vertical rather than horizontal rows may be featured part way up the wall.

One interesting basket presents certain differences as compared with the usual piece. In an over-two-under-two rhythm, four sets of seven elements each created diagonals in each quarter of the square base (see drawing). On the sides the patterning goes into the usual zigzags.

Rims of these baskets are of two types, a plain one and a slightly fancy type. In the first style, when the desired height is attained, one series of parallel weaving elements is bent to the outside and interplaited downward into the woven wall, then cut off, while the second series of elements is cut off at the basket rim. To make the second rim, the first step just described is given an extra "twist": instead of cutting off the elements after interplaiting them back into the wall, they are "turned diagonally toward the upper left and caught under the plaiting." This gives a slightly more finished appearance to the lower part of the rim; the resulting "collar" is about 1¾" to 2¼" deep.

The square bases of these baskets varied in size from a little over 4" to as much as almost 16" along each side. Heights ranged from 4½" to 7¾". One small basket, 4½" on each of its square-base sides and 4⅜" in rim diameter, had a lid which was 5" in diameter in its round base, 3¾" on each of its square-top sides, and 2½" deep.

The strainer of more open twilled weave continued to be used even after Shreve's report of 1943. When making their saguaro fruit wine, the Papago women preferred to use the basket in the straining process rather than a metal container. Basically this was because the liquid "tasted better"; obviously, a metal container might well react to the acid in the liquid and create a different flavor.

The long and narrow rectangular shape of plaited weave used as a container for the medicine man's equipment was woven in two parts, a base and a slightly larger lid. The latter dropped about two-thirds the way down over the container proper. Kissell reports that this basket was made by the wife or mother of the medicine man or by the medicine woman herself.[28] Shreve agrees that a relative makes this piece but adds that "today very few women plait so the medicine man will accept a basket from anyone who can make it satisfactorily,"[29] although he still preferred to have it woven by a relative. Seemingly, there was no ceremonial attachment to the weaving of the piece. In fact, some of the pieces have been produced to sell.

Medicine baskets vary in size; Kissell reports lengths from about 5⅛" to close to 33⅝" and widths from 2¾" to about 5⅞", and from 1⅝" to 8¼" for depths.[30] Shreve simply states that they are about 11¾" in length and about 4¾" wide and high, with a slightly larger top.[31] Of several examples observed, one had these measurements: for the botton, 10" long and 2½" wide, and the top 11½" long and 3" wide. This piece was made in an over-three-under-three rhythm and had vertical zigzags on its sidewalls. A second medicine basket was larger, the lower part measuring 18" by 5" and the lid 19¾" by 5½". Weave and design were like those in the first piece. Sometimes other designs are woven into both bottoms and lids of these baskets, several examples given by Kissell having "two or three squares placed side by side, each enclosing smaller graduated forms of the same shape."[32]

Medicine baskets were made to hold paraphernalia to be used in curing or in weather control. One observed medicine basket contained a dried-up piece of a plant and a simply carved figure of a snake. One reported by Kissell had a small "Apache effigy with head of wax and body of string and eagle feathers," some loose feathers, and a small skin bag for the effigy when it is not in use.[33] The contents of this bag would protect the Papagos from their enemies, the Apaches. A rain (medicine) basket which she describes contained "turkey feathers which, with proper chants, bring rain," three sticks which indicated the length of time the medicine man had practiced and which also caused rain and cured rheumatism, another stem with an attached buzzard feather, both connected with rain getting, extra feathers, a deer tail for curing headaches and fever, and "chicken hawk feathers, which, when all previous attempts to produce rain have failed, serve as a desperate call for rain for the village, and water and food for the children."[34] These are characteristic contents of medicine baskets, with, of course, quite a variety of additional materials in different baskets.

Shreve reports a few women making plaited baskets for sale in 1943. In their products, yucca was substituted for sotol; as was currently the practice in the coiled baskets, size was also decreased. One enterprising woman substituted green yucca in certain places to emphasize design in weave.[35] This seems to have been a short-lived trend, for plaited baskets as made by Papagos have disappeared.

PAPAGO LACE COILING

Although not a basket in certain aspects of its production, nonetheless the kiaha or "keeho" as referred to by the Papagos was used as a basket (Fig. 6.21). For unknown years it was produced by Pima and Papago Indians, serving both tribes as their chief and only burden basket. Apparently it disappeared from Pima use close to the turn of the century; forty years later it was no longer woven by the Papagos.

a.

b.

Fig. 6.21. Papago lace-coil burden basket or kiaha. Note the design in four parts. Originally pattern was emphasized by rubbing with red and blue colors. (a) Designs are concentric and diamondlike *(Bereneice Smith Collection)*; (b) a meandering line pattern *(private collection)*.

A delightful legend tells about the history of the presumed use of the kiaha. In the long ago, this burden basket moved about on its own three long spindly legs. One day a line of these lace pieces was helping the Papagos move from the desert to the mountains. The baskets were filled to the brim, but they moved along in light and happy manner. Coyote, who so frequently caused trouble, came along, sat on his haunches, and laughed and laughed. "What *are* you laughing at?" asked the baskets. "Oh—ha ha!—at you silly looking baskets, you with your long spider legs!" "Oh! oh!" said the baskets, "If that is the case, we will cease to carry burdens on our own! We won't walk again. The women must carry us on their backs from now on."[36] And with that they dumped their burdens on the desert floor, never again to carry them alone.

From then on the Papago women had to fill the baskets, get down on the ground and lift them onto their backs, holding them in place with a tump line and head strap. These women managed to carry rather considerable burdens in this manner (Fig. 6.22). As the horse and then wagons were acquired by them, and in time the automobile, the Papagos and Pimas gradually ceased to use the kiaha. Few were made after the early part of the nineteenth century, although Kissell reports that they were not uncommon in out-of-the-way villages when she did her research among these people in 1910–11.[37]

a. 

b. 

Fig. 6.22. (a) A baby sleeping contentedly in a kiaha, 1888 (*AHS #4799*). (b) Two women on the streets of Tucson with filled kiahas, 1900. (*Photo by W. L. Bowers, AHS #24808.*)

The kiaha was an all-purpose carrier. As Kissell says, in the "light but strong frame were carried fuel, food, and the materials for various manufactures" and "on top of any of these loads might be seen an infant strapped in its basket cradle."[38]

The agave used by the Papagos for the kiaha was gathered in the rainy season when the leaves are fleshy. They were originally worked at the spot where they grew in the mountains; later they were taken back to the village to be processed, often by boiling the leaves for a day. A group of women worked together. A large fire was built in a pit, allowed to burn down, and the coals were removed. The fleshy agave leaves were put in to roast all night. Skin and flesh could then be removed quite readily, leaving the long fine fibers. When washed and after several days in the sun, the fibers were ready for spinning the cordage out of which the kiaha was made. Kissell further describes this process, formerly done on the thigh, later on the leg just below the knee because of introduced clothing. Thus on her thigh or leg the spinner placed "two strands of fiber with her left hand, and with the palm of the right, rolls the two simultaneously away from her, thus giving them a hard twist. These two tightly twisted strands are released by slightly raising the hand, and then bringing it lightly toward her, thus uniting and twisting the two strands into a two-ply cord, by rolling in an opposite direction."[39]

In weaving the net for the kiaha proper, a technique was used which is referred to as knotless netting, coil-without-foundation, or lace coiling. The one mechanical aid used by Pimas and Papagos in this weaving was a wooden stick, or, after white man came, an umbrella rib with the end rubbed down to a point, and the eye in the piece preserved as in an upholsterer's needle; either is employed to push the cord through the loopings. "Seated on the ground in tailor fashion the Indian woman first makes a small fiber ring about seven centimeters (3/4") in diameter and holding this in her left hand she casts upon it the first row of loops. She loops a second row into the first row and a third into the second and so continues until a few inches of the work are completed; then, extending one foot, she slips over the big toe the beginning ring and in this position continues the looping, or lace coiling, until the kiaha is completed."[40] After several inches of the section of plain lace work are finished, the weaver starts her pattern, this accomplished by tighter and looser looping; she also used both plain and twisted looping.

After the net is completed, it is secured to a heavy, round or oval wooden ring of cat's-claw (*Acacia greggii*). Cordage was overcast around the ring and through the top loops of the net; agave was used earlier for this cord with which to fasten the net to the ring, and later horsehair was substituted. Four poles of saguaro (*Cereus giganteus*) ribs served as a frame to hold the net into a cone shape; these were secured to the net with either human or horsehair cordage. Where the four poles touch at the bottom of the cone, they are secured with hairs or fiber cordage, or, later, with old rags.

Heavy cordage ties the basket to the ends of a tump strap. This carrying strap, which is worn over the forehead, is twill plaited in a long narrow strip. It was made into a ring by interplaiting the ends; then, this was flattened into a double band about 2 3/4" wide and about 13 3/4" long. As it is done in an over-two-under-two weave, a simple pattern was produced, which looks like multiple rows of touching chevrons. A second band, the back mat, is attached to the carrying frame to protect the head and shoulders when the lace basket is on the woman's back. It is woven so that the two upper corners can be attached to the kiaha rim. Further, a hole is left near the lower end to accommodate two of the kiaha poles. Padding in the form of bark in earlier pieces, old rags later, was inserted between the mat and the crossing of the four poles, a spot which otherwise would have been uncomfortable to the basket carrier. This mat had rounded corners and averaged about 9" in width and about 23" to 27" in length. Woven in an over-three-under-three diagonal twill, this mat had a double edge which resulted from turning and interplaiting the elements back into the fabric. Designs included parallel bands of squares, or there were designs perpendicular to each other, or squares made up of smaller squares.

At the mouth, the kiaha varied in size. In a group of fourteen of these pieces, the dimensions were, for the largest, 29 1/2" by 26" and for the smallest, 9 1/2" by 8 1/4". The smallest pieces were probably made for children, as Russell indicates, "The young girls of 8 or 10 begin to use small kiahas made especially for them."[41]

Kissell points out certain differences between the Pima and the Papago kiaha. She says the Pima basket has a deeper, smaller, and more tapering cone, and that the design is simpler. The support poles, she says, show very slightly at the top and do not extend below the net at the bottom of the Pima piece while they show both above and below in the Papago kiaha. In fact, two of the poles at the bottom of the latter may extend almost 12" below their point of crossing. These, with a third loose pole which serves as a support, allow the kiaha to stand. The front poles, at the kiaha top, may extend almost 36" beyond the rim of the basket.[42] As the Pimas obtained kiahas from the Papagos after they ceased making them, these differences are significant in attempting to identify the works of the two tribes.

Designs in the kiaha are quite varied, despite the fact that they are usually in four repetitions of a single theme.[43] They run the gamut from simple to complex, but all appear most delicate, perhaps because of the lacy effect of the weave, plus the fact that they are basically line patterns and are carried in the more open portions of the weave. The design is woven into the piece, then emphasized by going over it in red and blue colors. Red was derived from a native clay, blue from the juice of the prickly pear, or indigo, or laundry blueing, the last three in order from earliest to latest.

All designs in the kiaha are banded, as the end of the central plain area forms the inner edge and the rim serves as the outer edge to create the band.[44] The manner of weaving would seem to indicate that the more open sections comprise design while the more solid portions represent background, this contrary to Kissell's suggestion. When putting color on the basket, it would seem that this was the weaver's notion, for she applied the reds and blues to the more open patterning.[45]

Within the banded scheme there were three secondary layouts; these methods of decorating are illustrated by the group of fourteen kiahas in the Arizona State Museum. One style consisted of a series of narrow or wide plain bands encircling the field of decoration, usually colored in alternating red and blue. Four-part arrangements can be divided into three substyles, namely, independent repeated units, continuous themes, and composite arrangements. Independent repeated units are sometimes static, but a choice of the main element in each unit may defeat this. An example would be an inward-folding fret in each unit which imparts a certain dynamism to the pattern. A second four-part layout, the continuous, was favored by the Papagos, perhaps for its more dynamic nature. One example is really a continuous band which twists itself into four closed frets in its wandering. The third four-part arrangement, the composite, combines the independent and four-times repeated element with an elaborate, meandering line. An all-over decoration of the band area seems not to have been so popular. In one instance, "The decorative area is completely covered with joined diamonds or almost-diamonds."[46] Seemingly there was a haphazard use of red and blue in this kiaha.

Design elements in kiahas are sometimes difficult to determine. However, the following can be more or less identified: diamonds and pentagons, lines, bands wide and narrow, frets open and closed, zigzags, a Maltese crosslike affair, stars, triangles, and rectangles. Then there are angular geometric figures which defy positive definition, usually created by meandering bands.

Withal, kiaha patterns are characterized by delicacy, by repetition, and by balance and rhythm (see Fig. 6.21). More of these designs are dynamic, with but few static ones. Regardless of secondary layout style, they are four-divisional.

Papago Indians have been most versatile in their production of basketry through the years. They have adapted to new materials, have changed vessel forms at the whims of the buying public, and have branched out in designing to suit their own tastes. Experimentation with techniques has resulted in delightfully new expressions such as the wheat stitch. Last along this line might be mentioned a very recent incident. A Papago woman browsing in a trader's shop saw a feathered Pomo basket. She returned several times to look at the piece, then one day came in proudly with a straight-walled Papago basket covered with delicately colored feathers woven into her yucca piece.[47]

BASKETRY OF THE PIMAS

When Breazeale wrote *The Pima and His Basket* in 1923, he was hopeful that this publication might aid in "stimulating interest in basketry and in the other fast-disappearing American arts."[48] Many of the baskets he wrote about were of fine weave and beautifully designed; to be sure, some of them were made before his visit to this tribe. In turn, before him, Russell wrote (at the turn of the century) that basket making was "practiced in nearly every Pima home."[49] Writing twenty years later, Breazeale says, "Probably not one woman out of ten knows how to weave a creditable basket."[50]

In 1935, it was written that Pima basketry was dying out. Baskets at that time were labeled "coarse and carrying little design," although the designs were along the lines of the past but much simplified. "When the present grandmothers are gone, there will be very few basketmakers surviving."[51] This situation was attributed largely to the fact that the weavers received so very little for their baskets, from $1.00 to $3.00 a piece. Breazeale quotes a Pima woman's thoughts: "Why should I labor for weeks upon a basket that may sell for two dollars, when I can make two dollars a day by picking cotton."[52] Cain, in 1962, noted that the Pimas were no longer using their own basketry, and writes that "The manufacture of a cheaper and cruder product . . . apparently has no appeal to the few Pima weavers still working." Further he states that this craft "almost inevitably will die out entirely within the next two decades unless something can be done to revive interest."[53]

And something has been done, for Pimas have been encouraged by traders to again produce baskets. Their products were, at the beginning of the 1980s, receiving just compensation, which will be one of the greatest incentives to the continuation of basket making within this tribe; also there is an increased interest on the part of the general public in basketry. These and other factors have come to bear upon the revival of Pima basketry. Its products are not yet as refined as was the work in the early part of the century and into the 1920s, but what is being done holds promise for a good future.

Pima basketry is somewhat like that of the old Papago style. So too is its history, except that the later chapters are quite different. For some reason the contacts that the Papagos had made were far more influential on the continuation of their basketry craft, while the lack of such probably encouraged the Pimas to let theirs slide. Undoubtedly the economic situation had something to do with all of this. For some reason, the Papagos had good contacts for selling their baskets, the Pimas did not; as both tribes substituted white man's pots and pans for their own baskets, it was sell them or not make them. This trend did not develop overnight, but in time not selling plus low prices for a fine product were accountable for the near-death of the Pima craft, and selling of a cheaper and more rapidly produced piece meant continued development of baskets by the Papagos. Further, the American fad in the 1970s for Indian crafts played a large part in the revival of Pima basketry.

In the overall picture Pima baskets have not been as varied in shape, design, or in materials of manufacture as have the Papagos'. Their utility shapes were trays, bowls, jars, and to these they added a few miscellaneous forms. Trays adhered to a basically graceful form, both deep and shallow, while bowls were deep and large for wine, smaller for other purposes. Jars ranged from the large storage types of earlier years to smaller sizes for trinkets. And, of course, there were miniatures of all three forms. Among miscellaneous forms that were not too abundantly made were cups, plaques, wastebaskets (these very popular for a short while), footed pieces, and several others.

Design Layouts

Design layouts in Pima basketry were rather limited, for quite generally pattern was related in trays to the center black circle in one way or another. An analysis made on fifty-six baskets in the original Breazeale collection revealed these: divided (largely banded), undivided (centered, all-over), and composite styles. Frequently an all-over layout resulted on trays when the design was definitely attached to the black circle and extended to the rim. The all-over style might be heavily or more sparsely expressed, utilizing lighter lines or darker elements emanating from the center theme, either in a balanced combination of lighter and more solid elements, or with one or the other dominant. Banded layouts sometimes involved the use of one or several bands between the black central circle and the rim. Actually, this might be called a composite layout, with a centered motif and bands; however, when the center circle is minimized, the bands become more prominent. In like manner, organizational bands occur between the black circle and rim; in like manner, too, this band may overshadow the central circle.

Sometimes the black circle becomes an overpowering centered motif, with diminished, repeated themes between it and the rim or attached to the rim. Or there may be "attachments" to the center circle such as heavy, continuous themes; a good example is the squash-blossom pattern, a beautifully synchronized design.

The above schemes are, of course, related to trays. On jars, and very deep forms, vertical or horizontal bands, organizational or regular, were common. Most frequently the pattern continued into the neck but occasionally there were separate neck-body bands on jars. One all-over wide band or several separate bands may be used. Several trays illustrated in Breazeale's collection also have banded patterns with no black centers; this trend is definitely later, as is the centered layout in a tray—for example, a large bird.

Materials

A fair variety of materials was employed by the Pima Indians in the production of their basketry, as indicated at the beginning of this chapter and as summarized here. For plaiting, river cane was used in early years, but from the first decade of the 1900s on they substituted Papago mats made of agave leaves because the cane no longer grew in this area. Russell says that the Pima used maguey fiber for the cordage for their burden baskets, and that saguaro sticks provided the heavy ribs which supported the lace-like body of this basket, as with the Papagos. In close coiling, some choice was possible, but willow was most commonly used for sewing, with less cottonwood employed. A little red appears in some earlier pieces, this is either mountain mahogany or manzanita. Foundations for this weave were usually of cattail stems, according to Russell.[54] Incidentally, the foundation bundle was flattened somewhat by the weaver, the resultant flat coil distinguishing the Pima from Apache and other baskets with a round coil. Coarse coiling employed a wheat-straw base as a rule, or sometimes arrowbush with open sewing done in the bark of the mesquite or, less frequently, the bark of other trees. A very crude "bird's nest" granary basket was produced in a single material, the stems (with leaves) of the arrowbush or arrowweed.

Technique

Techniques of making Pima baskets need not be discussed further inasmuch as there is little variation from Papago styles previously presented except in quality. Regular coil was far better developed by Pimas, resulting in the thinner walled and more flexible pieces; plaiting was comparable; and little or no difference occurred in the basic technology of lace coiling. Pima weavers did not branch out as did the Papagos in finer open and split stitch, nor did they develop the wheat stitch.

Coiled

Pimas produced some of the most beautiful close-coiled baskets in the Southwest. Certainly some of their vessel forms were the most graceful of any, this quality particularly to be noted in the delicate lines of many a tray. Add to this the fine sewing and thin lines, dynamic patterning so characteristic of many pieces, and there, indeed, is a work of art.

Close-coiled baskets were more limited in shapes than were those of the later Papago, undoubtedly because of the lack of the influence of the white man. This influence was so limited at times among the Pimas that it is hardly discernible; in fact, there is a greater evidence of Apache contact reflected in Pima baskets. For example, some volute or whirlwind motifs in trays and an all-over network on occasional bowls are very Apache-like. Of course, there was some intermarriage between the two tribes, and so it was inevitable that there would be exchange of ideas. This is rather like some of the Papago baskets on the extreme northern part of the Reservation where a strong Pima feeling appears in designs; or, for that matter, wherever there was intermarriage, regardless of location on the Reservation, the same is true. However, the Pima influence seems to have been stronger on the Papago basket weaver than the other way around. Perhaps this is partly because the Pima stopped making baskets when they ceased to use them; hence, few influences came from other tribes, and few "tourist" shapes and designs were developed. Further, when a group had such refined designs as did the Pimas and these adapted to specific forms, they could hardly be interested in the far less artistic work developed by the Papago. Thus, it is not surprising to find that trays, bowls, and jars are the dominant forms (Fig. 6.23). There are a few deep forms which could be interpreted as very deep bowls; some are wastebaskets. Russell claims that the latter form was recent and that "Nearly all the Pima baskets made during the winter of 1901–2 were of these shapes." He adds: "A notable feature of the ornament is the introduction of badly executed human figures." Thus, Russell pinpoints the introduction of both the wastebasket shape and certain life forms among the Pimas, both for white consumption.[55]

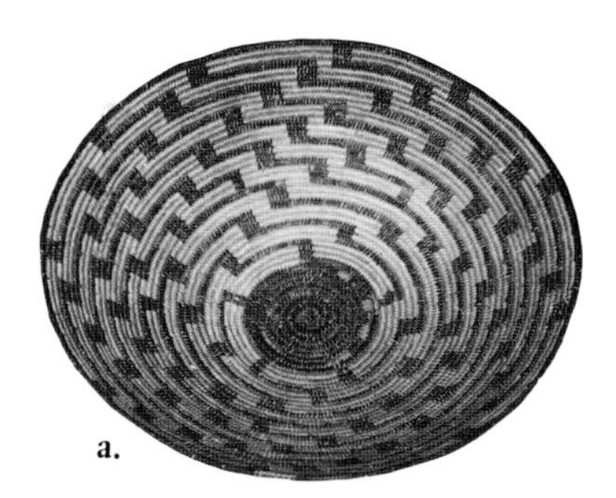

a.

Fig. 6.23. Pima basketry forms. (a) Tray *(ASM 700)*. (b) Jar *(private collection)*. (c) Bowl, with row of dancing men, with feathers (?) in their hair *(private collection)*. (d) A storage basket, with open stitching *(ASM 5317)*.

c.

d.

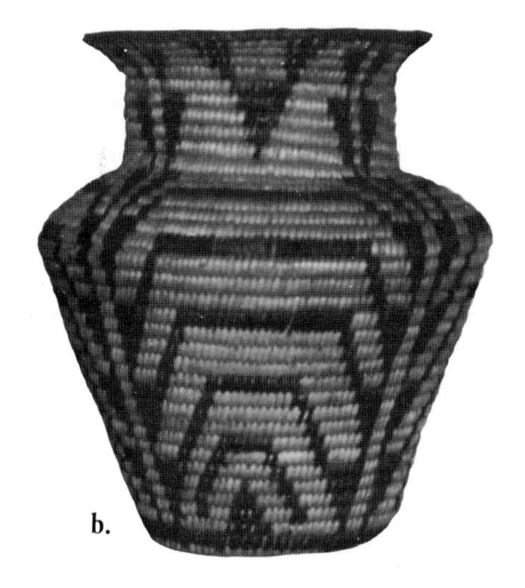

b.

Jars. Jars are illustrated by Russell in a number of plates. As these represent an early selection, some of their variations in forms will be given, all supported by pieces observed. A short neck, usually rounded body, and a flat base present a dominant style. The neck is usually straight, although in a few baskets it flares out at the lip; it may be wider or narrower, or, as in two examples, very narrow. Shoulder lines may be gently sloping, with a continuation of this line to the widest diameter which is high on the vessel, then an equally gentle turn and slope onto the base. In a few examples there is an abrupt shoulder which produces a very high widest diameter. Only one example has the widest diameter just below the center. Almost all body lines on jars are pleasing, with several straight-lined from high shoulder to flat base, and a few with a gentle curve from rim to base.[56]

A few additional variations in this form of later times may be mentioned. One is a very squat jar with a very low neck almost depressed into the shoulder. A second has almost no neck at all but does exhibit the usual graceful form with high shoulder and gentle body slope. A third is wider-mouthed than any illustrated in Russell; another is comparable to many in Russell except that it is much fuller-bodied. One jar is hourglass in form.

As to thread and stitch counts in jars, no mention of such matters is made by Russell, Kissell, or Breazeale. However, a later study was made of eighty-one baskets of the Breazeale collection by this writer; there were only two jars, thus stitch counts of five to ten and coils two to the inch do no more than indicate the general situation. Other jars from miscellaneous collections will indicate more realistically how these counts run. In one squat-shouldered piece, with 7″ rim, 13¾″ shoulder, and 8½″ height, the stitch count was six, the coil count four per inch. A high-shouldered piece, 10½″ tall and 7½″ at the rim, counted higher: ten stitches and a little over four coils, while a second of the same shape measures 5″ tall, has eleven stitches and three coils, and a third jar of this shape and 8½″ tall counted fourteen stitches and three coils to the inch. An average of these larger pieces gives ten stitches and four coils to the inch.

Smaller pieces, of course, often run higher; one piece 6″ in both height and shoulder diameter counted sixteen stitches and seven coils to the inch.

Designs are quite varied on jar walls but not so on bases. Some bottoms are plain, some are very simply decorated. One of the latter has nothing more than two black coils spaced out, one close to the turn. One has radiate, whirling lines emanating from a small black center, another has a small black circle in the center and four coyote tracks beyond it. All in all, bottom designs on Pima jars tend to be insignificant.

Wall designs on jars are much more elaborate; many tend to four vertical divisions, while others are six divisional (Fig. 6.24). Some have horizontal bands, for example, three of them; or on another jar, three on the body and a fourth on the neck. Many are all-over as far as the entire wall is concerned. There are a few other variations. Basket jars in the Russell reference[57] show the following: one almost straight-sided jar has all-over, parallel, horizontal zigzags made of blocks. Several have all-over netting, one plain, but the second with figures of men and/or coyote tracks within the net effect. Rather simple but effective are diagonal, encircling stepped blocks on a sharp-shouldered jar; on a second and more gently curving form is the same diagonal arrangement of paired coyote tracks enclosed in squares, with similarly arranged single coyote tracks. Two rows of joined interlocked line frets decorate the fairly straight wall of another vessel. Quite ornate is the vertical arrangement of stacked plantlike themes in multiple and joined rows on the entire wall and neck of a high-shouldered jar. Frets vertically or horizontally arranged, diamonds continuous or broken, horizontal bands of checks or coyote tracks, triangles, horses and humans in vertical or horizontal rows—these are other motifs which decorate jars.

a.

b.

c.

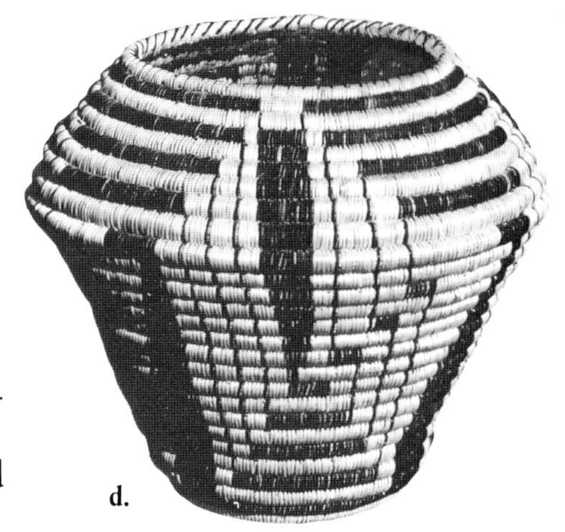

d.

Fig. 6.24. Examples of Pima jar baskets. (a) An old piece, as indicated in its form and design *(LA 7389)*. (b) Two old baskets, again as shape indicates *(ASM E302, 8036)*. (c) A wide and high-shouldered example *(ASM E3026)*. (d) Interestingly, this high-shouldered basket jar was made about 1975, and, although design is mindful of earlier styles, it is applied in a modern way *(Gallup Ceremonials, 1975)*.

A few comments may be made about jars in general. In one small selection the design went to the rim in all cases; this tends to be true in most Pima jars whether the neck is long or short. Layout styles in this collection included: dynamic, continuous, diagonal, repeated; quite static, isolated double-banded; and integrated all-over, simple to complex and usually dynamic. All of these are represented on other jars, some of them more complex, such as a triple-banded style. Also there can be added an all-over spotted or repeated style, with geometrics or life forms used. Black rims were often braided or so closely overcast that there was almost always a definite enclosing line at the rim. Rarely, blue trade beads appear on jar edges (Fig. 6.25).

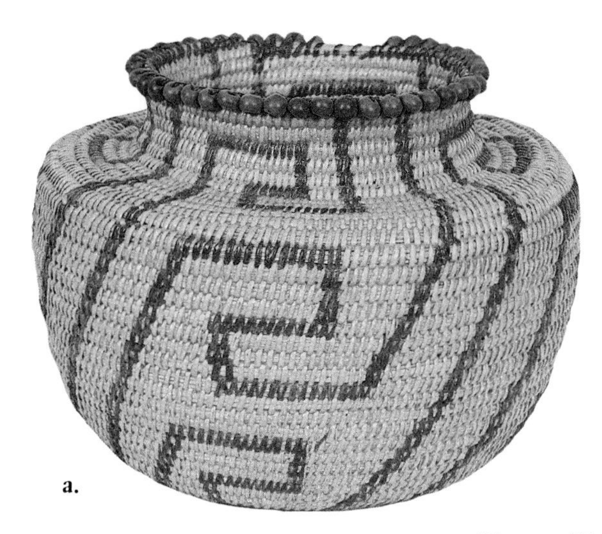
a.

b.

Fig. 6.25. (a) Old coiled jar, Pima made. The black woven meander design was balanced by the same in red painted on the finished piece. Large blue commercial beads decorate the rim *(ASM E562)*. (b) Another Pima jar ornamented with small blue beads at the rim, at and near the sharp shoulder, and on the shoulders of men in the lower row *(Rex Arrowsmith, Santa Fe)*.

Trays. Trays are undoubtedly the most common form of basket produced by the Pima Indians. In earlier years, they were more varied in size, shape, and decoration than any other form of basket. Of course, there is good reason for this because in the days of its use by the Pima Indians no form served as many purposes as did the tray. Kissell's four different trays illustrate variations from a gently curved rim-to-base style to a shallow cone with almost straight sides from rim to pointed base. In between is a tray with a rounded lower two-thirds and more of an outflare toward the rim, and a fourth tray is deeper, with an almost-recurve in the upper wall.

Russell illustrates all of his trays by a top view, thereby revealing nothing of their shape. In his text all are classified as bowls, including forms from "a perfectly flat disk to a bowl with rounded bottom having a depth of 20 cm." (7⅞").[58] Breazeale's method is much the same, although he does have several photographs of trays in profile; also some of his shots into trays are more revealing of both deeper and shallower forms or even some with wider and almost flat bases. The Pima tray form can be contrasted with the Papago in many ways. The latter stressed the perpendicular, and had wider, flatter bottoms. Only occasionally is there a flat-bottomed Pima tray, and even then this feature tends to be smaller than any of the flat bases of Papago baskets.

From numerous collections of Pima baskets, including Breazeale's, it can be reiterated that there was variety in tray forms. In a miscellaneous group of 102 baskets, these features relative to form can be noted. In diameters they ranged from 7" to 23" and in depth 1" to 10"; quite consistently, there were shallower depths for narrower diameters. Most of the baskets under 12" rim to rim were 3" or less in depth; from 12" to 15" some are as much as 4¾" deep, and in baskets over 15" in diameter the majority are between 4" and 6" with a sprinkling of lesser depths. In this selection there were cone-shaped trays, both shallow and deep; one was very deep, with a diameter of slightly over 20" and a depth of 10" and with very straight sides down to the pointed bottom. There were deep trays with rounded bottoms and with fairly straight or gently curving walls. The same characteristics are also to be noted in shallower trays. Some are bell-shaped. Several were flat-bottomed; one, in fact, was straight-sided, 2¼" deep, flat-bottomed, and 12½" in diameter; others have flat bottoms but more curved walls or very gently sloping walls. All in all, there was emphasis on grace in form.

Beginnings of Pima trays were of two sorts, one a simple coil, the second a small plaited square. In the first, a small section of foundation was wrapped, bent upon itself, then stitching into this began. In the second start a plaited knot was made, the elements involved were bent to the left to make the foundation, and sewing was started. Basically, rims were also of two types, either closely overcast or braided, and, characteristically, they were all black. Most of the braiding was very neatly done; overcasting was predominately vertical or almost vertical and touching, and usually quite fine. In the 102 baskets summarized, sixty-eight had overcast rims, twenty-seven were braided, and only seven were in regular stitching. So frequently the rim finish is indicative of the general quality of the basket; surely this is true of the Pima tray.

Generally, Pima sewing was quite carefully executed, the weaver being "very exact in this placing of the binding element, giving their baskets a more rigid surface, while the Papago are less particular, producing a rougher, less even surface."[59] It can be noted, too, that Pima coils are flattish but never as flat as the pounded Papago work in yucca. Stitching is quite consistently good throughout the tray, although the stitch count is not as high as might be expected. Of the 102 baskets, twenty-eight had a stitch count of eleven, sixteen had a count of twelve, and eleven counted thirteen stitches to the inch. On the lower side they dropped to seven examples with a count of ten, while as stitch count increased above thirteen, there was a heavy drop of examples, with five pieces counting fifteen stitches, four each counting fourteen and sixteen and not over three trays in any count above the last. The greatest clustering of coil counts was in the four, five, and six per inch groups, these with twenty-eight, twenty-three, and twenty-two, examples, respectively. Higher coil counts had drastically reduced representations.

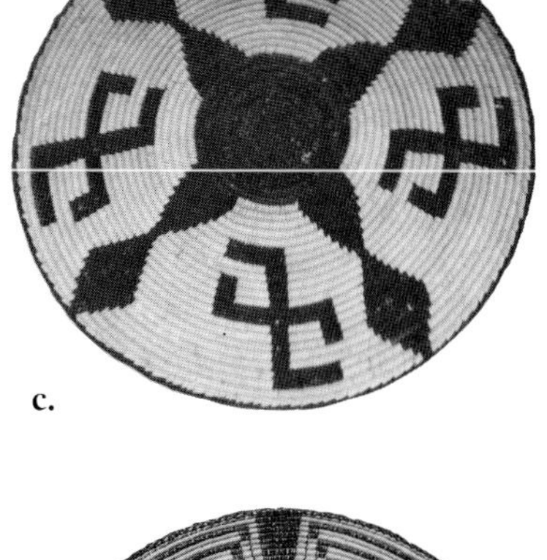

c.

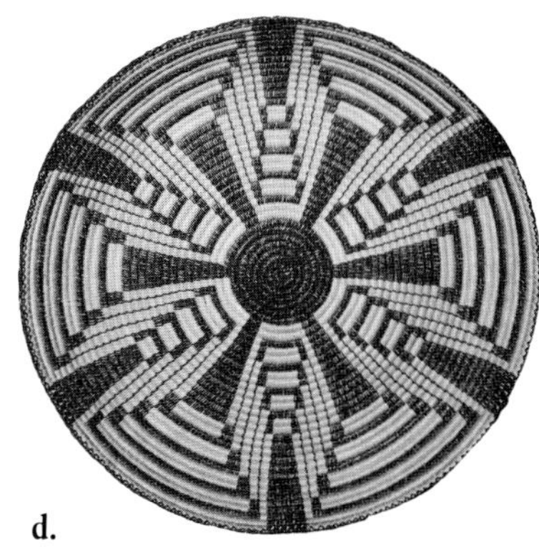

d.

a.

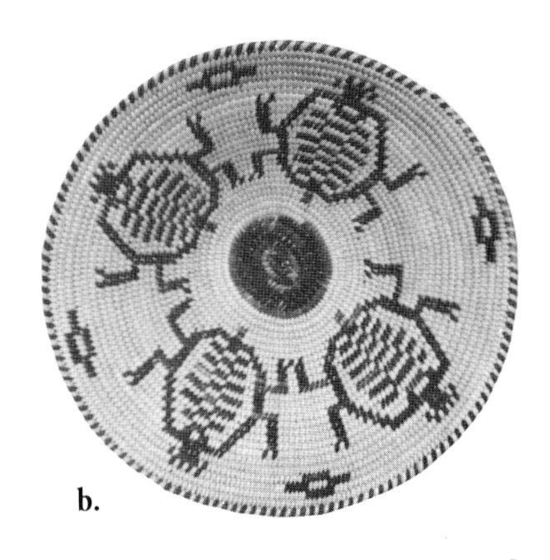

b.

e.

Fig. 6.26. Older Pima coiled trays which show some variety of design: (a) a very large black center with a banded, double meander *(ASM 670)*; (b) four delightful bugs *(ASM E330)*; (c) a floral center with "mixed up" swastikas between *(ASM E2098)*; (d) a beautifully woven squash blossom of six perfect petals *(ASM 19448)*; (e) another dynamic style that frequently characterize Pima patterning *(private collection)*.

Designs in Pima trays were indeed varied and outstanding (Fig. 6.26). The fine work which was being produced at the turn of the century continued into the 1920s but declined in succeeding decades. It was not until the 1960s that any appreciable revival of weaving took place among the Pimas and even this was on a relatively small scale. Some of this late work is outstanding, some is mediocre.

Russell illustrates typical Pima tray designs[60]; so well established were they at this time that the same general styles are again illustrated by Breazeale in 1923, with, of course, some new additions, and very little is added in ensuing years. A brief analysis of Russell's illustrations plus other baskets will be given to establish the basic Pima tray designs.

Some of the simplest of these patterns involve fairly large black central circles with line or line and square units separate from this. Lines alone usually created double frets; occasionally lines meander without actually making frets. There are both simple and complex line arrangements. Comparable lines or lines and squares were also used to create turtle shell patterns, alone or in combination with other motifs. Kissell implies in a comment that Pimas did not have negative patterns, for she says, "... light pattern on a black ground as only with the Papago."[61] Yet, among others, in one of the Russell pieces, turtle shell patterns have central negative coyote tracks. As a matter of fact, Kissell illustrates a Pima piece with all-over rectangles, each with a negative coyote track in it.[62]

Only one good squash-blossom pattern (but there are others elsewhere) is illustrated by Russell in trays; it has four petals and is beautifully presented. Relatively simple but effective is a floral theme done in concentric outlines and with the petals separated by four vertical, close-set double rows of triangles. Among the most dynamic of patterns illustrated by Russell are motifs taking off a black center and moving up left from here to the rim. Different motifs include wide and close-set steps made of lines, or joined stepped squares filled with negative coyote tracks, or larger touching squares in paired lines joined by horizontal lines. The last moves up to the right, an uncommon direction for Pima basketry motion. These are often called whirlwind motifs.

The most common design illustrated by Russell involves a black center circle from which three, four, or five elongate triangles take off, and from their tips evolve simpler line themes or more elaborate line-swastikas or other motifs. Sometimes a broad line, long or short, or some other geometric replaces the triangle, but all continue into some kind of elaborate theme. In a few instances the triangles serve as motifs about which concentric parallel lines circulate, sometimes creating flowerlike designs.

Most of the line work in all of these baskets illustrated by Russell tends to be light, made of one coil if on the horizontal, or of limited stitches if vertical or diagonal. This is one of the features which distinguishes Pima basketry from that of the Papagos. The latter would be more apt to use two coils for horizontals and more stitches for vertical and diagonal lines. Too, the center circle is usually larger in the Papago willow tray. To be sure, there are exceptions to these rules; in fact, Russell pictures one piece with two-coil horizontal lines and a very simple design. Basically, Kissell's illustrations support these details, with simpler and heavier Papago designs standing out in contrast to the more delicate Pima patterns. Some of the Pima baskets in her selection are even more dynamic and detailed than the ones in Russell's book.

Again, in the Breazeale collection are illustrated essentially the same general styles of tray decoration. There are plain, double, and interlocked frets; there are squash blossoms with three, four, and five petals, some complex, some less so; there are turtle shells with four or five "shells" in bands. There are floral motifs, some created by making horizontal lines of different lengths as described above. Swirling patterns of whirlwinds are, if possible, even more dynamic than in earlier years. Life forms also became a part of later baskets, as illustrated by Breazeale. Limited portrayals are illustrated by him of rattlesnakes, Gila monsters, eagle, horse, man, and several plants, including devil's-claw as well as saguaros and ocotillos with these plants.

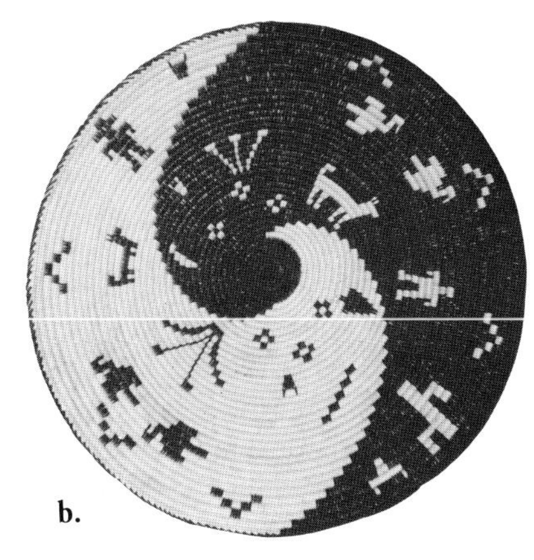

Fig. 6.27. Pima tray designs of later years. (a) A 1948 piece, a beautifully woven squash-blossom pattern *(ASM E540)*. (b) Quite unusual is this basket combining positive and negative small designs *(O'odham Tash, 1983)*.

The Pima woman was a master of line creation in basketry. Double rows of simple meandering lines cross in such a way as to bring into being swastikas, while in other instances single lines meander so as to form open boxes, larger toward the center, smaller near the rim. It is truly remarkable how these weavers could envision the finished product so as to be able to create the complicated intertwinings of the design as they went along. These line patterns demonstrate this ability as much as any pattern done by the Pima basket makers. Amazing, too, is the fact that so many of these line patterns, like other Pima designs, turn out so true, so completely well balanced (Fig. 6.27).

One piece illustrated by Breazeale is titled "The Spider and the Fly." It has a white center, a circle with broad black "spokes," a white circle, then five more joined circles each with narrow dividers which are suggestive of the web. The fly is caught between and within the last three "webs" and the spider is outside the web on the opposite side. Both spider and fly are strange little black creatures and both have big white eyes.[63]

Many of the fine designs and some of the quality craftsmanship continued for years after Breazeale's studies in the very early 1920s. However, quantity seems to have diminished. Robinson pictures a Pima woman with a beautiful tray basket with a thirteen-petaled, squash-blossom pattern woven into it.[64] It took her three months to weave. He also pictures a group of very fine trays woven in the same tradition as this one and numbering from eight to twelve petals. In fact, they are so "look alike" that they may well have been woven by the same woman. The baskets illustrated here are almost perfect in spacing and symmetry of forms, features so common to much Pima basketry.

The design in a basket pictured by Robinson is termed an original pattern or "an original design representing a dream"; this pattern is woven into two shallow tray baskets.[65] In both examples, the designs still involve elements and units familiar to the Pima weaver but they are put together in totally different ways. Robinson notes the "wholly intentional lack of balance in the design in one," which is very contrary to most Pima work. The second piece is much more symmetrical but does have one small unit of design which looks like an afterthought. Too, the total pattern is not quite as even and regular as is common in Pima baskets. In 1935, an article in *Indians At Work* refers to such patterning as "dream support" designs. A story is related in this article about a woman who started a basket, but no design seemed suitable. She laid the piece aside, lay down, and while asleep "saw a new design applied to one of the supports of the arbour. When she awoke she drew the design which she had dreamed." A second element of interest here is the drawing of the pattern, something not done by native southwestern basket weavers. In this article it is also noted that the "same motifs as of long ago" were still used but "only the simplified versions are made now."[66]

From a study of more recent pieces of Pima weaving the following comments can be made. There is a tendency toward greater simplicity of pattern. For example, in a thin-walled basket, there is a black center plus seven pairs of ladders with four "rungs" on each ladder. This is an old design. Another, by the same weaver, has a black center and beyond it an outlined starlike design made with squared-off tips. A third by this weaver shows the popular old swastika design but in a very simple form. Four of these motifs take off a black center and are no more than a simple single swastika without benefit of any of the complexities found in so many of the older pieces.

A Pima basket made in 1973 is also mindful of the more complex older pieces. Off the black center is a four-petaled flower, with swastikas taking off petal tips, and with tips of swastikas terminating in stepped triangles. Despite its more elaborate nature the design in this piece has a much lighter feeling than in the older examples. A 1975 basket which is also more reflective of the older styles is ornamented with a nine-point squash-blossom design; delicacy of pattern is to be noted in the single-stitch black verticals. The weave in this piece is excellent, averaging seventeen stitches to the inch. Another squash blossom, of eleven points, has a large black center; again the weave is most delicate, with a stitch count of sixteen per inch. This 1975 piece is large, measuring 19½″ in diameter but only 3½″ in depth.

A group of eight small Pima trays made early in 1975 reveals several traits which are mindful of the past in the weaving of this tribe. All have black rims, some braided. Stitch and coil counts are high. Designs include the maze, frets and meanders, star, butterfly, and squash blossom. A small piece (5½″ diameter) exhibited at the 1975 Gallup Ceremonials (made within the year) had a stitch count of twenty-five and a coil count of nine to the inch. It was ornamented with a five-point squash blossom. Another very shallow piece woven in 1975 measured 23⅞″ in diameter, averaged sixteen stitches and four coils to the inch, and had a most even design woven into it. The main motif of the pattern was a bug: there were four of them in the inner row, eight in the middle row, and sixteen of them in the outer row. A 1973 basket was 14″ in diameter and had a black center and eighteen stepped patterns from this to the rim. The steps were made up of thin vertical and horizontal lines with squares in alternate turns of the steps. The rim was overcast in black. Last to be mentioned is a basket which took the Grand Award in this craft at the 1976 Gallup Ceremonials. It was a shallow tray 16½″ in diameter and 2½″ deep. Stitches averaged sixteen and coils four to the inch, making the walls of the basket thin and flexible. A nine-petaled squash blossom decorated this piece; particularly appealing were the long and delicately slender blossoms and the triangles between them.

Perhaps several of the reasons for some of the fine Pima work of recent years (despite smaller quantities) would be trader interest and interest on the part of some organized groups through the years. As early as 1935 some revival of interest came through 4-H groups. Guildlike organizations have been ventured several times and have been influential in the revival of old basketry styles and in the maintenance of higher standards of weaving. During the mid and late 1970s several traders in Casa Grande, Arizona, were very influential in both the increase in quantity and the higher development of quality in Pima coiled weaving, particularly trays. So too was the Gila River Indian Arts and Crafts Center.

Bowls. Bowls are by no means as numerous as trays among the Pimas but quite a few were woven. In one selection of eighteen bowl baskets, the general range of size is representative: from 6½" to 18¾" in diameter and from 1" to 6½" in height. Older bowls tended to be larger in size, for they were woven primarily for use purposes. There is a fairly even distribution of sizes in the above selection, that is, with no clustering around limited dimensions.

Shapes vary from less attractive sharp- and straight-walled pieces to the graceful round-walled wine bowl. Kissell says that Pima bowls are deeper than those woven by the Papagos. Russell illustrates flat-bottomed, outflaring but straight-walled bowls of varying depths and several similar but less severe forms. Kissell shows the wine-bowl style, with a gentle curve from rim to center base and back to rim, and, of course, these are quite deep. Other bowls may be more conical in shape, deep and graceful, or curved-sided but flat-bottomed, or oval, or rarely with a slight outward curving near the rim. In general the more graceful forms, such as the wine bowl, were made for native use.

In a group of forty Pima bowl baskets, there was an interesting range in stitch and coil counts. Stitches ranged from four to twenty-seven per inch and coils from three to twelve per inch. There is clustering of stitches, with sixteen of the baskets numbering from nine to eleven in this group, and for coils, eighteen of the baskets numbered four to five.

Despite the fact that bowls are fewer in number, their designs present quite a variety (Fig. 6.28). Some of the very earliest patterns, recorded and illustrated in Bartlett, are combinations of vertical and horizontal lines, all joined.[67] A few bowls in Russell include patterns of simple paired zigzag lines, vertically placed, or opposed line frets, or diagonal stepped lines, or other simple geometrics; one is of the favored triangle-line-swastika combination, more complex than most bowl designs. In Kissell the wine baskets have fairly elaborate patterns. Two have medium black centers; from this, in one, emanate double and diagonal rows of blocks to the rim; they are joined by horizontal lines.

Several of the bowls pictured by Breazeale have unusual as well as typical Pima patterns. One has an all-over fret on the wall with an outlined diamond in each area created by the fret. Another has a black center surrounded by line patterns to the rim. This design is

Fig. 6.28. Like the Papagos, the Pimas made some bowls. (a) Most important was the large wine bowl, here simply decorated with encircling negative lines *(AHS)*. (b) A second old wine basket *(private collection)*. (c) Another old piece, oval in form, and decorated with men and horses *(AHS)*. (d) A much later piece with simple geometric decoration *(AHS)*. (e) Two small trays which reflect the popularity of life forms—a short Gila monster and a man *(ASM E321, E2260)*.

mindful of the Bartlett patterns in its use of horizontal and diagonal lines, some of the latter with triangles along their edges. Quite unusual is a fairly deep and straight-sided bowl with elongate black triangles pendant from the rim and the same but smaller ones coming up from the base. Between are two zigzags outlining the two sets of triangles. A low bowl with sloping straight sides is decorated with a deep meander one coil below the rim and one above the base; in each of the four spaces created by this meander is an outline Latin cross. One shallow bowl in a private collection and dated between 1908 and 1918 exhibits some of the early Pima life forms. In the center is a turtle surrounded by four coyote tracks, while on the wall of the piece are creatures whose short tails and horns would suggest young deer. Among other bowl patterns are squash blossoms, flowers, hourglass figures, women, and diamonds.

Several oval bowls woven by Pima women would indicate that both regular and unusual motifs were used for decoration on them. One such piece has six figures of women with what appear to be buckets, a rather different subject to say the least. A popular element but here used in a rather unusual manner is the triangle: in a bowl 11⅞″ by 8¾″ and 3″ deep there appear on the sidewalls twenty-two opposed and alternate triangles, while on the bottom of the piece were groups of white coils alternating with units of two black coils.

Miscellaneous Forms. Pima basket weavers did not do a great deal in the area of miscellaneous pieces except for occasional objects. To be sure, in pre-1900 years they produced a variety of storage jars, plaited pieces, and the kiaha. Then about the turn of the century, they made a fair quantity of miniatures. Although Russell cites no dimensions, he does refer, as noted above, to some large pieces such as wastebaskets, saying that they "are recent."[68] Again he decries the influence of traders who urged the use of life forms on these and other baskets; several that he pictures have horses or humans on them. One very small but deep basket with straight sides and flat bottom has several Gila monsters woven on its sides, all outlined above with an almost wavy line. Most of the wastebaskets he illustrates have geometric designs on them, several of them most attractive in their basically simple patterns; one has attractive multiple rows of wide-spaced and alternating single figures, a square with delicate line projections at each corner. Large, negative coyote tracks placed on the diagonal and joined by a fine line ornament another piece.

The Pimas' penchant for diagonal patterning on these large baskets resulted in an interesting arrangement of joined diagonal rows of paired lines with stepped triangles along them separating pairs of men, the top fellow upside down and the lower one right side up, and both with upraised hands. The straight-line wall of these baskets is usually drawn inward a little from wide rim to a slightly smaller base.

Seemingly, wastebaskets were never again as popular as implied by Russell. Kissell does not illustrate any such form for either Pimas or Papagos. They do appear later in museum and private collections in limited numbers: no doubt some of these were from the peak production years, 1901–02, as implied by Russell. Cain illustrates two baskets which are definitely wastebaskets[69] and a third which may be one.[70] The first has wider proportions and is decorated with fret and triangle elements; the second has an all-over heavy, netlike pattern made of large squares and rectangles. Because of its much smaller base, the third piece is noted as "maybe" a wastebasket. It is ornamented with four large H-like figures, solid black with light outlines.

One of the most interesting decorations which reputedly appears fairly often on Pima baskets is to be noted on a wastebasket form, a two-humped camel. The piece is small, 5" tall and 6" in rim diameter. The two-humped creature takes up the major part of a sidewall, while on the opposite side is a smaller one-humped camel plus a strange, tiny flat-backed animal near the rim. The story goes that one of the camels brought into northern Arizona many years ago wandered into Pima territory. Tom Bahti said that he had seen a number of Pima baskets decorated with a single-hump camel.[71] Perhaps this two-humped creature represents a bit of artistic license! Or was it seen in a circus? Or a picture? The fine example of a Papago yucca basket jar decorated with a lively two-humped camel (see Fig. 6.10) can serve for comparison with this animal's more common appearance on Pima pieces.

Deep wastebasket forms in the Arizona State Museum vary greatly in size, from 2½" to 19" in diameter and from 1" to 9½" deep. They have plain bottoms, or bottoms decorated with a small black center circle, or this circle with an added ring or two or with some other simple geometric pattern. Wall patterns include both life motifs and geometrics, and these may be dynamic or static (Fig. 6.29). Generally the designs tend to be simple, although a few are more complex. Repeated elements are common.

Russell refers to a "flat disc" as one of the other shapes which are "old style."[72] It is difficult to believe that this was one of the older forms; more likely, it was introduced about the time of the wastebasket. As Shreve said of the Papago, when baskets were made "for sale," they changed shapes, including the introduction of the "hot pads" or flat plaques.[73] This is a more likely situation among the Pimas, also.

Fig. 6.29. Pima coiled wastebaskets, some featuring diagonal geometric patterning and one with men, horses, saddle, and spurs. Shape varies a little: (a) tall (13¾″) and slender; (b) a little plump and 12″ high; (c) only 8½″ high, with a rim diameter of 12½″; (d) 11½″ high, with a rim diameter of 12½″. Two more deep forms: (e) this piece is decorated with great lizards and small men; (f) decoration here consists of diagonal geometrics *(ASM 13919, 19274, E3061, 13931, E3046,* and *E314).*

As might be expected, a flat plaque pictured by Breazeale has a simple maze pattern, or, as he labeled it, "the labyrinth." Breazeale says that no one knows how the maze came to the Pimas, but adds that "a few years ago the design was found scratched upon the adobe wall of one of the inside rooms of the ruins of Casa Grande."[74] He goes on to say that he has seen no use of the maze on older baskets, and that he could learn nothing from the Indians themselves about this design. However, they refer to it, he says, as "Montezuma's House"; this term supposedly was used by the Indian to refer to ancient buildings, such as "Casa Grande." Conceivably, then, this could be the origin of the maze in basketry, from the nearby prehistoric ruins (Fig. 6.30). Robinson pictures two baskets each with a maze design, one positive, one negative, and refers to the pattern as "very old and rare."[75] Most likely it does not date before the time of Russell. Breazeale concludes with this note: "Baskets with this design are usually woven by the younger members of the tribe."[76] Certainly the maze design is no longer "rare," particularly among the Papagos.

Cain pictures a miniature maze plaque which could not be more than 1¼″ in diameter.[77] It is fairly well woven but not so good a piece of work as the above. Contrary to these two maze plaques, a third one has a double fret in place of the maze and two men instead of one at the "entrance." This is a large piece 15″ in diameter. Its stitch count is twelve and coil five per inch; its rim is in regular sewing, in black.

Several plaques in the Breazeale collection count ten and twenty-two stitches and five and one-half and six and one-half coils to the inch. The first count was on a medium plaque, 8¾″ in diameter. Quite a few of the plaques are small in size; for example, one in a

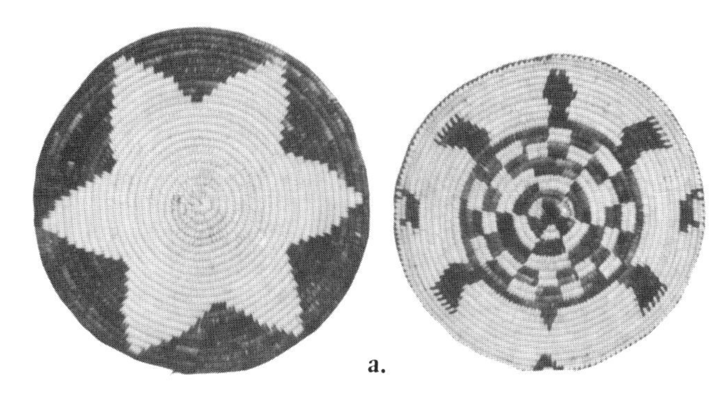
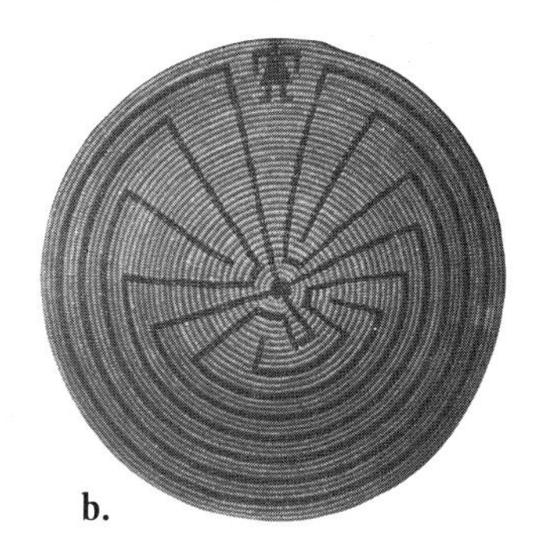

Fig. 6.30. Pima coiled plaques, with rather different patterns: (a) a large negative star at left *(ASM E9025)*, and at right a turtle with an elaborate back pattern *(ASM E4590)*; (b) a finely woven basket with a maze pattern *(ASM 781)*.

private collection is 3¼″ in diameter, another is 6″ across, the latter decorated with an eagle with outspread wings. At the 1976 Gallup Ceremonials one Pima plaque, 3½″ in diameter, was made of horsehair, and was decorated with the man in the maze pattern. A second one at the same exhibit was 7″ in diameter, made of willow and martynia, and decorated with the same subject as the first but in negative.

There are other large plaques, too. One oval piece in a private collection measured 17½″ by 18″ and averaged nine stitches and three coils to the inch; the rim was in regular sewing, all black. It is decorated with an inner band of a simple geometric and an outer band of deer alternating with another simple geometric. The animals are two-legged, with short tails hanging down, and with four-pronged antlers which touch the basket rim.

Occasionally cups have been woven by Pimas, either alone or complete with a saucer. They have handles too. One such piece, in the Breazeale collection but not in his book, was acquired about 1920–22. It measured 2⅜″ at the rim and was 1⅜″ high. This piece was very well woven, counting twenty stitches and six coils to the inch. A small black circle appears on the bottom of the cup, then at the turn onto the wall there starts a ten-petal, black flower. These petals are fairly straight on one side and stepped on the other. They extend to within one coil of the overcast rim.

Perhaps related to this form is a footed style shaped like an egg-cup. One of these is 4⅛″ at the rim and its height is 4⅜″. There is a tiny black center about 1″ in diameter. On the pleasingly shaped foot and gracefully outcurving cup are alternating bands of pale pink and white. Quite different is a second cup, for the foot is flat and the cup portion goes straight out from the base. A black band ornaments the juncture of the two parts, and on the wall of the cup are five figures of men, all black except for short projections from the tops of their heads which are alternately black and white. The rim is finished in alternate black and white stitches. A bowl and a plate woven as one, a footed tray, and two hats further illustrate other odd forms (Fig. 6.31).

Coiled Miniatures. Pima miniatures were made in considerable numbers earlier in this century, largely for sale to white men. Quite a few of these baskets labeled as miniatures are too large in size to be considered as such by this survey; nonetheless, they are included here. Seemingly, they had no real value to the Pima.

A remarkable collection, "one of the best if not the best," of Pima miniatures made around the turn of the century is housed in the Heard Museum in Phoenix. The pieces "range in size from six

a.

b.

c.

Fig. 6.31. Several odd shapes of basketry woven by Pimas: (a) a bowl with its own saucer attached and with geometric designs on each *(ASM 782)*; (b) a footed tray, also woven as one piece and with a braided edge to both tray and foot *(ASM 726)*; (c) two hats, with swastikas decorating the crown and a fret on the brim of the hat at the left, while the hat on the right is ornamented with triangles *(ASM 783, 2653)*.

inches in diameter down to several so small they will barely contain a single grain of wheat."[78] This selection of 128 pieces contains all of the shapes and designs typical of regular Pima baskets, bowls, trays, jars, plus a few straight-sided pieces. Among the designs are the squash-blossom pattern, meticulously executed in some of these small pieces. Another favored theme is a longer or shorter horizontal line attached by a square to a second line a coil or two above, these continuing and spiraling to the rim. Popular, too, was the Pima style with a large black center and, usually, four petals taking off this, then from the tips of these, lines to the left to form swastikas, one arm of which continues up and to the right to join another—in other words, an elaborately integrated pattern. Very small pieces have much simpler designs, such as a continuous band, or a stepped motif, or other small geometrics, or three repeated human figures. Even the maze is represented in some small pieces.

As to coil and stitch count, these Pima miniatures present some interesting figures. The 6″ tray, which is almost flat, had coil and stitch counts of twenty and twenty-seven, respectively. One 3½″ and one 3¼″ plaque averaged twenty coils and twenty-nine stitches to the inch. A tray which measured 1⅞″ in diameter had twenty-four coils and thirty stitches to the inch. Jars are somewhat more difficult to make, yet one which measures 1⅜″ high averaged eighteen coils and twenty-four stitches to the inch and another 2¼″ high jar was low on coil count, only ten to eleven, but the stitches were fine, counting thirty to the inch. Of the pieces under 1″, the best one, which measured ⅞″ in diameter and was ⅝″ high, had counts of twenty coils and twenty-four or -five stitches to the inch. Harvey and de Berge comment on Pima miniatures in their Hopi book, saying that the typical Pima basket of this type has twelve coils and eighteen to twenty-eight stitches to the inch.[79] Many in the Heard Collection were finer than this.

Decoration was surprisingly varied and extremely well executed in plaque miniatures, with all in black. One piece 3½″ and another 1⅞″ in diameter were both decorated with the maze motif, each complete with a tiny man. The smaller one was beautifully woven. Amazingly, one of the 3¼″ plaques had a black center, a row of five black dogs, and a second row of black dogs. Other motifs would include a dancing couple, running men, frets, and swastikas.

A few summary comments may be added regarding design on miniatures in this Heard Museum collection (Fig. 6.32). Spotted patterns are used, but as with the larger pieces, they are not as common as the joined or integrated motifs; certainly most tray designs are tied to the center black circle. On tall forms, bands on the sides are the most common arrangement; these are often vertical and are frequently organizational. In these deep forms, pattern covers most of the sidewall, and despite the small sizes of these pieces, there is much motion in quite a few of the designs. Almost all patterning is positive, although there is a little in negative style.

Open-Stitch Coiling

The Pima Indians did less in the way of open-stitch coiling than the Papagos, for they were not weaving many baskets when the more developed styles in this technique came into popularity. Dipping back into the past, however, it is to be noted that the Pimas made

Fig. 6.32. Pimas made quite a few miniatures at the turn of the century. This ASM group includes beautifully designed pieces of different shapes: trays, wastebasket, cup and saucer, and oval bowl. Note how design is adapted to each form. One tiny piece is covered with beads *(ASM E265, E292, E299, E544, E578, E4036, E9009, 23405)*.

both crude and coarse coiled baskets. Their baskets were often of different shapes. In the hands of the Pima woman, arrowbush twigs were wound upon themselves to create larger granaries which were nest-shaped. This piece does not have a base, for it was placed directly on the rooftop or on a platform on the ground, but it "is covered with a roof, slightly raised in low cone shape at the center and gently sloping to the overhanging rim."[80] As among the Papagos, so too among the Pimas, granaries vary in size but average between 16″ and 20″ in height and about 3 feet in diameter. They are smaller than some of the Papago storage bins, but they are more shapely, perhaps because of their lids; they were most attractive as they rested on rooftops.

Coarse Coiling

Pimas also made storage baskets of large size in coarse coiling. This involved a bundle foundation of wheat straw sewed with willow, mesquite, or acacia bark. Wide spacing of the sewing elements exposed the attractive sheen of wheat straw. Pima sewing is regular and even, with stitches one above the other; this adds to the perfection of the most attractive bell shapes of these granaries, and the shape was their chief artistic quality. There was also a braided rim to this granary. Larger bins are more globular in form than this bell-shaped piece. Pimas made a lid in the same weave as in their granaries.

One large coarse coil basket measured 36″ in its greatest diameter. Slightly misshapen from use, the height is impossible to obtain accurately, but it was approximately a little more than its greatest diameter, about 40″, and the rim about 21″ in diameter. It was woven in 1925, of wheat straw and mesquite bark. Stitches were ½″ to ¾″ apart, and they follow a more or less straight line from base to rim. A second used basket of this type measured 26½″ in body diameter and about 18″ at the rim. Materials and stitching were the same as in the first basket.

Russell reported that storage baskets "were and are yet of the highest utility to the Pimas."[81] Both the arrowbush and wheat-straw types were made at that time, the first used for storing mesquite beans and the second for corn and wheat. The crude coil type has a willow branch bottom; it is placed on the roofs of houses or sheds or on the ground where several may appear together and have a small fence built around them for protection. These early coarse-coiled Pima baskets, according to Russell, were sewn with willow bark, stitches were about 3⁄4″ apart, the coils 3⁄4″ or less in diameter, and the baskets were 1½ to 4 ½ feet in height.[82] Russell also mentions that the Pimas carry two coils along as they weave this basket, but Kissell says that "at times" this is done. But, she adds "while this method completes a basket more quickly, it produces a structure far less firm and strong, so that the single foundation coil is more frequently resorted to."[83] It is doubtful that the Pima used the double coil more than once in a while.

Plaiting

Russell notes that Pima women seldom made square-based, round-topped plaited baskets; rather did they obtain them from the Papagos.[84] Agave leaves were employed when these pieces were made, "deeper than they are broad," as Russell describes them. Medicine men's baskets were made of the same material and in the same manner, and seemingly were of the same sizes as their Papago counterparts. Implying that they were of the same material and weave, Russell also mentions food bowls "of remarkably fine workmanship and graceful shape" which were "carried by warriors on the warpath. They were used to mix piñole in and also served as drinking cups. They were light and indestructible."[85] It would seem that these would almost have to be of a tight-coiled weave if they were used for the purposes suggested here.

One example each of these pieces will be described. A square-bottomed, round-topped piece is much smaller than usual, the rim measuring 4″ in diameter, the square base 5″ on each of its four sides, and height is 4½″. As is common in such pieces, this basket starts out in an over-two-under-two rhythm, quickly turns to an over-three-under-three and continues in this to the rim. Concentric squares appear on the bottom, zigzags on the sides; a simple rim is plaited back into the sidewall; the lid to this piece is similar to the base. A medicine man's pouch measures 12½″ long and 4¾″ wide at the rim and is 5″ deep and it has an over-three-under-three alternation throughout, producing zigzags on the sidewall. The rim is like that of the above basket. The lid measures a little larger: 14⅛″ long and 7″ wide; otherwise, it is like the bottom of the basket in rhythm and design.

Lace Coiling

Pima Indians made a carrying basket, the kiaha, which resembles the Papago piece in most respects. As among the latter so too did young Pima girls start using the kiaha when about eight to ten years of age. Materials for both are similar, with a few local variations in sources. Saguaro ribs are used for the sticks; a double band of willow for the ring is employed in the top of the basket. Human hair is used to tie the sticks to the net. Back pad and head bands are of agave, while the cordage for the net is made from the fibers of sotol (or maguey?). Designs are woven into the Pima kiaha and are colored red and blue.[86]

Plain and twisted lace coil are combined in the making of the Pima kiaha as it is in the Papago piece; form tends to be a bit more shallow in the Papago piece; and design is difficult to analyze, for there are few positively identified patterns. Fourfold division of design prevails in the Pima kiaha as it did in that of the Papago. Generally there is a major, larger theme and a secondary, lesser motif, or perhaps just a line or two. All patterns are line designs created in the open part of the lace weave.

One pattern which is not greatly different from the Papago involves four long themes (see drawing), pendant from the rim plus four shorter ones, with continuous lines paralleling them, around and between them. Another is a triple triangular fret motif which is more or less continuously concentric, with this theme repeated four times. Illustrated in Russell is a third piece in which an almost-triangle is enclosed by an irregularly six-sided figure and then both are outlined by parallel enclosing lines which continue on around the center of the basket. There are four of these; then, there is a third partially outlining line which becomes a part of a second and lesser motif by outlining. Two other Pima kiahas will give some idea of their sizes. Both are more oval than round, probably because of use; one measures 22″ by 25″, the second 25″ by 27″ in their rim dimensions.

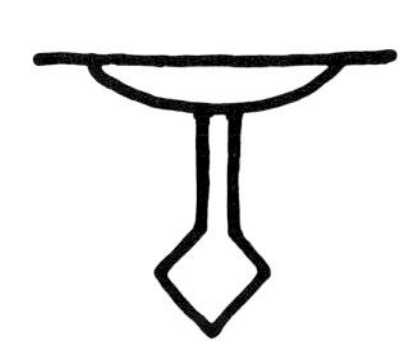

PAPAGO AND PIMA BASKETRY COMPARED

In many ways, the Pimas have remained more traditional in their basket weaving than have the Papagos. They adhered to the same basic materials early and late, and through the years there was little or no change in basic forms. There were some variations in design, but certain traditional ones were favored in early years and continued into recent times. They did not get caught up in the Papago use of yucca, nor in their trend for the ever new in basket forms and their emphasis on new and ever simpler designs.

In summary, the similarities and differences between Pima and Papago in the willow coiled baskets should be noted (Fig. 6.33). In general appearance they are very much alike; specifically, many individual pieces are difficult or impossible to differentiate. However, in pieces distinctive of each tribe there are specific qualities which identify their weaving.

In overall traits, the Pima basket is thinner walled, more flexible, the Papago wall thicker, more rigid, heavier, and more inflexible; in form the Papago is harsh, heavy, "pedestrian," the Pima flowing, graceful, delicate. Pima design is more dynamic, buoyant, lighter while Papago pattern is heavy, often static, and less imaginative.

a.

b.

c.

Fig. 6.33. Some examples of modern Pima and Papago baskets. (a) Papago pieces: old designs in new baskets, particularly the Gila monster (right) and the turtle shell pattern (upper left). All of these are done in yucca. (b) Four Pima baskets: upper right, a "dream basket"; to the left, a beautiful squash blossom; lower right, a marvelous "bug" design. (c) Papago pieces, with current shapes (flat forms prevailing) and designs, particularly the rattler in the upper left. *(Photos by Ray Manley.)*

Interestingly, the same motifs may be used, such as turtle backs, squash blossoms, elongate triangles merging into swastikas. Yet in these and other designs, emphasis on the following makes for tribal differences: lighter vertical and horizontal lines and more diagonals for Pimas, heavier lines and emphasis on verticals and horizontals by the Papagos. Stress on black, such as large center circles plus broader lines and larger mass areas in general, makes for a feeling of heaviness in the Papago basket pattern.

Perhaps the major differences in the basketry products of these two tribes are but reflections of their respective ways of life. Papago desert lands were harsh, difficult to deal with, unrelenting; water resources and food were scarce. Contrarily, Pimas were able to divert the waters of a then permanent river to raise a surplus of food which gave them leisure time; comparatively their lives were easier, they had time to dream. Papagos had to make the long trek into Pima country for willow; therefore, they used it sparingly while the black devil's-claw was close at hand and could be and was used in generous quantities.

Thus the lifeways of these two linguistically related peoples, the Pimas and Papagos, dictated many of the artistic differences in their basketry.

Chapter 7

Baskets of Yuman Tribes

HUALAPAIS, HAVASUPAIS, AND YAVAPAIS produced fine weavers and much basketry at certain times during later historic years. It is likely that all of these tribes did more basketry than is known, for they live in areas which are not conducive to the preservation of perishable materials. Perhaps the only pieces of any consequence in earlier years were those of strict utility, burden and tray baskets particularly. Then those who had the native ability, plus the inspiration through white contact, and a product which had potentials for sales, developed new styles and greater quantities of baskets from time to time.

The three Yuman tribes in the lower reaches of the Colorado River, the Mohave, Yuma, and Cocopa, made more pottery than baskets. Further, they obtained baskets from other tribes rather than make their own. These two facts may explain both a dearth of this craft and certain references to baskets among these tribes which were not woven by them. Maricopas, who moved into the Pima area about 1700, did little basketry and some of that was influenced by their new neighbors.

COCOPA BASKETS

Life was so difficult among the Cocopa that it is no wonder that they did not produce baskets. Kissell in 1916 mentions that these tribeswomen made a crude-coiled storage basket; these granaries "are used today upon the roof by the . . . Cocopa . . . ."[1] A little later Spier refers to the bird's-nest storage baskets used by this tribe. He says that they were "huge nest-like affairs crudely coiled of branches of arrowweed . . . three to five feet in diameter, three to four feet high . . . . These were, strictly speaking, not baskets at all, since they lacked a bottom, but (were) thick walled coiled cylinders . . . ."[2] Kelly goes on to add that they were made of willow, that they were placed in or upon the house, and that corn, beans, pumpkin strips, and mesquite beans were stored in them. Further, he notes that the Cocopa men made another crude storage jar solely of willow.[3]

YUMA BASKETS

Certainly basketry was extinct, or nearly so, among the Yuma tribesmen by the late 1920s.[4] Previously they had made a not-too-large, coarse-coiled storage jar of rushes. They also made an extremely large bird's nest storage jar; Douglas also says that they made coiled baskets with a foundation of two rods stacked.[5] Willow, arrowweed, and martynia were used in making the coiled baskets, the latter material for simple decoration. Shallow trays represent the only form in addition to storage jars, and they were 2 to 3 feet in diameter, 6″ to 9″ in height.[6]

MOHAVE BASKETS

Fig. 7.1. A Mohave basket: although labeled "storage jar," it is too small to have been so used except for small quantities or, perhaps, a few special seeds (8½″ high, 12½″ in diameter). The work on this piece is very good for open coil *(UCM 954)*.

Tantalizing references appear here and there to basketry of the Mohave Indians, but actually there is little available material on the weaving of this tribe. Kissell notes that they made crude-coil granaries and that they were set up on platforms.[7] She says that they used arrow bush *(Plucca borealis)* for the making of these cylindrical storage affairs.[8] Mason illustrates a Mohave carrying basket[9] which is about as crude as a basket can be. It is a long, narrow form, smaller at the base than at the rim. It seems that two bent withes formed four riblike affairs on which were wrapped stout cords which were then twined together vertically—and very crudely. Mason refers to this as "wrapped weaving."[10] Another withe formed the rim ring. Douglas says that the Mohaves made a few bowls of openwork coiling.[11] One such piece in the University of Colorado Museum, Boulder, is dated 1911 (Fig. 7.1), and is labeled "storage jar." It is a straight-sided basket 8½″ high, and wide-mouthed, 12½″ in diameter. Spaced stitching goes straight up the sidewalls.[12] No doubt the Mohaves traded for baskets as did other Yuman tribes.

MARICOPA BASKETS

Maricopas, as noted in Chapter 2, represent a Yuman-speaking people who moved away from the Colorado River into the vicinity of the Pima Indians about 1700. Spier says, "The Maricopa manufactured only burden baskets, obtaining from the Pima the flat bowl-like baskets needed for winnowing or serving food. Every household had one of each, but rarely more. Today a Pima basket forms a part of every woman's equipment and is highly prized."[13] A 1910 photograph (Fig. 7.2) shows an attractive Maricopa lady with a very large Pima basket on her head.[14] Reference is made to the fact that the lower Colorado Yumans were a pottery-making people, "where also baskets were obtained by trade rather than manufactured, and not much used,"[15] thus implying little basket production on the part of the Maricopa before they moved to the Gila River.

The Maricopa coiled burden basket is more the shape of a deep bowl with wide plain mouth and sides gently sloping to a flat bottom. Spier says the piece is about as high as it is wide, but calculating from his drawing and pictures of this form, the mouth diameter is one-third to one-half again as wide as the depth. He says the foundation is a "bundle of finely split tule" (*Scirpus* sp.) that is sewn with devil's-claw (*Proboscidea parviflora*) and willow (*Salix nigra*) splints. The bottom of the basket is solid black, probably for the same reason that it is so made by other tribes—it wears better. Side-

Fig. 7.2. A Maricopa woman (1910) carrying a large and finely coiled basket on her head. This was very likely a Pima piece, for Spier says that all trays used by Maricopas were woven by Pimas *(AHS #3239)*.

walls are often decorated with two bands. One illustration of a Maricopa burden basket (Fig. 7.3) shows a straighter-sided piece than Spier's drawing indicates, and also has a single wide design, a simple, four-part fret, from base to close to the rim. A simple black stitch appears on the rim. Apparently these baskets were quite finely woven with coil counts about the same as in Pima baskets.

The burden basket made by the Maricopa Indians was used primarily for the collection of mesquite beans. As it was carried on the head, on a ring made of willow splints, it had no loops on the sides for a carrying strap.[16]

Evidently Spier does not consider the bird's-nest granaries and coarse-coiled storage pieces as baskets, for, as quoted above, he says that the only baskets they made were the burdens. However, he goes on to describe the two cruder pieces. A granary resembled the Pima type in its cylindrical form, in its size of 3 to 5 feet diameter, in its lack of top and bottom, and in the fact that it was placed on a platform. It was woven of arrowweeds. This could have been a basket type long made by the Maricopas; however, the storage baskets adopted from the Pimas shortly before Spier's study were better made. A wheat-straw (*Triticum vulgare*) foundation sewed with willow bark was woven into a basket of rounded base and with sides sloping to a smaller mouth. Heights were about 30″, the mouth 14″, and the base twice that of the mouth.[17]

Fig. 7.3. A Maricopa woman of about 1900. The large basket on the left is quite like those described by Spier as burden baskets made by Maricopa women—straight-sided, wide-brimmed, and with a flat and fairly small base *(AHS #26031)*.

YAVAPAI BASKETS

In terms of their background and history, the Yavapais have shared culture with Mohaves, Apaches, Havasupais, and Hualapais, and this in spite of reference on the part of some of them to the latter two groups as "mean people."[18] Too, the Yavapais traded for baskets, and other items, with the Navajos. There were three Yavapai groups, Western, Northeastern, and Southeastern, but there was intermarriage between them. A few differences existed between them regarding the craft of basketry; for example, reputedly the Western Yavapais were the only ones who made baskets for boiling; they also parched with coals in baskets; they collected saguaro fruit in baskets, putting the juice of the fruit in water-tight pieces.[19] Their burden baskets were used to haul mescal heads and for maize storage—for the latter, as Gifford says, by setting the base of the conical basket in a hole about 1 foot deep, lining it with grass, and placing stones around the base to keep it upright.

Gifford's description of the awl used in basket making by this Western Yavapai tribe is mindful of prehistoric styles: they were made by "grinding and sharpening the lower leg bone of deer on rock," with the knob at the joints left on the end.[20] In writing about the Southeastern Yavapai, Gifford says that they used awls of "Yucca or mescal leaf points, or of hardwood. No bone awls were used."[21]

The "maternal grandmother taught the girl how to . . . make basketry" among the Northeastern Yavapais, but in Western Yavapai groups the mother taught her daughter this craft.[22] Gifford also notes that there was a "Three-rod coiled, pitched basket cup carried by older warrior in bag at right side; cup used to mix dried mescal and water."[23]

Gifford further notes that these two groups made twined and coiled work. In general he says that few designs existed earlier but that there were "more patterns created, [and] large deep baskets woven for Caucasian demand" when he worked among these people in 1936.[24] Plain twined and pitched water bottles were made of sumac (*Rhus emoryi*), stems, as usual, whole for warps and split for the wefts. Both flat-and pointed-bottomed types were produced: some were simply shaped, with a fairly wide mouth, medium neck, and more or less rounded body. The same materials were used for the conical burden basket; red decoration appeared on some of these, done with the inner bark of the root of yucca. A flatter-bottomed burden basket was woven of the same warp material, but mulberry (*Morus* sp.) was the source of the light weft elements, while decorative materials were martynia (*Proboscidea parviflora*) for black and mulberry colored with mineral pigments for the red. Bands decorated the sidewalls. Tightly woven burdens were used for small seeds.

Western Yavapais made a pitched water bottle in twined weave with a flat bottom; they also wove a conical burden basket like that of the Havasupai. Gifford says that lemonberry (probably *Rhus* sp.) was used for warps, mulberry for wefts, and martynia for black patterns in this piece with designs of horizontally nested chevrons. In the flatter-bottomed type, he illustrates lines and short diagonals in bands. This group also made winnowing trays in twined weave of circular form and 18″ in diameter, of the same materials as used in the conical burden basket.[25]

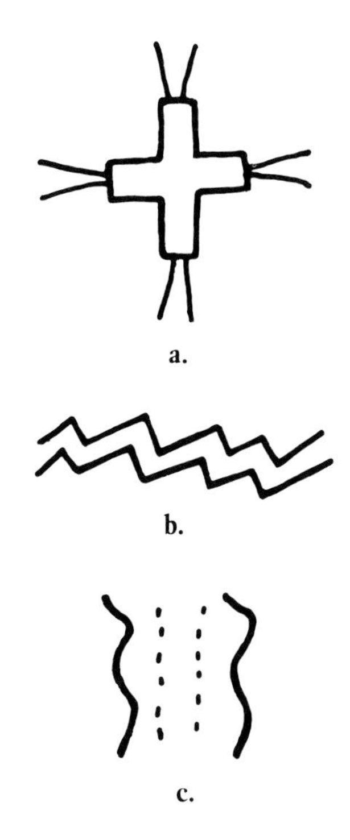

In coiled weave the Northeast Yavapai used a three-rod foundation for the making of water bottles, the cup mentioned above, dishes, and winnowing and parching trays. Materials at the time of Gifford's writing included *Salix lasioletis* and *Salix laevigata* for foundation and desert willow (*Chilopsis linearis*) for wefts, plus cottonwood (*Populus fremontii*) and mulberry for other sewing material. In some of the old pitched water bottles they used mulberry for both elements. Waterproofing in some old baskets was done with the juice of cooked mescal. As early as this time (1936) some Yavapai women were using a tin can lid with holes in it for keeping wefts even, referred to then as a "new innovation."[26]

According to Gifford, designs on Northeastern Yavapai coiled basketry were very simple. There were vertical lines in bands, straight encircling parallel lines, dots, independent chevrons, zigzags which were rather sharp, a so-called star (see drawing a), and also so-called crooked lightning (see drawing b).[27]

On Western Yavapai baskets, designs on coiled pieces became a little more elaborate (Fig. 7.4). On trays, for example, there was the motif shown in drawing c, with a deer on each side. One tray had a black center, a very uneven six-pointed star or flower, and beyond, a veritable shadow of the same created by six elongate rectangles pendant from the rim. Another piece had a simpler, smaller, four-pointed star or flower, each point capped with a deep V which looks almost like a bird, with a like theme repeated between points, and

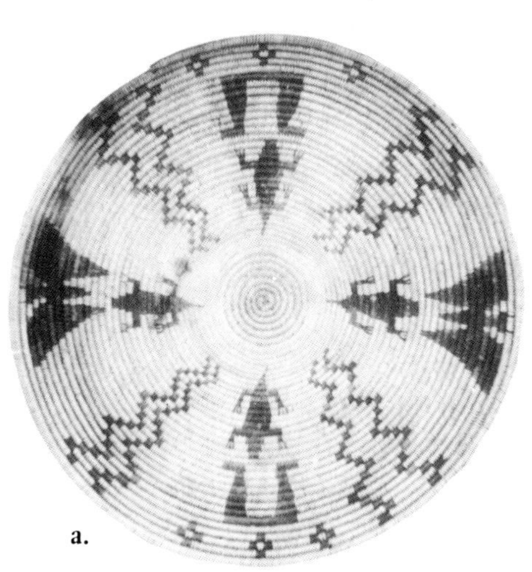

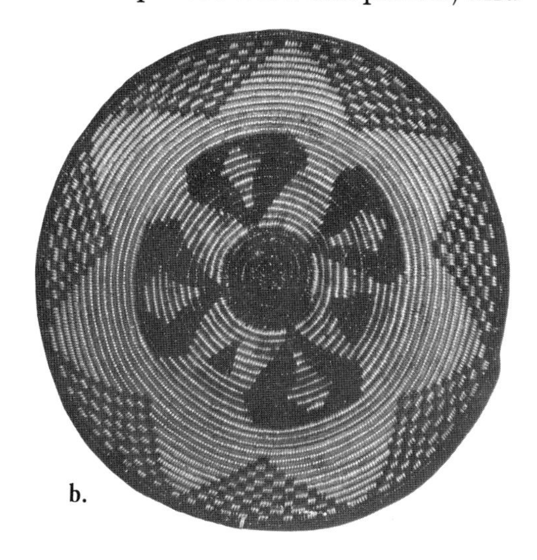

Fig. 7.4. Types of Yavapai baskets. (a) A very finely woven small piece (twenty-five stitches to the inch) with an a-b-a-c-a-b-a-c type of design *(ASM E3508)*. (b) Large black areas are typical of these tribal baskets *(UCM 17045)*. (c) Also typical are negative designs in the black sections *(UCM 17049)*.

the same heavy Vs at the rim. The latter resemble a zigzag because they are so close together.[28]

There was a Yavapai woman, Viola Jimulla, who lived in and near Prescott, Arizona, for many years; according to Barnett, she succeeded her husband who was chief of this group.[29] (Some Yavapais had no chiefs.) Her parents were among those Yavapais who lived on the San Carlos Apache Reservation, and Viola stayed there until she was fifteen years old. Later her mother and second husband moved to the Prescott area where Viola spent the rest of her life. According to Barnett, it was during her days on the San Carlos Reservation that she first learned basket making, and was, of course, continuously associated with and influenced by Apache styles of weaving.

Undoubtedly it was those years of living with the Apaches that influenced the coiled basketry style of many Yavapai women. Many pieces are like Apache baskets in shapes and designs. Yet there are differences. Both similarities and differences will be demonstrated, first in the works of Viola Jimulla as illustrated by Barnett, then in other Yavapai baskets researched in private collections and museums.

Forms produced by Viola included jars and trays. Two of the jars have the Apache elongate but rounded lines, with a wide mouth. Two more are also Apache-like in emphasized shoulders. A third jar style is not Apache in its low, squat form. Trays made by Viola seem to have been abundant; they are large and small and most attractively decorated. Some are much like the Apache, some quite different.

One basket jar, apparently a small one, has an arrangement of wide black bands placed diagonally across the piece from base into the wide-mouthed rim. Between the bands are several scattered elements including a dog, a man, and a solid black diamond. The second piece of this type has heavy horizontal zigzags whose touching points create a netlike effect over the vessel. Within each of the diamonds on the body and base, and in rim triangles created by them, are dogs and coyote tracks in smaller spaces, and several figures in the larger areas, such as men and crosses in one, or an eagle and a deer in another. The heaviness of the zigzags in this piece is not an Apache trait. One of the high-shouldered jars is pictured as Viola weaves on its wide neck; the body is ornamented with a large three-line zigzag with a checkered diamond on each outer tip. The simplicity of this jar decoration is not found often on Apache pieces of this time and type.

Trays are varied in their designing. One has the identical pattern described above for the jar: an encircling three-line stepped zigzag with diamonds tipping each point. In the tray it looks more like a flower; also on this piece it is even less Apache-like. One light pattern consists of all-over stepped, outlined diamonds with coyote track centers; this tray is totally un-Apache. Another piece with simpler decoration is a wide tray which has a small center circle and four bands of checkered circles; this piece could be Apache. A very Apache-like piece duplicates star or flowerlike themes: in the center is a six-pointed all-black motif, and touching it is a row of six black petals with a white coyote track in each and with black dogs (?) between them. Beyond is a second row of black flower leaves, these with a white figured man in each and a black human figure between leaves, and with coyote tracks just beyond the men's shoulders. The filling of all spaces is indeed like Apache basket decoration.

Other trays feature floral themes and triangles, or a flower and diamonds, or squares and little animals. Spacing is different in most of them, particularly as resulting in more clean-cut arrangements, or in more consistent repetition. In only one of these pieces is exact duplication of small elements broken: pairs of animals in an outer circle are back to back with each facing out in three repetitions, but in the fourth they are facing in the same direction—it would seem that a typical Apache trait had asserted itself in this piece. Most of Viola's baskets show good spacing but now and again one figure may be a little out of line.

It may be concluded then that Viola Jimulla represents a typical Yavapai basket weaver. Many of these women of the older generation (she died in 1966 at the age of 88) were definitely influenced by Apache styles, for women living and working together do influence one another. Barnett intimates that the Yavapais were the most influential in this situation when he says, "However, the Apache weavers lacked legend or background for their craft,"[30] and particularly when he credits the diamond pattern as originating with the Yavapais. Some Yavapais lived with the Apaches from about 1875 to 1900. It was about this time, certainly not later than the last years of this period, that the Apaches elaborated on their basketry designs and, apparently, began the use of life themes. It is still difficult to determine which was the "influencing tribe," which the "influenced."

In a photograph from *Arizona Highways* dated 1936,[31] a Yavapai woman is pictured holding a deep bowl. It is ornamented with the identical zigzags with points touched by diamonds as described above on a tray and on a deep jar, both woven by Viola. An oval bowl in a private collection has a white center with coyote tracks on the bottom. Sidewalls are decorated with outlined stepped diamonds at the ends and on each side with three solid-stepped and outlined triangles. This fairly recent piece is simply but effectively decorated. One tray dated between 1908 and 1915 was large, 18¾″ in diameter and about 4″ deep, and it had fifteen stitches and five coils to the inch. This piece was decorated with four rows of six triangles each, with each row touching the previous one. The triangles are particularly graceful with a smooth top and stepped sides.

Two baskets acquired in 1968, both appearing very new, present interesting designs. One is 11⅝″ in rim diameter, and has fifteen stitches and four coils per inch. A tiny black center has three white coils separting it from a first row of four bugs, then there is a second row with eight bugs to the rim. The second piece is small, 8¼″ in diameter and about 1¾″ deep. It is labeled on an accompanying tag, "First known Yavapai basket to have a snake design." The reptile starts in a black center with a V-shaped tongue and oversewn eyes; it then curves out in alternating black and white bands to the tail. The tail ends two coils from the rim, and it is distinguished from the body by being woven in alternate black and white stitches.

One deep, straight-sided bowl has a heavy black lower border with white horses (?) in it. Above is a white band with motifs which resemble joined triangles, this bordered at the top by black then white steps. Then comes a black zigzag; above it are, again, joined triangles filled with checkers. A white band at the edge has wide-spaced, small-stepped, and checkered triangles pendant from a black rim.

Yavapai basketry can thus be seen to resemble closely that made by the Apaches. Forms are very similar except for the conical burden basket and straight-sided deep bowls; some deep jars with low and protruding shoulders are also more typical of the Yavapais. Sizes and stitch and coil counts compare favorably. Many designs are distinguishable from Apache patterns, many others are not. The Yavapais favored concentric bands and less cluttering; the latter was expressed by Apaches through the addition of small independent elements; Yavapai lines are heavier and they favored more mass black. Often the Yavapais put together the same design elements and motifs used by the Apaches in a very different way, giving them a Yavapai feeling which is almost impossible to describe. Both tribes used the same geometric elements, featuring the circle, cross, diamond, triangle, zigzag, star and flower, coyote track, and the swastika. Both even featured the same curvilinear triangle and diamond. Both portrayed the same life forms: men and women, dogs, horses, deer, birds, saguaro, Gila monster (or lizard). But all in all, the Yavapais generally used fewer variations of elements in a single basket. Perhaps a subtle simplicity might characterize the Yavapai piece as contrasted with the zestful vigor of Apache design.

PAI BASKETS

Two tribes which could be treated together are the Hualapai and the Havasupai; in fact, they have been termed "Pai" in certain publications. Dobyns and Euler have used this term (1960)[32], and Bateman wrote of "Pai basketry" in 1972.[33] Dobyns says that they have been virtually one ethnic group since 1870.[34] So much intermarriage has taken place that baskets attributed to one tribe may well have been produced by a member of the other; thus, in many collections, a basket may be labeled Hualapai or Havasupai, but what is its real origin is another question. A case in point is a burden basket in a private collection. In height, background color, shape and number of elements in the starting knot, this basket is more like the Hualapai; in other details it is like the Havasupai. Too, there are, obviously, overlappings in most of these characteristics; thus, unless one knows the weaver, problems do exist regarding identification and clarification between the baskets of these two tribes. Kroeber stresses their similarities, noting only two identifying exceptions in Hualapai work: large baskets were started with six warps instead of the typical four, and the use of a different material, squawbush.

Even with qualifying characteristics one cannot be sure whether a basket was woven by a Hualapai or a Havasupai, for the problem of geneology comes into focus. Both of these tribes are patrilineal in their organization; therefore, if a Hualapai woman marries a Havasupai man, she goes to Havasu to live; thus, a basket woven by a woman living in this canyon is not necessarily a Havasupai basket. The same is true of a Havasupai woman married to a Hualapai man and living at Peach Springs.

Further, many reports on Hualapai or Havasupai basketry frequently overlook the fact that both of these tribes made coiled ware. As noted in the Kroeber report from a 1929 expedition, "some said Walapais never used coiled baskets for general purposes."[35] With this remark, plus a few words to the effect that bowls and trays were made and were decorated with "rather simple geometric or realistic designs," the subject of coiled work is dismissed. Too, the few coiled baskets observed during this period and referred to by Kroeber represent only a small part of the story of coiled work done by this tribe, for the time of this study was evidently a slack period. However, there were periods in Pai basket making during which there was great production, as is well illustrated for the Havasupai in the McKee collection of the 1930s discussed below. (And there are Hualapai pieces, or baskets made by Hualapai women, in this collection.)

Despite these discrepancies and problems each tribe will be treated independently, for each has its own way of doing a certain few things in the production of basketry. To begin with, however, a summary of Pai basketry, twined work specifically, will be presented to show how close some of these matters are. In fact, in many instances the specific tribes will not be identified, as the products will be called "Pai" baskets. Then follows a section on each tribe; these include further details on twined work plus coiled.

In both tribes, weaving was a woman's work. Both tribes were and are affected by tourists in their respective areas. Today both tribes still make basketry for sale; in fact, they have since the end of the 1880s. For native use, both tribes in the past did more weaving in wicker and particularly in diagonal twined; for the tourist trade both developed coiled weaving. Both produced conical burden baskets, parching trays, water bottles, bowls, and jars.

Shapes in Pai burden baskets presented by Bateman are basically conical (Fig. 7.5), some with pointed bases, some more blunt and wider, a few with a nipple-like base. General shape involves a fairly

a.

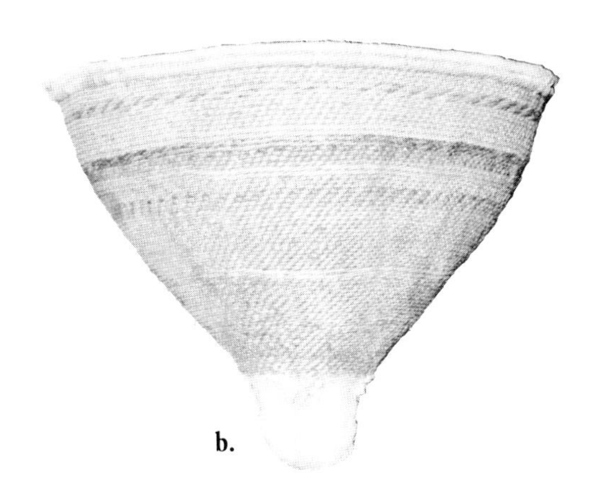
b.

Fig. 7.5. (a) "Pai" woman in this 1907 picture could be either Havasupai or Hualapai, for both tribes made the conical form of wicker burden basket on her back *(AHS #43232)*. (b) Havasupai burden basket with a "nipple" base *(LA 10974)*.

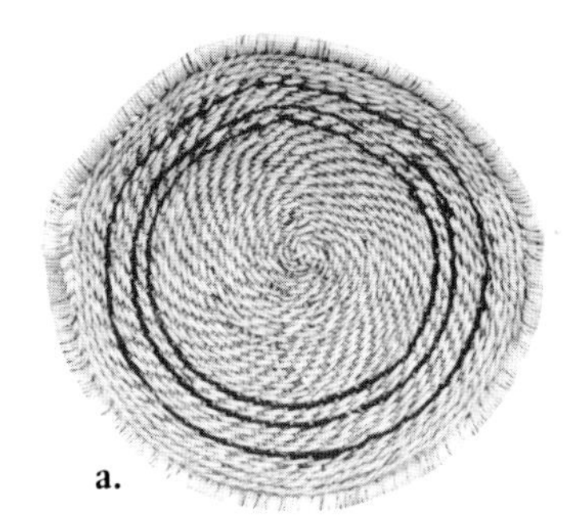

a.

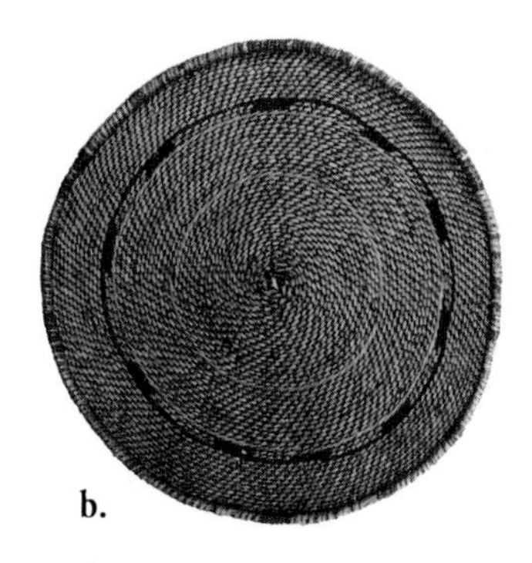

b.

Fig. 7.6. (a) Often Pai wicker winnowing trays were very simply decorated, either in varied weaves or, as here, in black lines. A sturdy rim is characteristic of these pieces *(ASM E9384)*. (b) A second tray with design in both weave and color *(AHS Sweeney Collection)*.

straight and smooth line from base to rim; a few examples have more of an outflare from about one-third of the way up to the rim. Many of these baskets are quite graceful in form.

Design tends to be simple in most of these pieces, with bands and half bands predominating in several different combinations. Half bands consist of short diagonal lines or triangles suspended from a continuous horizontal line. Bands may be made up of diagonals between two close-spaced lines; or, in another example, triangles are suspended from bordering lines toward the center to create a negative zigzag as they are alternating. Organizational bands are also represented, as in two horizontal rows of large parallelograms, or in a horizontal line with diagonals projecting from either side. Just plain lines are not uncommon, either in black or in the weave.

These burden baskets are of diagonal twined weave, basically with black patterns in devil's-claw. Pai burden baskets in general averaged in size from about 14″ to 26″ at the rim; some were larger. Bases were usually covered with a piece of rawhide; through buckskin loops was passed a tumpline of the same material.

Parching or winnowing trays were also made by Havasupais and Hualapais. Their techniques for making this basket include plain and diagonal twining plus some three-strand work. This tray varied in size from 12″ to 34″ in diameter and from 2″ to 5½″ in depth. Double rims are characteristic. Designs were in varied styles in black devil's-claw, or they were the result of triple twined wefts or other varied weaves (Fig. 7.6; also see Fig. 7.5). One example has an alternation of bands of plain and diagonal weave from near-rim to the center of the tray. Another parching tray has several similarly spaced plain-weave lines and a band of rather heavy short black lines placed effectively a little more than halfway from center to rim. Diagonals in the weave from center to rim serve as a subtle background for this band.

In a color-decorated tray basket, a wide brownish band with white flecking dominates over the diagonal weave; the brown results from twisting the weft elements which have the bark on one side. Another tray design involves a single row made up of black almost-rectangles on the outside and diagonal ones below, these alternating. This row is against diagonal twining, with occasional triple twined bands.

Fig. 7.7. A Pai wicker water bottle, more refined in shape than the typical jar of this type. Note two rows (five stitches each) of white against the dark brown of the rest of the bottle *(ASM E4230)*.

Pai water bottles (Fig. 7.7) vary in shape, the most common being flat-bottomed jar forms. Less common but more interesting is the biconic form, quite like that of the Paiutes but not as beautifully woven as the latter. In fact, water bottle weaves are comparatively crude as executed by the Pai groups, perhaps because they are heavily pitched, which conceals the weave. Yucca loops were used earlier, horsehair ones later, to receive the braided yucca or buckskin carrying strap. Mouths are small on all shapes of water bottles; however, like the Paiutes, the smallest mouths generally appeared on biconic forms. Color decoration is lacking, but there is some slight attention to weave variation which produced horizontal bands.

Pai twined basket bowls were so well woven that they held liquids; some did have mush rubbed in to aid in waterproofing. It is known that from the early 1880s to at least the turn of the century these bowls were used for food. By 1890 diagonally twined small bowls were woven, later to become abundant and popular commercial items. Some large pieces survived into the 1920s.

Shapes vary slightly in these bowls, although the majority are deep, round, and largely of the same or nearly the same diameter from rim to base. A heavy edge sometimes gives a wider rim diameter; some have a slight constriction immediately beneath this border, while others may be more drawn in at the rim. One older piece has a wider rim, a smaller base. Some shapes are carelessly executed. Rarely, some have handles.

Frequently the diagonal-twined bowls have a pattern in the weave alone, or sometimes there is a combination of weave and color decoration. Practically all of the later pieces were color decorated, probably a concession to sales. Earlier bowls may have black or brown decoration alone, while later ones feature either black alone, or red and black, or for tourist trade and still later, red and green, the last two colors particularly popular with Hualapai weavers. In bowls with varying weaves there may be two, three, or more lines or narrow bands of the triple twined weave alone or with color added. In some instances a single triple twine borders the color pattern.

Designs on bowls include the following. One small basket has a black pattern below middle in the form of a line with suspended diagonals. A second small piece has black spaced diagonals just under the rim and a wide red-brown band just below center consisting of diagonals on either side of a band. Unusual is a black-red pattern: a small black-red repeated motif at the rim; on the wall sets of four black nested chevrons above, joined below by the same in red, and the latter touching a narrow red line; then low on the wall a simple black-red-black band. One well-made bowl has two bands of alternating and touching diagonals in black and brown.

A few simple jar forms were produced by the Pai basket makers, usually in diagonal weave. One shape has a very wide mouth, a sharp incurve beneath the rim, and an exaggerated bulge in the lower body. Designs on these quite naturally feature diagonals because of the weave. On one attractive example there is a line with suspended, narrow diagonals at the base of the neck. Just above the greatest diameter of the body is a row of nested chevrons with a very narrow line running through their centers. On a second jar of the same shape there are two rows of repeated wide diagonals, one on the neck, one at midpoint on the body. Between these two is a heavy black line with suspended small repeated elements, a theme found again at the turn of the vessel base.

One last native form in wicker among the Pais should be mentioned, the seedbeater. Made of cat's-claw or sumac, these open pieces are tied at one end. They are woven of simple plain wicker.

Various odd shapes were made by the Pais in twined weave. For example, the straight-sided, flat-bottomed bowl may have an added handle. Or a footed cup shape (Fig. 7.8), much like an eggcup, was occasionally favored. One of these has a simple band of varied stitching on the cup proper and two fairly wide bands in black on the "foot." A second and larger example has, on the cup, two complete black bands, one with projecting black triangles and the second with spaced-out and irregularly-shaped, attached black

Fig. 7.8. A Pai wicker piece of pleasing lines and with simple decoration. This footed cup obviously reflects contact with the white man *(MNA 3177)*.

areas. Intermittent narrow black lines appear between these two. High on the foot is a plain red band. Obviously, this form was inspired through contact.

Miniatures were also produced by the Pais. Among other items these included conical burden baskets, complete with a simple black design, a capping on the bottom, and a carrying strap. One small burden basket has an exaggerated outflaring upper portion. Small water bottles are not uncommon; their forms are rather careless, and they are undecorated.

HAVASUPAI COILED BASKETRY

A brief history of Havasupai basket making will serve to introduce the work of this tribe. This has been derived from the writings of Spier,[36] Kroeber,[37] McKee,[38] and Bateman,[39] plus research on private and museum collections.

Prior to 1880 it seems that the Havasupai Indians were living largely as they had for centuries, a semi-wandering life which encouraged the production of a quantity of twined pieces and possibly a few undecorated coiled baskets. About this time, however, a large coiled tray decorated in black geometric designs seems to have appeared and was a popular trade item to Hopi and other puebloans.[40] McKee et al. feel that this development culminated in the 1930s[41], but there is reason to believe that there was a first high peak in the period 1890 to 1910 or a little later, this adequately recorded in the Sweeney Memorial Collection of baskets made from the late 1890s into the 1920s. At least for the earlier years in this period a great variety of forms and the greatest amount of varicolored decoration appeared in Havasupai coiled baskets. Twined work flourished as well.

There must have been a decline in coiled baskets just before and into the 1920s, for Spier gives them little attention in his 1928 publication. He tells of designs of great simplicity in baskets for native use and of a great borrowing of designs to be used on trade pieces. Of the latter he says there is little or no composition, that designs are crowded into baskets "without regard for their appropriateness." Certainly such comment is not applicable to the coiled basket designs of the early Sweeney or the later McKee collections of the 1930–40 period. Thus an upward turn in basketry production, and particularly in designing, must have taken place during this 1930–1940 decade, for coiling takes precedence over twining, with great variety and better quality in forms, sizes, and designs, and again life designs came into greater favor.

Then followed another great change. "By 1950 Havasupai basket making had declined drastically, not only in the production of utility ware, but also in the making of coiled ware."[42] By 1963, large conical baskets were no longer made, although small ones about 12" high were produced. Very little basket weaving was done during the 1950s according to Euler[43]; Smithson also says there were only a half dozen weavers at this time.[44] This low ebb in production continued to about the 1970s. Bateman refers to the late 1960s into the early 1970s as a recovery period for this basket weaving, with Peach Springs becoming a center of this revival. Here lived both

Havasupais and Hualapais, many of them intermarried. A class was organized here to teach the Indian women how to weave baskets,[45] and out of this came some of the finest weavers of the 1970s.

Both Peach Springs and Havasupai Canyon weavers were increasing and producing more basketry. Bateman summarizes this situation in several points of interest[46]: old forms were revived such as water bottles and parching trays, and other forms were retained; techniques which had been dropped were revived, such as the use of natural dyes; there was an honest response to the commercial which also carried prestige relative to the production of a traditional craft; and there was a revival of basket making among the women over fifty years of age. Despite these encouraging aspects, there are discouraging ones also, such as a shortage of materials and a lack of interest on the part of younger women. However, McKee et al. report in 1975, several years later than Bateman, that there were seventeen active basket makers at Havasuapi, five of them young women. They also report that smaller versions of the old utility forms were made, even toy versions of burden baskets and water jars, but that they were not as well woven.[47] Dobyns stated that baskets were taken out of Havasu Canyon as fast as they were made in the mid and later 1970s—hence little is known of the latest baskets made here.[48]

Materials

Materials used in making Havasupai baskets have been quite varied through the years. Among the more important ones are cat's-claw (*Acacia gregii*), cottonwood (*Populus fremontii*), and willow (both *Salix gooddingii* and *Salix bonplandiana*). Cat's-claw was basic in twining, although both cottonwood and willow might also be used (but the latter two were inferior, says Spier). The latter two materials were more important in coiled work; particularly was willow used in recent decades, according to McKee.[49] Squawberry (*Rhus trilobata*) was used in both twining and coiling, and a desert willow (*Chilopsis linearis*) was employed sometimes as a foundation material. Branches of the Apache plume (*Fallugia paradoxa*) and arrowweed (*Pluchea sericea*) provide rim material used in twined baskets. According to Spier, so too did acacia (*Acacia gregii*) and mesquite (*Prosopis veluntina*); either of these two was split and used in coil stitch running around the rim.[50] Serviceberry (*Amelanchier utahensis*) twigs were used for rims on twined baskets. Devil's-claw (*Proboscidea parviflora*) was the most common decorative material, providing the black in coiled and in some twined pieces.

Gathering and preparation of materials by the Havasupai women was an organized activity. Practically every material except devil's-claw was gathered at the appropriate season in the form of young branches or shoots cut in lengths of 2 to 3 feet and stored against future use. McKee et al. say that willow was best in late August but might also be collected in March or April, and that cottonwood was largely gathered in early spring but less of this material might be harvested in July and August.[51] Whether of the native wild and shorter variety or the introduced, cultivated and long type, devil's-claw apparently was gathered in August or September. The black outer part of this material was stripped off and stored in bundles. Whole rods of any of the above plants which were to be used as foundation material were stripped of their leaves and smoothed before storing. In like manner, any shoots which were to serve as weaving or sewing materials were split three ways, usually with fingernails and teeth. Often the inner pith was removed. The entire splint might then be scraped, in later years with a metal knife. In later years, too, a tin can lid with holes in it might be used for sizing the weft element. Often and particularly in earlier years, weaving splints for twined work frequently were not finished as herein described, for the natural colored bark of an element might be left on so that it could be manipulated to create a design. Bateman says that in 1972 the bark may or may not be left on[52], as does McKee in 1975.[53]

A few additional materials other than for weaving proper should be mentioned. There was the piece of rawhide put on the base of the carrying basket; after it was soaked in water, it was sewed on green, "with a through and through stitch" so that it was indeed secure. On some water bottles there are braided or bunched horsehair loops. A corncob may be rubbed over the surface of a water bottle to fill the interstices before soapweed paste and red paint are applied; then, of course, piñon (*Pinus monophyla*) pitch is used for the final waterproofing.

Dyes were used for Havasupai design. Bateman reports these sources for dye colors: the blueberry root or Oregon grape (*Barberis repens*) root gave a gold color, and walnut a brown shade; a red-brown seems also to have been derived from the Spanish bayonet root.[54] In many of the pieces produced between 1890 and 1910 there was considerable variety of colors, including reds, greens, yellows, purple, orange, pink, and black. Undoubtedly many of these were aniline in origin, except some of the black which was devil's-claw. Black, from devil's-claw, was used predominantly in the 1930–40 baskets.

a.

Fig. 7.9. Forms in Havasupai coiled baskets include: (a) trays, which are dominant; (b) jars, which are fairly abundant; and (c) bowls, these more common than in many tribes *(All AHS Sweeney Collection).*

b.

c.

Forms

In Havasupai coiled basketry there is great variety in vessel forms (Fig. 7.9). Dominant is the tray which was produced in a large range of sizes, from 5¾″ to 22″ in diameter and from ¾″ to 4⅞″ in depth. Probably the native tray tended toward the larger sizes but, as this form was produced more and more for sale, changes toward smaller pieces tended to occur. Not enough early Havasupai baskets remain to support this statement, but it is verified among those tribal groups where this craft lingered for native utility purposes into later years. Too, the more decorative nature of the pieces made for sale probably encouraged the making of more shallow pieces which would allow for a better display of pattern.

A second form is the bowl. This, too, varied in size, with measurements from 5¼″ to 15″ in rim diameter and 2½″ to 7″ in depth. The shape of this piece varied considerably, with two basic forms, round and oval. The majority have a feeling of roundness to them whether they are more or less straight-sided; a very few are straight-sided and flat-bottomed, lacking the rounded quality altogether. Some oval bowls have a more open feeling without an actual outflare. More unusual in Havasupai bowls are the following: a very deep form with a wider mouth and smaller base; more or less exaggerated footed styles; some with very rounded and bulging sides; a few of wide diameter high on the vessel; and, rarely, a style with a slight recurve close to the rim.

Jars make up a very small percentage of all Havasupai coiled baskets. Some are wide-mouthed and shallow, similar to bowls but with a neck. Some have pronounced everted rims and rounded bodies. One jar has a straight, wide neck, a rounded body, an abrupt turn to a short, straight-sided lower portion, and a flat bottom. Others have long necks and rounded or elongate straight-sided bodies. One example of the former general type has a definite wide neck and rounded body, very much in the Chemehuevi tradition. Another with longer lines in the body proper leans more in the direction of Apache forms. Definitely in Apache style is a jar with a fairly short neck, an abrupt out-turn into a very rounded shoulder, and a gracefully sloping line to a flat bottom.

Decoration

As far as design in general in Havasupai coiled baskets is concerned, first it may be said that there is great variety: from little or no pattern to great elaboration, from simple to complex layouts, from a few to many elements in a single piece. Coiled basketry, of course, carries the burden of design, while wicker is a distant second. Aniline dyes as well as some native ones came into focus, along with these trends, to make geometrics and life forms more elaborate than they had ever been before.

McKee's marvelous collection plus the Sweeney and other collections will serve as the bases of the following analyses of Havasupai basketry decoration. Too, it must be kept in mind that intermarriage between the Havasupai and Hualapai offers complications in relation to all discussions.

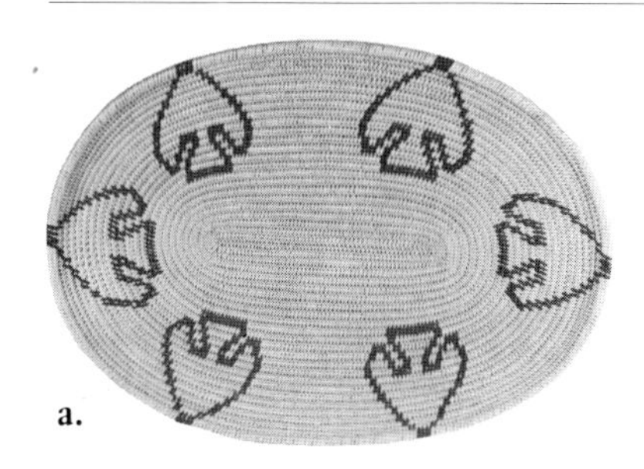
a.

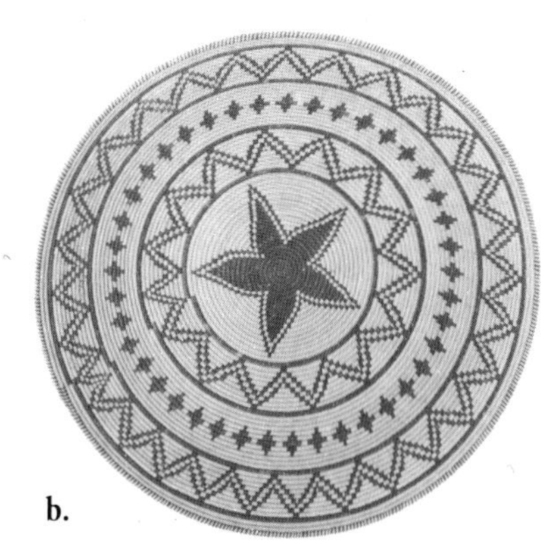
b.

c.

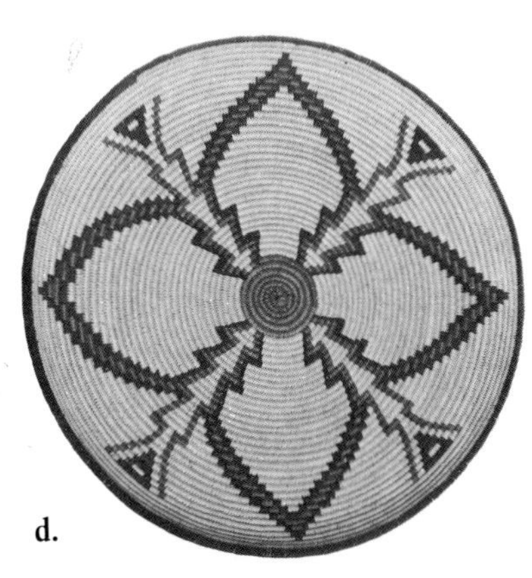
d.

e.

Design layouts in Havasupai baskets are more difficult to identify than is true of most tribal styles. There is a tendency toward all-over arrangements with some of these slightly more organized than others, thus suggesting that they may be, for example, organizational banded; others, however, overlap in such ways as to break down any scheme other than all-over (see Fig. 7.10).

Organizational and all-over banded layouts lead other styles by a great deal. In one collection of about 225 baskets there were at least one hundred examples of the former and over fifty of the latter. Repeated and banded layouts were next, with twelve and ten examples of each, respectively. All other styles had less than ten examples each; interestingly, they were all complex and included, among others, centered-banded, centered-multiple-banded, multiple-banded, and centered-repeated. So much variety is generally not found within a single tribe. Simple all-over layouts are also expressed in Havasupai basketry.

As to design elements and design, there is diversity equal to that in layout. The background of native elements and ways of using them served as a base to which were added Apache ideas, possibly Chemehuevi, Pima (or Papago?), and possibly some influences from other sources. Some may never be accurately identified.

Design elements in Havasupai basketry would begin with the inevitable styles which result from the right-angle crossing of warps and wefts so characteristic of coiled weaving. These would include the two basic elements, squares and rectangles, which, in turn, were built into many themes which function as units. Among these are triangles of right-angle or equilateral style, some with one or more sides which became curvilinear to a greater or lesser degree; diamonds often have comparable characteristics. Lines, frets, and zigzags may be thick or thin and arranged vertically or horizontally. Other basic elements or units would include coyote tracks, arrow points, life forms, the chevron, circles or near-circles, leaf or floral and tree themes, crosses, stars, and a few unidentifiables.

Squares or rectangles may be arranged in checker style to radiate in a straight mass from near center to the edge of the basket; in one instance, they cover the entire basket. In like manner or more dynamically they may form zigzags, sometimes to curve more than halfway around the basket to the rim. Or the same themes may be confined to short units within a band. Zigzags, often in double form, may encircle a basket in two or three rows in such manner as to create diamonds between them.

Triangles are extremely varied (see Fig. 7.9b, c). Their basic nature is mentioned above. Additionally they may be solid, or in single or double outline, or solid with an outline usually creating flower-like patterns. They may be stacked, two alone or many from near-center to rim, or they may serve, solid black and joined, to outline a nega-

Fig. 7.10. Layouts in Havasupai trays, bowls, and jars include the following: (a) organizational bands were most popular in trays, as in this oval style; (b) equally popular was all-over banded; (c) far fewer in number were centered-organizational banded styles; (d) simple all-over designs are also found but are not too common. Layouts on bowls and jars are comparable—namely, banded on the sidewall. These may be repeated as in (e) or continuous. *(All AHS Sweeney Collection.)*

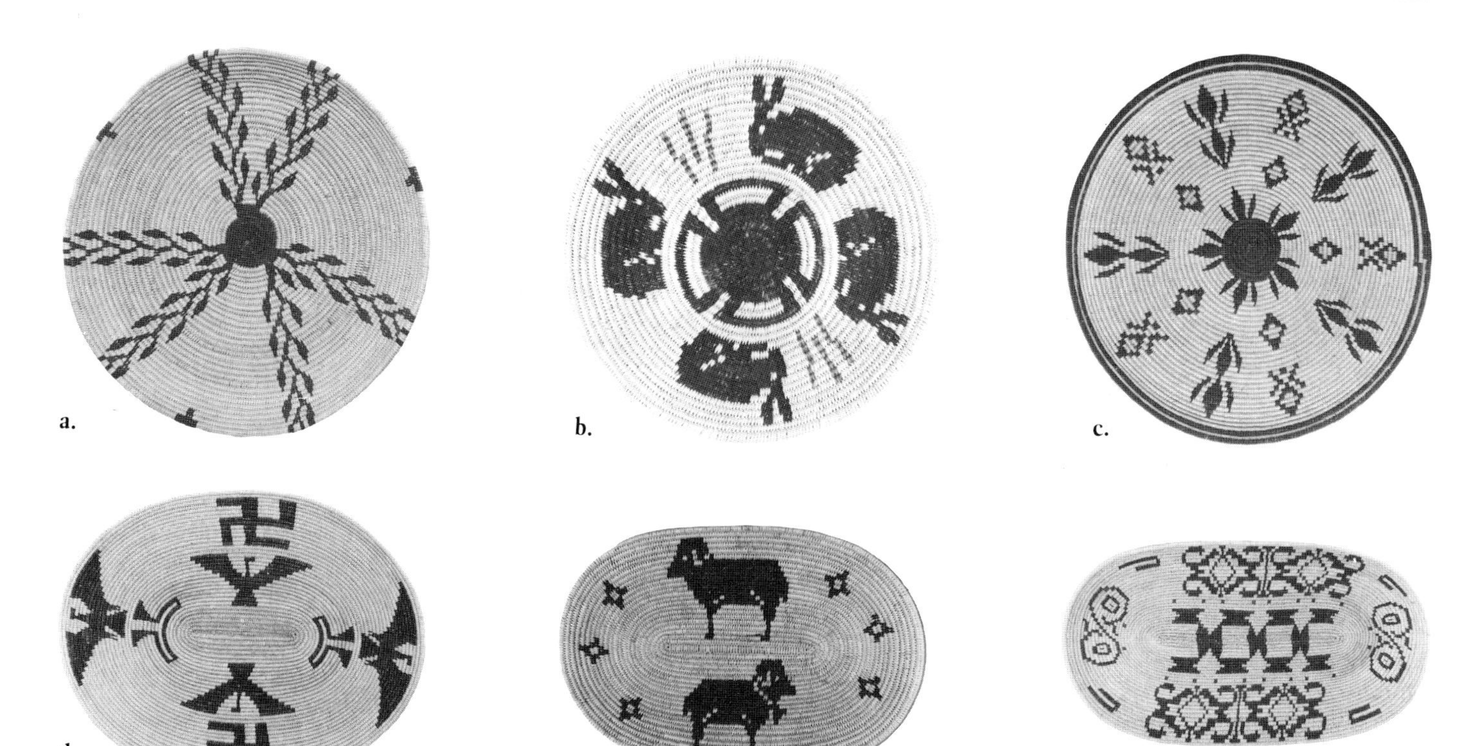

tive floral theme. Tips of triangles often point outward, particularly when they form a central star, although many have their bases facing the basket rim. Not infrequently the two styles appear in a single basket. Sides of triangles are often stepped.

Diamonds on Havasupai coiled baskets are frequently like triangles, stepped, solid, in single or double outline, or they may have a complex inner structure of small solids and open spaces, or a mere small square in the center. Whatever the style, they may be separate and repeated or joined and repeated. The lower half may be smaller than the upper half, occasionally so exaggerated as to lose its diamondlike nature. In one oblong basket, three black diamonds were placed in a horizontal row in the center bottom of the piece. Solid diamonds may be stacked vertically; they may be a bit squashed out of shape to elongate side-to-side dimensions. Occasionally a diamond may be formed of triangles. Perhaps one of the most complex of diamonds is composed of a large outline with an outline triangle inside at top and bottom, and a solid diamond within these on each side, and two T-shaped negative elements within each of these solids.

A floral-like theme has many variations: centered, it may be solid black with four to eight or even up to thirteen petals. These may be short and broad, or of long and slender leaves; some are more realistic. A few have a larger or smaller white center, with four to ten leaves beyond; these, too, may be more or less realistic.

Coyote tracks appear in two basic forms, positive and negative. They may be small and unobtrusive or large and rather overwhelming; in a stacked vertical arrangement, they may be smaller toward the center and larger as they approach the rim. Too, they may be added in spotted fashion, or vertical rows of them may alternately overlap.

Meandering lines take several forms. In one instance, opposed lines resemble the feet, the sides of a body, and arms of a human —but there is no head—is it really just a geometric? Another line

Fig. 7.11. Designs on Havasupai baskets range from simple to complex. (a) A simple vine design extends from near center to the rim. (b) Delightful crouching rabbits form a band around a geometric center. (c) Plantlike elements alternate with smaller geometrics. (d) An oval tray with vigorous birds (eagles?) and swastikas. (e) Docile sheep on opposite sides of an oval tray face in opposite directions, with geometrics at the ends. (f) Elaborate geometrics decorate this oval tray. *(All AHS Sweeney Collection.)*

meanders rather irregularly about the center of an oval bowl. Four pairs of short lines look almost—but not quite—like question marks. Some are almost Y-shaped. Others fall from the rim in a slight curve for a shorter or longer distance, some are short squiggles, some are L-shaped.

There are short vertical lines with alternating horizontals extending off both sides. T-shaped affairs are not uncommon. Frets made up of smooth-edged lines may be short and vertical, or horizontal and encircling the basket; they are usually double and of fairly heavy lines. Stepped themes may form dynamic slanting lines or encircling single or double zigzags, or they may radiate from center to rim in a direct or a curving line. These steps may be made up of squares or rectangles or short vertical and horizontal lines. They are generally positive but may be negative. Occasional lines are made into swastikas, with the arms moving clockwise, or they may form a chevronlike affair. Straight lines may outline other forms, such as joined vertical triangles. Short parallel horizontal lines may be contained between parallel verticals in ladderlike fashion.

In life forms,the bird is presented in formal, outspread-wing fashion with the head in profile; or the entire body and head are in profile; as ducklike figures; or as full-front big-eyed and big-eared owls. One probable bird has great, long, projecting tail feathers(?). Humans, both male and female, are most simply presented in full front, arms at the sides or raised, legs straight, and feet pointed outward. Proportions are fair to poor. Quadrupeds are square-bodied, with four legs attached equidistant along the lower side, with long tail and horse-like ears, or short tail and mountain sheeplike horns. Lizards are longer- or shorter-bodied. Butterflies are realistic even to projecting antennae and spots on their wings.

Full designs in Havasupai baskets are varied and wondrous (Fig. 7.11). They run the gamut from extreme simplicity to great complexity. In the former category would be a few fine stepped lines or broad and heavy ones running from near-center to the rim. These are in the minority. Far more characteristic are elaborate designs comprised of two or more elements in a variety of combinations. In a circular tray are seven black and very large leaf-shaped, separate elements about an open center, with seven detailed butterflies between leaf tips and touching the rim. An oval bowl has a central great lizard surrounded by very heavy, joined V-shaped units with groups of zigzags on either side and black rectangles at the ends enclosing opposed negative meanders. A third piece, a wide-mouthed jar, has vertical arrangements of a lizard with a horse above, stacked stepped triangles, double meanders, a man and a woman above him, then these irregularly alternated around the jar.

Positive design dominates in Havasupai basketry, but the use of negative themes is not uncommon; both may appear in a single basket. Designs are rarely static and may include lines of stacked coyote tracks from near center to rim or several motionless birds spotted on a bowl wall. Almost always they are dynamic, as the heavy usage of encircling zigzags, whirling steps, and moving frets would demonstrate. All-over integrated patterning can again be cited with these other traits as characteristic of Havasupai coiled basketry design. Also there is more balance in total design, with a rare example of an extra bit thrown in, the latter so typical of many Apache baskets.

Sweeney Memorial Collection

Certainly the major part of the McKee collection was Havasupai, yet, as noted above, it is known that at least several of the women making these baskets are definitely from Hualapai families.[55] Although the baskets in the Sweeney Collection are credited to Peach Springs and labeled "Hualapai," nonetheless this writer is of the opinion that most, if not all, of the pieces were really of Havasupai origins, for the Hualapais did not have such a rich design tradition in their coiled basketry, nor is fineness of weave in their background.[56]

Because of the earlier time involved with the Sweeney Collection and because of less knowledge pertaining to this period, more attention will be given some of these pieces. This large collection, involving more than ninety coiled baskets, was assembled in Kingman, Arizona, shortly before and after 1900. No designation for individual pieces will be given, for, as noted above, the two tribes, Hualapai and Havasupai, have been one for too long or have intermarried too much. In a sense, the term Pai might better be applied here as with Bateman's discussion; however, Havasupai remains the general designation, for it is believed that these tribeswomen were the chief weavers of the baskets in this collection.

Inasmuch as this type of coiled basketry was definitely for white trade, it is not surprising that basic forms include trays, bowls, and jars. There is considerable variation within each of these categories, for there were no restrictions as there would be for utility purposes. Trays are often very shallow, frequently with wide, flat bottoms; perhaps this is related to early requests from whites for this form. There were, of course, regular tray styles of deeper nature. Of forty-seven trays, fifteen were oval in form, a high percentage for this variation in native southwestern basketry as a whole. One very interesting tray is of the form shown in the margin. Could the weaver have seen an hors d'oeuvre tray or did some white person ask for such a form? Surely there was no use value for such a piece in native life.

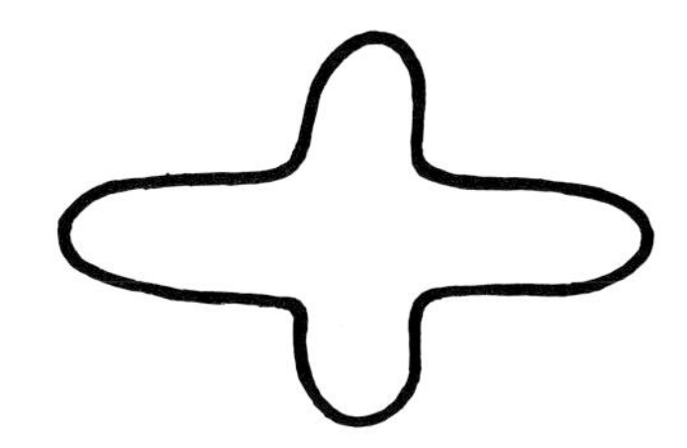

Bowls were also varied in shapes: seven out of eighteen were oval, one was rectangular, the rest circular. Most of them were deep, a few were quite shallow. Some had straight sidewalls meeting a flat bottom; in some, this wall curved gently into the base. It is interesting that there is such a high percentage of oval bowls, as is also true of the tray. Coiled jars present little variety of form; some are quite like bowls with a low neck added. In such cases, there is a slight incurve at the top of the body and a shallow, wide neck. Several jars only out of a dozen examples had slightly higher necks. Two of these basket jars had flat bottoms, the rest were gently curved from body into base.

Willow appears to be the basic material in these coiled baskets, both for the natural background and for a wide variety of dyed design colors. Devil's-claw was, in a majority of pieces, the only decorative material; in other baskets it shared with one or more other colors. In general, the latter included pale and more intense yellow, purple and lavender, pink and coral, red, green, and orange. Of the several colors combined with the natural and black, pink, red and yellow, or pink, orange, and yellow were favored.

The beginning of these baskets is a coiled circle which leaves a tiny central hole in a majority of pieces; or in oval forms, there is a long wrapped start. Weaving is counterclockwise. Rims present interesting variety, although almost all are in regular sewing; this is true of baskets of this collection, with but two pieces with tight, full braids, and one with a partly braided rim. Fifteen baskets were finished in white, nine in alternate black and white stitches, fifteen with the design into the rim, six with alternating pink or red and white stitches, three with alternating black and yellow stitches, one with larger black and white areas, one oval piece with black side rims and alternating black and white end rims, and the rest in black.

Stitch and coil counts are rather average in these pieces as compared with much southwestern Indian basketry. The range in eighty-two baskets for stitches was nine to twenty and for coils four to eight. Eighteen baskets had a stitch count of ten to the inch, twenty had eleven, and twenty-five pieces had fourteen. Very few baskets had nine, fifteen, sixteen, and seventeen stitches to the inch. Only one had a high of twenty stitches to the inch, and that was a small, well-woven rectangular bowl. Coil counts were largely five to the inch—there were forty-eight with this count. Nineteen pieces had four coils to the inch, thirteen had six, and one each counted seven and eight coils to the inch. Again the highest count, eight, was in the one rectangular bowl; indeed it was a fine piece of craftsmanship.

Vessel size varied quite a lot in trays, from 7½″ to 21½″ in diameter, while other shapes were more uniform. Tray rim widths were quite evenly distributed between these measurements, with examples as follows: six of 9″ and four each 13″, 14″, and 17″. All other diameters were represented by three or fewer examples each. Depths of trays varied less: there were seventeen trays just under 1″ to 2″, fourteen which were 2″ to 3″ deep, and one 4″ in depth. Oval trays ranged from 7¾″ by 5″ to 23⅜″ by 13⅜″, with a distribution between these measurements comparable to regular trays. Jars were small for the most part with nine of them from 6″ to 8″ in height, and three 12″ high; their rim diameters were: seven from 4″ to 5″, two 7″, and one each 6″, 11″, and 15″ wide. Bowls were a little more varied, with rim diameters and depths from 2″ to 7″. Oval bowl sizes were comparable to these regular bowl measurements.

Decoration of individual pieces of these coiled baskets included both geometric and life forms. In layout, trays utilized multiple-banded, all-over, and composite, the latter centered and organizational-banded. Jars and deeper bowls are either organizational-banded or of composite style of centered and banded.

The Sweeney Collection presents representative decoration of general styles for basic shapes (Fig. 7.12). One black and rather simply decorated tray is 14⅛″ in diameter, 2¼″ deep, and of good quality sewing. There are two basic motifs, the coyote track and a checkered stepped triangle, each theme presented four times in alternated and raylike rows from a small black center. A single white coil separates the design from the heavy black rim. A second tray has alternated but five-times-repeated rayed motifs, and because of overlappings, this design, like the first, is all-over. There is pleasing balance in the plan of the black-yellow total design. This second tray is larger, 16¼″ in diameter and more shallow, 1⅛″ deep, and better woven than the first. The triple coil rim is of interest in its black, yellow, and final heavy black coil.

a.

b.

c.

Fig. 7.12. Havasupai designs on jars and bowls. (a) Rather different is this geometric pattern on a straight-sided bowl. (b) Active patterning on this bowl is to be noted in a triple meander, with additions of deer and of large coyote tracks. (c) Butterflies with yellow wings and a plant decorate this flat-bottomed jar. *(AHS Sweeney Collection.)*

A third tray in this collection does not reflect the same balance and rhythm so well illustrated in accurate spacing in the above two designs. Rather there is poor spacing of three double-leaf themes, with "wide, wider, and widest" areas between them. The motif itself is most pleasing, with a leaf topping each point of vertical zigzags which reach from a black center into a white rim. Breaking the monotony of the otherwise white rim is a black T-shaped affair between leaf motifs.

One of the most delightful of tray decorations is represented on a fourth basket. Four crouching (or crunching) rabbits are presented in all black but woven so that the natural light material details eyes, legs, and feet. Even the tail is indicated in a stepped rump. These creatures are arranged in two pairs, each rabbit facing out toward a three-piece bit of what may represent grass, for its grows straight and is green. A white coil separates the figures from an all-white rim; sewing on this smaller basket (7½" wide) is very good, counting sixteen to eighteen stitches and six and one-half coils to the inch.

An oval tray is an exceptionally well-woven piece, with counts of more than fifteen stitches and seven coils to the inch, with rim measurements of 11" long and 7¼" wide. On each long side are figures of mountain sheep, so placed as to present one below, one above the other, the lower facing right, the upper to the left. Again the light ground is allowed to show through in stitches to represent the eye, the separate big horn, and some body markings. At each end are three almost-coyote tracks. All designing is in black, but in this oval tray is the common Pai all-white rim. Also like so many Pai baskets, this one is well woven, with a stitch count of fifteen and small coils averaging seven to the inch.

Similarly arranged but more repetitive is a second oval tray design, which features four eagles with outspread wings and with tails and profile heads turned to the viewer's right. The two end birds are situated above a geometric design, but the two at the sides are closer to center, and above each is a massive swastika. Irregularities occur in sizing and spacing; for example, one swastika has very irregular arms, and the bird at one end is smaller and not centered. As is true of a high percentage of oval bowls, the sewing is very fine, counting sixteen to seventeen stitches and eight coils to the inch.

A more coarsely woven (ten stitches to the inch) but large oval tray, 17¼" by 12", is decorated in a very simple manner. It has two outlined arrow points on each of its long sides and one of the same at each end. Quite different is a last oval tray, for it is as complex as the above is simple. It is quite large, 23⅜" by 13⅜", but of average weave. In the center are three butterfly-like black figures with their wing tips touching stepped geometrics on either side. Beyond this central motif and on either side are eight spaced-out small squares. Also on either side and beyond the squares are very elaborate double motifs, each half made up of a centered, stepped outline diamond which in turn is bound by the same general but more ornate shapes and in positive and negative, with two curved elements at each end. At the two ends of the basket are double, stepped, incurving frets. Much of the basket area is thus covered with design, and although there are several irregularities, it is, nonetheless, most attractive.

Simple indeed is a small (7" diameter) bowl with slightly bulging sidewall. It is well woven (twelve stitches to the inch) but simply decorated. The wall pattern begins on the bottom and consists of four colorful and separate zigzags composed of rather thick steps. Opposite steps have different alternations of colors, but both involve purple, yellow, and red. Design goes into an otherwise white rim. A bowl with an incurve-outcurve wall line is small, 8½″ in diameter and 6¾″ deep, but has quite an elaborate pattern. On the bottom is a four-pointed, all-black "flower," while on the wall a large triple fret dominates. Under each "peak" of the fret are large geometrics, and above each lower part is a deer with quite large horns. Large and small coyote tracks ornament the top beneath an unusual and a beautifully braided white rim. All designing is in black.

Jars are graceful in their outlines. Of four forms to be described, three have short necks and one does not. All four have full, rounded bodies, two have more generous flat bottoms, two slope downward to smaller bases. The first flat-bottomed piece is small, 7½″ at the rim and 5″ high; weaving is average in quality but well done, and decoration is simple. A five-petaled flower decorates its base; the only wall motif, all black, is a large double-outline triangle with the same but smaller ones at each top corner. The motif is repeated five times. Flat-bottomed also is a second jar, with a delicately outcurving neck. More elaborate too is the design: on the base is a single meander; on the wall are five paired butterflies, one above the other, and five single plant themes. The butterflies are black-bodied and have yellow wings outlined in black. Vertical zigzags with "leaves" at each point form the plants. One of the smaller-based jars has no design on the bottom but does have a lower double zigzag and an upper double meander on the wall; beneath the peaks on the former are crosses, between the two larger motifs are swastikas. All patterning is in black. This is a very small (5¼″ mouth, 4⅛″ high) but beautifully woven piece (nineteen to twenty stitches and seven to eight coils to the inch).

A last jar is the most graceful of pieces. A delicately curving neck flows into a rounded body, first outcurving then incurving to a small base. Bottom design is shown in the marginal drawing. Wall pattern included a series of six varied, six-pointed zigzags alternating with white coils to a rim stitched in alternate black and coral. From bottom to rim the zigzags are: one, single, black stepped; two, parallel bands of green, yellow, coral, and black; three, black, yellow, black; four, coral, white, green; five, black, coral, yellow, green; and six, black, yellow, black. Although in average weave, this is a most attractive piece, perhaps because of its bands of melded colors.

In summary of Havasupai coiled baskets as based on the Sweeney Collection, the following can be said: Walls of these baskets run the gamut from very thin to very heavy, with the average quite heavy. Shapes are distinctive of this group, occasional examples resembling those of other southwestern tribes. Some designs were unified, but small motifs were frequently scattered all over a basket or between large motifs. Life forms were more frequently in solid or near-solid, while geometrics were often line patterns. When colors were used, one color often outlined another, or they might appear as adjacent bands forming a geometric. More color was used in these Sweeney baskets than in any contemporary pieces which were researched except the Hopi, perhaps because of the popularity of aniline dyes at this time. Double outlines were common; organizational bands were very popular. White centers were numerous, but frequently there were designs on jar bottoms. Havasupai designing is characteristically dynamic, although there is some static patterning. Designs may go into the rim, or touch it, or end a coil or two below it. All in all, there are no distinguishing traits in these coiled pieces to tell which are Hualapai and which are Havasupai baskets; perhaps the finer ones, if not all, were made by Havasupais. Too, the fact that more definite knowledge exists for more elaborate Havasupai designs would place the majority of pieces in the Sweeney Collection in the realm of this tribe's production.

HAVASUPAI WICKER BASKETRY

In writing about the baskets of this tribe in 1928, Spier notes that each household would have two or three burden baskets, six food trays, one or two parching trays, a water bottle or two, and, in earlier years, a boiling basket.[57] The McKees reported the continued popular use during the 1930s of the winnowing tray, water bottle, and burden basket.[58] Obviously, there were no substitutes for these native-made twined pieces at this time; today one would rarely see any of these baskets in the Havasupai village.

Most of the baskets made and used by the Havasupais were woven in twined wicker, some in this weave alone, such as the burden basket, water bottles, and parching trays. However, as noted above, in discussion relative to the Pai in general, some shallow bowls and trays and some stone-boiling bowls (deep forms) were also made in coiled weave. Wicker weave as a whole tended to be crude, relatively speaking, in contrast to fine coiled work. However, where necessary, some pieces in twined weave were quite tightly woven and waterproofed by rubbing in mush or mescal juice. Water jars were often treated with piñon pitch and a paste made of crushed soapweed.[59] Later reports refer to coatings of peach or apricot pulp for parching trays, and the same plus an exterior coating of red clay and piñon pitch, inside and outside, for water jars.[60]

The Havasupai burden basket was basically conical in shape (see Fig. 7.5, both a and b), frequently having a nipple-like bulb at the base, as described for the Pai. A nipple effect is caused by putting the piece in another basket when starting the basket. In size, the utility burden baskets varied according to who was to use them, with the following approximate measurements: large ones, 24″ in diameter and 18″ high, for grown women; medium-sized burdens, 20″ in diameter and 18″ high, for older girls; and small ones, 14″ in diameter and 13″ high, for little girls. Smaller sizes have been woven through later years, particularly in the 1970s, as novelty pieces to be sold. Even miniature burdens were produced in these later years. Spier reported[61] that the utility burden basket was heavily weighted after completion to flatten one side so that it would not roll from side to side when being carried. The utility piece also had two loops placed about one-third of the way down to accommodate a carrying strap, these loops often made of thongs passing through the basket wall three, four, or five times. Too, some claim that the design is "interrupted at the back where the carrier's body would obscure the pattern"; Smithson corroborates this statement.[62] This may have been true of earlier pieces, around the turn of the century, but in later burden baskets the design is usually complete.

Design in the early 1900s was, reputedly, in the weave or of black in geometric bands, both of these styles used on burden and tray forms. Patterns in the weave were in three-strand twine, forming a single row or multiple rows, and placed at various points on the basket wall, frugally or more abundantly, closer together or farther apart. Some of the earlier black designs would include: a line one weft wide with oblique, short lines emanating from this, either above and below or on one side alone; a continuous horizontal zigzag; a horizontal band of equilateral triangles, "usually filled solid, and with basal angles in contact," or with bases touching a line around the basket; or "a band of two opposed dentate lines."[63] Sometimes, as on a boiling bowl, there might be a horizontal row of short, parallel diagonals.

HUALAPAI BASKETS

James reports in 1903 that a Miss Frances S. Calfee was sent to the Hualapai Indians as a field matron to work among them. Among other things, she "reintroduced the art of basket-making." He notes that she purchased "five specimens of their work that show considerable ability and make it certain that, if the art is cultivated, the Wallapais may soon rank as a great basket-making people."[64] James pictures a "Wallapai Basket Maker" with a large decorated coiled basket in her lap, a bowl-shaped piece with incurved rim.[65] Two very large wide zigzags decorate the wall, the upper one touching the rim and dipping into the depressions of the lower row. It would seem that two colors are used in this pattern, a lighter one for the center and a darker shade—but not black—for the outline. No mention is made of color, but Mason notes black and various shades of red as dominant.[66]

Kroeber, in his 1935 *Walapai Ethnography,* gives a summary of basketry developments of this tribe during the late 1920s, with occasional reference to earlier efforts.[67] "In modern times the industry has been somewhat modified by tourist demands," he says; then it is noted that there are both coiling and twining. Basket forms and their uses are given: cups or bowls (coiled) for mush, and, in twined, large openwork burden or firewood baskets, conical burdens for seed gathering, trays for parching and for mush, and water bottles.[68]

In his 1929 survey of Hualapais, little attention was given to coiling; this technique was the most subject to tourist demands, therefore seemingly of little interest to these investigators. Earlier coiling was done in mulberry, later in squawbush and willow. Close stitching on a three-rod foundation was both early and late. Typical of old work was a cup or bowl further waterproofed by rubbing mush into the interstices. Kroeber reiterates that in 1929, the coiled technique was used for the production of bowls and trays, "with rather simple geometric and realistic designs."[69] One such piece is 10½" in diameter, 1¼" deep, typical tray dimensions. An example of a coiled piece is illustrated in Kroeber[70]; it is straight-sided, flat-bottomed, and has a simple rim in white in the same stitch as the

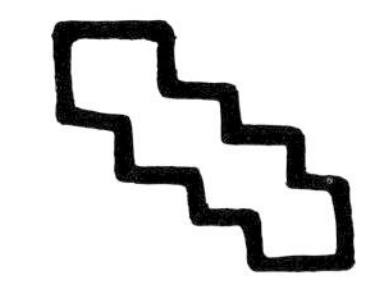

rest of the basket. The decoration is five or six very heavy stepped patterns (see drawing) in two colors, with a central lighter shade and a darker, heavy outline, a rather severe pattern but probably attractive in whatever colors were used (not mentioned). In general these colors are identified as black from martynia, "red, from Spanish bayonet root, yellow, from boiled umak root, brownish, from burnt mescal."[71] Several small trays in the Southwest Museum, Los Angeles, show the same heavier but more solid patterning; too, they illustrate the "realistic designs" in eagles and horses woven into them.

"The bulk of Walapai basketry was twined—above all diagonally," as described by Kroeber[72], it is identical to that done by the Havasupai; so too are the forms, at least for the most part. Kroeber stresses two sizes of seed (burden) baskets, the larger, conical type which curves into a nipple shape at the bottom, which is carried on the back, and a smaller piece carried in the hands which is used to fill the larger one. (This could be the seed beater.) The carrying basket varies in diameter from 12½″ to 19½″ and in depth from 13″ to 16″. Earlier this form carried designs in black only, later the decoration was in simple bands of brown (reddish?) and black, all in simple geometrics. Patterning also took the form of three-strand twined bands, which "is typical of all Walapai twined basketry."[73] A break in the design of the burden basket where it rested on the carrier's back has been pointed out as a Havasupai trait; Kroeber notes this feature once only in Hualapai pieces. Bateman in 1972 says that the "conical burden basket . . . was used extensively . . . within the last twenty years in Havasupai Canyon," but he does not credit such recency in the use of the Hualapai pieces.[74]

Flat trays for winnowing and the parching of seeds are diagonally twined. Concentric bands of three-strand twining were the only decoration on these pieces. Sizes ranged from 12″ to 18″ in diameter, with most measuring 16″, and in depth from 2¼″ to 4″, with a majority 2½″. Willow was used in making these baskets.[75]

Hualapai water bottles were also in diagonal twining. Often they were coated with red paint before they were pitched with piñon gum, inside and out. One shape was biconic; this style was represented by two sizes, 13½″ and 15″ in height and 2″ and 3″ in rim diameter. A smaller type was round-bodied and flat-bottomed; one of these was 8½″ high, about 7½″ in greatest diameter, and 2½″ across the mouth. There were loops on all of these for suspension cords made of braided horsehair or yucca.

The Hualapai seed beater is also labeled as "of Havasupai type."[76] They were from 1 to 1½ feet in length and 3″ to 6″ wide, with a "spoon-shaped curvature" 3″ to 4″ deep. Wide-spaced warps were twined together at intervals, to terminate in a handle formed by warps tied together. Some of the warps were "bent in a double angle" and did double duty as wefts as well. Bateman would place all of the above examples before 1929. He says that "plain twining disappeared from the Walapai area shortly after the turn of the century." He also says of burden baskets, water bottles, and parching trays that "The Walapai had ceased to manufacture such items years before the large museums did the bulk of their collecting."[77] The late nineteenth century collections of these items were all Havasupai, and these older burden baskets often had designs made

Fig. 7.13. Hualapai twined wicker baskets. (a) A straight-sided bowl. (b) A rounded form of bowl with the suggestion of a bird design *(ASM E3555)*. (c) Design is varied in this piece with sets of zigzags in contrasting colors on opposite sides. (d) Medium brown designs on a light ground create a soft effect in this piece *(ASM #E4436)*. Note the decorative three-element twine in all of these baskets. (e) A jar with a black design low on the wall.

by reversing the weft. Bateman says he never saw a Hualapai basket of this type—rather are all of them Havasupai.

Although the commercial twined wicker bowl (Fig. 7.13) is discussed with bare mention in Kroeber's *Walapai Ethnography,* a page of his illustrations tells a bit about them.[78] Forms in most of the nine baskets are severely straight-sided and flat-bottomed. Designs are confined to one or two bands, some narrow, several very broad. One has an organizational band with short pendant lines and four spaced-out units of seven chevrons between them. Two other baskets have a line immediately beneath the rim and a very wide band of short zigzags taking up most of the wall. A rather unusual pattern on a smaller and deeper piece includes a narrower solid line closer to the rim and wider band a little below center. Diagonals appear in several variations: simple and negative; or double along a line; or pendant from single lines; or mixed, the top row of lines all around the basket, and the lower row at intervals.

Bateman says that these pieces, in 1972, were made of sumac and willow by the Hualapai, with a greater variety of materials employed by the Havasupai: sumac, cat's-claw, mulberry (*Morus microphylla*), and willow.[79] It may be added that new forms appeared through the years, including bottle shapes and footed cups, and that a variety of colors was used by the Hualapais, stressing red and black, with the continued popularity of the bowl form.

Euler, in a personal conference in 1963,[80] said that at this time there were eight to ten Hualapai women who did basketry. They used little or none of it themselves. He had an example of a very

Fig. 7.14. Two additional Hualapai wicker baskets, both old. (a) A slightly taller example shows a typical regular band above and an organizational band below, both in deep brown *(private collection).* (b) A simpler arrangement on a bowl of average dimensions with decoration in black *(AHS Sweeney Collection).*

deep form, more like a wastebasket, done by one of these women. A like piece which measured 15½″ in height and 10″ in diameter had four bands of decoration rather evenly distributed about the wall of the basket. Still another piece was straight-sided but at the neck there was a slight incurve to the rim. The body of the basket was ornamented with five bands of decoration, from just under the rim to just above the wide flat base. Designs were simple diagonal line themes, in red and natural in the two top and bottom rows and in black in third and fourth rows (Fig. 7.14).

Thus wicker basketry was stressed by both Hualapai and Havasupai tribes in relation to their own lives. Forms were utilitarian, designing was present but limited, and technology was often poor but sometimes perfected. Although they continued with this style of basketry, production was greatly reduced after contact. Hualapais have continued to weave baskets in this tradition to the present but in smaller sizes and in shapes which appeal to the white man, the straight-sided or nearly straight-sided bowl. Both Hualapais and Havasupais were diverted to the making of more coiled baskets for the white man. Despite lack of evidence, this technique is too well expressed when first encountered to have been a late and new development. It is also likely that the Havasupais were foremost in the development of coiled basketry as indicated in major collections; hence, emphasis is placed on this tribe in discussions of the technique. It seems most likely that throughout this century the Hualapais have emphasized the production of wicker basketry while the Havasupais have stressed the weaving of coiled pieces (except for the burden basket), particularly on several occasions such as at the turn of the century, in the 1930s, and again in the 1970s.

Chapter 8

Navajo, Ute, Paiute, and Chemehuevi Baskets

Navajo Indians have made basketry for many years, perhaps ever since they arrived in the Southwest; there is the possibility that they brought this craft with them when they migrated from the north into this area. The first thought is supported by the fact that the foundation and stitching in some of their baskets compare with the same in Ute and Paiute pieces; in turn, the latter two tribes may well have acquired these details from prehistoric Southwesterners. Some of the patterning may have been adapted from prehistoric design also.

NAVAJO-UTE-PAIUTE COILED WEAVING

A variety of baskets has been produced by Navajos through the years. Matthews reports the continued production of the wedding style in 1894: "It is skillfully fabricated yet it is almost the only form and pattern of basket now made in this tribe."[1] About fifteen years later both coiled and wickerwork were referred to by the Franciscan Fathers. In the first technique they describe the wedding basket plus a variety of other designs in the same tray form. In wicker they reported that the Navajos made a water bottle and a carrying basket, the first "not plentiful" and the second even more rare at this early date.[2]

Writing in 1940, Tschopik notes that at the end of Bosque Redondo, in 1868 (see page 85), the Navajos were making and still using the coiled tray for both secular and sacred purposes, a coiled and pitch-covered bottle for transporting and storing of water, and a wicker gathering basket for collecting yucca fruit and wild edible seeds.[3] The tray was used as a food container and for seed beating, winnowing, and later for parching and roasting piñon nuts, for carrying seeds at planting time, tossing dice, and probably for some of the ceremonial purposes which are well known later on. Thus the basket tray then served in a great many more roles than today; too, there may have been a greater range of shapes and designs; and seemingly there were more women making them in 1868 than in 1940.

Tschopik goes on to note that function, use, and meaning of the tray basket changed quite a lot from 1868 to 1940. The three events he lists as "shaping the destiny" of this Navajo craft through the years were: one, the association with ritual behavior; two, contact with puebloans, which determined shape; and three, the later disappearance of a variety of utility forms.

After 1868 quite a change occurred in Navajo basket weaving. The variety of patterns settled down in time to what is now called the "wedding basket" theme (Fig. 8.1), with other designs eventually disappearing. The band design in this form involves a plain center, a design area consisting of a repeated series of an inner stepped black pattern which joins a plain red band, the latter, in turn, supports a second row of more numerous repeated black steps, and then there is a plain area to the rim. A single opening moves vertically through the entire band of design; it is directly opposite the end of the braided rim.

A word might be said regarding the symbolism attached to the design of Navajo wedding trays, for it is one of the few southwestern basketry decorations which probably has meaning. One very simple interpretation is that the inner black steps represent the underworld; the red band is the earth and life; and the outer black steps stand for the upper world. Fishler[4] recites the following interpretation which he obtained from one of his Navajo informants. The center spot (often a tiny opening) in the basket "represents the beginning of this earth as the Navajo emerged from the cane"; white around this is the earth. Stepped black designs represent the mountains, boundaries of Navajo lands; water bags and rainbows are draped on the mountains, clouds also rise from them. All the white in the basket represents dawn, all red the sun's rays, and all black the clouds, said the informant. Fishler adds much symbolism relative to numbers of coils; he then tells how Navajo legend relates that this wedding basket design was given to this tribe by White Shell Woman, and Thunder taught them to weave the water jar and carrying basket.[5] The braided rim is explained by the Navajos in terms of this legend: A Navajo woman was weaving under a juniper tree, trying to think of finishing the rim in some manner different from that of the regular stitch. A god tore a small sprig from the tree and tossed it into her basket. Immediately she thought of the braided rim.[6]

In completing this very brief historic background for Navajo basketry, it might be said that there were various regional occurrences of interest, as well as certain overall changes through the years. In time the taboos which were attached to the weaving of the basket became so heavy that Navajo women ceased to produce the piece. Ute and Paiute tribeswomen supplied the Navajos with the "wedding" style of basket which continued to be important for use in their rituals. There were local variations in ideas pertaining to its use for weddings, with the piece not appearing at all in some areas but retained in others. Not later than the 1930s and in various parts of the Reservation some Navajo women, often young ones, began to revive the making of the basket, most of them seemingly motivated by economic aspects and ignoring the taboos. Tschopik reports nine of these tribeswomen weaving baskets in the Ramah area in the late 1930s, seven of them young.[7] Adams tells of several full-blooded

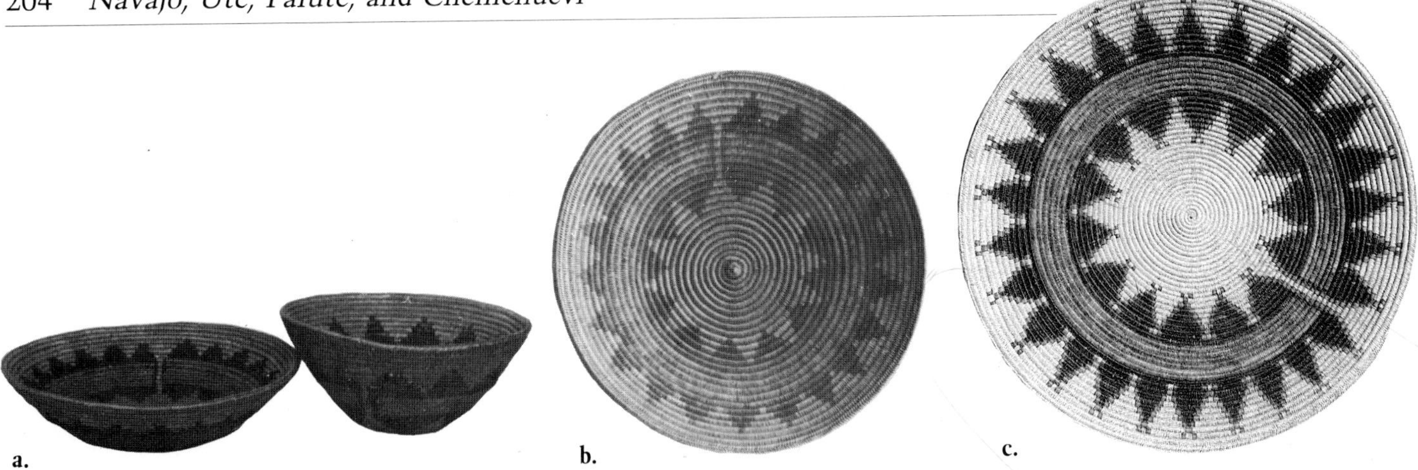

Fig. 8.1. Navajo ceremonial baskets, commonly called the wedding basket. (a) Variations in depths of this piece, with basket at left the more characteristic *(ASM E9007, E7511)*. (b) Full view of the typical wedding basket design; from the interior of the piece to the rim, there is always this sequence: black stepped units, a plain red or red-brown band, and exterior black stepped units. There is always an opening through the design *(James S. Griffith)*. (c) A 1965 example of a Navajo-made basket which is beautifully woven. Note the tiny red squares at the corners, and the red outlines of the inner and outer black steps *(Russ Lindgren)*.

Navajo women weaving baskets in the early 1950s at Shonto.[8] In the late 1960s a Navajo woman made a very large, beautifully designed and finely woven wedding basket in the Window Rock area. Occasional Navajo-made wedding baskets appeared in the Gallup Ceremonial shows during the late 1960s and into the 1970s. At the 1977 Casa Grande, Arizona, Indian Show, there were quite a few new Navajo-made wedding baskets. Thus there has been a gradual increase in the production of the wedding basket by Navajo women. A few variations appeared here and there, with an increase in size in some few pieces, and a greater elaboration in occasional design, such as a spread-wing bird on a 1981 piece.[9] Also there was a terrific increase in inferior weaving and rather wild aniline dyes.

The majority of other types of Navajo baskets tended to disappear. The carrying basket certainly was on its way out in the early part of the twentieth century, as implied by the Franciscan Fathers. Water bottles ceased to be important to the Indian at about the same time; however, these continued to be made in limited numbers, with two changes appearing: as a rule they were no longer pitched and the size was reduced considerably.

Altman notes that a Navajo bride cooks cornmeal in three colors, red for health, blue for happiness, and white for wealth.[10] During the marriage rite, the medicine man places the wedding basket with the cooked meal between the couple. Altman adds that the white serves as background, the red and blue over it in the form of a cross. Both the Franciscan Fathers[11] and Fishler agree that cross lines from east to west, south to north, and other lines around the edge of the mush were made of pollen. First the bride washes her groom's hands in a bowl with water in it; then he washes hers. This is followed by the bride taking a pinch of meal from the east side of the tray, the groom doing the same; then she takes meal from the south, west, and north of the pollen lines, each times the groom following her. Both together take meal from the center of the basket. The ceremonial piece is then passed around to all of the guests, each taking a pinch until the basket is empty. The last to take meal receives the basket. This use of the Navajo basket for a wedding is described by Altman in 1946.[12]

Adams says that apparently in the Shonto area the singer receives the basket at the termination of the rite.[13] In any event, there were around five hundred of these baskets in and out of this trading post during the years 1954–56. After any ritual use the basket was taken back to the trading post and sold, only to be bought again by another Navajo for some other ceremony. Adams also stresses the fact that these baskets hold cornmeal or pollen at these rituals.[14]

Matthews goes into a detailed description of the use of this basket as a drum. The same procedure is followed for marking the wedding basket around its edge and with a cross, with the same pattern duplicated on a rug on the floor of the ceremonial hogan. The basket is turned over, the east or west end of the rug folded over it, and it is beaten with a rather elaborately made yucca drumstick. Thus the basket is used for one of the most important of Navajo rituals, the Night Chant. Tschopik cites the following varied uses in the Ramah area. Here the basket is turned upside down to serve as a drum. Frequently it was used to hold ceremonial paraphernalia, such as rattles, prayer sticks, sacred meal, medicines, and other ceremonial objects, or it served as part of the mask in certain ceremonies. It is the utensil in which the ceremonial "bath" is given during certain rites. Despite the fact that the basket is required in specific sings,[15] it is best known as the receptacle to hold the sacred mush for the wedding rite; thus, understandably it has come to be known as the "wedding basket."

Inasmuch as this ceremonial basket has not always been made by Navajos, a word should be said regarding this situation. Seemingly the Navajo woman wove this piece until too much ceremony and too many taboos became attached to its production. Some ritual restrictions include the following: The basket must be started in the east, finished in the east. No one can watch a woman weave a basket. All work must be done some distance from the hogan; all weaving must be done on the concave surface, for the worker would otherwise lose her mind. If she worked in a high wind, her materials would split. A woman could not work on a basket when she was menstruating, nor could she sleep with her husband while weaving a basket. After the design was started and until the basket was finished, she could eat little meat and bread and no salt. And she must have a sing over her before and after starting the basket. These and other taboos were enough to discourage any woman from weaving a basket. Tschopik also stresses the fact that some Navajo singers have told the women that they would become ill if they wove baskets at all.[16]

Thus, for many years, fewer and fewer Navajo women produced this basket. Other tribes, such as southern Paiutes and Utes, placed no taboos on the production of the Navajo wedding basket, and as Stewart says, they found it to be a "lucrative and pleasant task." To quote Stewart further, he says that these tribes have "acquired a new art during the last decade or two. Not the art of basketmaking —they already had that—but the art of making a particular basket in a manner previously unknown to them. To make the wedding basket, the Ute and Southern Paiute acquired this new shape, the technique of elaborate decoration (which they lacked), and changed the direction of coiling and their method of sewing."[17]

Stewart notes further that the Navajos did not object to the lack of ritual on the part of the Utes and Paiutes when making the wedding basket. He states that their baskets and those of the Navajo "are almost identical," and indeed they are! It was requisite that certain details of the basket be adhered to: the same colors, the same design, and the braided rim which ended directly across from the opening in the design. Adams thought that perhaps the end of the rim which was more gently tapering was a diagnostic of the Ute-Paiute, while the abrupt end was the Navajo. Also he thought that about three-fourths of the baskets he saw during his year's work at Shonto in 1955 were made by Utes and Paiutes, for they had the gently tapering end at the rim. However, he said that this detail was a "general impression" which he had. Actually, there is nothing to support the notion that the abrupt rim end is either Navajo or Ute-Paiute. He estimated that about one in every twenty or thirty baskets coming into the post was new; this he supports by naming several Navajo women who were making this basket at the time and by referring to others in the Shonto area who were doing the same.[18]

Materials

Materials employed in the making of the Navajo tray baskets included sumac (*Rhus trilobata*) which was used whole for the two rods and split for the sewing splints.[19] Tschopik says a different species of sumac or even willow (*Salix* sp.) was used by the Paiutes[20]; *Yucca baccata* was cut into fine pieces for the bundle in the two-rod and bundle, bunched foundation.[21] The center starts with a short wrapped section, then splays out into the first sewn coil; the opening in the design is in line with this splay. Adams said that a wooden awl was used in the Shonto area in sewing coiled baskets. Counterclockwise sewing is employed, and stitches are non-interlocked. In the coiling process "the butt end of one rod must be placed against the tip of another."[22] Women are the weavers, although Tschopik reports that transvestites formerly made baskets.

In known wedding baskets of each of the three tribes, Ute, Paiute, and Navajo, the braid may be flat on top or it may be rounded and go partly down the sides of the top coil. Also there have been observed for all three baskets both types of endings at the rim, either very abrupt or gently sloping. As a whole, the latter predominates. Coil-stitch counts and sizes vary so greatly that they will be discussed below relative to tribal groups or different collections.

The background or light color in Navajo coiled baskets is the natural sumac. Black and red are usually dyed, the latter varying in shade from a bright red through dull shades of the same, into browns; orange is sometimes substituted. Black ranges from a true black to blue-black; of course, in many pieces it is faded and definitely of grayish tones. In earlier years both red and black were native dyes; Haile says they were the same as used for textiles.[23] The black reputedly was sumac leaves, twigs, and berries crushed and boiled with a powder made of a concoction of melted piñon gum and roasted ocher. For the red or reddish brown color, Haile says that mountain mahogany (*Cercocarpus* sp.) roots were crushed and boiled, then ashes of twigs of juniper and powdered bark of black alder were added. These "recipes" have been corroborated in more recent observations of dyeing basketry splints. Also, aniline dyes have been used in more recent years, often producing brighter reds or the orange mentioned above.

Forms

Haile adds that sumac or willow is the material which may have been used in the making of Navajo wicker baskets. Water bottles and carrying baskets were the two forms made in this technique;

the wicker water bottles "are not plentiful, and are being displaced more and more by the modern pail and bucket," he says.[24] The old wicker piece was often rubbed with red clay and pitched inside and out with piñon gum. The carrying basket (like pueblo peach baskets) was woven of willow in simple wicker weave.

It is of interest to speculate on how the wedding basket design evolved. Obviously, this is not definitely known, for the fragile basket does not leave many evidences of its historical development nor are records particularly revealing. Old baskets do show up now and then and some of these may well hold "chapters" in the story of the design in this piece, particularly if such pieces are dated.

Clay Lockett Collection

One such interesting collection of old Navajo baskets was in the Clay Lockett shop in Tucson, about 1942. It included one basket inspired by the wedding style and fourteen other pieces (Fig. 8.2a–o); some of the latter would seem to present possible steps in the evolution of the wedding basket design. The others appear to be unrelated to the wedding style and may well have been in the category of the general utility basket used by the Navajos intensively up to the end of Bosque Redondo times, tapering off in use after 1868. However, as noted, making certain baskets to trade or sell became important in the economy of the Navajo after they themselves ceased to use them. Even the wedding basket was taken to traders and sold, often to a white man, after its ritual use; from the 1930s into the 1980s these pieces were observed in many trading posts.

It is difficult to establish a complete sequence of types in this group of baskets. However, as is said in relation to a group of similar but not the same baskets illustrated in Amsden, "The designs suggest a progressive merging of the isolated figures—into the banded pattern."[25]

Beginning with baskets a and b in Figure 8.2, there are large, isolated elements. In examples c and d they are reduced in size; in the latter they are drawing closer together. Basket e shows the element larger again but closer together, while in basket f they are once more reduced in size but now actually touching, thus forming a continuous theme except for one point where an opening is left. In basket g a plain ring with an opening is formed, perhaps too far removed from the previous style and too simple to please the design inclinations of the Navajo. Interestingly, this same style with two outlining bands and with a single opening is pictured in *Anasazi Basketry,* and labeled Pueblo III[26]; seemingly this piece was the greater part of a tray basket; it has a two-rod and bundle foundation and uninterlocked stitches. In basket h, the banded theme is varied in a more meandering pattern, with an opening at one point. Perhaps this experiment still did not please, and so next was a red band with black edge and projections which are a bit barbaric (basket i). Then they tried a more gently undulating wide red band, still with a narrow black stepped edging (basket j). Then someone seemingly tried a pattern which was a cross between examples i and j, with more definitive stepped triangles than in the latter but without the sharp projections of the former (basket k). This piece was, perhaps, more to the liking of the designers, leaving but one step to a last style—the black-outlined red triangular extensions finally became black stepped triangles, on both inside and outside, and

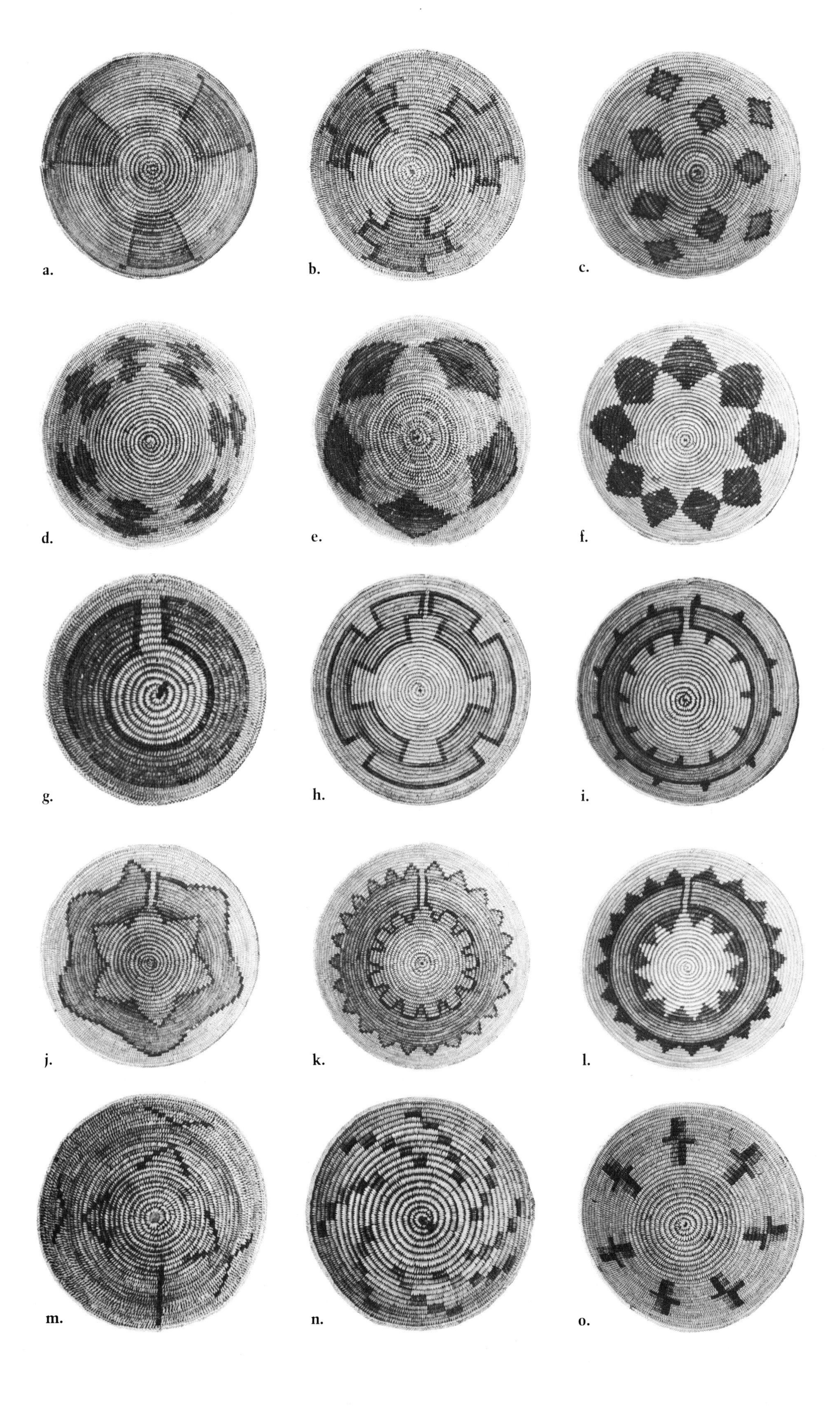
a.
b.
c.
d.
e.
f.
g.
h.
i.
j.
k.
l.
m.
n.
o.

between them the red area became a plain band. Thus the Navajo wedding basket (see basket l), may well have come into existence.

Other baskets (m, n, o) in this group may have been variations on the theme of individual scattered elements as seen in basket c. Basket m could belong to the above sequence, but baskets n and o seem less related to these arrangements. Neither in layout nor in potentials for design development do they seem to fit into the sequence. There were many other designs similar to baskets a and b, such as the large almost-square and the cross, both in red outlined in black and with tiny blocks at some (or all) corners.[27] Basket e is simulated in Amsden's Plate 4f, while his basket l in the same plate is similar to basket i except that they have projections with a tail, as shown in the marginal drawing. His basket i resembles number k.

Relative to the considerable speculation regarding what differences, if any, exist in the wedding basket as made by the Utes, Paiutes, and Navajos, the following comments are presented. As Fishler says, the Utes and Paiutes changed their foundation and the Paiutes stabilized the direction of the coil to the left in acquiescence to the desire of the Navajo,[28] and both tribes conceded to the shape and decoration required by the Navajos. Not all would agree with Fishler in these statements. Fishler would seem to credit the origin of certain designs unlike the wedding styles to Ute or Paiute Indians, or possibly to Navajo blankets. He seems hesitant to credit the Navajo women with developing these themes as they were "very reticent about effecting innovations in basketry design because of ritual and social pressure."[29] Against this thought it may be argued that the Navajo women were, perhaps, not yet subject to these ritual pressures, for most of the different designs were of earlier usage. In fact, it is quite likely that these designs were used largely on utility baskets, that the wedding basket pattern was an early development, possibly out of those suggested, and that the two co-existed. When the utility pieces disappeared, their designs were no longer used. It is quite likely that it was then that taboos began to be applied to the weaving of the remaining ceremonial piece so as to retain the "status quo," a common trend in religious art as a whole.

Possible Relation of Navajo Basket-Blanket Designs

The possibility that Navajo basket design may well have been derived from their blankets[30] can be supported in many cases in the grouping of early styles given in Figure 8.2, a–o, whether developed

Fig. 8.2 Suggested steps in the early development of the Navajo wedding basket: (a) and (b) are quite early, large and limited; (a) almost square units of design, and (b) crosses with tiny squares at the corners. In both examples design is in reddish brown outlined in black. (c) and (d) show much smaller elements, here diamonds, arranged in organizational bands. In (e) the units have become larger again, but they are closer together and in (f) smaller and touching at every point except one. In (g) the band has developed, a plain one with a definite opening at one point. In (h) the band changes to a wide meander; then (i) becomes plain again with stubby triangles projecting on either side. Probably experimentation made the band wavy (j) with suggested steps; then it was straightened out and definite steps were added to the projecting red triangles (k). The last step marks the full attainment of this design (l), with the outlining black becoming dominant in stepped triangles on both sides and the center band remaining plain red. Baskets (m), (n), and (o) show possible designs which resulted from experimentation along the way. *(From Clay Lockett Shop, photos by Fritz Kaeser.)*

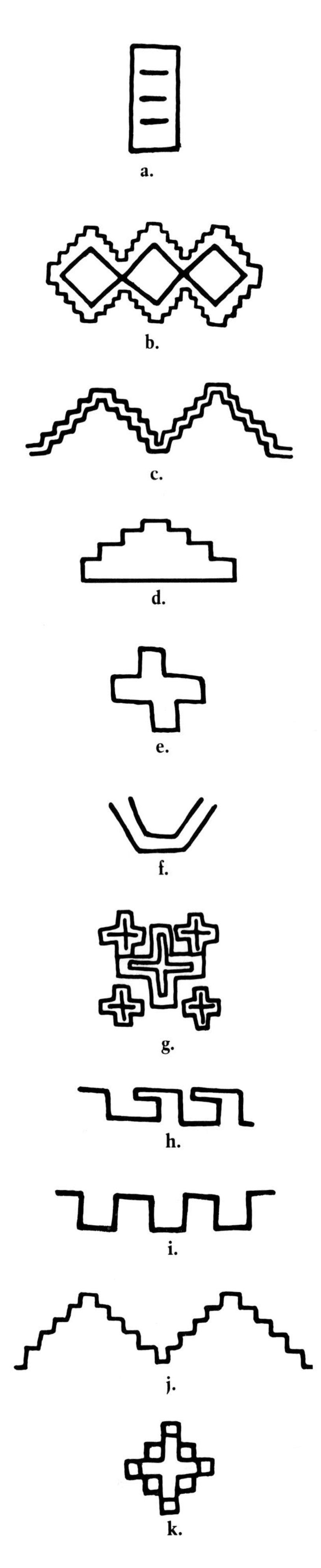

by Utes-Paiutes or the Navajos themselves. These first blanket comparisons are taken from Kahlenberg and Berlant's *The Navajo Blanket,* 1972.[31] In basket a the three rectangles are probably adaptations of such designs as found in blanket 16 which is dated 1850–1865 (see drawing a). In the same blanket are joined diamonds with stepped outlines comparable to the same in basket f (see drawing b), although in the latter the design becomes slightly more curved, no doubt owing in part to the shape of the basket itself. Stepped diamonds are common in Navajo textiles as illustrated in blanket 13 dated 1850–65; they are also found in baskets c, d, e, and f. In this blanket also are stacked diamonds which may have inspired the design in basket d. Meandering bands, such as in basket j with dark stepped edging, are to be noted in blanket 11[32] dated 1850–65 (drawing c). In the basket, the band center becomes wider, the edge narrower. Such adaptations are to be expected.

It would seem that there could be little doubt about the origin of the familiar wedding basket design, with its stepped triangles on either side of the red band (l). As early as the Period II Chief blanket style, 1855–65, illustration 2,[33] this stepped motif (drawing d) appeared in weaving. Whether or not it developed this early in the basket is not known, but surely the potential was there. A single line in basket o invites some speculation—a straight black line reaching to the rim, between simple patterns but not related to them: it would seem to be a forerunner of the opening through the wedding basket design. Its source may possibly be in the "weaver's pathway," a thread which goes from the interior through the border of a rug to the outside.[34] The same idea is expressed in other Navajo arts. Lines, single or double, also appear in blanket designs, as in Kahlenberg and Berlant[35], illustration 8, but usually no explanation is given of them; double lines date to at least as early as 1860–70.

Crosses of various sorts appear in blankets (illustrations 35, 49, 54),[36] including the one shown in drawing e; two colored ones in basket m could well have been inspired by this one. Bands are very common in blanket designs, with every conceivable version of wide bands of one color bordered by another, or composites of multiple bands, plus many other combinations. The plain red basket band bordered by black certainly finds its counterpart in many of these blankets pre- and post-dating 1850.

In Wheat's *Navajo Blankets*[37] are found counterparts of other motifs in these early Navajo baskets. Chevrons in basket o are not greatly different from those in blanket illustration 2,[38] dated 1830–50 (drawing f). Earlier crosses appear in blankets not later than around 1860 (blanket 8)[39] and are heavier in a few years (blanket 15)[40]. The latter show complex crosses with smaller ones near the four corners (see drawing g); could this style have been the inspiration for the heavy cross with tiny squares at each corner, simplified in the smaller basket b? Meanders appear not later than 1865–75, blanket illustration 10,[41] (drawing h), and in simple types of 1870–75, illustration 13[42] (drawing i); these are close in style to some in basket h. A more pointed version of this, almost a zigzag, with the same red center and a narrow black edging, now stepped, is to be noted in basket k; this style is also suggested in an 1850–60 blanket, illustration 13[43], drawing j. Stepped triangles and stepped diamonds are both found in the woman's blanket dress dated 1850–60, illustration 5[44]; the latter appears in the much elaborated style, almost a cross, shown in drawing k, and as discussed above (baskets c, d, e, f). These possible sources for Navajo basket designs are presented for what they may be worth, regardless of which craft did the "adapting."

Comparisons of Ute-Paiute Features in Navajo Baskets

Some points will be presented relative to a few characteristics in baskets definitely made by Utes or Paiutes. First is a collection of twenty-two baskets known to have been woven by Ute women; this study was made in June 1975, and all of the baskets were apparently new at this date. The pieces in this collection were cruder than older pieces made by the same tribe. There was a fair amount of variation in most of the characteristics except in coils which counted from only one and one-third to two to the inch, with half of them counting one and one-half to the inch. Stitches ranged from five to ten to the inch with half of the twenty-two baskets counting seven. Diameters were as follows: five baskets measured 13″ to 14″, fifteen were 15″–16″, one was 17″, and one was 19″ across. The last one is a fairly large wedding basket for contemporary times. Depths were from 2″ to 4″ with twelve baskets measuring 3″ to 4″ high in center measurement.

Designs were the usual interior and exterior black steps with a plain red band in between them. Most of the interior steps counted six or seven, with sixteen baskets in these two categories, one only of four steps and one only of ten steps. The outer steps had more of a range, from eleven to twenty-one, with two of the former and but one of the latter count. The greater number centered around thirteen (four), fourteen (six), and fifteen (four) outer steps. There seems to be no established ratio of inner to outer steps; for example, in three baskets there were eight and seventeen, five and ten, and six and thirteen. As usual the step was an equilateral triangle stepped on two sides in all but one case which was a right-angle triangle stepped on one side only. The red band was made up of two coils only in five examples while in seventeen baskets it was of three coils.

Some features in this collection tend to reflect inferior craftsmanship compared with some other Ute baskets. Coil count is low, for other baskets have been observed with a count of three per inch. Numbers of stepped patterns may exceed those given here, too. For example, in several known Ute-made pieces of 1976 there were as many as nineteen inner and thirty-seven outer steps. Stitching is very irregular in most of the baskets of this Ute collection, walls are heavy and stiff, and all but one of the pieces had a hole in the center. Most rim braids were rounded and sewed down onto the sides; three only had a flat braid on top of the rim coil.

Two very unusual pieces, one made by a known Ute woman, were in the 1976 Gallup Ceremonial competition. The unique features in each of these two baskets were two sets of the encircling design. Both baskets were average in size and in coil and stitch counts. In the inside encircling pattern of one basket were eight inner and sixteen outer steps, while the other pattern had fifteen inner and thirty outer stepped elements. The second piece counted nine and eighteen steps for the inside pattern, and nineteen and thirty-seven for the outer design. The first basket had red bands in both patterns while the second had red in the outside pattern and orange in the inner. One other basket in this same competition had eight crosses and coyote tracks in place of the inner theme and a regular wedding basket circle with a small opening for the outer design.

As far as rim braids are concerned, in general most of those observed, as in the above collection, are rounded but several are flat and on top of the last coil. The majority of the rim ends are gently sloping but a few terminate abruptly. As a whole, sewing in known Ute baskets is poor to fair, with better work in many earlier pieces. Thus, the above collection would seem to fit into the usual Ute pattern of basket weaving.

Of the many wedding baskets observed, very few could be positively identified as Paiute-made. These presented a few variations but no distinctive characteristics could be established; certainly the pieces would fall into a broad selection, but most were superior to the above 1975 Ute baskets. In the Paiute group both flat and round rim braids were noted, and most had a gently sloping rim end. Sizes were within Ute ranges, with diameters from 13½″ to 21½″; most of these pieces were slightly deeper than the Ute baskets, with variations from 3″ to 4⅝″. Stitches counted from nine to fifteen and coils two to four and one-half per inch, both of these features indicating finer sewing than is evident in the above Ute collection. All of the inner and outer motifs in the design were within the range of Ute pieces described above. There was a tendency to include more coils in the center band, for in the Paiute pieces there were from three to seven red coils forming this motif.

A small sample of eight baskets known to be Navajo-made and woven about 1975 shows no particular deviation from other styles of wedding basket weaving. More diameters are between 12″ and 14″ (five), and only one is 16″. Depths are little different—most clustering around 2″ to 3″ (five). Stitches reflect the average, with seven baskets of nine to ten stitches, and five baskets had two coils to the inch. Seven pieces had three red coils in the design, five had five to six inner stepped patterns and the same number had ten to thirteen outer steps. Six baskets had a hole in the center, two did not. All in all, these late Navajo-made pieces support older styles in a greater conservation in all features. However, the sewing in this modern group did not come up to the fine work of older Navajo pieces.

Additional Designs in Navajo Tray Baskets

As noted above, there are other designs in the Navajo tray, some of which are perhaps older than the wedding style. One of the most popular of the simpler patterns is the cross (Fig. 8.3). This appears in arrangements of three or four on a basket. Usually the cross is a large, equal-armed design, all four parts very thick and red, with a black outline. At each of the corners of the four arms are small black squares. Sometimes the arms may be thinner; in such instances the crosses may number more—for example, one piece has seven of them. Large, plain almost-squares which are smaller at the base appear in place of crosses but are not as common. Various arrangements of diamonds are to be noted, in single or double bands or scattered over most of the surface of the tray. Sometimes the single row may not be joined, particularly when the diamonds are

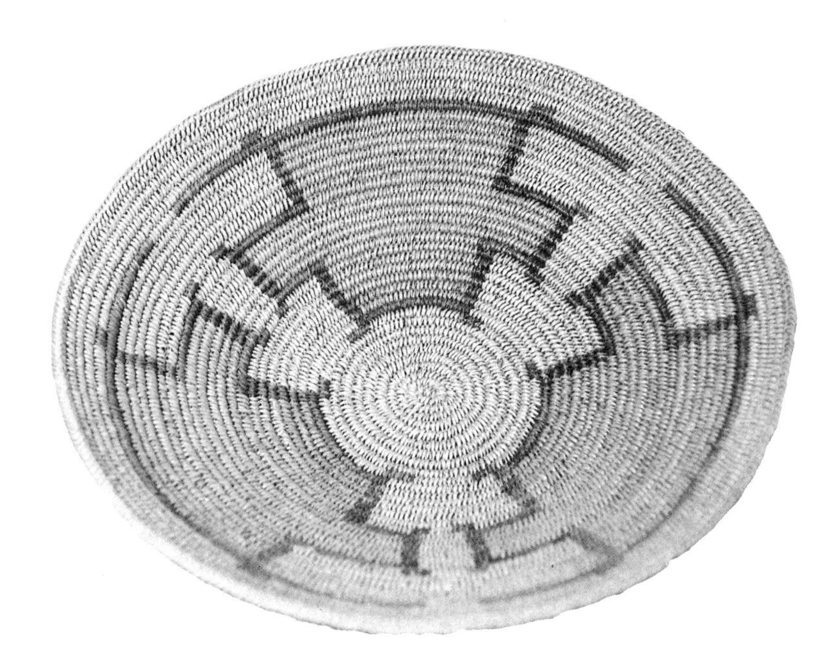

Fig. 8.3. A fairly popular old design for the Navajo coiled tray. Three or four of these crosses are woven in red with a thin-line black edging plus black squares or rectangles at the corners. Acquired in 1916 *(James S. Griffith).*

smaller in size. This form may be solid black, or red with a narrow black bordering line.

Another fairly common pattern is the band, plain and with or without projections or in angular or more pointed meandering arrangements. Almost invariably these bands are red inside with a narrow bordering black edge, and if present, projections are also black. A narrow opening characterizes this type, as is sometimes true of the row of diamonds. Many of the plain bands and angular meanders are very neatly done, but sometimes the projections are irregular in shape and not too well spaced. Some projections are mere continuations of the red area, with, of course, the black outline following their forms; some are thin or thick or mere right angles, with four of these a common number, or, as on one basket, four on the inside of the band, seven on the outside. Another tray has ten small stepped triangles on the inside of a plain band, seventeen of them on the outside; the band is red, the lines outside the band and triangles are black.

Other variations of these small designs include chevronlike figures placed at various points on a basket, usually repeated three times, or small stepped squares, sometimes in dynamic repeated curves. Other small elements, repeated from three to eight times are plain red "chongo hairdo" themes (the Navajo style) and all red (drawing a); arrow points (drawing b), also all red; triangles stacked in various ways, all red (drawing c), or half red and half black (drawing d). Sometimes there are oddly shaped geometrics (drawings e and f), drawing e in red outlined in black, and drawing f with a red center and black sides. In one basket were six rectangles woven at a slant, in red with thin black outlines. Inasmuch as many of these small patterns are scattered separately over the tray surface, there can be no opening; in place of it there is often a single or double line reaching from about mid-point in the sidewall out toward the rim (Fig. 8.4b, left). This is probably an indication that at least some of these baskets with designs other than the wedding style *might* have been used ceremonially, as noted above. Perhaps these lines were for the directional orientation of the piece as is the spirit opening in the wedding basket.

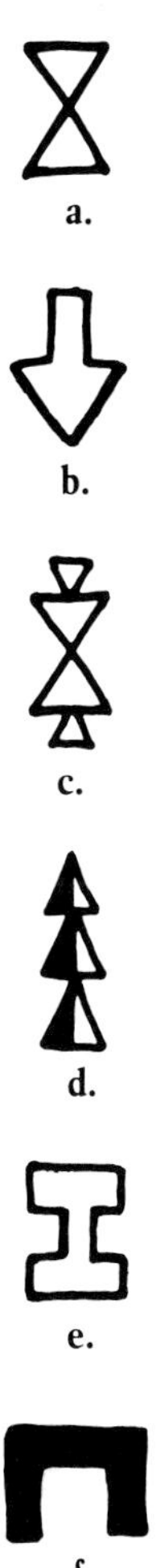

a.

b.

Fig. 8.4. Navajo tray baskets. In (a) is a regular wedding motif and to the right a more dynamic version of the same *(ASM 1837, 9002)*. (b) Left, the basket is decorated with simple stick figures; note two parallel lines which mark the "sacred outlet." To the right is another example of the use of the graceful Apache diamond *(ASM 1839, 8021)*.

Other forms of baskets in addition to the tray have been produced through the years by Ute, Paiute, and Navajo Indians. Again some of these are so similar that they are difficult or impossible to differentiate on a tribal basis. In 1963, Euler said that the Paiutes in northwestern Arizona no longer made any baskets at all; he also said that the last woman to make the simple twined basketlike beater "died several years ago."[45] This leaves the Utes of southwestern Colorado and the Paiutes of southeastern Utah, and some Navajos as forming the groups which continued in the old traditions, particularly in the making of the wedding basket.

Water Bottles

As to specific forms, certainly the most common is the coiled and pitch-covered water bottle. In 1942 Watkins described the bottle as having a long straight neck and handles, but there are variations on this piece; about the gathering basket, she says that it "is similar to those still used by the Hopis" and adds that it "may have been copied from the Pueblos."[46] Obviously she refers to the peach basket, a form evidently not made for many years.

The Navajo-made water bottle may have a longer (older) or shorter (more recent) neck and a rather full, rounded body. Also earlier styles seem to have had more rounded bases while later pieces were frequently flat-bottomed. Some of the Ute-made pieces had narrower necks; some of Paiute manufacture had very small necks and pointed bottoms. Size seems to have decreased as native use-value ceased. Many small pieces are made in later years.

The Navajo water bottle is generally in coiled weave (Fig. 8.5); it is represented in a dozen pieces of miscellaneous times and from a number of sources. Height ranges from 5½″ to 14″, with most of the baskets around 8″ to 9″ high. Greatest diameter in the body tends to be about the same as basket height, with a few both over and under this measurement. Neck diameters vary between 3½″ to 4¾″, while their heights run from 1¾″ to 3″. Stitch counts are low on most of these bottles, the majority of them three to four to the inch but with some up to nine to the inch; pitching took care of the poor sewing in the older pieces. Coils range largely from three to four per inch.

Forms in these water bottles have little in common except for a small neck and a larger body. Necks may be of medium height, fairly wide, and straight-sided. One slopes gently inward from rim to juncture with the body; another has a distinct outflare toward the body. Bodies may be perfectly rounded outward from neck to mid-body and from there inward to the base. One has an almost-ridge at mid-point; another has a gently out-curving line from neck to base.

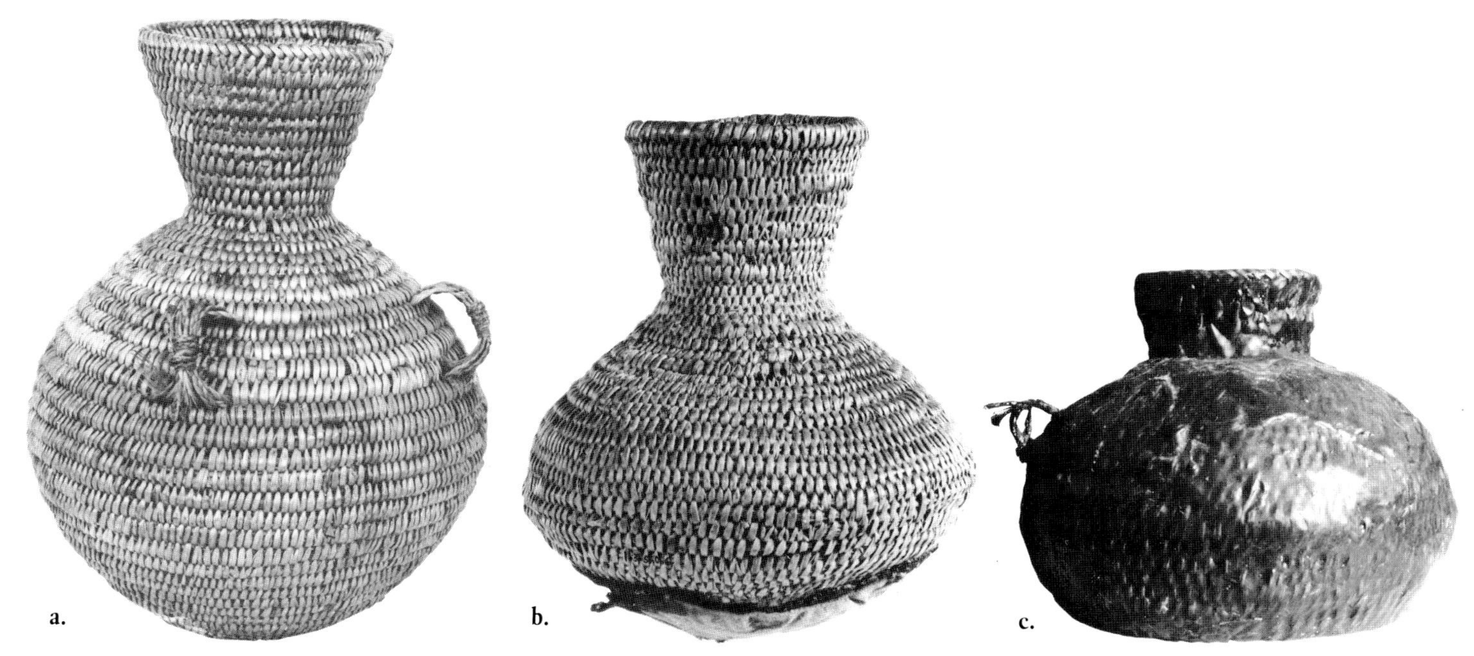

Fig. 8.5. (a) An attractively formed, coiled water jar, Navajo made. It is most symmetrical, has a braided rim and two handles. It lacks design, for originally it was pitch covered *(ASM 04328)*. (b) A second jar with a more squat body and a sharper line into the lower portion. Note patch on base *(ASM 13506)*. (c) A round-bodied, flat-based Navajo jar woven in 1962 and pitch covered *(private collection)*.

Still another has a squat neck and body and a flat base, in contrast to a basket with a long and more graceful neck flowing into a thinner body.

Most of these water jars have handles, usually two to a bottle, and generally they are placed fairly close together. All handles but one are of horsehair; some are braided and at least one has a double braid for each loop. Originally all of the bottles were probably pitched, and in some instances this pitch is carried onto the handles. Pitch is so heavy on some baskets that such features as coil and stitch count and rim finish cannot be determined. In several baskets there are herringbone braided rims.

In most instances the coiled water bottle is undecorated. In this group, however, one carried a quite complex design. This basket was woven by a Navajo woman in the early 1970s and deviates from normal features in several ways. First, it is of natural and dyed yucca. The neck pattern is merely alternated brown and natural stitches for one coil; then the end of the body pattern is in the bottom neck coil. An irregular pattern on the rounded body consists of rows of stepped, almost-triangles, solid and outline, or so arranged as to form diamonds; or they are all solid; or, in one row, there is a rather odd-shaped, almost rectangular theme. This bottle had a lid which was also designed.

It is probable that coiled water jar forms were more regular and larger, that stitching was better and closer, and that the finished product was more usable in earlier pieces. But as these Indians apparently made the coiled bottle more frequently for sale, size and quality were both reduced. In the first place, the coiled jar quite generally replaced the wicker style; when the former was developed, it was undoubtedly used natively to some degree. As late as 1910 Haile notes that prior to their association with the Navajo, basket making among the Paiute "was confined to a rudely constructed wicker bottle."[47] However, Mason shows two evenly woven, well-shaped Paiute coiled bottles[48] and mentions that many more were to be noted in collections[49]; too, he shows two Navajo women carrying coiled water jars.[50] Actually the question may be asked: who made the coiled water bottle first? Whatever the answer, both tribes were using it at the turn of the century.

Several examples of the wicker bottle will suffice to characterize this piece. One Paiute example is rather graceful; it has an unusually small neck and a gently outflowing body line from neck to bottom; it is twined wicker and pitched. One such Ute piece is 9″ high, 18½″ in circumferences at its widest point, and has a 1½″ neck at the rim. There are two braided horsehair handles on this point-bottomed piece, and it is pitched, of course. A Navajo piece is very irregular in shape. From a medium neck it follows a relatively straight—but bumpy—line to the widest diameter, then turns inward, following an equally irregular line to a flat base which is wider than the rim. Sewing is in a regular, plain twine weave, not too well done.

Ute, Paiute, and Navajo baskets have been, since the turn of the century, basically coiled. Perhaps there were more twined pieces than ever suspected in earlier years, but they surely did not survive the first decade of this century. Even coiled work changed, for decoration of the tray settled down to the "wedding" style alone. The few variations of this theme which have occurred in recent years might promise new directions in the design of the wedding basket; this statement would not include the baskets woven in bilious colors and in uncontrolled designs. However, baskets like one woven by a Navajo woman in 1981 would support a more hopeful future. Centered in this piece is a deep red and white eagle on a yellow ground. Mindful of wedding-basket tradition are the next two decorative areas, one with black and red steps against a white ground and two, black double steps against a yellow ground. All is secured within a braided rim.

CHEMEHUEVI BASKETS

Chemehuevi basketry is one of the least known of all southwestern types. Practically nothing has been written on the subject; in fact, there is little authentic information on this tribe and its culture in general. Like so many groups with a background of wandering, they were basket makers. Interestingly, they are referred to as the "poor relations" of the Paiutes. As they lived in open desert country, the chances of the preservation of any early baskets would be negligible; therefore, practically nothing is known of this craft until their later contacts with Anglos shortly before and after 1900.

There are certain outstanding traits which distinguish Chemehuevi coiled baskets from most others, particularly as these characteristics may be taken as a group. Any one, or perhaps several, of them might apply to a basket of another tribe but together they signify "Chemehuevi." There is a roundness of form in jars, a whiteness in the willow used, a clear-cut sharpness in design in these baskets. Patterns tend to be limited or spotted rather than continuous, although there are some of the latter; stitching is consistently close and even. Jars predominantly have short but very definite necks; in one selection of eighty-five baskets of this form, fifteen had no necks. And there are many floral or flowerlike and plant patterns.

Numerous other traits can be added to the above list to distinguish Chemehuevi basketry. One is discrete spacing, both in relation to the total basket pattern and in conjunction with elements of design. There is more repetition than there is continuity of pattern.

Very common are outline designs rather than solids; this gives a lightness to their basket decoration, and adds a clean and fresh look to the entire piece. Repetition is commonly alternating, a-b-a-b, with emphasis on four-part designs. Although coils frequently grow a little larger toward the rim, stitches in these baskets remain remarkably the same throughout a single piece. Weaving is consistently of high quality; the sewing surface is extremely smooth, but cut stitches or element ends can be felt sometimes on the nonsewing surface. Black rims predominate; in fact, in forty-nine of the baskets noted above, all were black except five, and these included two all white, one each alternate black and white, white with black overstitching, and white with design into it.

Many of the above points, plus others below, are based on a study of baskets in the Birdie Brown Collection. Mr. and Mrs. Brown lived at Parker, Arizona, at the turn of the century, running a trading post frequented by the Chemehuevi Indians from whom they collected many hundreds of baskets.[51] Between three and four hundred of these, plus many others from additional collections, served as a basis for this study.

Forms

Chemehuevi basket forms are usually trays, jars, and bowls, with large pieces practically non-existent (Fig. 8.6). This may be due to early commercialization of the craft and the production of pieces suitable to white man's uses. Oval jars are perhaps more common than among most southwestern tribes, although this form has been noted in Yavapai and Papago basket collections. There is not the great variety within a single form which is a common trait in some groups, for example, the Papago. Jars are usually bulbous but once in a while they become more elongate; a few trays are oval. And there did not develop among the Chemehuevis the miscellaneous forms which sometimes accompany commercialization, as among the Papagos.

Fig. 8.6. Forms in Chemehuevi baskets are predominantly trays and jars. (a) Trays had curved walls and were decorated in more sparse and ordered style, as on the right; bowls might be more abundantly ornamented in scattered or organized fashion, as on the left *(ASM GP48365-X-1, E2553)*. (b) Usually jars had short necks and rounded bodies; design might be on or close to the greatest diameter and in an organizational band, left, or more scattered, right *(ASM E8487, E2550)* or (c), design might also be both above and below center *(ASM GP48367)*. Most jars were round (b), but some were oval (c).

Technical Background

Materials used in Chemehuevi baskets include basically willow (*Salix* sp.), devil's-claw (*Martynia fragrens*), and juncus. Whole, small willow rods can be gathered at any time to form the foundation. Willow for sewing splints, however, had to be gathered in middle March or late September, for then they had fewer leaves and were easier to split. Splitting is done with the usual thumb-forefinger-teeth combination, with each rod split into two or three pieces. A second splitting removed the fine inner bark (which became weft material) from the pithy core and the tough outer bark. Weft elements were pulled through holes in a tin can lid to make them uniform. Devil's-claw was cultivated. The third material, juncus, which is a water plant, came largely through trade, and later, specifically from the Banning, California, area, and a little from along the Colorado River. It was gathered in the fall; it was dark brown at the base, and shaded into a lighter color at the top of the stalk, sometimes a light yellow. This variation in color was often used to advantage in designing.

Occasional other materials might be used by the Chemehuevi weaver, such as water grasses, tules, cottonwood (*Populus fremonti*), and feathers. Topknots of quail might appear around the basket rim. The quills of the Red-shafted Flicker were scraped and used, imparting a pink or yellow tone to designs. These were noted several times in the Brown Collection. For the weft a variety of these materials might be used: willow or cottonwood formed the basic light background, with juncus sometimes used and imparting a mottled brown or brown-to-yellow base color. For designing, devil's-claw was the most common material, with juncus next, and water grasses and particularly feathers used rarely.[52]

Sizes of Chemehuevi baskets were definitely small to medium with many small and miniature pieces woven. Jars were largely from 6″ to 9″ high; one in a group of fourteen was 15″ tall; one other piece in another collection was 20¼″ in height, the latter the largest recorded jar in this survey. Trays varied, although they tended toward medium to slightly larger sizes, such as 6″ to 8″, and up to 15″ in diameter. In one group of thirty trays there was a clustering of sizes from 6″ to 8″ in diameters and a second, lesser clustering from 13″ to 15″, with a scattering between these two groups and limited examples both above and below. The largest basket in this group was 23″ in diameter. Bowls tended to be smaller than trays. In one group of fourteen, there were three each 6″, 7″, and 8″ in diameter, two each 10″ and 11″, and one 9″ piece.

Clockwise coiling is unique to Chemehuevi basket weaving. Robinson notes, "One characteristic peculiar to the Chemehuevi craft is that the coiling proceeds to the right."[53] However, not all of their work was in this direction. For instance, out of a selection of forty-nine baskets, fourteen were counterclockwise. Coiling is the only described technique developed by this tribe, although Douglas notes that they also made a twined type of basketry.[54] Kroeber reports that they made a twined, peaked or conical cap and a conical carrying baskets.[55] None of the latter was encountered in this survey. In coiled work a three-rod foundation in used consistently (Mason says "a rod"[56]) with sewing wefts enclosing the top element in the coil below and completely wrapping about the current coil. Weaving is close in most baskets; although the sewing wefts may be wider in larger pieces, they too are close together. Evenness of width is characteristic in all stitches, wide or narrow.

Coil and stitch counts are varied but quite generally higher than in other baskets. In the group of forty-nine baskets referred to above, coil counts ranged from four to eight with a concentration in five, six, or seven to the inch. There were thirteen baskets of five coils to the inch, fourteen with six coils, and fifteen with seven. Stitches were fairly well spread out from twelve to seventeen to the inch with the following representation: five each with twelve, thirteen, and sixteen, ten with fourteen stitches, sixteen with fifteen stitches, and four baskets with seventeen stitches to the inch. Size played a part in stitch variation, with wider and therefore fewer of them in larger baskets. By the same token miniatures had very high stitch counts. Although analyzed below, it may be noted here that stitch counts in these small pieces ranged from nine to thirty-three per inch and coils from four to ten per inch.

Decoration

Designs are quite distinctive in Chemehuevi baskets (Fig. 8.7). In addition to or in support of certain general and outstanding characteristics given above, the following can be noted before individual pieces are described. In one group of eighty-five baskets, twenty-five had continuous patterns and sixty had repeated main motifs. Although most patterning is horizontal on both trays and jars, there is some diagonal arrangement on the latter form. Both trays and bowls may have either flat or gently curved bottoms; jars may have either, although there is more apt to be a definite and continued curve from the wall into the base. These details affect the placement of design. Pattern is not often carried to the rim coil, although it may be so treated in both jars and trays. A distinctive Chemehuevi feature is the placement of design on a number of jars directly on, or on and below, or below the widest diameter. In a few pieces this widest measurement is high on the vessel wall and all design is below it. Black centers are not common on trays; if anything is present, it is usually a flower or star. Bottom decoration on jars was neglected, with but a few noted in the several hundreds of jars examined.

Layouts in decorating Chemehuevi baskets are varied, but bands and organizational bands would seem to dominate. Frequently the major part of the sidewall of a jar has a wide organizational band within it, or a much smaller band of the same style at or below the widest diameter. Repeated layouts are also found on jar sides. True or organizational bands just below the rim are common on trays or on the sidewall of bowls, in both instances leaving a large undecorated central area. Repeated designs appear in like manner on trays, and all-over designs are found largely on this form. Composite layouts, mainly centered-banded or centered-organizational-banded, are also to be noted on tray forms.

Designs on Chemehuevi baskets may be either geometric or naturalistic (Fig. 8.8). Perhaps most common of the latter are butterflies and snakes, although there are quite a few bugs. A few other creatures are represented, and, rarely, humans. Plants are fairly common, particularly flowers and vine-like growth. Geometric

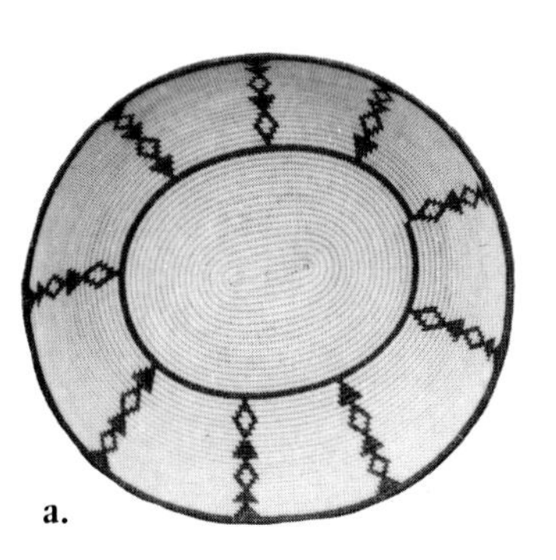
a.

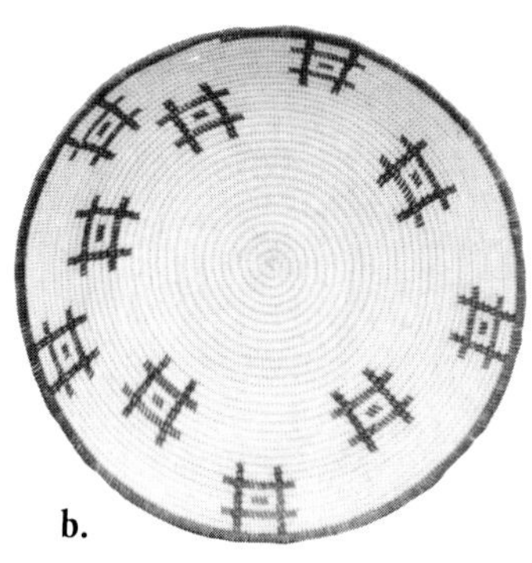
b.

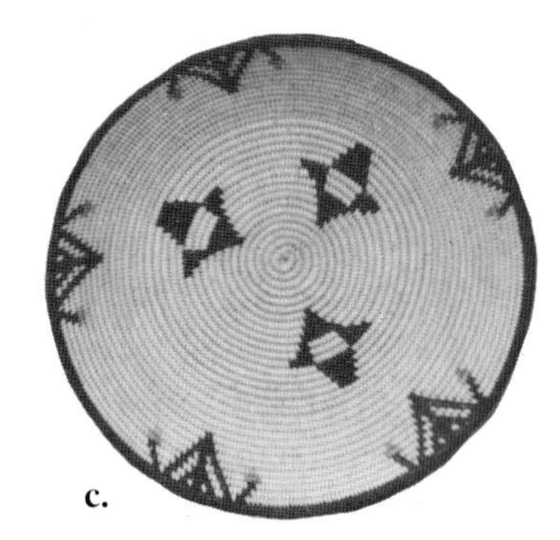
c.

d.

e.

f.

Fig. 8.7. Chemehuevi trays and bowls. (a) A regular band *(MNA 3500),* and (b) an organizational band *(MNA 3497),* both with simple repetitive motifs. (c) Two motifs decorate this tray in all-over style *(MNA 3491).* (d) A composite design of centered and banded motifs. (e) Jars have single repetitive geometrics such as this rather large one *(photo by Ray Manley);* (f) smaller pieces, also jars, utilized plant themes (lower left) or butterflies (upper right). *(Photo by Ray Manley.)*

units and motifs are numerous, although some are favored over others. Diamonds are in outline usually, but some are solid; they are single or concentric, plain or stepped, and frequently they are combined with other elements to form motifs. They appear in composite forms in bands; often they are filled with other diamonds, or triangles, or checkers, or coyote tracks. Triangles are comparable: single or multiple, alone, or stacked, or in rows, combined to form stars, or edging diamonds, plain or stepped. Coyote tracks are single or multiple stacked; they appear alone or in combination with other geometric units. Hexagons are used like the filled diamond. An equal-armed cross is to be noted, alone or in diamonds. One basket was decorated with diagonal nested rows of chevrons.

Although much of the patterning on Chemehuevi baskets is static, there is some dynamism, particularly as expressed in diagonal stepped patterns. Steps are double or triple, and certainly they conform to the outline feeling so popular for these baskets. Zigzags are sometimes used in the same diagonal fashion or they may be horizontal in alignment. There are a few other geometrics used in these baskets but the above comprise the major ones.

In 1904 Mason noted that Chemehuevis used only two colors, black and natural; "however, feathers are introduced under the stitches," he adds.[57] He illustrates typical jars and trays, the latter apparently large sized.[58] Zigzags appear in diagonal arrangements on one jar and in bands on two others. On another jar are joined coyote tracks arranged in stepped rectangles placed diagonally and low on the vessel. Rows of joined stepped triangles are arranged like

Fig. 8.8. Chemehuevi life designs on baskets. (a) The tray is decorated with four diamond-back rattlesnakes; a bowl basket with butterflies in different positions. (b) A bowl to the left with pert rabbits; center, another bowl with a snake and butterfly; and to the right, butterflies and plants on a bowl. In the background is a large bowl decorated with butterflies in yellow and black. *(Photos by Ray Manley.)*

rayed bands on a tray; another features a band of diamonds in negative. This basic motif on another tray (shown in drawing a) is a typical Chemehuevi basket decoration.

The Birdie Brown baskets were not dated (collecting started shortly after 1900), but all of them seem to be typically Chemehuevi in style. In fact, not much change seems to have occurred through the years. If Mason is correct in his above statement, then juncus might have been added at a later date, and, if his comment regarding design is meant to exclude life forms intentionally, then perhaps these too were added along the way. But much of this has to do with the size of his sample. A few comments on designs from the Birdie Brown Collection follow.

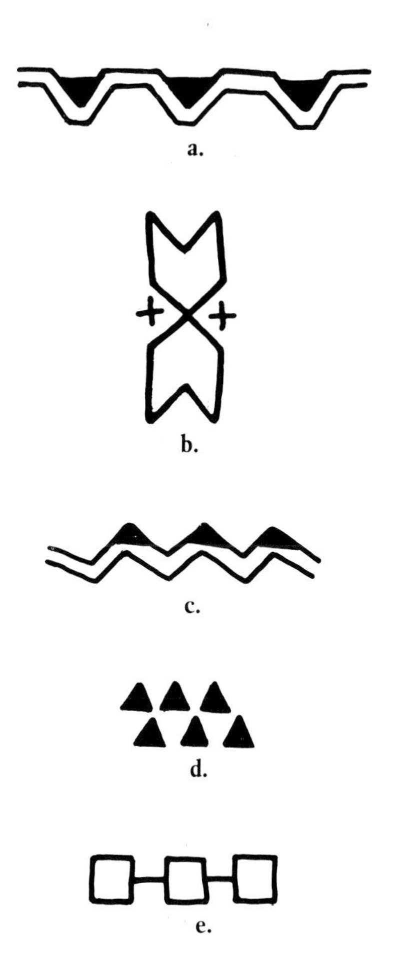

Jars present a variety of designs. One has four sets of stacked outline triangles, with tiny triangles within them. Alternating with these are stacked geometrics of a different shape, the main theme, as shown in drawing b. These reach to within several coils of the black rim. A more squat jar has an organizational band of zigzags arranged in the same manner (drawing c), this appearing below center on the jar. Below a high shoulder on another jar are two rows of severely prim solid triangles (drawing d), not quite touching, and encircling the jar. Bugs and birds in overlapping rows ornament the walls of one jar, these in black against a mottled background of varicolored juncus. Another jar has a ring of joined outline squares (drawing e) near the bottom; the sidewall is decorated with a two-part, double, vertical meander from the base to a black line several coils below the rim coil. A different decoration is floral: six stems each with three leaves and a blossom on top, all done in black and

f.

g.

h.

i.

j.

k.

l.

m.

yellow-brown, and all appearing from above mid-point to the base of the jar. Two large repeated butterflies ornament another of these jars low on the wall.

Three bowls from this collection are very simply decorated. One has rows of triangles projecting from two lines which encircle the basket wall. A second has one row of touching diamonds double outlined and with a cross in the center, this repeated eight times. A third bowl is wall-decorated with four large curved-edged triangles filled with tiny triangles.

Trays have endless types of decoration, from highly balanced, symmetrical styles to snake themes which are neither symmetrical nor balanced. In one of the later, two snakes appear on the same basket, one with its head to the right, the other with its head to the left. Triangles suggest body markings, lines indicate rattles. Background is mottled juncus. Another similarly decorated piece has white diamonds on the snakes' black bodies.

Simple banded layouts in trays are common. Usually the band is close to the rim, with an inner black line and the black rim as the second enclosing line. One such band has line-joined outline diamonds enclosing solid diamonds and with tips filled in (see drawing f). Another tray has six sets of double stacked triangles (drawing g); a second of this type has nine of these motifs, and a third has seven. Seemingly this was a favored theme. Slightly more elaborate is this same pattern repeated six times but alternating with a single row of stacked triangles. Another tray has a comparable vertical but simpler repeated motif, seven of these (drawing h).

Organizational bands are represented by several patterns. One tray has alternating swastikas and diamonds, the latter made up of four solid stepped smaller diamonds. Another has a row of black outlined diamonds with brownish-yellow interiors. Six long vertically placed rectangles with dividers (drawing i) fill an organizational band which joins the rim in another tray. Six yellow flowers on black stems occupy the same position on one tray. Positioned in the same type of organizational band are four cats alternating with the "devil himself" (drawing j)! Another life form is a bit more recognizable—four solid black Gila monsters alternating with open center "stars" (drawing k). A simple, double-stepped zigzag is positioned like the above themes. Double bands were fairly common as tray decoration.

A few all-over layouts appear on trays. Two of them have a central five-pointed star, then bugs all over the tray. One has a plain background plus Gila monsters at the rim, but the second has additional themes, three snakes(?), as in drawing l, and two arrows, as in drawing m. The two trays are almost identical in size. They could have been made by the same weaver, for it was traditional among the Chemehuevi that certain designs, such as bugs, "belonged" to certain women. Some say that these designs were passed down from generation to generation through family lines.

Popular for this tray basket was a composite layout, usually involving a central motif combined with either a band, an organizational band or a half band. Simple indeed was one tray decoration with a central star (or flower) with an organizational band beyond it made up of joined outline diamonds each enclosing a small solid

n.

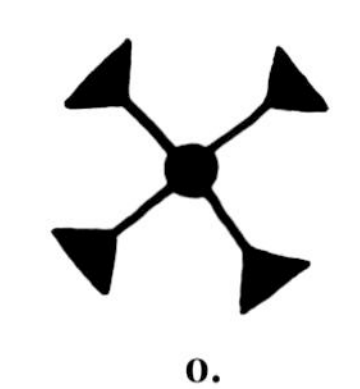
o.

diamond. Two trays are similarly decorated with two bands of paired diamonds, but they are different in the central motif, one having a double-line circle, the second a line circle emitting four pairs of arrow points (drawing n). A last example of the composite tray decoration has a central, open eight-pointed star and an organizational band beyond it. In the latter are three butterflies in black, yellow, and brown, with coyote tracks above them and triangles at their sides. Between butterflies is a single large motif (shown in drawing o). One of the most elaborate decorations involves a five-pointed star center with a ring beyond it which creates a wide band. Within the band are two rows of birds (eagles?), four in the first row, and five in the second. Simple and odd line geometrics appear between the birds.

There are, of course, many other combinations of a variety of units and motifs, such as single bands of black and white checkers, or a great variety of arrangements of triangles, or simple and complex bands of diamonds. There are other diagonal zigzags, or direct radiate themes; there are encircling frets. On jars there are plants up the sides, or stacked squares, or encircling paired squares or simple zigzags, or there are simple repeated crosses or diamonds, or joined coyote tracks, or other geometrics.

All in all, Chemehuevi basketry design is basically simple, basically restrained. It is clear and clean, leaving ample space for each motif to be seen, for each element to be defined, and frequently there is much undecorated space. It is well planned and often equally well executed.

Miniatures

More than sixty-five Chemehuevi miniatures in the Birdie Brown Collection were examined. In size they varied from ¼″ to 5″ in either rim diameter if trays or height if jars. The largest piece in this selection was a jar under 5″ in height and just over 5″ in diameter.

Forms in miniatures are primarily jars and trays. However, one group of thirty-seven pieces consists of nothing but jars, from minute ones to the largest under 2″. Out of the above selection of sixty-five pieces there was a single bowl only; this, of course, fits in with the overall picture of percentages of various forms. There is some variation within basic miniature forms, particularly of jars. Some jars have no necks; all necks are low, some just barely exist. Too, some of the miniature jar forms are more rounded while others are more elongate. The amazing thing is that even the tiniest of miniatures are beautifully formed, symmetrical and aesthetically pleasing, and many of these small pieces carry a full complement of design comparable to full-sized pieces. Description of a few pieces will support this statement.

Stitch and coil counts on Chemehuevi miniatures testify to the superior craftsmanship on these pieces. In a group of thirty-three baskets, the range of stitches starts at fourteen per inch and goes to twenty-seven, with one each at twenty-six and twenty-seven. There are one and two examples each for fourteen, fifteen, sixteen, twenty-one, and twenty-two stitches per inch with the mass of these baskets in between: five, six, six, and five examples for seventeen, eighteen, nineteen, and twenty stitches to the inch, respectively. Coils are also fine, with eleven and ten examples counting seven and eight, respectively, only two specimens counting six, and four and five baskets with nine and ten coils, respectively.

Layouts on miniature jars compare favorably to the same on larger pieces, with emphasis on repeated and alternated (a-a-a-a or a-b-a-b) and an organizational band or bands the most common; on trays are the same plus true bands.

Geometric decoration on miniature jars runs the gamut from a simple stepped zigzag just below center to varied groupings of clustered triangles over most of the wall surface on several vessels, and in both positive and negative. A wide band on the center of one jar has the design shown in drawing p repeated eleven times. Three bands of checkers, wide-narrow-wide, decorate most of the wall of another piece. Four very large versions of drawing q decorate the rounded wall of a jar. Vertically arranged alternating patterns (drawing r) appear on one jar, each repeated four times. Floral themes were popular on these tiny jars. One has a yellow and pink rose-like flower repeated four times. Repeated three times is another flower, small and yellow, on a stem with two heavy green leaves. Four tree-like affairs have one redwing blackbird on the top of each. Another jar is decorated with birds and dragonflies, each again repeated four times. Butterflies and flowers ornament one jar; a large black stork overpowers a vertical stack of geometrics on another. Life forms are favored to decorate jars, one with three beautifully done yellow butterflies outlined in black, and another with four repeated large roses. Tree-like designs appear on two miniature jars, four on one, and eight crowded onto another wall. One of the most interesting of these tiny pieces has a mottled ground on which appear five large bugs.

p.

q.

r.

Most unusual are two designs which appear on separate jars. One resembles a five-branched candelabrum, roughly as shown in drawing s. This is repeated three times on the wall of the jar. The second motif is an elaborate sugar bowl with two high handles and a lid, done in black and yellow. Three of these alternate with double vertical rows of stacked black triangles, with a narrow white line between them.

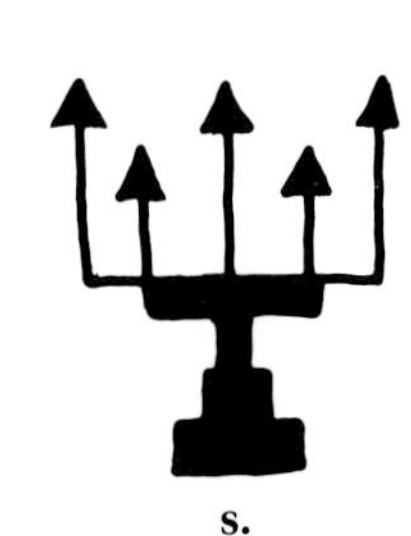

s.

The only bowl in this group of sixty-five miniatures is extremely well formed and has eighteen spaced black diamonds in a horizontal row at the center. One of the rare cases of a nonbalanced design is on a tray: two almost opposed butterflies, and between them, on one side, two leaflike affairs on either side of a cluster of crosses, and on the other side, the same leaves with a smaller flower between them. One tray has four repeated bugs on its upper wall, all black. Geometrics are common on the miniature tray form: a wall zigzag; a black wall band with two rows of negative diamonds; a wall band with three each alternating diagonals of solid black and checkered stepped squares; and four repeated "stars" made of six triangles, around a circle, drawing t. One other tray is ornamented with four lizards, opposites alike but with variations in black, yellow, and brown toes and tails in the two pairs.

t.

Certainly these few examples of miniature decoration will give some idea of the great variety of subjects treated on these small pieces. Even the smallest bears some design, often no more than a simple geometric theme.

Chemehuevi basket design can be characterized by clean-cut presentations of limited, discrete patterning. Although dominantly black, occasional other colors do appear. Life forms are fairly abundant, but geometrics are favored above them. In spite of the fact that it is likely that more wicker and plainer coiled pieces were used in their wandering days, it is indicated in excellent craftsmanship that the Chemehuevis have long produced beautiful coiled baskets.

Chapter Notes

Chapter 2

1. Wormington 1957.
2. Aikens 1970.
3. Jennings 1957.
4. Sayles 1941.
5. Haury 1976; Kidder 1962.
6. Kidder 1962.
7. Ibid.
8. Morris and Burgh 1941.

Chapter 3

1. Random House Dictionary 1971: 124.
2. The majority of names of plants used herein were compiled by Denwood Butler, a student in the College of Agriculture, University of Arizona, who was also interested in Southwestern Indian Art (1976).
3. Williamson 1937: 34.
4. Stevenson, M. C., 1915: 81.
5. Jeancon and Douglas 1930: 18, 20.
6. McKee *et al.* 1975: 12.
7. Gifford 1932: 219.
8. Jeancon and Douglas 1930: 19.
9. Douglas 1933a: 23.
10. Colton 1965: 22.
11. Colton (1965) gives a detailed discussion of this process of dyeing, from materials used to variations in methods.
12. Ibid.: 16, 17, 23.
13. Douglas 1933b: 30–32.
14. Douglas 1934: 46.
15. Kissell 1916: 156.
16. Ibid.
17. Adovasio is incorrect in including wicker under plaiting; instead it should be related to twining. He says of plaited, "there are usually no functionally distinct horizontal and vertical elements" (1977: 104–05). In this statement he is correct, but also in this comment he eliminates wicker from the classification of plaiting. Wicker has distinct vertical stationary warps and horizontal moving wefts, both traits the same as in twining.
18. Roberts 1929: 137.
19. Wrapped weave was used for the making of objects other than baskets in the Southwest; for example, Hopis made fences in this weave and Papagos used it to produce shelves and other such items.
20. Kissell 1916: 206–9.
21. Tanner 1982: Fig. 4.1a.
22. Ibid.: Fig. 4.1b.
23. Roberts 1929: 173; Kissell 1916: 196.

Chapter 4

1. Webb and Weinstein 1973: Photo 18; see also Hough 1918.
2. Jeancon and Douglas 1931a: 66.
3. Conferences with E. B. Danson, then Director of the Museum of Northern Arizona, Flagstaff, 1963. This improvement was due largely to the dedicated efforts of the staff members of the Museum who worked with the Hopi Indians throughout the year, year after year, to encourage them to improve their craft arts.
4. Butler says that some botanists (i.e., Webber) say that *Yucca angustifolia* and *Y. angustissima* should be changed to *Y. glauca*; then they remark that the last is distributed no farther west than eastern New Mexico!
5. Colton 1951: 13.

6. Ibid.: 35. Kearney and Peebles give *Thelesperma megapotamicum* rather than *T. gracile,* the latter given by Underhill (1944) and others.
7. Bartlett 1951: 98.
8. Danson, Conference 2-23-63. He showed this writer several examples in the Museum of Northern Arizona which featured this pattern and these colors.
9. This stitching is usually straight and horizontal, but it also may be vertical or diagonal; sometimes, eyes are emphasized in stitching in a circle.
10. An article in the *Casa Grande Dispatch,* Arizona, 1-27-69, is here quoted and the article, plus a picture of the original basket, provided a basis for comments.
11. Harvey and de Berge 1969: 1.
12. Ibid.: 3.
13. Ibid.; 10, 11.
14. Ibid.: 11.
15. Ibid.: 19, 28.
16. Ibid.: 37.
17. This situation changed with the later establishment of classes to teach basketry on the Hopi Reservation.
18. Jeancon and Douglas 1931a.
19. *Rhus trilobata,* or sumac, is the same as wild currant.
20. Other varieties have been given by different writers; these two, *C. greenei* and *C. nauseosus,* are from Kearney and Peebles, as given by Butler.
21. Bartlett, Conference 2-22-63.
22. In judging baskets on several occasions at the Museum of Northern Arizona, it was difficult to distinguish some of the anilines and native dyes. Both were observed as used in several individual baskets.
23. Underhill 1944: 22.
24. Colton 1965: 83.
25. Ibid.: 52, 58, 62.
26. Ibid.: 22–23.
27. Ibid.: 81.
28. Ibid.: 35.
29. Colton 1938: 14.
30. Ibid.: 13.
31. Jeancon and Douglas 1931a: 67.
32. Bartlett 1951: 97.
33. Underhill 1944: 20, 22.
34. This piece was on its way to the Museum of Northern Arizona when observed (courtesy B. Wright).
35. Bartlett, Conference 2-22-63; also see Bartlett (1948: 33–41) for discussion of plaited baskets.
36. Webb and Weinstein 1973: photos 48–55.
37. Ibid.: photo 58.
38. Jeancon and Douglas 1931a.
39. Wright, Conference 3-17-77.
40. Judd 1954: 162, 163.
41. Whitaker 1974: 136–45.
42. Goddard 1931: 95.
43. Stevenson, J., 1883: Figs. 484, 485, 488.
44. Ibid.: 368, 369.
45. Ibid.: 368.
46. Mason 1904: Fig. 10.
47. Ibid.: 265, Fig. 70.
48. Ibid.: Plate 213.
49. Ibid.: 500.
50. M. C. Stevenson 1904: 373.
51. Underhill 1944: 22.
52. Williamson 1937: 37, 38.
53. Ibid.
54. Ibid.: 37, 38.
55. Ibid.
56. Ibid.
57. *Indians at Work* 10-15-37; see also Williamson 1937.
58. Ellis and Walpole 1959: 181.
59. Ibid.: 182.
60. Hough 1918.
61. Ellis and Walpole 1959: 183.
62. Bahti 1968: 26.
63. Curtis 1972: 63.
64. Ellis, Conference 4-27-63.
65. Ellis and Walpole 1959: 183.
66. Anonymous: 1936.
67. Ellis and Walpole 1959: 183.
68. A. G. E. in *El Palacio,* Dec. 1945: 290.
69. Ellis and Walpole 1959: 183.
70. Certainly there was much trade among puebloans and between them and other tribes. Old photos of pueblo rooms decorated with baskets from other tribes would testify to this.
71. Ellis and Walpole 1959: Fig. 3.
72. Ibid.: 187.
73. Ibid.: Fig. 7
74. Ibid.: 182, 183.
75. Vivian 1957: 152; Ellis and Walpole 1959: 197.
76. Ellis and Walpole 1959: 182.
77. Mason 1904: 500 and Plate 212.
78. Ellis and Walpole 1959: 193.
79. Ibid.: 192–93.

Chapter 5

1. Opler 1941: 97.
2. Ibid.: 130.
3. Ibid.: 381.
4. Ibid.
5. Tanner 1982.
6. Mason 1904: Plate 227, top.
7. The trader at Dulce, New Mexico, was influential in getting the Jicarillas to revive their basketry craft.

The success of this show, where quite a few baskets were sold, was an inspiration to these basket weavers.
8. Tanner 1982: Figs. 5.4a,b.
9. The use of a basket for a drum has been common practice among several tribes. In some groups any basket will do, but among others specific pieces must be used.
10. Kendall and Dorothy Cumming were stationed on the Jicarilla Apache Reservation at this time and were greatly interested in the revival of basketry among these Indians. Correspondence with and pictures sent by Mrs. Cumming provided additional and valuable information to the research on original baskets regarding this design development.
11. Roberts 1929: 148.
12. Ibid.: Fig. 13.
13. Ibid.: 166.
14. Ibid.: 166, 167.
15. Ibid.: Fig. 8a–e.
16. Ibid.: 150.
17. Tanner 1982: Fig. 4.4.
18. Roberts 1929: 152.
19. Ibid.: Fig. 5a–f.
20. Ibid.: Fig. 18.
21. Tanner 1982: Fig. 4.1a.
22. Roberts 1929: Figs. 16a–e, 17a, b, d.
23. Ibid.: Figs. 15a–d.
24. Tanner 1982: Fig. 4.2.
25. Roberts 1929: 171.
26. Tanner 1982: Fig. 3.3.
27. Ibid.: Figs. 3.6–3.26.
28. Wade and Strickland 1981: 110. Many years ago "Rupkey" was woven into a basket for a trader at San Carlos.
29. This strengthening at certain points on the basket by the use of three-ply twine is a device resorted to by several tribal weavers, although Apaches are most outstanding in the use of this feature.
30. Kissell did not include this form in utility pieces of the San Carlos Indians; Keith Basso (an outstanding researcher among Western Apaches) and various other ethnologists have not observed the use of the coiled jar about Apache wickiups. The thesis that it was woven for sale thus seems to have good support.

Chapter 6

1. Kissell 1916: 172–90.
2. Ibid.: 183.
3. Shreve 1943: 53, Figs. 12 and 13.
4. Ibid.: 53, 54.
5. Ibid.: 55.
6. Shreve 1943: 6.
7. Kissell 1916: 232.
8. Shreve 1943: 7.
9. Ibid.: 96, Table II, Part 2.
10. Kissell 1916: 193.
11. Shreve 1943: 57.
12. Kissell 1916: 191.
13. Shreve 1943: 58.
14. Ibid.: Fig. 17*e, f.*
15. These two baskets are so like fine Pima work in form, delicacy of design, and thinness of wall that one can suspect a Pima woman married to a Papago man and living in this far corner of the Papago Reservation.
16. Shreve 1943: Fig. 29.
17. Kissell 1916: Fig. 28.
18. Ibid.: 178.
19. Shreve 1943: 98.
20. W. Bowers purchased this jar basket in 1928 at Casa Grande, Arizona. He was a student at the University of Arizona at the time.
21. Kissell 1916: 190–91.
22. After this analysis, the Bowsers added greatly to their miniature collection, including many finer pieces of craftsmanship.
23. Shreve 1943: 43.
24. Kissell 1916: 153.
25. Shreve 1943: 43.
26. Kissell 1916: 159.
27. Shreve 1943: 45.
28. Kissell 1916: 168, 169.
29. Shreve 1943: 46.
30. Kissell 1916: 169.
31. Shreve 1943: 46.
32. Kissell 1916: 169.
33. Ibid.: 171.
34. Ibid.
35. Shreve 1943: 48.
36. Underhill 1951: 21.
37. Kissell 1916: 228.
38. Ibid.
39. Ibid.: 229.
40. Ibid.: 231, 232.
41. Russell 1908: 141.
42. Kissell 1916: 135, 136.
43. Tanner 1965.
44. Ibid.: Figs. 2–4.
45. Ibid.: 71.
46. Ibid.: 74.
47. This is the only example of a feathered Papago basket this writer has ever seen. The Indian lady apparently purchased her feathers at a "dime" store. The shop involved was the Bowser's in Casa Grande, Arizona.
48. Breazeale 1923: 7.
49. Russell 1908: 131.
50. Breazeale 1923: 37.
51. Hart 1935: 16.

52. Breazeale 1923: 125.
53. Cain 1962: 33.
54. Russell 1908: 131, 133.
55. Ibid.: 139.
56. Ibid.: Plates XXIX–XXXII.
57. Ibid.
58. Ibid.: 135.
59. Kissell 1916: 209. The term "rigid" is not quite correct, for characteristically the Pima basket walls are thin and more flexible. Perhaps Kissell meant smooth and even, for that they are. Frequently, age adds a degree of rigidity.
60. Russell 1908: Plates XXII–XXVIII.
61. Kissell 1916: 222.
62. Ibid.: Fig. 62*a*.
63. Breazeale 1923: Fig. 77.
64. Robinson 1954: Plate VI.
65. Ibid.: Plates XV, XVI.
66. Hart 1935.
67. Bartlett 1854: 227.
68. Russell 1908: 139.
69. Cain 1962: Fig. 15*a, e*.
70. Ibid.: Fig. 15*c*.
71. Tom Bahti, an Indian trader in Tucson, Arizona, said that he had seen a number of baskets with camels woven into them, but did not remember where the baskets were at the time (1966).
72. Russell 1908: 135.
73. Shreve 1943: 103.
74. Breazeale 1923: 79, 80.
75. Robinson 1954: Plate XII.
76. Breazeale 1923: 80, 81.
77. Cain 1962: Plate 5.
78. Ibid.: 16.
79. Harvey and de Berge 1969: 11.
80. Kissell 1916: 178.
81. Russell 1908: 143.
82. Ibid.: 144.
83. Kissell 1916: 190.
84. Russell 1908: 145.
85. Ibid.: 145, 146.
86. Ibid.: 140–143.

Chapter 7

1. Kissell 1916: 173.
2. Spier 1933: 90.
3. Kelly 1977: 48–51.
4. No Yuma coiled pieces were observed; hence, it is likely that they were defunct long before the 1920s (a wide selection of sources was covered).
5. Douglas 1939: 152.
6. Forde 1931: 124.
7. Kissell 1916: 173.
8. Ibid.: 177.
9. Mason 1904: Plate 17.
10. Ibid.: 231.
11. Douglas 1939: 152.
12. Although pieces of Mohave coiled work are occasionally referred to in writing, their provenience is not indicated; no such work was observed. The photograph of this one coiled piece is interesting; perhaps it was used for storage of special seeds, for it is too small to be used for much else.
13. Spier 1933: 122.
14. Several baskets labeled "Maricopa" were observed by this writer, but they were typically Pima in all characteristics.
15. Spier 1933: 122.
16. Ibid.: 122, 123.
17. Ibid.: 124.
18. Gifford 1936: 250.
19. Ibid.: 260.
20. Ibid.: 273.
21. Ibid.: 219.
22. Ibid.: 301.
23. Ibid.: 303.
24. Ibid.: 281.
25. Ibid.: 282.
26. Ibid.
27. Ibid.: 283.
28. Ibid.: Plate 13.
29. Barnett 1968: viii.
30. Ibid.: 33.
31. *Arizona Highways* 1936.
32. Dobyns and Euler 1960.
33. Bateman did intensive study of Hualapai and Havasupai baskets; the results are recorded in his M.A. thesis (1972) at Northern Arizona University, Flagstaff.
34. In a discussion relative to this subject (1-31-77), Dobyns said that the two tribes, the Hualapai and the Havasupai, wandered together for many years before they settled down in their present locations. As a result of this, there was much intermarriage.
35. Kroeber 1935: 79.
36. Spier 1928.
37. Kroeber 1935.
38. McKee *et al.* 1975.
39. Bateman 1972.
40. Again, photographs of pueblo interiors might be mentioned, and it can be added that some of the designs on the baskets, on walls of some rooms, appear to be Havasupai.
41. McKee *et al.* 1975: 2.
42. Ibid.: 7.
43. In several conferences with Euler in 1963, he noted that he had been in direct contact with Havasupais for a long time and that they had produced but a few pieces of wicker and coiled basketry for some years.

44. Smithson 1959: 143.
45. Bateman 1972: 62.
46. Ibid.: 77.
47. McKee *et al.* 1975: 9.
48. Dobyns (1-31-77) said that an estimated 10,000 visitors walked into Havasu Canyon in the previous year, and many of these literally bought baskets before they were finished, waited for them, and took them immediately.
49. McKee *et al.* 1975: 12.
50. Spier 1928: 132.
51. McKee *et al.* 1975: 14.
52. Bateman 1972: 30.
53. McKee *et al.* 1975: 16.
54. Bateman 1972: 37.
55. Dobyns (1-31-77) said that he recognized some Hualapai names among those given for Havasupai basket makers.
56. Several basketry experts, including Jerold Collings (discussion 2-19-77), are of the opinion that the Sweeney Collection is basically Havasupai and not Hualapai.
57. Spier 1928: 124.
58. McKee *et al.* 1975: xvi.
59. Spier 1928: 127.
60. McKee *et al.* 1975: 17, 18.
61. Spier 1928: 127.
62. Smithson 1959: 145.
63. Spier 1928: 137.
64. James 1903: 67–69.
65. Ibid.: Fig. 62.
66. Mason 1904: 517.
67. Kroeber 1935: 79–81.
68. Ibid.
69. Ibid.: 79.
70. Ibid.: Plate 7.
71. Ibid.: 81.
72. Ibid.: 79.
73. Ibid.: 80.
74. Bateman 1972: 10–11.
75. Kroeber 1935: 80.
76. Ibid.: 81.
77. Bateman 1975: 21.
78. Kroeber 1935: Plate 8.
79. Bateman 1972: 24.
80. Euler, personal conference, 3-30-63.

Chapter 8

1. Matthews 1894: 202.
2. Franciscan Fathers 1910: 297, 298.
3. Tschopik 1940: 458–60.
4. Fishler 1954: 208, 209.
5. Ibid.: 209, 210.
6. Matthews 1894: 205.
7. Tschopik 1940: 446.
8. W. Y. Adams was at Shonto Trading Post, Shonto, Arizona, for one year; he told of Navajo women in this area in the early 1950s who were weaving baskets (conference with Adams, 2-27-57; see also Adams, 1963).
9. Large Navajo trays observed at Flagstaff in the late 1970s and at Casa Grande in 1981 would support this statement. Garish colors characterized the earlier pieces, but color and design both were under control in the several 1981 baskets noted.
10. Altman 1946: 162.
11. Franciscan Fathers 1910: 447–48.
12. Altman 1946: 160–63.
13. The singer would either keep the basket or take it to the trading post and sell it.
14. It may be added that many of the baskets which were sold to white men still had cornmeal or pollen well embedded in basket bottoms.
15. Tschopik 1940: 447.
16. Tschopik 1938: 261.
17. Stewart 1938: 758, 759.
18. It is of interest to note these several references by Adams to Navajo women who were still weaving baskets, for other writers so frequently stress the fact that these women all but ceased to make baskets because of the development of ever more restrictive taboos.
19. Jeancon and Douglas 1931b: 83.
20. Tschopik 1940: 448.
21. Tschopik 1938: 257.
22. Tschopik 1940: 449.
23. Haile, in Franciscan Fathers 1910: 230, 232.
24. Ibid.: 297.
25. Amsden 1934: Plate 4.
26. Morris and Burgh 1941: Figs. 17*a* and 27*d*.
27. Amsden 1934: Plate 4*b–e*.
28. Fishler 1954: 211.
29. Ibid.: 212.
30. Ibid.
31. Kahlenberg and Berlant (1972) have no page numbers in this publication; therefore, the illustration numbers only will be given in the text.
32. Ibid.
33. Ibid.
34. Bennett 1974: 2.
35. Kahlenberg and Berlant 1972.
36. Ibid.
37. Wheat 1974. Wheat also says of the Navajos that "In the early 1600s they were trading baskets, tanned hides, and other articles to the Pueblos in exchange for woven goods." This, surely, laid the foundation for a brisk exchange of

design elements between the two crafts, baskets and blankets. Wheat supports this belief in the statement, "since Navajo baskets were well known before the Navajo began to weave blankets, it seems probable that the basketry design system was simply transferred to the woolen and cotton textiles."

38. Ibid.
39. Ibid.
40. Ibid.
41. Ibid.
42. Ibid.
43. Ibid.
44. Ibid.
45. Conference with Euler, 3-30-63. It might be noted in passing that the only Paiutes included here are those just mentioned plus others in southern Utah, and not the more northerly tribes whose culture and baskets are definitely more in the California tradition.
46. Watkins 1942: 13.
47. Franciscan Fathers 1910: 291.
48. Mason 1904: Plate 117.
49. Ibid.: 361.
50. Ibid.: Plate 118.
51. Mrs. Birdie Brown told this writer that she had around 5,000 baskets in her collection, this including many tiny pieces in glass tubes. The majority of these baskets were Chemehuevi.
52. In their original state these feathers probably imparted even more to the color of these baskets.
53. Robinson 1954: 144.
54. Douglas 1940: 197.
55. Kroeber 1908: 42.
56. Mason 1904: 519.
57. Ibid.
58. Ibid.: Plate 232.

Bibliography

A.G.E.
1945 *El Palacio* (December).

Adams, William Y.
1963 "Shonto: A Study of the Role of the Trader in a Modern Navaho Community." Smithsonian Institution, *Bureau of American Ethnology Bulletin* 188. U. S. Printing Office, Washington, D.C.

Adovasio, J. M.
1977 *Basketry Technology.* Aldine Manuals on Archaeology, Aldine Publishing Company, Chicago.

Aikens, C. Melvin
1970 *Hogup Cave.* Anthropological Papers No. 93, Department of Anthropology, University of Utah, Salt Lake City.

Altman, George J.
1946 "A Navajo Wedding." *Masterkey,* Volume XX, No. 5. Southwest Museum, Los Angeles.

Amsden, Charles Avery
1934 *Navaho Weaving—Its Technic and History.* The Fine Arts Press, Santa Ana, California, in cooperation with The Southwest Museum.

Anonymous
1936 "Basket Making Among the Indians of the Southwest."

Bahti, Tom
1968 *Southwestern Indian Tribes.* K. C. Publications, Flagstaff, Arizona.

Barnett, Franklin
1968 *Viola Jimulla: The Indian Chieftess.* Prescott Yavapai Indians, Southwest Printers, Yuma, Arizona.

Bartlett, John R.
1854 *Personal Narrative of Explorations and Incidents in Texas, New Mexico, California, Sonora, and Chihuahua Connected with the United States and Mexican Boundary.* Two Volumes, George Routledge and Company, London.

Bartlett, Katharine
1948 "Hopi Yucca Baskets." Museum of Northern Arizona *Plateau,* Volume 21, No. 3, pp. 33–41. Northern Arizona Society of Science and Art, Flagstaff, Arizona.
1951 "How to Appreciate Hopi Handicrafts." In *Hopi Indian Arts and Crafts,* Museum of Northern Arizona Reprint Series No. 3. Northern Arizona Society of Science and Art, Flagstaff, Arizona.

Bateman, Paul
1972 *Culture Change and Revival in Pai Basketry.* M. A. Thesis, Northern Arizona University, Flagstaff, Arizona.

Bennett, Noel
1974 *The Weaver's Pathway.* Northland Press, Flagstaff, Arizona.
Breazeale, J. F.
1923 *The Pima and his Basket.* Arizona Archaeological and Historical Society, Tucson.
Butler, Denwood
1976 "The Plant Materials Used in the Basketry of the Southwestern American Indians." Unpublished paper.
Cain, H. Thomas
1962 *Pima Indian Basketry.* Heard Museum of Anthropology and Primitive Art, Phoenix, Arizona.
Colton, Mary-Russell F.
1938 "Arts and Crafts of the Hopi Indians." Museum of Northern Arizona, *Museum Notes,* Volume 11, No. 1, Northern Arizona Society of Science and Art, Flagstaff, Arizona. (July 1938)
1951 "Hopi Indian Arts and Crafts." *Museum of Northern Arizona Reprint Series* No. 3. Northern Arizona Society of Science and Art, Flagstaff, Arizona.
1965 "Hopi Dyes." The *Museum of Northern Arizona Bulletin* No. 41. Northern Arizona Society of Science and Art, Flagstaff, Arizona.
Curtis, Edward S.
1972 *Portraits from North American Indian Life.* Outerbridge and Lazard, Inc., in association with American Museum of Natural History, New York.
Dobyns, Henry F., and Robert C. Euler
1960 "A Brief History of the Northeastern Pai." Museum of Northern Arizona *Plateau,* Volume 32, No. 3. Northern Arizona Society of Science and Art, Flagstaff, Arizona.
Douglas, F. H.
1933a "Colors in Indian Arts; Their Sources and Uses." *Denver Art Museum Indian Art Leaflet* 56, Denver, Colorado. (March 1933)
1933b "Indian Basketry, Varieties and Distributions." *Denver Art Museum Indian Art Leaflet* 58, Denver, Colorado. (May 1933)
1934 "Design Areas in Indian Art." *Denver Art Museum Indian Art Leaflet* 62, Denver, Colorado. (July 1934)
1939 "Types of Southwestern Coiled Basketry." *Denver Art Museum Indian Art Leaflet* 88, Denver, Colorado. (December 1939)
1940 "Southwestern Twined, Wicker and Plaited Basketry." *Denver Art Museum Indian Art Leaflets* 99–100, Denver, Colorado. (February 1940)
Ellis, Florence H., and Mary Walpole
1959 "Possible Pueblo, Navajo, and Jicarilla Basketry Relationships." *El Palacio,* Volume 66, No. 6. The Museum of New Mexico, Santa Fe, New Mexico. (December 1959)
Fishler, Stanley A.
1954 "Symbolism of a Navajo 'Wedding' Basket." *Masterkey,* Volume 28, No. 6. Southwest Museum, Los Angeles.
Forde, C. Daryll
1931 *Ethnography of the Yuma Indians.* University of California Publications in American Archaeology and Ethnology, Volume 28, No. 4, Berkeley.
Franciscan Fathers
1910 *An Ethnologic Dictionary of the Navaho Language.* Saint Michaels, Arizona.
Gifford, E. W.
1932 *The Southeastern Yavapai.* University of California Publications in American Archaeology and Ethnology, Volume 29, No. 3, Berkeley.
1936 *Northeastern and Western Yavapai.* University of California Publications in American Archaeology and Ethnology, Volume 34, No.4, Berkeley.
Goddard, Pliny E.
1931 *Indians of the Southwest.* Handbook No. 2, American Museum of Natural History, New York.
Hart Elizabeth
1935 "Arts and Crafts of the Pima Jurisdiction." *Indians at Work,* Vol. II, No. 19, pp. 16–18. Office of Indian Affairs, Washington, D.C. (May 15, 1935)

Harvey, Byron, and Suzanne de Berge
1969 *Hopi Miniature Baskets.* Arequipa Press, Phoenix, Arizona.
Haury, Emil W.
1936 The Mogollon Culture of Southwestern New Mexico. *Medallion Papers* No. XX. Gila Pueblo, Globe, Arizona.
1976 *The Hohokam, Desert Farmers and Craftsmen.* University of Arizona Press, Tucson.
Hough, Walter
1918 "The Hopi Indian Collection in the United States National Museum." Vol. 54, No. 2235. *Proceedings of the United States National Museum.* Government Printing Office, Washington, D.C.
James, George Wharton
1903 *Indian Basketry.* Privately printed, Pasadena, California.
Jeancon, Jean Allard, and F. H. Douglas
1930 "Pima Indian Close Coiled Basketry." *Denver Art Museum Indian Art Leaflet* No. 5. Denver, Colorado.
1931a "Hopi Indian Basketry." *Denver Art Museum Indian Art Leaflet* No. 17, Denver, Colorado.
1931b "The Navajo Indians." *Denver Art Museum Indian Art Leaflet* No. 21, Denver, Colorado. (April 1931)
Jennings, Jessie D.
1957 *Danger Cave.* Anthropological Papers No. 27, Department of Anthropology, University of Utah, Salt Lake City.
Judd, Neil M.
1954 *The Material Culture of Pueblo Bonito.* Smithsonian Miscellaneous Collections, Volume 124. Smithsonian Institution, Washington, D.C.
Kahlenberg, Mary Hunt, and Anthony Berlant
1972 *The Navajo Blanket.* Praeger Publishers, Inc., New York, in association with the Los Angeles County Museum.
Kearney, Thomas H., and Robert H. Peebles
1951 *Arizona Flora.* University of California Press, Berkeley.
Kelly, William H.
1977 "Cocopa Ethnography." *Anthropological Papers of the University of Arizona,* No. 29. University of Arizona Press, Tucson.
Kidder, Alfred Vincent
1962 *An Introduction to the Study of Southwestern Archaeology.* Yale University Press, New Haven.
Kissell, Mary Lois
1916 "Basketry of the Papago and Pima Indians." *American Museum of Natural History Anthropological Papers,* Volume XVII, Part IV, New York.
Kroeber, Alfred L.
1908 *Ethnography of the Cahuilla Indians.* University of California Publications in American Archaeology and Ethnology, Volume 8, No. 2, Berkeley.
1935 *Walapai Ethnology.* Memoirs, American Anthropological Association, No. 42, Menasha, Wisconsin.
Mason, Otis Tufton
1904 *Aboriginal American Basketry.* Smithsonian Institution Annual Report, 1902. Report of the U.S. National Museum, Washington, D.C.
Matthews, Washington
1894 "The Basket Dance." *American Anthropologist,* Volume 7, No. 2, pp. 202–8.
McKee, Barbara, and Edwin and Joyce Herold
1975 *Havasupai Baskets and their Makers: 1930–1940.* Northland Press, Flagstaff, Arizona.
Mori, Joyce and John
1972 "Modern Hopi Coiled Basketry." *Masterkey,* Volume 46, No. 4.
Morris, Earl H., and Robert F. Burgh
1941 *Anasazi Basketry: Basket Maker II through Pueblo III*—A Study Based on Specimens from the San Juan River Country. Carnegie Institution of Washington, Publication 533, Washington, D.C.
Opler, Morris Edward
1941 *An Apache Life-Way.* University of Chicago Press, Chicago.

Random House Dictionary of The English Language
1971 Unabridged Edition, Random House, New York.
Roberts, Helen H.
1929 *Basketry of the San Carlos Apache.* American Museum of Natural History, Anthropological Papers, Volume XXXI, Part II, New York.
Robinson, Bert
1954 *The Basket Weavers of Arizona.* University of New Mexico Press, Albuquerque.
Russell, Frank
1908 The Pima Indians. *Bureau of American Ethnology Annual Report 26.* Government Printing Office, Washington, D.C.
Sayles, E. B., and Ernst Antevs
1941 The Cochise Culture. *Medallion Papers* No. XXIX. Gila Pueblo, Globe, Arizona.
Schapiro, Meyer
1953 "Style" in Kroeber, A. L., *Anthropology Today.* University of Chicago Press, Chicago.
Shreve, Margaret B.
1943 *Modern Papago Basketry.* M.A. Thesis, University of Arizona, Tucson.
Sloan, John, and Oliver LaFarge
1931 *Introduction to American Indian Art,* Parts I and II. The Exposition of Indian Tribal Arts, Inc., New York.
Smithson, Carma Lee
1959 *The Havasupai Woman.* Anthropological Papers No. 38, Department of Anthropology, University of Utah, Salt Lake City.
Spier, Leslie
1928 *Havasupai Ethnography.* Anthropological Papers, Volume XXIX, Part III, American Museum of Natural History, New York.
1933 *Yuman Tribes of the Gila River.* University of Chicago Press, Chicago.
Stevens, G. A.
1935 "Educational Significance of Indigenous African Art." In *Arts and Crafts of West Africa,* edited by Sir Michael Sadler. Oxford University Press, London.
Stevenson, James
1883 "Illustrated Catalogue of the Collections Obtained from the Indians of New Mexico and Arizona in 1879." *Bureau of American Ethnology Annual Report* 2, Government Printing Office, Washington, D.C.
Stevenson, Matilda Coxe
1904 "The Zuñi Indians." *Bureau of American Ethnology Annual Report* 23, Government Printing Office, Washington, D.C.
1915 "Ethnobotany of the Zuñi Indians." *Bureau of American Ethnology Annual Report* 30, Government Printing Office, Washington, D.C.
Stewart, Omer C.
1938 "The Navajo Wedding Basket." Museum of Northern Arizona, *Museum Notes,* Volume 10, No. 9, pp. 25–28, Flagstaff, Arizona.
Tanner, Clara Lee
1965 "Papago Burden Baskets in the Arizona State Museum." *The Kiva,* Volume 30, No. 3. Arizona Archaeological and Historical Society, Tucson.
1982 *Apache Indian Baskets.* University of Arizona Press, Tucson.
Tschopik, Harry, Jr.
1938 "Taboo as a Possible Factor Involved in the Obsolescence of Navaho Pottery and Basketry." *American Anthropologist,* Volume 40, No. 2.
1940 "Navaho Basketry: A Study of Culture Change." *American Anthropologist,* Volume 42, No. 3, Part. 1.
Underhill, Ruth
1944 *Pueblo Crafts.* United States Department of the Interior. Bureau of Indian Affairs. Branch of Education, Washington, D.C.
1951 *People of the Crimson Evening.* United States Department of the Interior. Bureau of Indian Affairs, Office of Education Programs. Haskell Institute, Lawrence, Kansas.
Vaillant, George C.
1939 *Indian Arts in North America.* Harper and Bros, New York.

Vivian, Gordon
1957 "Two Navaho Baskets". *El Palacio,* Volume 64, Nos. 5–6, pp. 145–155. The Museum of New Mexico, Santa Fe.
Wade, Edwin L., and Rennard Strickland
1981 *Magic Images.* Philbrook Art Center and University of Oklahoma Press, Norman.
Watkins, Frances E.
1942 *The Navaho. Masterkey,* Volume XVI, No. 5, Southwest Museum, Los Angeles.
Webb, William and Rober A. Weinstein
1973 *Dwellers at the Source*—Southwestern Indian Photographs of A. C. Vroman 1895–1904. Grossman Publishers, New York.
Webber, John Milton
1953 *Yucca of the Southwest.* Agriculture Monograph No. 17. U.S. Department of Agriculture, Washington, D.C.
Wheat, Joseph Ben
1974 *Navajo Blankets from the Collection of Anthony Berlant.* University of Arizona Museum of Art, Tucson.
Whitaker, Kathleen
1974 "Zuñi Shalako Festival." *Masterkey,* Volume 48, No. 4. Southwest Museum, Los Angeles.
Williamson, Ten Broeck
1937 "The Jémez Yucca Ring Basket." *El Palacio,* Volume XLII, Nos. 7, 8, 9. The Museum of New Mexico, Santa Fe. (also in *Indians at Work,* 10-15-37.)
Wormington, H. M.
1957 *Ancient Man in North America.* Denver Museum of Natural History, Popular Series No. 4, Fourth Edition, Denver, Colorado.

CONFERENCES

Adams, W. Y., February 27, 1957
Bahti, Tom, 1966 (several during the year)
Bartlett, Katharine, February 22, 1963
Collings, Gerald, February 19, 1977 (plus others)
Cummings, Dorothy, Correspondence, May 15, 1963
Danson, E.B., February 23, 1963 (plus others)
Dobyns, Henry, January 31, 1977
Ellis, Florence H., April 27, 1963
Euler, Robert, March 30, 1963
Penfield, Susan, Conferences 1974 (many throughout year)
Wright, Barton, March 17, 1977

Index

Note: *Page references in italics indicate special emphasis on topic.*